COMMUNITY-LED DEVELOPMENT IN PRACTICE

In the last decade, the international development sector has been re-examining its ways of thinking, being, and doing, and we have seen a growing consensus around the need to centre communities in development. However, there is little clarity on what such centring entails and how it can be achieved. This edited volume addresses this gap by highlighting what community-led practices look like and how they compare across different sociocultural and organisational landscapes.

Bringing together the work of over 30 international authors, ranging from experienced community-led development practitioners to acclaimed scholars, the book reflects on and critically analyses grassroots initiatives, national-level organisations, and larger-scale international operations. The case studies demonstrate the similarities and differences in community-led practices according to organisational size and spread, while documenting the process of human change that these practices unleash. The volume's overarching structure reflects the characteristics and processes of community-led development, captured via nine different dimensions: participation inclusion and voice; local resources; sustainability and exit strategies; accountability; responsiveness to context; collaboration (including working with sub-national governments); community-led monitoring and evaluation practices; and facilitation.

The book will be of interest to funders, organisations, and practitioners looking for non-Western, non-dominant, everyday stories of change. It will also be useful to policymakers, students, and researchers from the fields of community development and international development theory and practice.

Elene Cloete is Senior Director of Research and Advocacy for Outreach International, Kansas City, USA. Her practice and research interests include the following: the role of motivation, basic psychological needs, and self-regulation in development; community leadership; the hidden benefits of improved sanitation; and locally led monitoring and evaluation practice. Elene is a social anthropologist by training.

Gunjan Veda is Global Secretary for the Movement for Community-led Development, a Majority World-led network of networks with 2000+ local organisations and their INGO allies. Her work includes creating collaborative partnerships, and interrogating structural violence in existing systems, forms of knowledge production and publication to make them more inclusive and equitable. Gunjan has previously worked within the non-profit sector in India and was a policymaker in the Indian Government's Planning Commission. She has published two books: *Beautiful Country*: Stories from Another India, and *The Museum of Broken Tea Cups*.

Rethinking Development

Rethinking Development offers accessible and thought-provoking overviews of contemporary topics in international development and aid. Providing original empirical and analytical insights, the books in this series push thinking in new directions by challenging current conceptualizations and developing new ones.

This is a dynamic and inspiring series for all those engaged with today's debates surrounding development issues, whether they be students, scholars, policy makers and practitioners internationally. These interdisciplinary books provide an invaluable resource for discussion in advanced undergraduate and postgraduate courses in development studies as well as in anthropology, economics, politics, geography, media studies and sociology.

Reformers in International Development
Five Remarkable Lives
David M. de Ferranti

Young People in the Global South
Voice, Agency and Citizenship
Edited by Kate Pincock, Nicola Jones, Lorraine Van Blerk and Nyaradzayi Gumbonzvanda

Community-Led Development in Practice
We Power Our Own Change
Edited by Elene Cloete and Gunjan Veda

For more information about this series, please visit: www.routledge.com/Rethinking-Development/book-series/RDVPT

COMMUNITY-LED DEVELOPMENT IN PRACTICE

We Power Our Own Change

Edited by Elene Cloete and Gunjan Veda

Routledge
Taylor & Francis Group
LONDON AND NEW YORK

Designed cover image: Artwork by Favianna Rodriguez, © 2012

First published 2025
by Routledge
4 Park Square, Milton Park, Abingdon, Oxon OX14 4RN

and by Routledge
605 Third Avenue, New York, NY 10158

Routledge is an imprint of the Taylor & Francis Group, an informa business

British Library Cataloguing-in-Publication Data
A catalogue record for this book is available from the British Library

Library of Congress Cataloging-in-Publication Data
Names: Cloete, Elene, editor. | Veda, Gunjan, editor.
Title: Community-led development in practice : we power our own change / edited by Elene Cloete and Gunjan Veda.
Description: Abingdon, Oxon ; New York, NY : Routledge, 2025. |
Series: Rethinking development | Includes bibliographical references and index.
Identifiers: LCCN 2024033820 (print) | LCCN 2024033821 (ebook) |
ISBN 9781032456263 (hardback) | ISBN 9781032456232 (paperback) |
ISBN 9781003377917 (ebook)
Subjects: LCSH: Community development–Case studies.
Classification: LCC HN49.C6 C6525 2025 (print) | LCC HN49.C6 (ebook) |
DDC 307.1/4–dc23/eng/20241029
LC record available at https://lccn.loc.gov/2024033820
LC ebook record available at https://lccn.loc.gov/2024033821

ISBN: 9781032456263 (hbk)
ISBN: 9781032456232 (pbk)
ISBN: 9781003377917 (ebk)

DOI: 10.4324/9781003377917

Typeset in Times New Roman
by Newgen Publishing UK

We dedicate this volume to those at the centre of community-led development, the people.

CONTENTS

ILLUSTRATIONS

Figures

Maps

Tables

NOTES ON CONTRIBUTORS

Amani Initiative – Established in 2012 in Maracha District, Uganda's West Nile Sub-Region, Amani Initiative prevents and responds to teenage pregnancy and child marriage through integrated community-led interventions. It works across 15 districts, collaborating with 12 health facilities, 15 women-led self-support groups, 3,000 schools, and 30 community change agents.

Vinya Ariyaratne is the Honorary President of the Sarvodaya Shramadana Movement, Sri Lanka's pioneering community development organisation. As a Board-Certified Specialist in Community Medicine and a development practitioner, he leads the national-level organisation with significant influence and dynamism. A pivotal figure in Sri Lankan civil society, Ariyaratne contributes to local and international discussions and practice in community development, rights, and public policy. Notably, he engages in health rights advocacy and currently focuses on emergency response programmes related to food security and nutrition amidst the socio-economic crisis in Sri Lanka.

Monisha Behal, an activist and social worker from Assam, founded North East Network, a women's organisation in North East India in 1995, bringing local issues of gender and marginalisation of the region to global attention.

Chad Bissonnette is President and Co-founder of Roots of Development, a US-based non-profit organisation dedicated to fostering sustainable, community-led development. Bissonnette holds a degree in International Relations from The American University in Washington D.C. and has spent almost two decades working in grassroots development.

Moigua Bockarie is a farmer and tribal authority who lives in Grima with two wives and six children. He is a OneVillage Partners' Community volunteer and project committee member who leads community development processes for inclusive collaboration and participation. He is a strong advocate for women's inclusion in community decision-making.

Matthew Breay Bolton is a professor of political science at Pace University in New York City. He was part of the International Campaign to Abolish Nuclear Weapons (ICAN) team that was awarded the 2017 Nobel Peace Prize. He has published six books, including *Political Minefields* and *Imagining Disarmament.*

CLD-Benin – Established in 2017 and working in partnership with Benin's House of Civil Society, CLD-Benin represents over 1,000 civil society organisations nationwide. CLD-Benin prioritises five thematic areas: Agriculture and nutrition, responsive local governance, climate change and environment, health and community well-being, and local economic development.

John Coonrod founded the Movement for Community-led Development. A PhD physicist, he left physics during the 1984 Africa famine to join The Hunger Project staff, where he helped develop locally led programmes in Africa, Asia, and Latin America. He is the author of *How the Road Built Me.*

Simon Eli, Leadership & Partnership Director, Nuru Nigeria, is committed to community development, specialising in curriculum development and capacity strengthening. His work has benefited smallholder farmers in Northeast Nigeria, empowering cooperative leaders to drive positive change. Simon holds a BTech in Urban and Regional Planning and an MTech in Infrastructure.

Udesh Fernando is the Director of the Sarvodaya Institute of Higher Learning (SIHL), the higher learning arm of the Sarvodaya Movement. A scholar-practitioner in development, he provides programmatic leadership to SIHL with over 12 years of experience in community development and civil society sectors.

Philip Forth spent the early part of his career as a geophysicist in the oil and gas industry. He has been involved with the Constellation since its formation. He became a member of its board in 2010 and became Chair of the Constellation in 2014.

Amy Gaman is an impact-driven leader with extensive experience in humanitarian and development work. She specialises in gender, nutrition, building local organisations, and agribusiness. Her national contributions include the reintegration of Chibok Girls, national gender policy, and response to COVID-19 impacts. Amy holds an MBA from Business School Netherlands.

Sheku Mohamed Gassimu Jr. is the Partnership and Program Director at OneVillage Partners. He has experience in implementing CLD programmes designed and implemented by communities. Sheku is adaptable and resilient, and his laughter is infectious! He holds a Bachelor of Science (Hons) in Sociology and a Master of Community Development from Njala University, Sierra Leone.

Casey Harrison believes rural community development is vital to a more sustainable and peaceful future. He works to support Nuru local NGOs through innovation and learning. Casey holds a dual MA in Natural Resource Management and International Affairs and was a Peace Corps Volunteer in Zambia.

David J. Howlett is a visiting assistant professor of religion at Smith College in Northampton, Massachusetts, USA. He is the author of *Kirtland Temple: The Biography of a Shared Mormon Sacred Space* (University of Illinois Press, 2014) and *Mormonism: The Basics* (Routledge, 2017).

Fatmata Lansana is a qualified MCHAID nurse who was a dedicated staff member at the Grima Community Health Center. In 2010, she was deployed as the first health care professional stationed there and directed health services there for more than 10 years. She is married and has four children.

Matt Lineal works at the cross-section of implementation, scaling up, and resilience to cultivate lasting, meaningful choices in rural communities. Matt is a tropical forester by training and got his start in international work as a Peace Corps volunteer in Honduras.

Chad McCordic is the Country Director of OneVillage Partners in Sierra Leone and has led the design of all of their community-led development work since 2014. He has over 15 years of experience working with grassroots non-profit organisations across Africa.

Philemon Vandi McSenesie, a program officer at OneVillage Partners with 7 years' experience in Community-Led Development, trains communities on project management, communications, and leadership skills. He is passionate about initiatives that bring sustainable changes within to improve community well-being.

Abiy Meshesha is an innovative problem-solver dedicated to achieving scalable, sustainable impact in marginalised communities. With two decades of experience at Save the Children, Medicins Sans Frontiers, and Nuru Ethiopia, he chaired the Nuru Collective Global Advisory Committee in 2023. Abiy holds an MA in Sociology and BA in Education.

Brent Metz is Professor of Anthropology and Director of the Center for Latin American & Caribbean Studies at the University of Kansas. His research focuses on indigenous identity and development, particularly among the Ch'orti' Maya of Guatemala and Honduras, about whom he has published four books and many articles.

Nyagajia Rogers Mustapha is the LEAD Program Supervisor at OneVillage Partners with experience and knowledge in designing and coaching Community-Led Development projects implemented by communities. He is a holder of National Diploma and a Bachelor's Degree in Commercial Studies with advanced option in Business Administration.

Rituu B. Nanda is the Participatory Program Advisor for South Asia at Global Fund for Children. She brings systems thinking and a gender lens to facilitating community-owned processes and participatory MEL. Rituu is a founding member of the Evaluation Community of India and serves as a facilitator of research groups at the Asia Pacific Evaluation Association (APEA).

Hanna Nel is an emeritus professor in the Department of Social Work and Community Development at the University of Johannesburg, South Africa. Over the last 15 years, her research has focused on community development, specifically asset-based citizen-led development (ABCD) in South Africa. Hanna has guided 59 master's and doctoral students.

Essa Mohamed Rafique is a voting member of The Constellation. Rafique, who twice won the MacArthur Foundation Fellowship Award for Leadership, has worked with communities in Bangladesh, Nepal, and India. Rafique, a WHO Consultant, is a Dermatologo-Venereologist. He is also qualified in Front-End Programming and Islamic Studies.

Matt Reeves lives in Nairobi, Kenya, and provides strategic leadership to the Aga Khan Foundation's global civil society portfolio. He has supported community-led development initiatives in 25+ countries across Africa, Asia, Europe, and North America.

Louino 'Robi' Robillard is an activist and a community leader who works on community-driven social change shaped by the principles of the traditional Haitian practice of "konbit". Robillard is a founding member of the national movement Gwoup Konbit and Program Director of Rasin Devlopman.

Marlou de Rouw is a co-founder and board member of The Constellation. She has worked with communities in Africa, Asia, and Europe on topics such as living together, integration, HIV/AIDS, climate, and sexual health of girls. Marlou is trained as a journalist and anthropologist specialising in intercultural dialogue.

Aida Ramos Viera holds a PhD in Cultural Geography from The University of Kansas. Her research and publications centre on indigenous territoriality in Mexico and Central America, with a focus on indigenous land tenure, management, and conservation.

Pauline Wambeti believes in "not waiting for other people to make the changes for us, but to make the changes ourselves." She worked for 20 years in community development in Kenya, studied social work and community development with a postgraduate in development studies. She is a 2018 East Africa Acumen Fellow.

Vanessa Woode, Communications Supervisor at OneVillage Partners, is a gender and race advocate with 6+ years' experience in policy evaluation, strategic communication, and community engagement. When not reading the latest Afro-authors, she's passionate about decolonising international aid and storytelling that shifts the status quo.

WHERE WOMEN HAVE A VOICE

Message from H.E. Dr. Joyce Banda

Since serving as Malawi's president (2012–2014), I have devoted my energies to two vital and linked issues – women's leadership and community-led development. These have been key priorities for my work with the Joyce Banda Foundation, which has supported more than 3,000 women and girls, as well as in the African Union's African Women's Leadership Network.

How are community-led development and gender justice linked? In Africa, the vast majority of people are rural, and many travel on foot. If there is not a responsive local government within walking distance, they have no meaningful voice in the issues that affect their daily lives: food, water, education, health, and public safety. These are the public services that women particularly care about. Bringing the collective voice of women and girls to grassroots policy decisions is vital. Having a voice in governance is key to these public services, and a fundamental human right – a right that is too often denied.

Fortunately, Africa is heading in the right direction, albeit too slowly. Since the 1995 Fourth World Conference on Women in Beijing – organised by an African woman, my dear sister Gertrude Mongella[1] – the growth of women's civil society groups has been tremendous and impactful.

In 2003, Africa adopted the Maputo Protocol on Women's Rights, which has now been ratified by nearly every African country.[2] Africa's Vision 2063 calls for half of all elected seats at every level, including the community level, to be held by women. Worldwide, only three countries have reached that goal, and women make up only 27% of seats in Africa.[3] Rwanda has the highest women representation in decision-making positions in the world,[4] and the benefits are there for us all to see and learn from.

There is a long way to go, however. Africa's post-colonial governments have tended to be highly centralised, despite the recognition that women's leadership and decentralisation are vital for overcoming poverty in Africa. Mobilising the power of Africa's civil society to advocate for the principles of community-led development is therefore critical.

The level of funding for community-based organisations, particularly women-led organisations, is abysmally small and must change. As of the 2023 UN High-Level Political Forum, the international community has awakened to the fact that 65% of the Sustainable Development Goal targets can only be achieved at the community level.[5] Yet only 1% of official development assistance devoted to gender issues is going to grassroots women's organisations.[6] International funders have finally made commitments to shift far more funding to organisations based in the Majority World ("global south"). That must happen and happen urgently. The world must also ensure that the majority of those funds go to women-led organisations. As the famous economist Ester Boserup wrote 50 years ago, when the majority of aid goes to men, that aid is actually widening the gender gap, not closing it.[7] When a woman is empowered, the whole community benefits.

In 2014, the African Union passed the African Charter on the Values and Principles of Decentralisation, Local Governance and Local Development, which came into force in 2019.[8] It calls upon all governments to transfer percentages of their national budget to local communities and strengthen the ability of local governments to raise and disburse funds. Kenya has led the way on this, with a guarantee of 15% of the national budget devolved directly to county governments.[9] Other countries are beginning to follow suit.[10]

In 2024 the world will gather at the Summit of the Future. If that future is going to truly be bright for billions of women and girls living in rural areas, we must invest in those women and girls and in the communities where they live. I believe that this book will make important contributions to all those devoted to this noble cause. It will show practitioners and policymakers a different way of doing things, one that is rooted in the agency of girls, women, and communities around the world.

Notes

1 Vuzo, Stella. 2020. "Meet Tanzania'S Gertrude Mongella, 75, Who Led the World to Historic Beijing Conference on Women in 1995." Africa Renewal. October 29, 2020. www.un.org/africarenewal/magazine/october-2020/meet-tanzanias-gertrude-mongella-75-who-led-world-historic-beijing-conference

2 Equality Now. 2023. African Countries Show Progress in Advancing Women's Rights: Landmark Report on the Maputo Protocol. July 13, 2023. https://equalitynow.org/press_release/african-countries-show-progress-in-advancing-womens-rights-landmark-report-on-the-maputo-protocol

3 Prinsen, Larisse. 2023. "The Maputo Protocol: A Reason to Hope". *Public Law Corner: A Blog of the Southern African Public Law Journal.* November 1, 2023. https://unisapressjournals.co.za/index.php/SAPL/article/download/13933/7339

4 UN Women. 2018. "Revisiting Rwanda five years after record-breaking parliamentary elections." UN Women, August 13, 2018. www.unwomen.org/en/news/stories/2018/8/feature-rwanda-women-in-parliament
5 OECD. 2022. "OECD toolkit for a territorial approach to the SDGs", *OECD Regional Development Papers*, No. 33, OECD Publishing, Paris. www.oecd.org/regional/cities/OECD_Toolkit_for_A_Territorial_Approach_to_the_SDGs.pdf
6 Staszweka, Kasia, Tenzin Dolker and Kellea Miller. 2019. "Only 1% of gender equality funding is going to women's organisations – why?" *The Guardian*, July 2, 2019. www.theguardian.com/global-development/2019/jul/02/gender-equality-support-1bn-boost-how-to-spend-it
7 Boserup, Ester. 1970. *Woman's Role in Economic Development*. London: St. Martin's Press..
8 African Union. 2019. *African Charter on the Values and Principles of Decentralisation, Local Governance and Local Development*. African Union. https://au.int/en/treaties/african-charter-values-and-principles-decentralisation-local-governance-and-local
9 Kimenyi, Mwangi S. 2013. "Devolution and Resource Sharing in Kenya." *Brookings Open-Ed*. October 22, 2013. www.brookings.edu/articles/devolution-and-resource-sharing-in-kenya/
10 Commonwealth Local Government Forum. 2021. "Devolution in East Africa." Commonwealth Local Government Forum. July 8, 2021. www.clgf.org.uk/whats-new/news/devolution-in-east-africa/

FOREWORD

Scott Guggenheim

The reason why I so much enjoy talking to people who work on community-led development is because so many of them are at heart deep idealists. They truly love their work, and they can see that what they do can make a difference to the lives of poor or marginalised people.

People are pretty depressed about development these days, and rightfully so. Development theory seems to be a never-ending series of big "aha" moments that take over development agencies, think tanks, and universities, and then, like deflating balloons, lose steam as gritty reality quickly falls short of the golden promises. Neo-liberal theories of free trade promised to do away with inefficiencies so that unencumbered markets could deliver prosperity. Prosperity may have followed for some, but far too many countries instead got rapidly rising inequality, corruption, and an apparent never-ending cycle of financial crises that could only be overcome by constantly rising levels of debt. Even as neo-liberalism's charms lost their lustre, new models for tackling problems of "fragile states" and "governance" appeared, arguing that institutions mattered as much as markets alone. Having acknowledged their importance, though, not much happened as people discovered that naming the problem is not the same as fixing it, and they simply did not have adequate models and tools to do much about these problems. Of late, even the concept of growth itself has come under challenge: the long-term environmental costs turn out to have been wildly under-estimated and are increasingly coming home to roost. Once again, it is poor countries and poor people who get to bear the worst of these costs.

Too much development theory is predicated on the idea that people, culture, and societies are a "problem" that development expertise must fix. This model is failing, in rich countries as well as developing ones. Distrust of development expertise and institutions is at an all-time high. Something is deeply wrong when development programmes intended to help poor communities instead leave them displaced, indebted, marginalised – or angry.

We need to start over again. People matter. People's agency matters. A century ago, anthropologists and sociologists wrote about the importance of community, of norms, and of trust, and the problems that arise when "modernization" undermines and devalues these but does not succeed in replacing them with new forms of solidarity that can give people's lives meaning.

The community-led development movement is as much a philosophy about development as it is a methodology or a string of projects. It believes that people should have a strong if not determinant voice in their own development. Or, as OneVillage Partners asked villagers in Sierra Leone why they were dancing enthusiastically in the midst of a village meeting to discuss a health clinic, "When we had a chance, we asked Philemon why everyone was this happy. 'We've had seven NGOs do projects here,' he said. 'This is the first time anyone has asked us what we want!' Then he went back to dancing."

Every chapter in this book carries the same message. People give value to having a say. Including local knowledge, local understanding, and local decision-making in development must go beyond something to do just to tick a box, at least not if development programmes want to respond to perceived needs and see some ownership of what gets done. Community-led development is about inclusion, the idea that every effort should be made to hear everybody's voice, not just the voices of the rich, the powerful, or the well-connected.

The community-led development movement supplements the importance of giving voice with a commitment to working with and through communities. Communities are as much a social as they are a physical space. They are where social capital gets formed and used. Good development builds on that social capital, not just rides roughshod over it. This belief that socially defined communities have a reality and role that goes beyond the choice-making individual gives the community-led movement its unique character as well as a methodology for action.

Community-led development goes in and out of favour. In general, there are three particularly well-founded criticisms of community development as an overall model, and a very large number of bad ones. Daniel Immerwahr, a popular historian who studied the "small is beautiful" projects of the development industry of the 1950s, wrote about how the romanticisation of community's presumed egalitarianism came to grief in the highly stratified, often oppressive, communities of real-life, particularly in caste-inflected village India (2015). A second criticism comes from equating community programmes with "small" programmes. It is great for non-governmental groups to spend a decade working in 10 or 15 villages, but to see social change, local development needs to be able to work at scale. The third criticism focuses more on the technological simplicity of most community programs. It is fine to build village roads and markets, but development will only happen when poor countries industrialise and can build nationwide electrical systems, highway networks, and factories.

These criticisms are all fair. They are also largely out of date. Community programmes do run the risk of elite capture. But it is very hard to argue that other types of programmes haven't been running the same risks for a very long time now. During my time in the World Bank, I used to look at the social impacts stemming from population displacement. It would never cease to amaze me how World Bank projects could calmly rationalise displacing 50,000 poor people for an urban water supply project but would then design a highway that splits down the middle to avoid displacing the family of one senior politician.

Elite – and, commonly, male – capture of community development cannot be avoided, but it can be mitigated, particularly when community development links up with other movements for social reform. Several of the articles in this book give sensitive, granular portrayals of how exclusion operates. Monisha Behal recounts the formation of the North East Network in India's remote Nagaland, which gradually but effectively changed patriarchal norms over women's roles in public decision-making. And Brent Metz's reconstruction of why insuperable community divisions caused a well-intentioned Engineers Without Borders water project to fail shows that overcoming community conflict is never as easy as just bringing along good intentions.

The issue of whether community-led development can achieve scale is also a bit of a relic, but it nevertheless continues to resurface in development discussions. Susan Wong and I have written elsewhere (2018) about how big and long-lasting national community projects can be found across the World Bank's portfolio of programmes, but the World Bank is not the only agency realising that a relatively small project done in 75,000 villages is actually quite a big project. One thing I really enjoyed reading through the chapters in this volume is seeing the wonderful Aga Khan rural support programmes spread a community-led approach for bringing basic services to some 30,000 neglected communities across Asia and East Africa. Sri Lanka's Sarvodaya Shramadana Movement has worked in 15,000 communities, and the Amani Initiative creatively engages with some 3,000 neglected communities in Uganda. The point here, though, is not just that community-led programmes can be quite big, but the critique that other development programmes that operate at a local level cannot adopt a more people-focused approach does not really hold water.

The third criticism, that left to their own devices, community people would make a nation of NGO-run village republics, is a deep exaggeration but it is not entirely untrue, either. As John Coonrod's chapter in this book shows, much of the community-led movement originated in countries with authoritarian, colonial, or post-colonial governments, where the political drivers were to consolidate a central government's control, not to delegate decision-making downwards or, worse, just hand cash over to villages to make their own investments. Development agencies followed this centralising lead, building government capacities to control territory and nominally providing services through big, centrally directed state ministries and agencies, but at the expense of local autonomy and virtually any sort of voice from the local people. This is why community development has so often felt like an insurgent movement rising from within the technocratic empire of state-focused development. While it is helpful to remember the context, for community facilitators, the result has been a tendency to put our heads down and plough ahead, letting the development elite do their thing.

This is less and less true, however. As community-led approaches gain credibility, members of the community development movement become more confident about engaging with government players and acknowledging the importance of the broader policy context, not just because "it's important" but because national policies and programmes can offer and shape a community's opportunities. Virtually every chapter in this book provides insights into how a second generation of community-led development has worked out creative and effective ways to engage local and even national governments. They describe how responsive and helpful those governments can be, but at the same time, they illustrate how much better outcomes are when government engagements are negotiated rather than just accepted or imposed. Nel's chapter on women's groups in South Africa describes not just how a local community organised, but how it brought together resources from NGOs, the Walter Sisulu University, and South Africa's Department of Agriculture – a far cry from the image of community autarky.

For that negotiation to happen, communities require an ability to act collectively. Most of the chapters in this volume are told from the perspective of an outside organisation learning to overcome barriers to group organising. Bissonette and Robillard make some very good points about how in Haiti, localising management to a Haitian grassroots group suddenly provided the deep understandings of language, metaphor, and styles of storytelling that made organising meaningful. Aida Ramos's chapter is an especially sophisticated analysis of how community social structures define and manage state engagements in a particularly exciting and contemporary area within global development policy: whether and how to provide payments to communities for providing environmental services.

Even though I've spent most of my adult life engaged in community-led development programmes of one sort or another, as I read the essays contributed to this collection, I found myself saying, "Gee, I wish I'd thought of something like that back in the day." Amani's use of village motorcycle drivers as "change agents" is nothing short of brilliant. If anybody can bring ideas (and useful gossip!) across village boundaries, they can. Aga Khan's honest, insightful reflection on what they have learned from their support for community-led development in countries ranging from Portugal to Afghanistan should be required reading for all development workers. I wish that I had read it at the start rather than end of my career! The chapter on the Nuru collectives' accountability-based methodology to providing support to farmer cooperatives along different segments of the value chain, and then evolving that support over time, seems like a remarkably thoughtful approach to the perpetually challenging problem of how to improve rural livelihoods. As Amani seems to have done so effectively with the Parent-Teacher Associations in Uganda, I've also been thinking about whether and when it is feasible to take some of the moribund but familiar organisational shells left by previous government or donor projects and re-purpose them.

The essays in this book are valuable reports from the field worth reading on their own merits. But they also provide a uniquely interesting way to dive into the nitty gritty of what it really means to be a community development worker. Is community-led development the answer to the world's problems of poverty, alienation, environmental destruction? Of course not. But, bit by bit, the stories collected by people like the contributors to this collection do offer a way to re-think some assumptions about who needs to be involved in those discussions and how they can become part of a new, people-centred way of thinking.

References

Immerwahr, Daniel. *Thinking Small: The United States and the Lure of Community Development*. Cambridge, MA: Harvard University Press, 2015.

Wong, Susan, and Scott Guggenheim. *Community Development: Myths and Realities*. Policy Research Paper 8435. Washington, DC: The World Bank, May 2018. https://documents1.worldbank.org/curated/en/677351525887961626/pdf/WPS8435.pdf.

ACKNOWLEDGEMENT

All the co-authors and chapter contributors of this volume have one thing in common: a resounding "Yes!" Two years ago, when we reached out to them to learn about their interest in an edited volume on community-led development, their response was unequivocal. They have since demonstrated an abiding commitment to this project. We are thankful to them for the time and effort they spent in crafting their chapters to share their learnings with a wider network of practitioners, students, and communities of practice. Without them, this volume could not have happened. Their experiences *are* this volume. By sharing them through chapters, these busy practitioners and academics helped exemplify the core characteristics of community-led development – what it is, how it functions, where, and for who.

We also want to thank our respective organisations, the Movement for Community-Led Development (MCLD) and Outreach International, and our colleagues, including John Coonrod, for their continued support. They have been with us throughout the project, from the initial conception to celebrating how it came together. We know when the volume is published, they will reflect our work to a broader audience.

We are grateful to our advisors, particularly Scott Guggenheim and Nazneen Kanji for encouraging us, challenging us, and connecting us to the right people for this volume. And to the hundreds of community-based organisations and practitioners we work with, your stories, your dedication, and your passion have nurtured our own. Thank you for showing us and the world that an alternate way is possible!

The idea for this volume emerged from a collective project that we, the co-editors, were a part of. For three years we worked together with dedicated professionals committed to community-led development from all over the world to better understand this approach and its nuances. In MCLD's collaborative research team, we found not just new ideas, tools, and the framework which grounds this book, but a community that has since stood with us. Thank you to the entire collaborative research team – particularly the scoping group – for your friendship, support, and solidarity. Holta Trandafili, Nelly Mecklenburg, Janet Edmond, Martha Cruz Zuniga, and Diana Delgadillo Ramírez – you continue to inspire us!

And to our families, who stood by us as we worked through weekends and holidays, as we spent all our after-work hours discussing, researching, editing, and writing, we could never have done this without you. Thank you for keeping us grounded and for always being there for us!

And finally, as co-editors, we have had each other throughout the project. We were each other's sounding boards, testing grounds, launching pads. We were critics and cheerleaders. We have grown together in not only our appreciation for community-led development but also our curiosity for how we can sustain momentum towards a hopeful future.

Introduction

1

INTRODUCTION

The Current Landscape and Practice of Community-Led Development

Gunjan Veda and Elene Cloete

On November 4, 2021, Samantha Power, the Administrator of USAID, the world's largest bilateral agency, made two commitments: to provide 25% of all USAID funds directly to local organisations by 2025, and to ensure that by 2030, at least half of all USAID funding goes to programmes that place local communities in the lead in co-designing, priority setting, implementing or evaluating the work (USAID 2021). The first of these commitments has been the stated intent of one USAID administrator after another since the launch of USAID Forward in 2010 (Ingram 2022; USAID 2015). It was also an ask of the 2016 Grand Bargain, an agreement between funders, UN agencies and humanitarian organisations to improve the effectiveness and efficiency of humanitarian action and get more means into the hands of people in need (Metcalfe-Hough et al. 2023). The second part of Administrator Power's commitment, however, reflected an emerging realisation that shifting money to local organisations was critical but insufficient to address the structural and systemic inequities that underpin the international development and humanitarian sectors. It recognised the agency of communities and community leaders.

Community-led development is not a novel idea. Simply put, it

> is a development approach in which local community members work together to identify goals that are important to them, develop and implement plans to achieve those goals, and create collaborative relationships internally and with external actors – all while building on community strengths and local leadership.
>
> *(Veda et al. 2021b, 135)*

DOI: 10.4324/9781003377917-2

Yet, it is a concept that sits uneasily within the development and humanitarian sectors whose foundations are steeped in white saviourism (Fanon 1970; Cammarota 2011; Pailey 2019; Sumner 2022; Khan et al. 2023) and false generosity (Freire 1970).

This false generosity which places the international (often just another term for organisations based in the Minority World, commonly referred to as the Global North) actor in the role of the protagonist and the Majority World communities in the role of passive recipients or beneficiaries, obscures the agency, knowledge and resourcefulness of these communities. In the early 1990s, Bangladeshi photographer Shahidul Alam began using the term Majority World to describe populations that were hitherto referred to as "developing," "emerging," or the Global South. The term is a political statement designed to remind the world that the people we are talking about comprise a majority of the world's population. Yet, they are forced to follow the dictates of people living in the places referred to as "developed" or the Global North, who are a minority of the global population (Alam 2008). We, the editors of this volume, have consciously adopted this term as a reminder of the power of people and communities.

But let us return to the notion of false generosity embedded in the development and humanitarian sectors. By obfuscating (at best) and denying (at worst), the agency of Majority World actors, it perpetuates the very systems of oppression it purports to fight so that the oppressor can continue to exercise their benevolence in service of the oppressed. Consequently, the professionals who seek to fight injustice and systemic inequities become instruments of colonial continuity (International Development Committee 2022; Khan et al. 2023). Initiatives for systemic change become little more than piece-meal attempts to improve, rather than transform, the current system as evidenced by the oft-stated-yet-not-implemented commitments to transfer funds to local organisations. The promise of short-term gains through incremental changes and the fear of losing the little progress that has been made mitigates the urgency for systemic change, relegating it to the realm of the desirable but improbable. Yet as feminist civil rights activist Audre Lorde noted during her speech in 1979, "The master's tools will never dismantle the master's house. They may allow us to temporarily beat him at his own game, but they will never enable us to bring about genuine change" (Lorde 1984). Community-led development requires systemic change through a transformation in the mindsets, not just of communities but of development funders and implementing agencies. It recognises the agency of communities and their leadership in bringing to life their vision for a better world through their own initiative, knowledge and resources. Yet, it should not be seen as an abrogation of the state's responsibility to its citizens. Instead, it is an approach where the state discharges its responsibility towards its citizens in partnership with them.

The first section of this introduction, *Language Matters*, defines the different terms that are currently being used to speak to power inequities in the system. The second section, *The Need*, examines the current scenario in the international development and humanitarian sectors to articulate why we, the co-editors of this volume, believe that there is an emerging intent towards this transformation. The third section, *The Beginning of a Partnership*, traces the journey of this volume and why we decided to collate it. The fourth section, *A Framework for Community-Led Development*, delves into the nine dimensions of community-led development around which this volume has been structured, and the fifth section, *The Sum of All Parts*, outlines the different chapters included in this volume.

Language Matters

Language is power. It is "both a means of communication and a carrier of culture" (Ngũgĩ 1986, 387). For a long time, the language of the international development and humanitarian sectors reflected the racist and colonial influences that shaped these sectors and sought to normalise them. The growing realisation of the systemic violence perpetuated by the current systems led to a frenzy of efforts to make the language more congruent with the principles of equity, justice and agency. It is notable that this frenzy was once again led by international actors and has resulted in a plethora of buzzwords which are used interchangeably even though they refer to different albeit interconnected ideas (Cornwall 2007). We clarify here how we use some allied terms like decolonisation, localisation, locally-led development (LLD), community-driven development (CDD) and shift-the-power in this volume. Before we begin, however, we would like to acknowledge our own role in perpetuating existing linguistic hegemonies by publishing in a colonial language that remains inaccessible to many. We also want to note that many contributors in this volume have used terms like donors, beneficiaries, bottom-up, welfare and capacity building – all of which reflect the systemic inequities that have shaped our sector. We have made a conscious decision not to change those terms, though we discussed them with the authors. This is because the conversation around the change in terminology has been happening mostly in the Minority World. We felt by changing the terminology used by the contributors we would be changing their voice.

Sondarjee and Andrews (2022, 551) describe decoloniality as

> a political project of human emancipation through collective struggles, entailing at least the following: 1) abolishing racial hierarchies within the hetero-patriarchal and capitalist world order, 2) dismantling the geopolitics of knowledge production, and 3) rehumanising our relationships with Others and nature.

Decolonising development is, therefore, a political project that seeks to dismantle the hegemonic power structures which privilege the ways of thinking, being and doing of the Minority World and dehumanise the Majority World. Among other things, it emphasises the richness of indigenous development frameworks and ways of knowledge production, questions the whiteness of knowledge and the ensuing tyranny of merit, challenges the existing grant-making, governance and salary structures that discriminate against Majority World actors, critically examines linguistic hegemony and reiterates the importance of local and national leadership in reversing historical wrongs (Ngũgĩ 1986; Maral-Hanak 2009; Sultana 2019; Sandel 2020; Sutherland 2023). Tavernaro-Haidarian (2018), however, contends that this framing of decolonisation, rooted in "normative adversarialism" (Kalberg 2004) and violence inherent in the notions of dismantling and rejecting, is itself colonial. Instead, she draws on the African philosophy of Ubuntu and the Baha'i idea of constructive resilience to propose an integrative approach where decolonisation "entails constructing something that transcends the narrow confines of inherited structures and systems without pouring energy into their dismantling" (p.113) and "transcending coloniality by doing what colonialism never did, which is to respect, contribute, engage, and connect" (p.114). We recognise that much of the current discourse on decolonisation continues to view it as a form of resistance and revolution. However, we, the co-editors, find Tavernaro-Haidarian's approach to decolonisation better aligned with community-led development and adopt it as our framing.

According to the UN Inter-Agency Standing Committee (IASC), localisation "enables the meaningful engagement and leadership of local and national actors in humanitarian response, enhancing capacity exchange and increasing direct funding" (Inter-Agency Standing Committee [IASC] n.d.). Instead of addressing issues of power differentials and structural racism that are critical for systems transformation, it focuses on the flow of resources to Majority World organisations that have been systematically starved by the humanitarian sector.

> Localisation looks at the inequities in the system with one eye closed, looking solely at a small handful of the symptoms of the problem (such as lack of funding and unequal partnerships) without asking the difficult questions about the deeply problematic assumptions and attitudes that gave rise to the problem … and which continue to underpin the system.
>
> *(Peace Direct 2022, 4)*

At best, localisation is an act of appeasement and, at worst, a manifestation of the false generosity of Minority World actors who shift the conversation away from power to funding. As this realisation has begun to seep in, organisations and agencies have begun to re-examine their own definitions of localisation. USAID now defines it as "the set of internal reforms, actions, and behavior changes USAID is undertaking to ensure our work puts local actors in the lead, strengthens local systems, and is responsive to local communities" (USAID 2022b).

USAID defines LLD as

> The process by which a diverse group of local actors set their own development agendas; develop and implement solutions; use their capacities, leadership, and

> resources to promote equitable change; and ensure that positive outcomes can be sustained by local actors, for local actors.
>
> *(USAID 2022b)*

This term, often used as the development sector counterpart to "localisation," is however broader than localisation. It goes beyond the technocratic discussion on funding flows and recognises the agency and leadership of local actors. However, unlike decolonisation, it does not critically address issues of structural racism. The use of the term locally-led has also led to intense debates about who is local and who defines them. It has perpetuated existing power differentials as the Minority World power holders once again sit in judgement over Majority World actors to decide whether they are local enough. LLD also overlooks the structural inequities that exist within countries, assuming that a national organisation represents all the populations of the country.

Community-led development, on the other hand, bypasses the contestation around who is local by focusing on the agency of those directly affected by the decisions being made. It addresses structural inequities at both the global and the national level by ensuring that every person has a voice and choice in decisions that affect their lives. True community-led development cannot take place without addressing questions of power, structural racism and injustice. It centres inclusion and agency of the communities, celebrates their relational infrastructure, knowledge and resources and recognises their ownership over knowledge, resources and programming – all of which require critical engagement with structural inequities and power hegemonies. Yet, community-led development does not seek to dismantle the colonial hegemonies in the same way that decolonisation does. Therefore, we find it much closer to Tavernaro-Haidarian's invitational and constructive approach to decolonisation.

Two other phrases that frequently appear in conversations around decolonisation and community-led development merit mention here: Community-Driven Development (CDD) (Guggenheim 2021) and ShiftThePower.

The World Bank Group, which channels over a tenth of its lending through CDD programming, defines CDD as "an approach to local development that emphasizes community control over planning decisions and investment resources…This approach enables communities to work in partnership with national and local governments to identify and manage community-level investments" (2022, 2). The major difference between CDD and community-led development is in the resourcing, scope and relationship with governments. Heavily resourced and much larger in scale, CDD programmes are "frequently used to deliver basic services, construct and maintain local public goods and infrastructure, maintain common property resources, and plan and manage community budgets" (Holmlund and Rao 2021, para 4). They work through or in partnership with governments (national and local) and require a "'sandwich' of capable institutions at the bottom and the top, and full integration with the relevant line ministries" (Holmlund and Rao 2021, para 12). Community-led development programmes recognise the importance of working with local governments, but that is seldom their starting point. Their focus is, first and foremost, on strengthening community leadership and mobilisation. They can also be at varying scales and are often conducted with more limited resources, as the chapters in this volume will demonstrate.

ShiftThePower (Hodgson 2021) started as a hashtag to promote the Global Summit on Community Philanthropy in Johannesburg in 2016. Its purpose was to provoke and inspire. It serves as

> both a call for new behaviours, mindsets and ways of working and a reminder .. that often, those we seek to "help" have much more power – knowledge, skills, networks – than they are given credit for. It is the job of those institutions that are serious about real, lasting change to know when to give up their own power, stand back and help make that happen.
>
> *(Global Fund for Community Foundations na, para 3)*

Finally, no discussion on community-led development can be complete without a look at the term *community*. Systems theory defines community "as a structure of relationship whose members are inter-related and function through social interaction. Community relationship could be based on shared identity that is derived from place, ethnicity, culture, interest, or ideology" (Goel 2014, 2). Consequently, there are various types of communities, and a person is, at any time, a member of multiple communities. "In CLD programming, 'community' often refers to people living within a particular geographic area who share a sense of membership, social interactions and access to material resources, even as they inhabit multiple other 'communities' of practice, faith and kinship" (Veda et al. 2021a, 7). However, it is important to remember that this place-based idea of inclusive communities where "no one is left behind" is a construct by organisations supporting community-led development programming. Communities are, by nature, not just heterogeneous but exclusionary (Chouinard and Milley 2018). In community-led programming, the idea of community is constantly being negotiated and broadened in conversation with the people who inhabit the place of programming.

The Need: Translating Intent into Practice

Even as recently as 2019, whenever we spoke of community-led development, we were always met with patronising smiles followed by, "Of course, it sounds wonderful, but what is the evidence that it works?" Since 2022, no one has asked us this question. And yet, this is not because the last few years have seen a systematic attempt to document the impact of community-led projects and to prove their efficacy over top-down, outsider-driven projects. What then has changed?

Administrator Power's commitment and the steps USAID has taken to operationalise it have definitely strengthened the momentum towards LLD. They have not just led to the adoption of better policies within USAID – for example, the Local Capacity Strengthening Policy or the amendment to the Acquisitions and Assistance Strategy – but also the emergence of a donor statement on LLD signed by 20 bilateral agencies and 15 foundations as of February 2024 (USAID 2023). New alliances of funders and international implementers like WINGS and the RINGO (Reimagining the International NGO) Project are emerging, and International Non-Governmental Organisations (INGOs) are inking new promises of transformation like the Pledge for Change. Grand Bargain 2.0 also recognised the need for greater engagement with and influence of local and national actors (Metcalfe-Hough et al. 2023).

But while Power's announcement may have galvanised the move towards LLD, it is not what triggered the change. In 2020, the Development Assistance Committee of OECD, comprising members from 32 countries, recommended that its members increase systematic engagement with local organisations and channel greater funding directly to them (OECD 2020). In the same year, the World Bank was already channelling USD 33 billion, representing 11% of its lending through CDD programmes (Holmlund and Rao 2021).

In some ways, the current push towards LLD and the release of new metrics by USAID to gauge progress on them has also created the danger of turning the intent for LLD into a mere numbers game. It has led to heightened debates in the Minority World on who constitutes local and who does not.

What changed in the last few years, we assert, is that there was a real impetus towards decolonisation and LLD that came from the communities and Majority World actors themselves – in other words, the need for change is demand-driven. Majority World actors are increasingly beginning to step up and exercise their power by speaking at global fora, forming new coalitions and creating elements like partnership charters to spell out their ideas of fairness. For example, over 2000 Majority World actors have signed on to a letter that was sent to funders, foundations and international organisations in November 2023, on how to organise events on LLD. The letter articulates their frustration at the performative aspect of these events that continued to sideline them (Perrone 2023). It is this exercise of power by Majority World actors and their unwillingness to step back that has led the world's biggest funders and their implementing partners to reconsider their ways.

The death of George Floyd on May 25, 2020 and the BlackLivesMatter (BLM) movement forced many in the Minority World to undertake self-reflection (International Development Committee 2022). It put the spotlight on the deeply embedded structural racism and violence prevalent in Minority World countries that started with slavery and colonialism and has continued unmitigated, leading to calls for restorative justice (Shaw and Kidwai 2020). At the same time, it provided a space to forge a global solidarity based on transnational connective action (Bennett and Sergerberg 2012) in the Majority World (Shahin et al. 2021). Increasingly, Majority World actors began to use this space to articulate the systemic discrimination prevalent, not just within countries but also between them, strengthening the decolonising aid movement (Osofisan 2020; Patel 2021). These parallel processes together resulted in critical discourse on structural inequities and strengthened the intent towards systemic transformation. Since decolonisation remains a difficult subject for many in the Minority World, the focus has turned towards LLD.

This intent to recognise the power and contribution of local actors and communities was further cemented with the onset of the COVID-19 pandemic, which demonstrated that communities are the first responders in a crisis. Therefore, it was vital to recognise and strengthen their agency. However, decades of a top-down colonial system have meant that funders and implementing organisations alike do not know how to partner with communities and support them in their efforts to create the future that they envision for themselves. It is this need that triggered the current volume.

During the course of our four decades of collective experience in this sector, in the Majority World and in international and translocal spaces, we, the co-editors of this volume, have witnessed community-led development in action in different parts of the world, most notably in our own countries. We have also experienced the very real challenges that make the practice of community-led development difficult. Through this volume, we seek to present learnings from various types of organisations – local, international and translocal – and networks who have undertaken community-led development to provide insights on how to translate the intent of centring communities in our work into practice. At the same time, we also wish to demonstrate that there is no one formula for successful community-led development. Instead, the practice of community-led development, and indeed the extent to which it is possible, will depend on the context in which it is being carried out.

The Beginning of a Partnership

It was in April 2020 that we, the co-editors of this volume, first met. The world around us was in a state of panic and chaos. Just a month earlier, on March 11, 2020, the World Health Organization declared COVID-19 as a pandemic. The number of reported COVID-19 cases had crossed 3 million (WHO 2020), international borders had been shut down and more than half the world's population was under some form of lockdown. As development and humanitarian professionals were being parachuted out of their places of work to the relative safety of their home countries, communities and community-based organisations (CBOs) all over the world were faced with a crisis like never before. They rallied together, despite famines, ongoing conflicts, poverty, floods, rising unemployment and a complete breakdown in information to spread awareness, create makeshift hand washing stations, stitch masks and make and distribute sanitisers. They used everything at their disposal, from loudspeakers fixed on two-wheelers and cycle rickshaws to old scraps of cloth. They pooled together food and essential supplies for their neighbours and began to search for information to fight the pandemic.

At this time, the Movement for Community-led Development (MCLD), a translocal consortium of hundreds of local and community-based organisations and 75 INGOs (in April 2020) began to facilitate virtual meetings to pool together information, learning and resources and create a peer support network. Launched on the sidelines of the UN General Assembly in New York in September 2015 when the world was adopting the Sustainable Development Goals, MCLD started as an initiative of 18 INGOs to ensure that every person has a voice and choice in decisions that affect their lives. Gradually it morphed into "a vibrant, collaborative space for collective action" (Veda 2023, 3), serving as a container for change (Cabaj and Weaver, 2016, 9) for member organisations and individuals who sought to address power imbalances within the development and humanitarian sectors and among themselves.

MCLD meetings had mostly been virtual to ensure access for CBOs and local organisations. When the COVID-19 virus began to spread, MCLD members realised that they were facing similar problems: how to balance the safety of development and humanitarian professionals with the need of communities, how to continue our work in the face of lockdowns and restrictions, how to ensure a steady supply of vital resources to the communities which continued to experience disasters – natural and human-made. This led to the call for a peer support platform where CBOs, INGOs and community leaders could come together to share experiences, brainstorm on common concerns and offer emotional support to each other. The first meeting of the "Adapting to COVID 19 and Beyond" platform was held in April 2020.

Elene, representing Outreach International, an international nonprofit with its US office based in Kansas City, attended this first meeting. An anthropologist by training, Elene had worked closely with numerous Majority-World communities, including some in South Africa, her home country. Shortly after the meeting, she contacted Gunjan, who was co-facilitating the adapting to COVID-19 series for MCLD and led its collaborative research team.

Gunjan had begun her career as a grassroots activist with a small feminist organisation called the North East Network in India. As a 22-year-old, she had witnessed first-hand the power of civil society, particularly women and youth, in India's conflict-affected northeast. A journalist by training, Gunjan had worked for almost two decades with social movements in India, both as part of the nonprofit sector and the government, before joining MCLD to study the impact of community-led development.

In February 2019, when Gunjan first joined MCLD, the world was still not convinced about the need to put communities front and centre in development. Following the Grand Bargain and the launch of the #ShiftThePower movement (Wilkinson 2017; Hodgson 2021), development and humanitarian professionals had begun to get uncomfortable with their existing ways of thinking, being and doing. Uneasy laughter and a reference to local organisations had begun to find its way into conversations on how the sector was doing. Yet when it came to community-led development, the conversation always centred around evidence. This was particularly true for the positivists who sought evidence on the complex and multi-layered process of human change through randomised control trials (RCTs) (White et al. 2018). Such evidence was not widespread, mostly because community-led development was often carried out by small local organisations who did not have the resources to undertake systematic evaluations, let alone RCTs. The World Bank funded large-scale CDD projects, particularly those that had been embraced by national governments like the KALAHI CIDDS in the Philippines and the National Program for Community Empowerment (PNPM) in Indonesia offered impact data (Edillon et al. 2011; Voss 2012; World Bank 2022) but not enough to convince the development and humanitarian sectors of the need for transformation.

It was against this backdrop that Gunjan created the collaborative research team in April 2019. Composed of 35 monitoring, evaluation, research, learning and programme professionals from 23 organisations, this team sought to study the impact of community-led development through a systematic review of the evaluation reports of community-led development programmes conducted by INGOs. Our goal was to systematically study community-led programming from around the world to understand where it has worked, how, why and for whom. However, during discussions and consultations with various CBOs, INGOs and thought leaders in the field, we realised the need to first arrive at a common understanding of community-led development because it is, "common sense but elusive. It's hard to describe and capture because it never looks the same in two places" (Inspiring Communities 2013, 15).

Elene joined MCLD's collaborative research team in May 2020 and thus began a partnership that has contributed to the development of practitioner-led tools, trainings on community-led development and now, this volume. Together we used MCLD's extensive network as well as a process of snow-balling to invite contributions for the volume. We saw this volume as an opportunity to serve as a moment of disruption, where scholarship and knowledge from the Majority World is presented in its own voice. This volume brings together voices of both Minority and Majority World practitioners and academics. In doing so, we recognise not just the power differentials that exist but seek to illustrate how community-led development provides a means of addressing such inequalities through collaborative and participatory approaches. In putting together this volume, we facilitated a process of sense-making with all authors and contributors so that we could expand our collective understanding of community-led development and its principles. We saw the sense-making exercise as a process of "mutual empowerment," an act of "constructive resilience" that is "building on" and "integrating the various ways of knowing that exist in the repository of the world's cultures and values" (Tavernaro-Haidarian in Sutherland 2023).

We decided to structure the volume around a framework which is currently being used by hundreds of CBOs, INGOs and even local governments around the world. In the following section we describe this framework.

A Framework for CLD

MCLD's collaborative research team followed a process of inductive reasoning to arrive at 11 characteristics that define community-led development. These are accountability, adaptability, capacity strengthening,[1] collaboration, collective planning and action, community assets, community leadership, participation and inclusion, sustainability, transformative capacity and voice.

> Recognizing that CLD will look different depending on context, the team designed a rubric to reflect how these 11 characteristics would appear in the program lifecycle...This rubric contained nine dimensions and provided a benchmark for measuring progress towards them, even as it acknowledged the diversity and varying scope of CLD programming.
>
> *(Veda et al. 2021a, 8)*

The choice of a rubric was deliberate. Aston (2020) notes that rubrics "provide a harness but not a straitjacket for assessing complex change, and they help stakeholders build a shared understanding of what success looks like... Rubrics allow us to think about membership rather than measurement." Through the use of a rubric, the collaborative research team sought to acknowledge the range of community-led development practices, even as it began to develop benchmarks for practitioners.

After extensive consultations with community-led development practitioners, thought leaders, academics and limited literature reviews conducted over 18 months, the aforementioned 11 characteristics were distilled into the Participatory CLD Assessment tool (Veda et al, 2021c) with nine dimensions reflecting the principles and processes integral to the practice of community-led development. These are indicated in Figure 1.1. The first seven are characteristics and principles of community-led development. The remaining two – facilitation and CLD-congruent monitoring and evaluation (M&E) – are processes that are necessary to operationalise community-led development.

The first dimension of the tool, *participation, inclusion and voice*, is in many ways the foundation of community-led development, which seeks to ensure that every person has a voice in decisions that affect their lives. The tool combines these three key concepts into a single dimension because they are intrinsically intertwined. Participation is an "infinitely malleable concept" that means different things to different people in different settings (Cornwall 2008). It takes place across a spectrum ranging from tokenism to partnership and citizen control (Arnstein 1969). In development, participation is often viewed as an exercise to elicit the

FIGURE 1.1 The nine dimensions of community-led development.

"voices of the poor" for reasons ranging from tokenism to making development interventions more effective and responsive (Goetz and Jenkins 2002). Brohman (1996, 251) argues that participation is an inherently complex and political act, raising questions around who participates, in what, why and how. It is ultimately about power and control (Arnstein 1969; Cornwall 2008).

Voice is important because it brings in the unique representation that individuals have of "their distinctive position in social space and in relation to other[s]" (Bourdieu 1971 in Bonnin 2021), combining the knowledge and capital that they have accumulated over time. Every human being has a voice (not in the spoken sense). Yet colonialism and a history of structural violence have forced many to believe that they do not have a voice, their voice does not matter or they need to stay silent in order to survive. Moreover, in participatory processes "attempts to elicit the voices of ordinary or marginalised people are ultimately conducted on terms dictated by the organisers. They are 'by invitation only'. They are the powerless answering to the powerful" (Goetz and Jenkins 2002, 10). Thus "having a voice, in a way that matters, requires attention to both processes of voice and the valuing of voice" (Tachhi 2016, 117). It also necessitates an intentional process of inclusion through the creation of safe spaces so that the most marginalised can exercise their voice.

Participation without inclusion can strengthen inequities and marginalisation (Chattopadhyay 2015; Fraser in World Culture Report 2000). Inclusion however is an inherently difficult process because "communities are heterogeneous entities defined as much by their differences, not only in terms of composition, but also by their interests and concerns" (Chouinard and Milley 2018, 73). The process of inclusion, therefore, requires continuous and critical self-reflection by both practitioners and power holders, a self-reflection often muddied by fear. Yet inclusion is not just a passive act carried out on the marginalised. It requires recognition by both the power holders (of the value of the marginalised) and the marginalised (self-esteem). It happens when the exercise of voice by the marginalised is matched by the critical self-reflection of the power holders, leading to recognition and redistribution (Fraser 2000; Chouinard and Milley 2018).

The second dimension of the tool is *local knowledge and resources*. MCLD defines local knowledge as

> knowledge embedded in a community. It refers to the intergenerational traditional wisdom, life experiences, artistic expressions, skills, relationships, systems of communication (traditional and emergent), decision-making and conflict resolution, and understanding of the local context that exists within every community. It encompasses both tacit and explicit knowledge, and is locally and collectively produced, applied, and innovated. Local knowledge can be intergenerational or emergent – new, co-created, curated and incorporated into the shared wisdom.
>
> *(MCLD in USAID, 2022a)*

Local resources comprise natural resources (like sand, rocks or forests), human resources (including skills, knowledge, labour and time), physical infrastructure (roads, buildings etc.) and social infrastructure (like relationships, traditional institutions and community groups).

All programmes, including the most top-down ones, use local knowledge and resources. The difference between regular programming and community-led programming is in how local knowledge and resources are treated. Are they just used to fulfil the agendas of external agents, be they funders, governments or civil society organisations? Or are local knowledge and resources the foundation on which programmes are built? Community-led development programmes do not see local knowledge as less than Western and outsider-driven knowledge. Nor do they see communities as a source of resources to fulfil their programming needs. Instead, in community-led programmes communities mobilise their own resources and knowledge because they feel ownership over the programme and are committed to the change it seeks to make. Some community-led approaches like Asset Based Community Development (ABCD) start "with what the people have" and enable communities to recognise and build on their resources through intentional facilitation (Mathie et al. 2017).

The third dimension of community-led development, *sustainability and exit strategies*, recognises that development and humanitarian assistance are almost always temporary. At some point, determined almost always by funders or the political situation of a country, external support to a programme ceases and the implementing organisation exits (Ahmed et al. 2018). For long, the challenge in the development sector has been to ensure that this exit is efficient and responsible, that is, the exit happens in a manner that the positive change brought about by a programme is sustained either through a continuation of activities or through a change in behaviours and mindsets. In practice, exit decisions are seldom made with sustainability in mind and often involve a last-minute handover of programme infrastructure to local groups or leaders, with limited and in some cases, no attempt to prepare the groups to continue the programme work (Heldgaar 2008; Ahmed et al. 2018).

In theory, sustainability is in-built into community-led development programmes because a community does not exit a programme. Therefore, when programmes are designed, implemented and owned by communities, the likelihood of their continuing after the cessation of external support is high. However, in practice, sustainability requires intentional planning. Measures need to be embedded into community-led programmes right at the planning stage. Communities need to work with external stakeholders and local governments, where feasible, to build infrastructure to sustain both the momentum and the positive change once the external stakeholders exit. More recently, there has been talk about shifting from the idea of exit to transition. This is based on the realisation that a cessation of a financial relationship does not necessarily need to signal the end of all relationships between an external organisation and a community. Instead, it can mark the transition towards a more equitable partnership where the external agency continues to serve as an ally to the community, enabling it to get access and visibility through its own network and connections.

Accountability is the fourth characteristic of community-led development in the tool. In simple terms, accountability is "the obligation to explain, justify, and take responsibility for one's actions" (USAID 2023, 1). In community-led development, accountability is the mechanism that builds and sustains trust, which is vital to exercising individual and collective agency. Done right, it nurtures a sense of shared responsibility and political power, which, in turn, sustains participation. However, Chouinard (2013, 239) argues that "accountability has lost its traditional democratic meaning of shared responsibility and shifted to a predominantly technocratic conception focused on control, regulation, and compliance (Greene 1999; Perrin 2007)." By viewing accountability as an economic act focused on expenditure and performance monitoring, the technocratic concept of "mutual accountability" made popular by the aid effectiveness agenda, reduces citizens to consumers (Biesta 2004; Chouinard 2013; Jones 2017). In contrast, in community-led development accountability is political, relational, multi-directional (not top-down or bottom-up) and collective.

Context matters. "What works effectively in one setting does not automatically or easily transfer to an alternative setting, even within the same organisation"

(Harvey 2022, 1587). This realisation has led to new approaches in international development including *Thinking and Working Politically* (McCulloch and Piron 2019), *Doing Development Differently* (Harvard Kennedy School 2014) and *Problem Driven Iterative Adaptation* (Andrews et al. in Whaites et al. 2015, 123–133). In 2019, The Organisation for Economic Co-operation and Development's Development Assistance Committee (OECD-DAC) recognised adapting to context as a Guiding Principle on Managing for Sustainable Development Results, calling for more flexible and iterative approaches to programming (Sharp and Wild 2021). Therefore, it is no surprise that the fifth dimension of community-led development is *adaptability or responsiveness to context.* This refers not just to "an ability to assess, identify and respond to contextual barriers and enablers" (Harvey 2022, 1588), including culture, power dynamics, resource access, political environment, but also the ability to continuously learn and adapt by embracing failure. It recognises the dynamic nature of local contexts, particularly in a world that is becoming increasingly fragile and unpredictable and emphasises the need to continually assess the appropriateness of programming to respond to changes in local contexts, in partnership with communities. Finally, it "erases the boundaries between design, implementation, and evaluation and reframes thinking to consider the complexity of development problems and nonlinear change pathways" (Brinkerhoff et al. 2018).

In Aotearoa (the Maori language name for New Zealand), there is a saying, "Nā tō rourou, nā taku rourou ka ora ai te iwi. With your basket and my basket we will sustain the people" (Inspiring Communities na). This saying aptly represents dimension six of the tool – *collaboration.* In community-led development, collaboration can be of various types: collaboration within and between people of similar socioeconomic and cultural backgrounds (horizontal), collaboration between people and groups representing different political, social and economic power (vertical), collaboration between communities and broader movements and finally, collaboration between government-civil society and communities. The latter is important both for the sustainability and scalability of community-led interventions. It is therefore regarded as a separate dimension unto itself.

Wood and Grey (1991, 146) define collaboration as "occurring when a group of autonomous stakeholders of a problem domain engage in an interactive process, using shared rules, norms, and structures, to act on or decide on issues related to that domain." Collaboration and connection are at the heart of the collective planning and action that defines community-led development. They happen with the active participation of different stakeholders and can strengthen voice, trust and inclusion, thereby building community ownership. Collaboration is important not just because it enhances social capital and collective power, but also because it can mitigate marginalisation, isolation and othering by creating empathy, acceptance, belonging and mutuality. Through the process of bridging, collaboration reminds us that "we are inextricably interconnected and it helps us build a large 'we' that does not demand assimilation" (Powell and Heydemann 2020, para 9).

Collaboration between government, civil society and communities has been a long-standing feature of CDD programmes, as noted earlier. While community-led development programmes may not necessitate this collaboration as their starting point, in the long run, they do require strong local governments that are responsive to the needs of their citizens. Therefore, building systematic engagement between communities and local governments is the seventh dimension of community-led development, and particularly important when looking at the question of sustainability.

While the first seven dimensions of community-led development in the Participatory CLD Assessment Tool focus on principles of community-led development, the final two dimensions cover processes that are integral to the practice of community-led development: M&E that is community-led development congruent, and facilitation.

M&E has long been a part of development practice. In its current form, M&E often serves as an extractive tool, where communities are treated merely as sources of data to fulfil the accountability needs of funders and implementing organisations. As such, it exacerbates the systemic injustices embedded in the international system. Masvaure and Motlanthe assert that "The evaluation field is a microcosm and an appendage of Western hegemonic influence on international development" (2022, abstract). Yet, M&E carried out in congruence with community-led principles can serve as a powerful tool for dismantling power inequities (Ahrens et al. 2023; SPCC et al. 2024). When a community decides what success looks like, how it should be measured, when and towards what end, it not only engages in a cycle of continuous learning and adaptation, it also overcomes the sense of learned helplessness (Gordon 1985) perpetuated by traditional development sector initiatives. In community-led development congruent M&E, external actors and implementing partners can play the role of facilitators, strengthening the community's capacity to measure the performance of its programmes. However, the ownership of the data and decision-making around what data is collected and how it is used, remains with the community (SPCC et al. 2024).

Facilitation is the final dimension of the tool and integral to the practice of community-led development. It is through facilitation that participation happens, inclusion is realised, collective planning and action are implemented. Skilled facilitation that is responsive to local power dynamics can lead to solidarity, trust and bridging, paving the way for collaboration and connection. In this case,

> Facilitation is a co-creative and adaptive process in which a facilitator enables local actors to set common goals, take ownership of these goals, build on existing strengths, and work towards achieving their goals. Key components of effective facilitation are guiding discussion, asking questions, consensus building, mediation and ensuring diverse voices are heard, all within a relationship of mutual learning and partnership.
>
> *(Veda et al. 2021b, 52)*

The essence of facilitation is in enabling, not doing; in holding space, not taking space; in standing, not speaking (Weisbord and Janoff 2007). Facilitators can be both external to a community or members of the community itself. Wheeler et al. (2020) identify three types of blind spots that facilitators of participatory processes have to tackle:

> i) getting beneath the surface of labels and names while also recognising our own positionality and that of others; ii) navigating a process which enables diverse and invisibilised experiences to emerge through different ways of knowing, while also enabling participants and practitioners control over how and when and what is communicated; and iii) building inclusive collective action, which does not reify experiences or homogenise difference, but provides a firmer foundation for collectivity to be sustained.
>
> *(2020, 4)*

A skilled facilitator not only understands the power and politics that exist in a community but also recognises their own biases and blindspots.

After multiple rounds of pilot testing and inter-rater reliability studies with student interns and community-led development practitioners across various countries, these nine dimensions and the rubric that sought to measure progress on them were refined into the Participatory CLD Assessment Tool (see Annex).

A learning-focused tool, it enables organisations and local governments to see how community-led their work is and to adjust their programming in partnership with community members. It encourages professionals and organisations to engage with and think deeply about the principles of community-led development. At the time of the volume's publication, the tool was available in ten languages and being used by local governments, INGOs and CBOs worldwide.

The Structure of the Book

The last few decades have seen some robust debates on the need for community-led development and allied approaches like LLD, with justifications ranging from the normative to the instrumental and the emancipatory. This volume does not seek to add to this body of literature by delving into the why of community-led development. Instead it focuses on the how – how does one practise community-led development? Therefore the current volume is structured around the nine dimensions of the aforementioned Participatory CLD Assessment Tool. Extensive consultations, literature reviews on specific dimensions and the widespread use of the tool have demonstrated that these nine dimensions are vital for the practice of community-led development. While many of the dimensions seem intuitive, operationalising them poses unique challenges.

As team members of MCLD's global collaborative research effort, we undertook a landscape review of 173 community-led development programmes across 65 countries (Veda 2022a). While the review was insightful in describing the breadth of the community-led development programme types and the presence of community-led dimensions within these programmes, it could not capture the organisations' unique approaches to community-led development and their responsiveness to local contexts. The complexity and context-specific nature of such practices, therefore, remain less explored. Speaking to this gap, each chapter in this volume exemplifies a specific dimension, illustrating the dimension's theoretical foundations, challenges and practical manifestations, while situating such discussions within the work of a specific organisation.

Here we want to emphasise that even though every chapter focuses on one or two dimensions, the presence of one dimension does not guarantee community-led development. On the contrary, all nine dimensions must work together in tandem to ensure sustained and quality community-led development. Thus, while every case study in this volume focuses on a particular dimension to explain what it looks like in practice, it also illustrates how that particular dimension works in combination with the others to ensure ongoing collective action.

The book is divided into five parts in addition to the introductory and concluding sections. Each of the five parts begin with a brief introduction to the dimensions they focus on. In these parts, we briefly pause to situate the dimension in discussions within the development sector and beyond, setting the stage for our contributors' respective chapters. As our intention with each chapter is to illustrate the "how" of the different dimension, we purposely selected contributors steeped in community-led development. Thus most chapters are written directly in the voice of practitioners, many of whom are from the Majority World.

The introductory section contains this introduction and a chapter by Dr John Coonrod, co-founder of MCLD. Titled *The Quest for Human Dignity*, Coonrod's chapter tells the story of community-led development through the eyes of a practitioner, a physicist who was so inspired by the ideals of human dignity that he left the labs at Princeton University to work with communities around the world. In keeping with the constructive resilience that this volume seeks to embody, his chapter does not seek to provide a comprehensive or authoritative history of community-led development. Rather, it focuses on key moments and champions that have significantly impacted the trajectory of community-led development. Coonrod starts with Gandhi's Village Republic, recounts the story of Jimmy Yen's Rural Reconstruction Movement in China and the Naam Movement in Burkina Faso and engages with Freire's concepts of generosity. His journey encompasses encounters with Robert Chambers, often described as the father of Participatory Development, the feminist movement, the community-driven programmes across Asia, and finally results in the formation of MCLD in 2015.

Part I of this volume delves into collaboration, within communities, between them, and with other key stakeholders, particularly the government. We begin with this dimension because at its core, community-led development is about collective planning and action through shared leadership and responsibility. Through four chapters set in Sierra Leone, Uganda, Mexico and Benin, this section looks at how organisations can create spaces for community members to come together, bond and collectively exercise their leadership. They speak to the importance of working with governments, particularly local governments, which is not just important for scale and sustainability, but also to ensure that community-led development does not become an excuse for the state to abrogate its responsibilities towards its citizens.

In *The OneVillage Partners Method: Building New Community Spaces for Consensus and Collaboration*, the team from OneVillage Partners in Sierra Leone demonstrates how through the philosophy of partnerism, an organisation can facilitate the development and strengthening of collaboration among all stakeholders. The authors share the organisation's community-led development methodology as it takes shape and continues to evolve within the postcolonial context of Sierra Leone, a country subjected to "Humanitarian Imperialism." They show how collaboration and consensus-building can build social capital sustainably even as it leads to improvements in health and quality of life.

Aida Ramos, a human geographer, delves into how a state's responsibility to its citizens and community-led development can work hand in hand in her chapter titled *Communal Land Organisations and Payments for Environmental Services in the Huasteca Potosina Region of Mexico*. The recognition and appreciation of local resources by both development interventions and local communities is an essential aspect of community-led development. But in some cases, such recognition can deepen inequalities, as Ramos' analysis of the self-governing mechanisms of Mexico's once state-granted communal lands, or ejidos, illustrates. Situating her analysis within the context of neoliberal reform, Ramos explores the promises and problems of a market approach to community-led initiatives, focusing specifically on local resources management and natural conservation under the Payments for Environmental Services (PES) programme among two communities in Mexico's Huasteca region.

How can a small CBO started by a youth from the community use collaboration to address complex challenges like child marriage and teenage pregnancy? The Amani Initiative, a nonprofit organisation from Uganda tells this story in *The Power of Synergy: Unlocking Sustainable Development through Collaboration in Uganda*. Told through the words of Nixon Ochatre, the founder of Amani, and various change agents from the communities in the West Nile region of Uganda where the organisation began, this chapter explores the different kinds of collaboration that are possible and even needed within communities to bring about sustainable change on complex issues. In the spirit of community-led development and local ownership, this chapter makes no attempt to summarise, synthesise or annotate the voices from the community. It is a departure from publication standards, but we believe it embodies the call for change that underpins conversations on decolonisation.

To Transform Systems, Start with the Heart: CLD Benin's Story of Collective Power and Collective Impact is the final chapter in this section, collaboratively developed by members of the Movement for Community-led Development Benin (CLD-Benin), a local nonprofit organisation. In this chapter members explain how their voluntary network, connecting over a 1000 CBOs, leverages relational capital to build and sustain collaborations. Through their own journey and collective action initiatives on local superfoods and COVID-19 awareness, they share how integrating the principles of community-led development like inclusion, local resources and knowledge transformed their ways of working and eventually enabled them to impact the systems they are a part of. In its initial years, CLD-Benin members applied Kania et al.'s Water of Systems Change Framework (2018) to their work. Gradually however they began to adapt this framing for community-led work. Together with 300 colleagues from Benin and around the world, they developed the Community-led Worldview of Systems Change which they share in their chapter.

Part II delves into the dimension of responsiveness to context or adaptability. The two chapters in this section demonstrate how INGOs committed to community-led development have learnt to adapt their work to the local context. In *When the Helped Help the Helpers Help: The Global Diffusion and Transformation of Community-Led Development Practices in an American Faith-Based NGO*, co-authors David J. Howlett and Matthew Breay Bolton draw from postcolonial theory to trace the genealogy of the participatory development model used by Outreach International, an INGO based out of Kansas City, US. In doing so, they show how Outreach's community-led methodology has been shaped by local political contexts, in particular the radical community organising methods used by local Filipino activists and development workers mobilising against poverty and authoritarian governance. Filipino field staff transformed the very organisation that had hired them, as Outreach increasingly adopted their Participatory Human Development model as the standard field methodology.

In *Aga Khan Foundation: Adapting Community-Led Development to Diverse Contexts,* Matt Reeves, Global Lead for Civil Society at the Foundation uses a series of vignettes to showcase how the organisation adapted its methodology across geographies and time, identifying aspects of their approach that are core, as well as those that are flexible. Based on conversations with colleagues from around the world, Matt's chapter touches on critical areas including (i) when to work with existing organisations and when to create new groups, (ii) the power of community philanthropy and local resource mobilisation, (iii) the resilience of community leadership at times of significant societal disruption and (iv) the potential and pitfalls of technology in transforming community development.

Part III of this volume focuses on two dimensions: participation, inclusion and voice, and local resources and knowledge. Participation and inclusion are, at least in theory, the basis for most development and humanitarian projects since the 1990s. Yet, structural inequities present in most societies often compounded by colonial histories and capitalistic systems of exploitation, the chequered track record of development organisations, internal strife and the almost institutionalised invisibility of the most marginalised groups make this one of the most challenging aspects of community work. Participation requires trust and "effective voice" (Couldry 2010); inclusion, an ability to see and value the most invisibilised. They represent a journey that requires humility, courage and intentionality. Participation, inclusion and voice are also deeply entwined with local knowledge and resources. Respecting their knowledge and assets not only enables marginalised groups within communities to feel valued, it also increases their ownership over a programme.

The first two chapters in this section, one located in India and the other in Guatemala, demonstrate the challenges to participation and inclusion and the pivotal role that community organisations play in overcoming them. The third chapter in this section uses examples from South Africa to show how local knowledge and resources can be centred in community-led development practice.

Monisha Behal, a grassroots feminist activist provides an autoethnographic account of how a small isolated community in Nagaland, Northeast India, led by its women and youth, stepped into its own agency and built the road to resilience in *The Chronicles of Chizami: How Women from a Small Naga Village Built the Road to Resilience*. She outlines the challenges to participation, particularly for women in a patriarchal and strife-ridden society and shares learnings on operationalising inclusion through an integrated approach. Behal notes the importance of seemingly non-productive activities, like cooking together or singing around a bonfire in building trust and relationships, that are at the heart of all community-led work.

In *What Participation Means in a Divided Indigenous Community: The Case of an Engineers without Borders Water Project among the Ch'orti' Maya of Eastern Guatemala* Brent E. Metz, Professor of Anthropology at the University of Kansas, US, defines participation as multi-party collaboration and provides a critical perspective on the challenges of inclusive participation, particularly in indigenous communities dealing with a history of colonisation. Metz's chapter captures the struggles a Ch'orti Maya group in Guatemala faced in accessing water sustainably. It also reflects on the challenges local communities endure when navigating international funding partnerships that are intended to facilitate inclusive planning and participation and yet can sow the seeds of distrust and division.

In *Local knowledge and resources for community-led development in South Africa – looking through an asset-based lens,* Hanna Nel, Associate Professor in the Department of Social Work at the University of Johannesburg, shares tools and approaches to operationalise asset-based community development (ABCD), a community-led approach that enables community members to move from a dependency mindset, focused on outside resources, to become citizens who are self-reliant and owners of their development efforts. She draws on examples and a case study from South Africa to demonstrate how the five-step ABCD process prevents exploitation, restores people's power, pride and independence and raises their consciousness about taking control of their future.

Part IV of the volume encompasses the dimensions of sustainability and accountability highlighted through two chapters, one based in Haiti and the other in a collective model from Kenya, Ethiopia and Nigeria. *From Roots to Rasin: The Story of Transition and Transformation* addresses the much talked about questions of exit and sustainability by demonstrating how ethical and responsible transitions can take place and power be shifted to communities. It focuses on the partnership between a Haitian organisation *Rasin Devlopman* and their US partner, *Roots of Development.* The co-authors, Chad Bissonnette, an American who started Roots of Development and Louino "Robi" Robillard, a Haitian who leads Raisin, reflect on the two organisations' combined histories to describe why and how Roots of Development created and transferred total responsibility for its programme in Haiti over to a Haitian organisation. Such a transfer of responsibilities acts as a powerful example of how a Western-based organisation realised its own blindspots and sought to address them in a sustainable and meaningful way. Told in a conversational style to preserve the perspectives of the authors, the chapter highlights the value of local leadership and serves as a guide on how to make the work of international organisations more respectful, more sustainable and ultimately more impactful while remaining accountable to local partners.

In *Accountability in Community and Local Leadership: The Nuru Collective Approach to Uniting People through Place and Purpose*, Casey Harrison, Pauline Wambeti, Amy Gaman, Matt Lineal, Simon Eli and Abiy Meshesha from Nuru Collective document their work spanning Kenya, Ethiopia and Nigeria. Through the work of Nuru Collective, a group of not-for-profit, non-governmental organisations with a shared vision, this chapter demonstrates how an organisation can apply the principles of accountability to its work and put into place practices that embed it into the ways of thinking and doing of both its staff and the communities that it supports. The chapter shows how formal processes and structures can aid accountability by assuring people that their collective agency in holding leaders and other stakeholders to account has some institutional backing, thereby increasing their odds of success.

Part V of this volume delves into the two processes that are vital to operationalise community-led development: CLD congruent M&E and facilitation. In *Who Owns the Response? How Self-Assessment Catalyses Ownership in the work of The Constellation*, the team from The Constellation, a nonprofit organisation that works with communities in more than 70 countries, share two approaches that its practitioners use to support community ownership. The first, the Community Life Competence Process (CLCP), is a learning cycle whereby communities assess, and subsequently learn from their actions. The second, characterised by the acronym SALT: Support, Appreciate, Learn and Transfer is an appreciative facilitation approach. By elaborating on the philosophy underscoring these approaches and then providing examples of how these approaches take shape in real life, the Constellation team illustrates how integral community-led processes of self-monitoring, evaluation and facilitation are to create sustainable and resilient communities.

The final contribution in this volume is from Udesh Fernando and Vinya S. Ariyaratne of the Sarvodaya Shramadana Movement, a self-governance movement from Sri Lanka founded by A.T. Ariyaratne in 1958. In their chapter titled, *We Build the Road and the Road Builds Us: The Sarvodaya Shramadana Movement's Participatory Community Development Model*, Fernando and Ariyaratne share a development approach arising from the Majority World. They demonstrate how Sarvodaya has been using quality facilitation to support communities in realising their potential and co-creating a community-led development approach that is holistic and spanning six-dimensions – spiritual, moral, cultural, social, economic and political.

In the conclusion to this book, we, the co-editors, bring together some key lessons from these diverse case studies. We examine the inter-relationships between the dimensions and how they manifest in practice, how community-led development and its practice change with context and locality, and explore what scale means for community-led programming. We conclude by recognising that community-led development is hard work and requires intentionality at every step, from all the actors involved. It is not a magic bullet and should not be viewed as a panacea for all that ails the international development and humanitarian sectors. Yet, when done right and with the right intentions, it has the potential to transform our current system, one community at a time.

Note

1 At the time of the research it was capacity building. Since then, MCLD has moved to capacity strengthening following consultations with its members.

References

Ahmed, Farzana, Haley Dillan, and Jim Robinson. "Planning for Success from Start to Exit: A Review of Literature, Policy and Practice." Stopping As Success, 2018. www.stoppingassuccess.org/wp-content/uploads/2020/01/Planning-for-success-FINAL.pdf

Ahrens, Vivien, Evelyn Cruz, Mariana Pasturczak, Lori L. Bakken, and Travis R. Moore. "Between Funding Requirements and Community Priorities: Centro Hispano of Dane County's Transformative Approach to Program Evaluation." *Journal of MultiDisciplinary Evaluation* 19, no. 44 (July 20, 2023). https://doi.org/10.56645/jmde.v19i44.787

Alam, Shahidul. "Majority World: Challenging the West's Rhetoric of Democracy." *Amerasia Journal* 34, no. 1 (2008): 88–98.

Andrews, Matt, Lant Pritchett, Salimah Samji, and Michael Woolcock. "Building Capability by Delivering Results: Putting Problem-Driven Iterative Adaptation (PDIA) Principles into Practice." In *A Governance Practitioner's Notebook: Alternative Ideas and Approaches*, edited by Alan Whaites, Eduardo Gonzalez, Sara Fyson and Graham Teskey, 123–33. Paris: OECD, 2015.

Arnstein, Sherry R. "A Ladder of Citizen Participation." *Journal of the American Institute of Planners* 35, no. 4 (July 1969): 216–24. https://doi.org/10.1080/01944366908977225

Aston, T. 2020. Rubrics as a Harness for Complexity, April 7. Retrieved March 11, 2021, from www.linkedin.com/pulse/rubrics-harness-complexity-thomas-aston/

Bennett, Lance, and Alexandra Segerberg. "The Logic of Connective Action." *Information, Communication &Society* (April 10, 2012). https://doi.org/10.1017/cbo9781139198752

Biesta, Gert J. J. "Education, Accountability, and the Ethical Demand: Can the Democratic Potential of Accountability Be Regained?" *Educational Theory* 54, no. 3 (July 15, 2004): 233–50. https://doi.org/10.1111/j.0013-2004.2004.00017.x

Bonnin, Juan Eduardo. "Discourse Analysis for Social Change: Voice, Agency and Hope." *International Journal of the Sociology of Language* 2021, no. 267–268 (2021): 69–84. https://doi.org/10.1515/ijsl-2020-0081

Brinkerhoff, Derick W., Sarah Frazer, and Lisa Marie McGregor. 2018. Adapting to Learn and Learning to Adapt: Practical Insights from International Development Projects. RTI Press. RTI Press Policy Brief No. PB-0015-1801. https://doi.org/10.3768/rtipress.2018.pb.0015.1801

Brohman, John. *Popular Development: Rethinking the Theory and Practice of Development.* Oxford: Wiley Blackwell, 1996.

Cabaj, Mark, and Liz Weaver. 2016. Collective impact 3.0 an evolving framework for Community Change. Tamarack Institute. Retrieved January 14, 2024, from https://cdn2.hubspot.net/hubfs/316071/Events/CCI/2016_CCI_Toronto/CCI_Publications/Collective_Impact_3.0_FINAL_PDF.pdf

Cammarota, Julio. "Blindsided by the Avatar: White Saviors and Allies Out of Hollywood and in Education." *Review of Education, Pedagogy, and Cultural Studies*, 33, no. 3 (2011): 242–59.

Chattopadhyay, Soumyadip. "Contesting Inclusiveness: Policies, Politics and Processes of Participatory Urban Governance in Indian Cities." *Progress in Development Studies* 15, no. 1 (2015): 22–36.

Chouinard, Jill Ann. "The Case for Participatory Evaluation in an Era of Accountability." *American Journal of Evaluation* 34, no. 2 (2013): 237–53. https://doi.org/10.1177/1098214013478142

Chouinard, Jill Anne, and Peter Milley. "Uncovering the Mysteries of Inclusion: Empirical and Methodological Possibilities in Participatory Evaluation in an International Context." *Evaluation and Program Planning, Elsevier* 67, no. C (2018): 70–78.

Cornwall, Andrea. "Buzzwords and Fuzzwords: Deconstructing Development Discourse." *Development in Practice* 17, no. 4/5 (2007): 471–84. www.jstor.org/stable/25548244

Cornwall, Andrea. "Unpacking 'Participation': Models, Meanings and Practices." *Community Development Journal* 43, no. 3 (June 5, 2008): 269–83. https://doi.org/10.1093/cdj/bsn010

Couldry, Nick. "Voice as Value." In *Why Voice Matters: Culture and Politics after Neoliberalism*, 1–20. London: SAGE Publications Ltd, 2010. https://doi.org/10.4135/9781446269114

U.S. Agency for International Development. "Donor Statement on Supporting Locally LED Development:" U.S. Agency for International Development, November 2023. www.usaid.gov/localization/donor-statement-on-supporting-locally-led-development

Edillon, Rosemarie, Sharon Faye Piza, and Carlos Abad Santos. *Impact Evaluation KALAHI-CIDSS Final Survey*. The World Bank Group and Asia Pacific Policy Centre, June 2011. https://kalahi.dswd.gov.ph/press/downloads/category/61-world-bank-evaluation-reports

Fanon, Frantz. *Black Skin, White Masks*. London: Paladin, 1970.

Fraser, Nancy. "Redistribution, Recognition and Participation: Towards an Integrated Concept of Justice." Essay. In *World Culture Report, 2000: Cultural Diversity, Conflict and Pluralism*, 48–57. Paris: UNESCO, 2000.

Freire, Paulo, and Myra B. Ramos. *Pedagogy of the Oppressed*. New York: Seabury Press, 1970.

Goel, Kalpana. "Understanding Community and Community Development." Essay. In *Community Work: Theories, Experiences and Challenges*, 1st ed., 1–15. India: Niruta Publishers, 2014.

Goetz, Annemarie, and Rob Jenkins. 2002. Voice, Accountability and Human Development: The Emergence of a New Agenda. Human Development Occasional Papers. UNDP.

Gordon, Adele. "Learned Helplessness and Community Development: A Case Study." *Journal of Community Psychology* 13, no. 4 (October 1985): 327–37. https://doi.org/10.1002/1520-6629(198510)13:4<327::aid-jcop2290130402>3.0.co;2-v

Guggenheim, Scott. Indonesia and the Kecamatan Development Program. April 2021. https://documents1.worldbank.org/curated/en/548791632334335638/pdf/Origins-of-Community-Driven-Development-Indonesia-and-the-Kecamatan-Development-Program.pdf

Harvey, Gillian. "Context Matters, so How Do We Get Better at Working with Context in Implementation Research and Practice? Comment on "Stakeholder Perspectives of Attributes and Features of Context Relevant to Knowledge Translation in Health Settings: A Multi-country Analysis."" *International Journal of Health Policy and Management* 11, no. 8 (2022): 1587–89. https://doi.org/10.34172/ijhpm.2022.7088

Heldgaar, Jesper. Managing Aid Exit and Transformation, SIDA, May 2008. www.oecd.org/derec/norway/42208151.pdf

Hodgson, Jenny. "The Birth of #ShiftThePower." *Alliance Magazine* (August 31, 2021). www.alliancemagazine.org/opinion/the-birth-of-shiftthepower/

Holmlund, Marcus, and Vijayendra Rao. "Where and When Is Community-Driven Development (CDD) Effective?" Web log. *Development Impact* (blog). World Bank (October 26, 2021). https://blogs.worldbank.org/en/impactevaluations/where-and-when-community-driven-development-cdd-effective

Ingram, George. *Locally Driven Development: Overcoming the Obstacles*. Brookings Global Working Paper, 173. New York: Brookings Institute, 2022.

Inspiring Communities. *Learning by Doing: Community-Led Change in Aotearoa NZ*. New Zealand: Inspiring Communities Trust, 2013.

Inspiring Communities. "What Is Community-Led Development?: Inspiring Communities." Inspiring Communities | Supporting Community-Led Development. Accessed May 5, 2024. https://inspiringcommunities.org.nz/ic_resource/what-is-community-led-development/

Inter-Agency Standing Committee (IASC). The Grand Bargain, n.d.. https://interagencystandingcommittee.org/grand-bargain. Accessed February 4, 2024.

International Development Committee. "Racism in the Aid Sector." House of Commons UK. June 23, 2022. https://committees.parliament.uk/publications/22698/documents/166821/default

Jones, Timo Mahn. *Accountability for Development Cooperation under the 2030 Agenda*. Bonn: Deutsches Institut für Entwicklungspolitik. October 2017. www.issuelab.org/resources/27662/27662.pdf

Kania, John, Mark Kramer, and Peter Senge. The Water of Systems Change, June 2018. www.fsg.org/wp-content/uploads/2021/08/The-Water-of-Systems-Change_rc.pdf

Karlberg, Michael Robert. *Beyond the Culture of Contest: From Adversarialism to Mutualism in an Age of Interdependence*. Oxford: George Ronald, 2004.

Khan, Themrise, Kanakulya Dickson, and Maïka Sondarjee. *White Saviorism in International Development: Theories, Practices and Lived Experiences*. Wakefield, Québec: Daraja Press, 2023.

Lorde, Audre. "The Master's Tools Will Never Dismantle the Master's House." 1984. *Sister Outsider: Essays and Speeches*, Ed., 110–114. Berkeley: Crossing Press, 2007. Print.

Maral-Hanak, Irmi. "Cultural Hegemony? The Example of Language Use in International Development Co-Operation in Tanzania/East Africa." *Spectrum: Journal of Global Studies* 1, no. 1 (2009): 53–68.

Masvaure, Steven, and Sonny M. Motlanthe. "Reshaping How We Think about Evaluation: A Made in Africa Evaluation Perspective." *African Evaluation Journal* 10, no. 1 (August 25, 2022). https://doi.org/10.4102/aej.v10i1.618

Mathie, Alison, Jenny Cameron, and Katherine Gibson. "Asset-Based and Citizen-Led Development: Using a Diffracted Power Lens to Analyze the Possibilities and Challenges." *Progress in Development Studies* 17, no. 1 (2017): 54–66.

McCulloch, Neil, and Laure-Hélène Piron. "Thinking and Working Politically: Learning from Practice. Overview to Special Issue." *Devlopment Policy Review* 37 (2019): O1–O15. https:// doi.org/10.1111/dpr.12439

Metcalfe-Hough, Victoria, Wendy Fenton, and Farah Manji. 2023. *The Grand Bargain in 2022: An Independent Review*. HPG Commissioned Report. London: ODI. www.odi.org/en/publications/thegrand-bargain-in-2022-an-independent-review

Ngũgĩ wa Thiong'o. *Decolonising the Mind: The Politics of Language in African Literature*. London; Portsmouth, NH: J. Currey; Heinemann, 1986.

OECD. "Development Assistance Committee Members and Civil Society." *The Development Dimension* (April 30, 2020). https://doi.org/10.1787/51eb6df1-en

Osofisan, Wale. "Opinion: Why the Black Lives Matter Movement Should Have Us Rethinking Humanitarian Aid." *Devex*, November 20, 2020. www.devex.com/news/opinion-why-the-black-lives-matter-movement-should-have-us-rethinking-humanitarian-aid-98570

Pailey, Robtel Neajai. "De-Centring the 'White Gaze' of Development." *Development and Change* 51, no. 3 (2019): 729–45.

Patel, Smruti. "Localisation, Racism and Decolonisation: Hollow Talk or Real Look in the Mirror?" *Humanitarian Practice Network* (September 29, 2021). https://odihpn.org/publication/localisation-racism-and-decolonisation-hollow-talk-or-real-look-in-the-mirror/

Peace Direct. 2022. *Localisation and Decolonisation: The Difference that makes the Difference*. Discussion Paper. www.peacedirect.org/wp-content/uploads/2023/09/PD-Localisation-and-Decolonisation-Report-v3.pdf

Perrone, Alessio. "The Call to End 'abject Humiliation' over Development Conferences." *Devex*, November 30, 2023. www.devex.com/news/the-call-to-end-abject-humiliation-over-development-conferences-106699

Powell, John A., and Rachel Heydemann. "On Bridging: Evidence and Guidance from Real-World Cases." Othering & Belonging Institute, August 19, 2020. https://belonging.berkeley.edu/on-bridging

Samahan para sa Pagsulong at Pag -unlad ng Capaculan (SPCC), Nancy Bobadilla, and Gunjan Veda. "Our Data, Our Process: Re-Imagining the Community-Led Monitoring and Evaluation Discussion." *Asia Pacific Journal of Evaluation (APJE)*, Special Issue, 2, no. 1 (April 16, 2024).

Sandel, Michael J. 2020. *The Tyranny of Merit: What's Become of the Common Good?* Business Book Summary. First edition. New York: Farrar, Straus and Giroux.

Shahin, Saif, Junki Nakahara, and Mariana Sánchez. "Black Lives Matter Goes Global: Connective Action Meets Cultural Hybridity in Brazil, India, and Japan." *New Media & Society* 26, no. 1 (November 18, 2021): 216–35. https://doi.org/10.1177/14614448211057106

Sharp, Samuel, and Leni Wild. "Opportunities and Challenges for DAC Members in 'Adapting to Context.'" ODI, 2021. www.jstor.org/stable/resrep51224

Shaw, Daniel Odin, and Saman Ayesha Kidwai. "The Global Impact of the Black Lives Matter (BLM) Movement." *The Geopolitics* (August 21, 2020). https://thegeopolitics.com/the-global-impact-of-the-black-lives-matter-movement/

Sondarjee, Maïka, and Nathan Andrews. "Decolonizing International Relations and Development Studies: What's in a Buzzword?." *International Journal* 77, no. 4 (2022): 551–71.

Sultana, Farhana. "Decolonizing Development Education and the Pursuit of Social Justice." *Human Geography* 12, no. 3 (2019): 31–46.

Sumner, Andrew. "What Is Development Studies?" EADI, 2022. www.eadi.org/fileadmin/user_upload/EADI/03_Publications/EADI_Policy_Paper/What_is_Development_Studies.pdf

Sunderland, Ryan. "Unlearning the "Master's Tools": Can International Development Be Decolonized?" *Yale Journal of International Affairs* (2023). www.yalejournal.org/publications/unlearning-the-masters-tools-can-international-development-be-decolonized. Accessed, February 4, 2024.

Tachhi, Jo. "When and How Does Voice Matter? And How Do We Know?" In *Voice & Matter: Communication, Development and the Cultural Return*, edited by Hemer, O. and Tufte, T., 117–28. Goteborg: Nordicom, 2016.

Tavernaro-Haidarian, Leyla. "Why Efforts to Decolonise Can Deepen Coloniality and What Ubuntu Can Do to Help." *Critical Arts* 32, no. 5–6 (2018): 104–18. doi:10.1080/02560046.2018.1560341

"The Doing Development Differently Manifesto." October 5, 2014. Harvard Kennedy School. https://bsc.hks.harvard.edu/the-ddd-manifesto/

USAID. 2015. USAID Forward. https://2012-2017.usaid.gov/usaidforward Accessed, February 4, 2024.

USAID. Administrator Samantha Power on a New Vision for Global Development. 2021. www.usaid.gov/news-information/speeches/nov-04-2021-administrator-samantha-power-new-vision-global-development Accessed, February 4, 2024.

USAID. Integrating Local Knowledge in Development Programming. July 2022a. https://usaidlearninglab.org/system/files/2022-10/integrating_local_knowledge_07112022-400pm_1.pdf

USAID. Localization at USAID: The Vision and Approach. 2022b. www.usaid.gov/sites/default/files/2022-12/USAIDs_Localization_Vision-508.pdf

USAID. "Listening to Local Voices: Accountability and Feedback Plans." 2023. Accessed April 28, 2024. www.usaid.gov/sites/default/files/2023-01/USAID_NPI_ALPGuideSeries-4_5-27-2022b.pdf

Veda, Gunjan. "Chronicles of a Transformative Movement: Strengthening Our Interconnectedness." *Interdisciplinary Journal of Partnership Studies* 10, no. 1 (2023): Article 4. https://doi.org/10.24926/ijps.v10i1.5458

Veda, Gunjan, Holta Trandafili, Martha Cruz Zuniga, Janet Edmond, Nelly Mecklenburg, Elene Cloete, Diana Delgadillo, Randy Lyness. 2021a. *Unpacking Community-led Development.* New York: The Movement for Community-led Development.

Veda, Gunjan, Cara Donohue, Gill Westhorp, Ruth Nicholls, Amy Williams, Diana Delgadillo, Elene Cloete, Matthew Cruse, Molly Wright, Holta Trandafili. 2021b. "Impact of Community-Led Development on Food Security (InCLuDE): A Rapid Realist Review." www.fsnnetwork.org/resource/impact-community-led-development-food-security-lnclude-rapid-realist-review

Veda, Gunjan, Holta Trandafili, Brigitta Bode, Nelly Mecklenburg, Elene Cloete, Janet Edmond, Diana Delgadillo, Martha Cruz Zuniga, Julie Carandang, Randy Lyness. 2021c. *Participatory CLD Assessment Tool,* New York: The Movement for Community-led Development. https://mcldtools.github.io/en.html

Voss, John. *PNPM rural impact evaluation* (English). Washington, D.C.: World Bank Group, 2012. http://documents.worldbank.org/curated/en/543401468259751080/PNPM-rural-impact-evaluation

Weisbord, Marvin R., and Sandra Janoff. *Don't Just Do Something, Stand There!: Ten Principles for Leading Meetings that Matter.* San Francisco: Berrett-Koehler Publishers, 2007.

Wheeler, Joanna, Jackie Shaw, and Jo Howard. "Politics and Practices of Inclusion: Intersectional Participatory Action Research." *Community Development Journal* 55, no. 1 (January 2020): 45–63. https://doi.org/10.1093/cdj/bsz036

White, Howard, Radhika Menon, and Hugh Waddington. *Community-Driven Development: Does It Build Social Cohesion or Infrastructure? A Mixed-Method Evidence Synthesis*, March 2018. https://doi.org/10.23846/wp0030

WHO. *Coronavirus Disease 2019 Situation Report 10*1. 2020. www.who.int/docs/default-source/coronaviruse/situation-reports/20200430-sitrep-101-covid-19.pdf?sfvrsn=2ba4e093_2

Wilkinson, Susan. "#ShiftThePower: Community Giving as a Critical Consciousness-Raising Tool." *The Foundation Review* 9, no. 3 (2017). https://doi.org/10.9707/1944-5660.1378

Wood, Donna. J., and Gray, Barbara. "Toward a Comprehensive Theory of Collaboration." *Journal of Applied Behavioral Science* 27, no. 2 (1991): 139–162. DOI: 10.1177/0021886391272001

World Bank Group. Evidence Note on Community Driven Development (CDD). *A Summary of Key Findings on World Bank Financed CDD Operations.* World Bank Group, June 2022. https://collaboration.worldbank.org/content/usergenerated/asi/cloud/attachments/sites/collaboration-for-development/en/groups/community-driven-development-global-solutions-group/documents/jcr:content/content/primary/blog/evidence_note_oncommunitydrivendevelopmentcdd-ca2s/CDD%20Evidence%20Note%20-%20final.pdf

2

THE QUEST FOR HUMAN DIGNITY

A Practitioner's History of Community-Led Development

John Coonrod

It was in 1969 that I first understood the importance of community-led development (CLD). The civil rights and anti-war movements of my student activism emphasised participatory local democracy and questioned the very existence of nation states. Since then I have dedicated my life to transforming the current international systems from top-down to community-led, first with The Hunger Project, a non-profit organisation headquartered in the US, and then with The Movement for Community-led Development, a Majority World led network of networks. In this chapter, I tell the story of CLD as I understand it and through the works of key champions who have inspired me in my 50-year long journey on this path.

Why History Matters

On December 6, 2022, the newly re-elected US Senator Warnock stated,

> I believe that democracy is the political enactment of a spiritual idea: the notion that each of us has within us a spark of the divine…We all have value. And if we have value, we ought to have a voice.

Sadly, that is not how many of us behave. While some view history as the process of expanding opportunity for every human person, others see it as a deadly competition requiring authoritarian leaders. These conflicting views are how we must understand the history of CLD and its importance.

DOI: 10.4324/9781003377917-3

From Ancient Times

My favourite story about the conflicting views on human civilisation comes from the Hebrew scriptures (New International Version, 1973, Samuel 8: 4–20):

> So all the elders of Israel gathered together and came to Samuel at Ramah. They said to him, "You are old, and your sons do not walk in your ways; now appoint a king to lead us, such as all the other nations have…."
>
> Samuel said "This is what the king who will reign over you will do: He will take your sons and make them serve with his chariots and horses… he will take your daughters to be perfumers and cooks and bakers. He will take the best of your fields and vineyards and olive groves and give them to his attendants… When that day comes, you will cry out for relief from the king you have chosen, and the Lord will not answer you on that day."
>
> But the people refused to listen to Samuel. "No!" they said. "We want a king over us. Then we will be like all the other nations, with a king to lead us and to go out before us and fight our battles."

Some say this dichotomy is baked into our DNA. Steven Spielberg's television series *Why We Hate* cited studies explaining that chimpanzees and bonobos evolved on two sides of the Congo River (Pusey 2022). On the bonobo side, the land was fertile, and food was abundant. Bonobos lived in peace and harmony. On the chimpanzee side, the environment was harsh, and tribes of chimpanzees competed and went to war. We evolved from the chimps.

For more than 2 million years, human society was in small nomadic ice-age communities that only seemed to battle woolly mammoths and sabre-tooth tigers – a collective impact project. Hunter/gatherer societies (including those that survive today) were quite egalitarian. There was no concept of "ownership."

Around 14,000 years ago, the earth began warming, and people began establishing settled agriculture. Suddenly, it became advantageous to "own" land – often arbitrated by elders in the community – and since women did most of the farming, it began to be advantageous for men to marry multiple women. The agricultural revolution introduced patriarchy (Davis 2018) and more formal systems of community governance. Villages were established, regulated by norms and rules with decisions taken either by consensus or by elders – or both.

The norms and rules often became religions, such as practised by Samuel or embedded in Vedic writings that described village self-government, which by the year 100 CE were termed panchayats comprising five elders (Udgaonkar 1969).

Then around 5,000 years ago, people learned to make bronze – a much better weapon for patriarchs with imperial aspirations. Samuel lost his argument, and kings began to coalesce villages into relatively small kingdoms and fight wars. Kings needed a communication system to convey their glory and commands beyond their personal reach, so writing became a major invention in the Bronze Age. Yet most daily decisions remained local.

Kingships were not typically inherited and were either based on brute force or some sort of oligarchic decision-making process. While the Greeks get the credit for coming up with democracy in 509 BCE (in response to middle-class unrest), there is evidence that there was also democracy in Bangladesh 300 years earlier when a king died without a replacement, and panchayats governed themselves quite happily until another king came along (van Schendel 2009).

This relationship between kings and somewhat autonomous communities is fairly universal. Even the feudal system of the Middle Ages in Europe, the empires of Rome, Asia and the Americas and the kingdoms of Africa gave local communities a fair amount of autonomy.

The big shift to the centralised state and concentrated private wealth seems to have occurred with the Renaissance and then the Industrial Revolution. As the anthropologist Laura Nader points out, until the 1500s, everywhere on earth had a similar level of economic development. Any unusually successful business would be promptly taken over by local royalty or religious leaders (Prak and Zanden 2023).

With the Protestant Reformation, first in the Netherlands, private capital could be accumulated and protected by the State. The era of exploration provided new opportunities for plunder, international slave trade and colonisation – fertile ground to fully express toxic masculinity.

These forces reached new peaks with the Treaty of Westphalia, which established the concept of national sovereignty, ending 80 years of warfare that interfered with the concentration of wealth. From there, they moved on to the British Empire and its takeover of India in 1858.[1]

The contradiction between free markets, autocratic colonialism and slavery was the boiling stew that gave rise not only to the American and French Revolutions, the American Civil War, the Slave Rebellion in Haiti and the Russian Revolution but also to intellectual fervour fuelling the global abolition movement.

The history of CLD in the modern era begins with the English social philosopher John Ruskin. In 1860, Ruskin wrote a series of essays that criticised the capitalist system because it created a hierarchical social structure, hyper-competitive culture, mechanical worldview and undermined the dignity of labour. As an alternative, he suggested building economic systems that facilitate fair wages, and meaningful work, focusing on enabling the least powerful, not the most. He published this collection of essays in 1862 as a book, entitled *Unto This Last* (Ruskin 1862).

Max Weber, the definitive scholar on the rise of national bureaucracies at this time, defined government as a "monopoly on violence" (Weber 1919). The violent enforcement of colonialism, slavery and unbridled capitalism was entirely inconsistent with professed religions. Something had to give.

The remainder of this chapter is the story of a few of the champions for a shift in power. There are many inspiring examples worldwide. I will focus on those with whom I've had the most personal contact in the 50 years that I have been engaged with CLD.

Gandhi and the Village Republics

> I have not pictured a poverty-stricken India containing ignorant millions. I have pictured to myself an India continually progressing along the lines best suited to her genius. I do not, however, picture it as a third-class or even a first-class copy of the dying civilisation of the West.
>
> *(Gandhi 1959, p. 3)*

The Indian National Congress was established in 1885 by the British for better dialogue with educated Indians – not as a freedom movement. Like Gandhi himself at the time, the Congress saw the British Empire as a civilising force in the world. Between 1885 and 1905, it made various humble proposals for improved human rights, including repeal of the Salt Tax, the subject of Gandhi's famous 1930 Salt March.

It was in 1893 that Gandhi began his law practice in South Africa. He was awakened to racism on May 31 when he was thrown off the whites-only first-class coach of the train at Pietermaritzburg Station. That same year he read and reported being revolutionised by Tolstoy's *The Kingdom of God Is Within You* with its radical demands for nonviolence. He founded the Natal Indian Congress and began protesting racism in South Africa in 1894.

Gandhi's first ideas for CLD were inspired by the lifestyle of vegetarian Trappist monks as well as his reading of Tolstoy. He learned of the Trappists while still a student in England and visited a Trappist community near Durban in 1895. He described it as "a quiet little model village, owned on the truest republican principles. The principles of liberty, equality, and fraternity are carried out in their entirety. Every man is a brother, every woman a sister…" (Gandhi, 1895, p. 225). Gandhi admired the "patterns of simplicity, virtue and gentleness." Everything he saw at the settlement impressed him. The males of the predominantly Zulu population were trained in the various workshops to be blacksmiths, tinsmiths, shoemakers, carpenters and tanners, whilst the girls joined the sisters in ironing, sewing, straw-hat manufacturing and knitting. The community had its own printing press, a flour mill operated by waterpower and an oil press. Without distinction of race, all the men laboured in the fields where many varieties of tropical fruits and vegetables were grown. Efficient management of the workshops and farm enabled the settlement to be almost self-supporting.

In 1904, Gandhi was given a copy of Ruskin's *Unto This Last* by Henry Polak, a newspaper editor in Johannesburg. Gandhi read it during an overnight train ride and recalled in his autobiography that it caused "an instantaneous and practical transformation of my life." He continued, "I believe that I discovered some of my deepest convictions reflected in this great book of Ruskin" (Gandhi 1929, p. 335).

The lessons that Gandhi understood from *Unto This Last* were:

- The good of the individual is contained within the good of all.
- All people have the same right to earn a livelihood from their work, regardless of trade.
- A life of labour as a farmer or hand-craftsman is a dignified and valuable life.

To share these insights with his fellow citizens in India, Gandhi translated *Unto This Last* into Gujarati language in 1908 and entitled it *Sarvodaya* (the well-being of all).

Gandhi saw community development as inextricably linked to both morality and political liberation. As his protests in South Africa increased, he established a newspaper – the *Indian Opinion*, in 1903. It soon ran into financial problems, and his solution was to move to the countryside in 1904 and run it as a commune at the Phoenix Settlement. There, each resident also cultivated their own small plot of land.

Growing racist oppression in South Africa led to increased protests, and he was jailed. Upon his release in 1909, he travelled to England as part of an Indian Delegation, and on the ship, he wrote *Hind Swaraj* (Indian Self-rule), calling not only for the removal of the British but the removal of their so-called modern culture.

Back in South Africa, he established his second experiment, Tolstoy Farm in the Transvaal, where residents farmed collectively rather than individually. It was there that he met Gopal Krishna Gokhale, who was instrumental in transforming the Indian National Congress into a freedom movement.

Gandhi returned to India, and as part of his growing leadership within the Freedom Movement, he emphasised village self-government (*Gram Swaraj*) as a strategy for improving people's lives and as a model for the future of India. He wrote:

> In this structure composed of innumerable villages there will be ever-widening, never ascending circles. Life will not be a pyramid with the apex sustained by the bottom but an oceanic circle whose centre will be the individual, always ready to perish for the village, the latter ready to perish for the circle of villages and so on, sharing the majesty of the oceanic circle of which they are integral units.
>
> *(Gandhi 1962, p. 80)*

In 1931, Gandhi published detailed principles for how panchayats ought to be run, reflecting both his commitment to local solutions and shrewd perceptions of the dangers of village power dynamics. "The disability to impose fines or social boycott is a necessity of the case in the initial stages. Social boycott in villages has been found to be a dangerous weapon in the hands of ignorant or unscrupulous men" (Gandhi 1959, p. 6).

Gandhian village development continues to this day. One of my mentors, Prof. Ramlal Parikh, a youth leader in the Indian freedom movement and later chancellor of a university founded by Gandhi, summarised it nicely in his mobilising mottos: "Work for all, education for all, health for all, food for all."

Following India's independence in August 1947 and Gandhi's assassination in January 1948, panchayats had no constitutional standing. India's constitution (the longest in the world) was adopted by a constituent assembly and came into force on January 26, 1950. It established a federal system delegating powers to states (aligned roughly with language boundaries), thus (as in the US) local issues were left to the states. Some states had elected panchayats, some had traditional, non-democratic panchayats enforcing norms of the caste system and some had both.

India adopted a Soviet-style system of five-year plans for rapid, state-supported industrialisation. However, the second five-year plan recommended officially establishing Panchayati Raj in India.

Little was done until Rajiv Gandhi – no relation to the Mahatma – championed Panchayats by introducing a constitutional amendment in 1989. The assassination of Rajiv Gandhi in May 1991 catalysed pro-panchayat activists to successfully pass the 73rd amendment to India's constitution, which made Panchayati Raj the law of the land when it entered force in April 1993. It also reserved one-third of all seats and presidencies in panchayats for women. Till then, only three states (Maharashtra, Gujarat since 1963 and West Bengal since 1978) had been holding panchayat elections. Some states continued to resist, with Bihar not holding elections until 2001 (Kumar 2001).

My boss at that time, the CEO of a non-profit organisation called The Hunger Project, Joan Holmes, commented that the election to office of more than 1 million rural women was the greatest social revolution of our time. In 1992, I participated with my Indian colleagues in the State of West Bengal to create an orientation programme on health, education and good governance for tens of thousands of newly elected panchayat members.

Kerala has the distinction of having the most successful panchayats in the country. While many panchayats were starved of resources, Kerala invested heavily in its panchayats and supported them through KILA, the Kerala Institute of Local Administration. In 1996, Kerala launched the "People Plan" campaign for bottom-up planning in all 900 panchayats. I visited panchayats across India, and most had one small hut and one paid secretary. In Kerala, the panchayats professionally manage budgets upwards of US$1 million, are well-staffed and sustain the best social indicators in the country.[2]

Today, several central government schemes are channelled directly through panchayats. Transparency has been improved with the passage (after massive civil society activism) of the Right to Information Act of 2005.

Rural Reconstruction in China

During World War I, as Gandhi was mobilising an ambulance corps, another community development pioneer was in the trenches in France, confronting the mindset he grew up with.

Y.C. James "Jimmy" Yen was nearly the same age as the Nobel Laureate in Literature Pearl S. Buck, and both grew up in China at the same time, although they never met in person until World War II. Pearl Buck was so eager to tell Yen's story that she took him to her farm in Pennsylvania for two days and published his story in the small book *Tell the People*. Alas, it is long out of print.

Yen came from the scholarly class in China – people who could read and write classical Chinese with its 30,000 characters. He received his degree from Yale, which connected him for life with a cohort of Wall Street people. During World War I, he was hired by the Young Men's Christian Association (YMCA) to go to France.

When we think of World War I, we think of the horrors of trench warfare. But who dug the trenches? Not the French, English and Germans, but thousands of migrant, unskilled Chinese labourers. Yen was hired to "minister" to these men. As a member of the scholar class, Yen had been raised to see these labourers as subhuman creatures who could not be educated.

Each morning, when Yen opened his tent, a line of men wanted him to write letters home. The line grew longer every morning, and he realised this was untenable. So, in his tent in France, he devised a simplified 1,000-character version of Chinese and taught the men to read and write.

As Paulo Freire discovered 50 years later, learning to read and write is not simply a matter of skill – it's a transformation in who people experience themselves to be in the world – from victim to change agent (Freire 1970, p. 98). And it was an enormous transformation for Yen. He realised that these men were as smart or smarter than he was. By marginalising them, China was sitting on an untapped gold mine of talent.

When Yen returned to China after the war, he launched the volunteer-based Mass Education Movement to spread literacy. China's future leaders Mao Tse-tung and Zhou Enlai were among his student volunteers.

Poverty in rural China was extreme. As rural people experienced the transformative power of literacy, they sought to change every aspect of their oppressive environment. The Mass Education Movement evolved into an integrated program of "rural reconstruction" – what we call CLD today. The Rural Reconstruction movement began in the county now known as Dingzhou in Hebei province and spread to thousands of villages. Yen's methodology of community mobilisation based on self-reliance was highly successful. Rural Reconstruction villages became so resilient that when Japan invaded China in 1931, the Japanese avoided them.

Many people first heard the wisdom of Yen via the Credo of the Rural Reconstruction Movement.

Go to the people
Live among them
Learn from them
Love them
Serve them
Plan with them
Start with what they know
Build on what they have.
Y.C. James Yen.

The Rural Reconstruction Movement continued for a time following World War II and the triumph of the Chinese Communist Party, until there was a falling out with Mao. Yen moved to the Philippines, where he established the International Institute of Rural Reconstruction (IIRR), which continues to this day. He led IIRR to carry the seeds of CLD to Vietnam, the Philippines, Indonesia and South Korea.

The philosophy of Rural Reconstruction continues to this day in China through an academic current known as the "New Rural Reconstruction Movement" led by Prof. Wen Tiejun, whose approach contributed to China's "New Socialist Countryside" policy (Tiejun 2015).

A.T. Ariyaratne and the Sarvodaya Shramadana Movement

Dr. A.T. Ariyaratne of Sri Lanka was another CLD pioneer. Ari, as he was known to his admirers, was inspired by the principles of nonviolence and village self-government carried out in India.

Born in 1931 in the village of Unawatuna, Ari began organising impoverished coconut workers when he was just 14 years old. He heard of Mahatma Gandhi only through the news of his assassination and later travelled to India to learn about the principles of Gandhian rural development.

Ari adopted these to his own Buddhist context in what he termed Sarvodaya Shramadana – the Awakening of All through Shared Labour. As a middle-school teacher, he brought his students to work side-by-side with some of the most impoverished villagers. As in China and India, this produced transformative results in both the material and spiritual quality of people's lives.

Sarvodaya's approach, which currently covers 15,000 villages in Sri Lanka, is explored in detail in Chapter 15. Like Gandhi, Ari was awakened to new possibilities through travel outside his home country. And like Gandhi and Yen, Ari recognised that village development required inspiring a transformed mindset.

However, unlike Gandhi, Ari saw that this awakening would be the first in a series of stages. Sarvodaya therefore describes a graduation process of five stages:

1. Psychological infrastructure – a village awakening
2. Social infrastructure – formation of groups for children, youth, mothers, farmers and elders.
3. Satisfaction of basic human needs and formation of Sarvodaya Shramadana Society
4. Initiation of programs on legal, economic and technological empowerment
5. Sharing with neighbouring villages – a well-developed village, rather than Sarvodaya staff, accompanies surrounding villages in their development.

Fanon and Decolonising the Mind

While Gandhi was the chief philosopher for CLD in Asia, in Africa it was Frantz Fanon, an anti-racist, anti-colonial writer most famous for his 1960 book *The Wretched of the Earth*. Unlike Mahatma Gandhi, Fanon was decidedly not nonviolent and fought in the wars of independence in both Algeria and Sudan. He was born in French Martinique and trained in France as a psychiatrist. His rage at the racism he experienced in both France and the US mobilised him and shaped his thinking and writing.

What he shared with Gandhi was the recognition that decolonisation required decolonising the mind of the oppressed as well as the necessity of vanquishing the oppressor.

> It is Fanon's expansive conception of humanity and his decision to craft the moral core of decolonisation theory as a commitment to the individual human dignity of each member of populations typically dismissed as "the masses" that stands as his enduring legacy.
>
> *(Nicholls 2000, p. 1)*

The Naam Movement of Burkina Faso

As in Asia, the quest for post-colonial CLD sprung up in Africa, applying many of the same principles.

While Gandhi hoped the post-colonial world would avoid the top-down approach, virtually all post-colonial governments embraced it. The Indian politician Ramakrishna Hegde once said to me, "In 1858, the British created a system to enslave us, and we have carefully preserved it ever since." The same was true in countries across Africa. I once was in a meeting with Tanzania's first president, Julius Nyerere, as he visited India. He explained to an Indian official "the difference is that India has villages – we just have rural people."

That, of course, was not really true, yet African villages were much smaller and far less integrated in the national governance systems than India's panchayats. Many African governments launched top-down, government-led rural development programs post-independence, employing government extension workers.

One such worker was Bernard Lédea Ouedraogo in Burkina Faso, then Upper Volta. In the 1960s, he became increasingly frustrated with the failure of government-staff-led rural development to take hold – people were simply not accepting it. At best, villages attempted to game the system to see what they could get from it.

Bernard's journey is described by the Swiss activist Pierre Pradervand in *Listening to Africa* (1989). Today's funding agencies would be well advised to read this book, as he goes into great detail on how such agencies can authentically partner with grassroots movements.

Like Gandhi and Ari, Bernard studied and built on ancient strengths within his society. In fact, he visited Sarvodaya in Sri Lanka and drew inspiration from that visit.

Burkina Faso possessed an ancient tradition of *Kambi-Naam*: youth groups for cultural and moral development through collective action. Bernard began experimenting with awakening people to this tradition and transforming it into a systematic, integrated process that was very intentionally inclusive of all members of the village. He formally established the Naam Movement in 1967 and nurtured it to grow organically to reach 4000 villages by 1987. He received The Hunger Project's Africa Prize for Leadership in 1989 and the Right Livelihood Award in 1990. His favourite phrase was "Development Without Damage" (Ouedraogo 1988).

I first visited Naam villages in 1989, accompanied by Pierre Pradervand. The villages were abuzz not only with agricultural activities but also small-scale industry, including bicycle production, which was a liberating force in a society where women typically transported huge bundles on their heads.

From the 1960s onwards, the Sahel region was increasingly drought-prone. In 1975, Bernard met with like-minded leaders of farmers' federations from the region, and with Bernard Leconte, he established a new "network of networks" – the Six-S Movement – that, with backing from Swiss Development Cooperation, created an innovative structure of flexible funding and capacity strengthening.

Six-S stands for "se servir de la saison sèche en savane et au Sahel" or in English "making use of the dry season in the savannah and the Sahel." In the dry season, farmers could not farm. Six-S provided training and flexible funding for farmers to design and implement dry-season livelihood opportunities and other village improvement programs.

Money can often be a spoiler in the quest for self-reliance, and Six-S pioneered a rigorous set of principles – the "Six-S Spirit" – to ensure farmer-led organisations build themselves up without dependency. They required associations to demonstrate commitment through savings before gaining membership. They required and provided management training. They rigorously required financial and decision-making transparency of all members.

For agencies such as USAID (United States Agency for International Development) struggling to learn how to support small community-based organisations, Six-S provides a blueprint. The Swiss Development Cooperation staff would attend Six-S annual meetings as peers – listening and participating as equals. Farmers would have no hesitation in disagreeing with them when they felt called to do so. It was truly an example of Freirean Co-learning – as described next.

Paulo Freire in Latin America and beyond

CLD is a science. It builds on a socio-political critique of Western modernism, an anthropological study of indigenous strengths and a strong spiritual and philosophical commitment to human dignity. Like any science, it attempts to share knowledge through clear and finite sets of principles.

One of the most influential thinkers in this science is Paulo Freire, the Brazilian educator most famous for his book *Pedagogy of the Oppressed.* Freire was greatly influenced by the writings of Fanon as well as those of psychologist Erich Fromm (Freire 1970, p. 63).

Unlike Y.C. James Yen, Freire grew up poor and often hungry when the global depression of 1929 wiped out his family's previous middle-class status. He experienced personally how his poverty made it very difficult for him to study (Stevens 2012).

As his family's income improved, he attended law school. He was appointed in 1946 to serve as the education director of the Department of Education and Culture in the Brazilian state of Pernambuco, where he focused on literacy among people experiencing poverty. At that time, literacy was a requirement to be a voter. That work came to a halt in 1964 with a coup in Brazil, and Freire was imprisoned as a traitor for 70 days. He then left Brazil and travelled first to Bolivia and then to Chile for five years.

After Chile, Freire was hired at Harvard and eventually moved to Geneva to the World Council of Churches and the FAO (Food and Agriculture Organization). These platforms gave him an opportunity to share his experience and philosophy with the world. His books are widely included in the curricula for training school teachers but rarely (and to my mind, tragically) ignored in the training of development practitioners.

Like virtually every modality of CLD I've studied, Freire describes the process as beginning with the awakening of the critical consciousness of the "oppressed"

> This, then, is the great humanistic and historical task of the oppressed: to liberate themselves and their oppressors as well. The oppressors, who oppress, exploit and rape by virtue of their power, cannot find in this power the strength

> to liberate either the oppressed or themselves. Only power that springs from the weakness of the oppressed will be sufficiently strong to free both.
>
> *(Freire 1970, p. 44)*

Freire draws a powerful distinction in the role of outsiders in development – between false and true generosity.

> Any attempt to "soften" the power of the oppressor in deference to the weakness of the oppressed almost always manifests itself in the form of false generosity; indeed, the attempt never goes beyond this. In order to have the continued opportunity to express their "generosity," the oppressors must perpetuate injustice as well. An unjust social order is the permanent fount of this "generosity," which is nourished by death, despair, and poverty. That is why the dispensers of false generosity become desperate at the slightest threat to its source.
>
> True generosity consists precisely in fighting to destroy the causes which nourish false charity.
>
> *(Ibid, p. 45)*

Like Gandhi, Freire feared that the oppressed, entrenched in the context of oppression, will strive to become the oppressor. He describes this as "fear of freedom."

> The oppressed, having internalized the image of the oppressor and adopted his guidelines, are fearful of freedom. Freedom would require them to eject this image and replace it with autonomy and responsibility.
>
> *(Ibid, p. 47)*

All of this and much more is just in Chapter 1 of *Pedagogy of the Oppressed*. The rest of the book, and many other works by Freire, detail the process of facilitating this journey – the process of conscientisation and "co-learning" through a dialectical "praxis" of reflection and action.

These principles and processes are immediately familiar to many who have devoted their lives to practices that truly respect the dignity and equality of every human person. Freire's concepts have become vital tools not only for development practitioners but also for the indigenous rights movement and feminists.

"Where are the Women?"

Throughout these first decades of the 20th century, there were courageous women around the world fighting for basic human rights. They marched alongside Mahatma Gandhi – often in the frontline absorbing the brutality of the British, but to this point they rarely appear in the leadership of the emerging modes of CLD. Part of that was undoubtedly due to the deeply patriarchal nature of societies. Part of it was a conscious choice, an assumption that women's rights might flow naturally with broader liberation. Dakshayani Velayudhan, the only Dalit woman member of India's constituent assembly, had said, "Personally, I am not in favour of any kind of reservation in any place whatsoever" (Economic Times 2023). By the 1960s, they realised this was an error. This "back seat" role can be seen throughout the quest for human dignity. After the US Civil War, for example, Frederick Douglass had initially advocated for a 15th Amendment to include voting rights not only for African-American men but also for women, but changed his mind when it appeared including women would defeat the bill. After passage, he resumed supporting women's voting rights (Gordon n.d.).

One of the models for the US Constitution was the Iroquois Confederation, the oldest living system of participatory democracy in the world, dating from the "Great Peace" of 1142 (Hansen 2009). Iroquois women were involved in all decision-making. Clan mothers appointed the chiefs, and women could veto any declaration of war (Nordell 2016). This aspect was obviously not adopted by the US Constitutional framers.

Feminists were at the forefront of the quest to establish the League of Nations and the United Nations. Eleanor Roosevelt may have chaired the writing committee for the Universal Declaration of Human Rights (UDHR), however, Majority World women played key roles. Hansa Mehta, a staunch fighter for women's rights in India, is widely credited with making a significant change in the language of Article 1 of the UDHR, by replacing the phrase "All men are born free and equal" to "All human beings are born free and equal" (OHCHR 2018).

The UN Commission on the Status of Women (CSW) was established in 1946. In 1965, CSW began working in earnest towards CEDAW, the Convention on the Elimination of All Forms of Discrimination Against Women. A Declaration to that effect was adopted in 1967, and work began to make 1975 the International Year of the Woman with the first International Women's Conference held in Mexico City.

In addition to generating the will to have the UN adopt CEDAW in 1979, the Mexico City Conference was the first where a majority of delegations were headed by women, including the newly independent nations across Africa. This was a first great opportunity for many women civil society leaders to come together, and one outcome was the establishment of Women's World Banking by Esther Ocloo of Ghana, another early winner of the Africa Prize for Leadership.

The World Community Briefly Takes Note

Interestingly, one of the most detailed books on the history of CLD is an anti-CLD book –*Thinking Small: The United States and the Lure of Community Development* by Daniel Immerwahr (2015). In my assessment, Immerwahr sees CLD as an American, or even a CIA, plot to undermine insurgencies intent on overthrowing governments – a rather hard case to make post-9/11 but one I hear often from advocates for a strong benevolent state. Indeed, the 1931 papal endorsement of subsidiarity is often seen as a counter to Soviet state socialism. Immerwahr singles out US government support of James Yen to export the Rural Reconstruction approach to South Korea, Thailand, Ghana and India.

It is true that preventing regional, tribal, religious and other forms of political violence has been a strong motivation for countries that adopt CLD programs, the theory being that when local people have a peaceful pathway to meeting local aspirations, they will take it.

The success of these movements did not go unnoticed and began to receive more formal support both from their own governments and from the international "donor" community. One of the most successful efforts that was both country-owned and donor-funded was *Saemaul Undong* – the New Village Movement of South Korea during the 1970s.

Like civil society CLD programs, Saemaul Undong began by transforming mindsets – from dependency to self-reliance – among both government personnel and rural populations (Asian Development Bank [ADB], 2012). It supported community action projects on a competitive basis, with major support from USAID. Within four years, rural income surpassed urban income for the first time. Within nine years, rural income increased six-fold. South Korea transformed from one of the lowest-income countries to being a major source of development aid over a 20-year period.

Many other community-led initiatives were supported by Organization for Economic Co-operation and Development (OECD) governments during this period. Even the Green Revolution was implemented through community leaders via farmer-to-farmer mentoring.

The Former Colonies Teach the Colonisers

One of the most influential activists for community-led programming is a former (and one of the last) members of the British Overseas Civil Service in Kenya, Robert Chambers. In the 1980s, Chambers published a series of books drawing from his experience in Africa and challenging the then-growing top-down approach to development. His 1983 book *Rural Development: Putting the Last First* waged war on the smugness of "outsiders" in the development process and articulated the principles and practices of facilitating participatory development. Subsequent books introduced Participatory Rural Appraisal (PRA). Robert is both a leading academic – helping make the Institute of Development Studies (IDS) at Sussex University one of the most progressive in the world – and a fervent practitioner, most recently leading global campaigns for Community-led Total Sanitation (CLTS). In 2022, IDS published *Revolutionizing Development: Reflections on the Work of Robert Chambers*, covering his 50 years at IDS – the book is freely available online (Cornwell and Scoones 2022).

Support Stops, and Slowly Restarts

Despite undeniable successes and the voices of champions such as Chambers, international funding for CLD largely stopped in the mid-1980s. First, there was a global financial crisis triggered by an oil embargo that contributed to World Bank and IMF policies of structural adjustment – belt-tightening by Majority World governments. When these countries slashed budgets, community development programs were among the first to go.

This was also the time of the "Child Survival Revolution" led by James Grant at UNICEF. It was observed that top-down campaigns for "GOBI" (Growth Charts, Oral Rehydration, Breastfeeding Promotion and Immunization) could dramatically reduce infant mortality, which, in turn, improves overall health and slows population growth. James Grant was a champion of "going to scale." Grant and others invested heavily in transforming BRAC, then a community-development-focused organisation in Bangladesh into a large-scale service provider.

The harshness of structural adjustment, with its macroeconomic focus, received pushback from civil society, such as the "50 years is enough" movement calling for the shutdown of the World Bank.

This swinging pendulum led to the concept of "Human Development" – a push by United Nations Development Programme (UNDP) to measure not by Gross Domestic Product (GDP) growth but by a Human Development Index, summarised each year in a Human Development Report (HDR). The 1993 HDR focused on people's participation and called for at least 20% of development funding going directly to the grassroots – a norm that sadly never caught on (Nassef et al. 1993) and in 2015 became one of the five goals of the MCLD (more on this later).

A noted critique of top-down planning is Prof. William Easterly, one of the few economists ever fired by the World Bank. Easterly has a brutal wit and, like Chambers, fights against top-down planners, particularly in his book *The Tyranny of Experts* (Easterly 2013).

Another critic of big government was British Prime Minister John Major, who introduced a new framework for citizen engagement in local government – the Citizen Charter. Citizen Charters give citizens precise information on the entitlements and what to do when the government fails to deliver them.

In the early 2000s, the World Bank established its Community Driven Development (CDD) Program, giving communities a direct voice in decision-making over project resources. Many CDD projects focused on infrastructure, such as the large-scale National Solidarity Programme (NSP) in Afghanistan. NSP established Village Development Committees that included women with the power to set their own priorities and implement their own projects. This evolved into a more holistic "Citizen Charter" program in years just before the Taliban takeover (World Bank 2020).

Other successful CDD programs that evolved into nationally supported CLD programs include KDP in Indonesia (Guggenheim 2021) and the Kalahi-CIDSS in the Philippines (Department of Social Welfare and Development [DSWD] 2003).

Advocacy for Widespread Adoption

Initiatives to advocate for community-led approaches to international development have emerged, contributed and then faded. The International Community Leadership Project brought together 31 pioneering practitioners from across the globe in March 1983, who also met with community organisers from Harlem and Arkansas. The Institute for Cultural Affairs organised an International Exhibition of Rural Development in 1984.

Those of us committed to CLD found hope – and then frustration – in the 2000 UN Millennium Declaration and the multisectoral nature of the Millennium Development Goals (the MDGs). The MDGs were successful in motivating stronger top-down, sectoral approaches and led to increased official development assistance, increased demand for mutual accountability and aid effectiveness through country ownership and the Paris Principles. Yet there was no mention of communities.

Successful policy advocacy requires robust literature with strong evidence. Sadly, CLD has been stuck in a "Catch 22" situation – since there has been no significant funding for CLD, there has been no community of practice, no research, little evidence, and thus no effective advocacy to devolve budgets and decentralise decision-making authority.

CLD practitioners did not even have a shared language for it. We had each developed our own private methodologies and private language. We felt alone, misunderstood and – frankly – a bit self-righteous.

The earliest use of the phrase "Community-led Development" I can now find is from 2002 in regard to rural development programs with the US Department of Agriculture (Reid 2002). President Obama, a former community organiser himself, used the phrase frequently but only in the context of domestic policy.

In 2012, several like-minded NGOs began advocating at the UN for communities to be a focus of the follow-up to the MDGs, the Sustainable Development Goals (SDGs) for the period 2016–2030. We discovered several articles from New Zealand defining the phrase "community-led development" as the "process of working together in place to achieve locally owned visions and goals" (Inspiring Communities 2012). This was an "aha" moment. Here was a phrase which expressed what we all stood for.

We began holding events at the World Bank, the UN and USAID to promote CLD. The World Bank CDD program is a natural ally, as is United Cities and Local Governments (UCLG), a network of local government associations. UCLG is particularly influential at the UN.

In 2014, the decision was made to create the Movement for Community-led Development (MCLD). MCLD participated in preparatory conferences for the SDGs, pushing for SDG 11 to not only be "sustainable cities" but "sustainable communities." We pushed for communities to be included in SDG16 – good governance "at every level" starting at the community level.

MCLD held a side event at the Financing for Development Conference in Addis Ababa, Ethiopia, in July 2015, where OECD countries promised to increase aid to communities. We then formally launched MCLD during a plenary at the UN Sustainable Development Summit (2015) and explored it further at a UN General Assembly side event hosted by the government of the Philippines.

Remarkably, there were two other CLD-flavoured side events that same day – one by UCLG with the UN Capital Development Fund (a source of funds for local governments) and one by South Korea and the UN Development Program promoting their partnership to modernise and bring Saemaul Undong to other countries.

From its inception, MCLD combined actors focusing on humanitarian response, peace-building and development – a combination known as the Humanitarian Development and Peace (HDP) Nexus. Local actors dislike this term, as they are generally the same actors pivoting from D when H or P are called for.

The next milestone was the 2016 UN Humanitarian Summit at which Majority World and OECD countries agreed to a "Grand Bargain" to increase humanitarian funding with greater investment in strengthening local capacity. The NEAR Network was established as a network of Majority World humanitarian actors in support of the Grand Bargain.

During this period, the Obama administration established a commitment to "localization" as part of their "USAID Forward" initiative, although their definition of "local" tended to mean national organisations within a host country, not a local community. This was continued under the Trump Administration as the "Journey to Self-Reliance" and increased the focus a bit towards communities. In 2021, human rights activist and former UN Ambassador Samantha Power became administrator of USAID and, in November 2021, declared her vision that by 2030, one-half of USAID's budget would be devoted to community-led programs (Power 2021).

Conclusion

The world has declared strong ambitions for ending hunger and poverty. Yet the agencies devoted to achieving those goals seem to shift from fad to fad, seeking "silver bullet" top-down solutions rather than building on the wisdom and experience of the past hundred years. Those living in poverty do not have the luxury of time or "fads." The world community must quickly shift resources and decision-making authority to those most proximate to the challenges and best positioned to meet them. The time for CLD is now.

Notes

1 The UK Parliament passed the Government of India Act on August 2, 1858, abolishing the East India Company and transferring its functions to the British Crown.
2 In 2021, Kerala ranked 9th on the Social Progress Index among 32 states and union territories.

References

Asian Development Bank (ADB). 2012. *The Saemaul Undong Movement in the Republic of Korea.* Asian Development Bank.

Cornwall, Andrea and Scoones, Ian. 2022. *Revolutionizing Development.* University of Sussex. URL: www.taylorfrancis.com/books/oa-edit/10.4324/9781003298632/revolutionizing-development-ian-scoones-andrea-cornwall

Davis, Matthew. 2018. "Can Inequality Be Blamed on the Agricultural Revolution?" World Economic Forum. www.weforum.org/agenda/2018/10/how-the-agricultural-revolution-made-us-inequal

DSWD: Department of Social Welfare and Development. 2003. accessed September 8, 2024, https://kalahi.dswd.gov.ph/about/kalahi-cidss

Easterly, William. 2013. *The Tyranny of Experts.* Basic Books. ISBN: 478-0-465-03125-2

Economic Times. 2023. "Women's Reservation Bill: The Evolution and What It Has Come to." URL: https://economictimes.indiatimes.com/news/india/womens-reservation-bill-the-evolution-and-what-it-has-come-to/constituent-assembly/slideshow/103799908.cms

Freire, Paulo. 1970/2018. *Pedagogy of the Oppressed.* 50th anniversary edition. Bloomsbury Academic.

Gandhi, Mohandas Karamchand. 1895. *Collected Works, Vol. 1.* All Available at www.gandhiashramsevagram.org/gandhi-literature/collected-works-of-mahatma-gandhi-volume-1-to-98.php

Gandhi, Mohandas Karamchand. 1929. *An Autobiography or My Experiments with the Truth.* URL: www.mkgandhi.org/ebks/An-Autobiography.pdf

Gandhi, Mohandas Karamchand. 1959. *Panchayat Raj.* Navajivan Publishing House. www.mkgandhi.org/ebks/panchayat_raj.pdf

Gandhi, Mohandas Karamchand. 1962. *Village Swaraj.* Navajivan Publishing House. https://gandhiashramsevagram.org/pdf-books/village-swaraj.pdf

Gordon, Ann D. 2020. "Fraught Friendship: Susan B. Anthony and Frederick Douglass." *On Their Shoulders: The Radical Stories of Women's Fight for the Vote*, National Park Services. www.nps.gov/articles/000/fraught-friendship-susan-b-anthony-and-frederick-douglass.htm

Guggenheim, Scott. 2021. Putting People First in Practice: Indonhesia and the Kecamatan Development Program. In: Koch-Weser, Maritta, Guggenheim, Scott. (eds) *Social Development in the World Bank.* Springer Cham. https://doi.org/10.1007/978-3-030-57426-0_12

Hansen, Terri. 2009. "How the Iroquois Great Law of Peace Shaped U.S. Democracy | Native America." How the Iroquois Great Law of Peace Shaped U.S. Democracy | Native America. 2009. www.pbs.org/native-america/blogs/native-voices/how-the-iroquois-great-law-of-peace-shaped-us-democracy/

Immerwahr, Daniel. 2015. *Thinking Small – The United States and the Lure of Community Development.* Harvard University Press.

Inspiring Communities. 2012. Community-led Development Think Piece. July, 2012. Inspiring Communities. https://inspiringcommunities.org.nz/wp-content/uploads/2015/06/CLD-Think-Piece-July-2012.pdf

Kumar, Girish. "Review of Panchayat Elections: Overcoming State's Resistance." *Economic and Political Weekly* 36, no. 20 (2001): 1681.

Nassef, Abel Fattah, Osman, Osman M., Habib, Sohier K., Ryhan, Hamed M. and Hopkins, Michael. 1993. Human Development Report 1993: People's Participation. New York.

Nicholls, Tracey. 2000."Frantz Fanon | Internet Encyclopedia of Philosophy." *Internet Encyclopedia of Philosophy*. URL: https://iep.utm.edu/fanon/

Nordell, Jessica. 2016. *Millions of women voted in this election. They have the Iroquois to thank.* Washington Post, November 11, 2016. URL: www.washingtonpost.com/posteverything/wp/2016/11/24/millions-of-women-voted-for-hillary-clinton-they-have-the-iroquois-to-thank/

Ouedraogo, Bernard. 1988. "'Development Without Damage': The NAAM Groups Tackle Drought." *Wajibu. A Journal of Social and Religious Concern* 3, no. 4: 11–13. https://journals.co.za/doi/pdf/10.10520/AJA10169717_116

Power, Samantha. 2021. *Administrator Samanthan Power On A New Vision for Global Development.* URL: www.usaid.gov/news-information/speeches/nov-04-2021-administrator-samantha-power-new-vision-global-development

Pradervand, Pierre. 1989. *Listening to Africa*. Praeger.

Prak, Maarten, and van Zanden, Jan Luiten. 2023. *Pioneers of Capitalism: The Netherlands 1000–1800*. Princeton University Press.

Pusey, Anne E. "Warlike Chimpanzees and Peacemaking Bonobos." *Proceedings of the National Academy of Sciences of the United States of America* 119, no. 31 (2022): e2208865119. https://doi.org/10.1073/pnas.2208865119

Reid, J. Norman, ed. 2002. *Advancing Knowledge and Capacity for Community-Led*. AgEcon Search. https://ageconsearch.umn.edu/record/33541

Ruskin, John. 1862. *Unto This Last*. Pennsylvania State University Library.

Stevens, Christy. 2012. "Paulo Freire." In: *Critical Pedagogy on the Web*. University of Iowa. The Holy Bible: New International Version. 1973.

OHCHR. 2018. "The Role of Women in Shaping the Universal Declaration of Human Rights." *United Nations*, March 6, 2018. www.ohchr.org/en/stories/2018/03/role-women-shaping-universal-declaration-human-rights

Tiejun, Wen. 2015. *Addressing Rural Crisis in Developing Countries*. Institute of Chinese Studies.

Udgaonkar, Padma B. 1969. *Political Institutions & Administration of Northern India During Medieval Times, from 750 to 1200 A.D.* Motilal Banarsidass Publishers, p. 210.

van Schendel, Willem. 2009. *A History of Bangladesh*. Cambridge University Press.

Weber, Max. 1919. *Politics as Vocation*. www.academia.edu. www.academia.edu/26954620/Politics_as_Vocation.pdf

World Bank. 2020. Afghanistan's Citizens' Charter Program: Empowering Communities for Better Service. URL: www.worldbank.org/en/results/2020/10/20/afghanistans-citizens-charter-program-empowering-communities-for-better-services

PART I

Collaboration/Working with Sub-National Governments

Elene Cloete and Gunjan Veda

The chapters in this section demonstrate how community-led collaboration takes shape and enables positive change. Such collaboration includes connecting with and leveraging mutually beneficial relationships with sub-national governments. Depending on the political context, such relationships are not always possible, but when they are, they are productive in sustaining an intervention's momentum and long-term impact.

What Is Collaboration and Why Does It Matter?

A definition of collaboration sets the groundwork for the chapters in this section. It also helps in identifying alignment with broader community-led principles of meaningful participation, inclusion, voice, and ownership. But what exactly is collaboration? At a minimum, it involves creating mutually beneficial relationships to achieve common goals. In this process, responsibilities, authority, and accountability are shared. While it is important that the goals of collaboration should benefit all parties involved, it is even more important that those goals are shared (Chrislip and Larson, 1994, 5, in Bowen 2005). Wood and Gray's (1991, 146) seminal work on collaboration adds additional elements to consider when reflecting on what the concept is and how it functions, particularly within the realm of community-led development. They describe collaboration as occurring "when a group of autonomous stakeholders of a problem domain engage in an interactive process, using shared rules, norms, and structures, to act on or decide on issues related to that domain."

There are at least five elements built into this definition, which need consideration. First, a meaningful collaboration will promote the *autonomy* of all stakeholders. Autonomy, in this case, not only refers to independent decision-making power

DOI: 10.4324/9781003377917-4

and therefore not being subjected to power differences or manipulation, but also to the choice to participate in the collaboration in the first place. Without such autonomy, the relationship will not be collaborative. Instead, it might start to look more like a merger or amalgamation. Second, collaboration emerges mostly in response to a *problem* or *challenge, and stakeholders' individual and shared interest* in addressing such a challenge. These interests can change or shift as the collaboration changes over time. Third, *shared rules, norms and structures* typically guide collaboration. For a collaboration to be successful, it is important that such rules and structures become explicit at the start to ensure clarity and transparency among all stakeholders, including roles and responsibilities. Fourth, collaboration is an *interactive process*. As collaborations evolve, roles and responsibilities shift, and timelines change. Throughout the process, all stakeholders are interactively involved in shaping the trajectory of their collaboration. Lastly, collaboration is directed towards an objective that requires collaborators to *act and make decisions*. Wood and Gray (1991) confirm that objectives are not crucial to be met or finalised because, after all, things can change. However, collaboration still requires action, and actors have to decide on activities, objectives, and goals.

Collaboration, like accountability, is multidirectional. It can include horizontal interaction between people of similar socioeconomic and cultural backgrounds, but it can also be vertical, encompassing connections between people and groups representing different political, social, and economic power. One primary example of the latter includes connections between local community groups and political or government units. The spatial metaphor linked to collaboration as well as the relational aspect of the concept aligns closely with social capital, particularly how scholars have both described and also operationalised it to describe relationships within the community development context. Such work includes the chapter by McCordic et al. in this volume as well as previous work they have done to describe the community-led approach of OneVillage Partners (McCordic et al. 2020). Exemplary is also the chapter of CLD-Benin and their experiences developing collaborative engagements with different government entities in Benin.

Social capital is especially helpful in describing the relationships, agility, potential, and strength of collaborations across different social and political landscapes. Social capital is, according to Robert Putnam, "features of social organisation such as networks, norms, and social trust that facilitate coordination and cooperation for mutual benefit" (Krishna 2001, 930). It is, therefore, about the connections between people, existing "in the relations among persons" (Coleman, 1988, S100–S101). When considering the dynamics of social capital and its various degrees and relational characteristics, scholars identify at least three different dimensions – Bonding, bridging, and linking capital (Woolcock and Narayan 2000, Woolcock 2001). These dimensions represent, but also align with, collaboration as it takes shape across different socio-political and societal power hierarchies.

Collaboration that happens on a horizontal level corresponds to bonding social capital. Bonding social capital refers to the connections within a group or community characterised by high levels of similarity in demographic characteristics, attitudes, and available information and resources. These connections exist between people who are similar to each other and are typically characterised by strong, close relationships. Examples of bonding social capital include family members, close friends, and neighbours (Claridge 2018). The Amani authors' description of the relationships and also the collaboration happening among members of the women's savings groups, between taxi-riders, or *boda-boda* operators, and among youth active within the youth clubs exemplify how their interventions leverage these relationships to implement their community-led activities. What is especially noteworthy from the Amani authors is how bonding capital and the corresponding sense of connectedness and social cohesion can positively influence behaviour change. Similarly, Ramos' chapter on communal land organisations in Mexico confirms the potential of strengthening and then leveraging internal connections and relationships. The youth in Cristiano, for example, have drawn from their collaboration to mobilise their community towards greater access to resources.

Yet another form of collaboration takes place among actors representing different groups. While bonding capital is about the relationships *within* a particular group, bridging social capital is about connections *between* different communities, groups, and organisations (Claridge 2018). Within the context of community-led development, collaborating across these identified divides is crucial, not only to leverage the resource and knowledge sharing that can emerge from such connections but also to ensure increased inclusivity, participation, and voice. In the case of Amani, establishing and then strengthening connections between the women's groups, and other groups such as the *boda-bodas*, youth clubs, and others, strengthened the intervention's impact and also its longevity. Similarly, CLD-Benin's extensive reach was a direct result of mobilising different networks (existing collaborations), formal and informal, representing different population groups, to come together.

A last set of collaborations denotes more vertical ties or linking social capital. Bridging capital can have a vertical aspect to it because differences in cultural background and socioeconomic identities often create power indifferences and hierarchies. But linking capital is perhaps more explicit in how the relationships it represents take shape across different social strata with a visible power hierarchy (Woolcock 2001). A typical example of these relationships is the connections between community groups and government units and actors. In the work of the Amani Collective, such collaboration exists between women's groups and government officials, religious leaders, and cultural leaders. We also recognise such vertical collaboration between community groups in Sierra Leone and different government entities. As McCordic et al.'s chapter illustrates, these vertical connections are integral to their interventions as they facilitate the flow of resources while also establishing different forms of accountability. Another example of such vertical collaboration is the Payment for Environmental Services (PES) program in Mexico, as described in Ramos' chapter.

Having connections with other people and networks across different vertical and horizontal planes is one thing. Actively using them to initiate change is another. Krishna (2003) reminds us that having social capital, even at high levels, does not mean much if people do not draw from it. Strengthening communities' capacity to draw from, use, and deploy their social capital is a crucial first step before the benefits of collaboration can emerge. For example, the strength of a vertical connection with local government truly becomes active if local community groups can make officials attentive to the need for particular policy changes at a local level while also seeing such policies being developed, implemented, and reported on. Alternatively, it is also beneficial for local government units to connect with local community groups to establish buy-in and the community-wide adoption of policies. Communities drawing from their connections with government officials to access resources is another example of how existing connections with government turn from merely "knowing each other" to actually enabling change. A vertical connection with local government officials established and strengthened through community-led activities is crucial in strengthening communities' networking capacity. Such activities start with identifying relevant networks of support and then initiating the flow among such networks towards mutually beneficial outcomes. Most important, as is evident from the CLD-Benin authors, is the intentionality of collaboration. If such intentionality is present, not only will collaboration be more likely to sustain, but it will also foster greater interconnectedness, and mutual benefits in the long run.

From Collaboration to Partnership

Another approach to conceptualising collaboration is to consider it in relation to cooperation and partnership. In this case, Bowen (2005, 74) argues that these concepts sit on a continuum. On the one end is cooperation, suggesting that people "exchange ideas and information and do not get in one another's way." In the middle of the continuum is collaboration, indicating that people also act together. Partnership is towards the opposite end, denoting "a more mutually interdependent nature in the relationship among the actors that one would expect to find in joint initiatives" (Fiszbein and Lowden 1999, 4, in Bowen 2005). The emphasis on interdependency captures intentions of equity and equality and an awareness of not only the value all stakeholders bring to a collaboration but also that such value can be further magnified through collaboration with others. The emphasis on partnerships that emerge from and through collaboration is the theoretical basis for McCordic et al.'s chapter. Structuring their description of OneVillage Partners' on the concept of partnerism, their programming reflects the ultimate goal of community-led collaborations.

References

Bowen, Glenn A. 2005. "Local-level stakeholder collaboration: A substantive theory of community-driven development." *Community Development* 36, no. 2: 73–88.

Chrislip, David D. and Carl E. Larson. 1994. *Collaborative Leadership: How Citizens and Civic Leaders Can Make a Difference.* San Francisco: Jossey-Bass.

Claridge, Tristan. 2018. "Functions of social capital–bonding, bridging, linking." *Social Capital Research* 20, no. 1: 1–7.

Coleman, James S. 1988. "Social capital in the creation of human capital." *American Journal of Sociology* 94: S95–S120.

Krishna, Anirudh. 2001. "Moving from the stock of social capital to the flow of benefits: the role of agency." *World Development* 29, no. 6: 925–943.

Krishna, Anirudh. 2003. "Partnerships between local governments and community-based organisations: exploring the scope for synergy." *Public Administration and Development: The International Journal of Management Research and Practice* 23, no. 4: 361–371.

Wood, Donna J. and Barbara Gray. 1991. "Toward a comprehensive theory of collaboration." *The Journal of Applied Behavioral Science* 27, no. 2: 139–162.

Woolcock, Michael. 2001. "Microenterprise and social capital: a framework for theory, research, and policy." *The Journal of Socio-Economics* 30:193–198.

Woolcock, Michael and Deepa Narayan. 2000. "Social capital: implications for development theory, research, and policy." *The World Bank Research Observer* 15, no. 2: 225–249.

3

"THE ONEVILLAGE PARTNERS METHOD"

Building New Community Spaces for Consensus and Collaboration

Chad McCordic, Sheku Mohamed Gassimu Jr., Nyagajia Rogers Mustapha, and Vanessa Woode with Philemon Vandi McSenesie, Fatmata Lansana, and Moigua Bockarie

"The Thinking Place"

Philemon McSenesie's[1] home is Grima, a village carved out of the thick forest of eastern Sierra Leone. His ancestors began the community here.

> It was my grandfather's father and two of his friends who found that spot when they were hunting. They had it as a spot to rest, and they realised that it would be a good space to start a community. They sat and thought about what to call this new village. After some time, one of them said, "We've sat and thought about the name for this place for so long, let's just call it 'The Thinking Place'," and that's how it has the name in Mende, Ge-Lie-Ma, shortened to Grima.

Grima is on a hilltop, and its peaceful setting makes it a place to come together and think. At this time, Sierra Leone was a British colony, and as the years went on, despite its tranquil isolation, the turmoil of both colonisation and post-colonial conflict affected this village. Grima, like many rural communities, was practically demolished during the Civil War in the 1990s. As the community rebuilt, NGOs came in with projects to provide basic needs, but without much consultation with the community. Each time, the NGO told the community what the project was and asked for their input: mud bricks and their labour. Philemon remembers, "The projects were never what we prioritised, but we accepted the help." Eventually, in 2010, a local politician funded what the community wanted: a safe place for women to give birth.

The clinic was built of packed mud bricks with cement plaster, which was not exactly a comfortable environment. Moigua Fatmata was the first nurse officially stationed in Grima, and she quickly became aware of the challenges. "At the

DOI: 10.4324/9781003377917-5

time I moved there, Grima was very remote. And it wasn't easy to live there." The community's isolation meant that goods and services were difficult to attain, much less electricity and running water, and women were affected most by the lack of resources. "The health of pregnant women and mothers with newborns was not good," Fatmata shared, "Most households and pregnant women had poor knowledge about how to keep healthy" (Rogers 2022a). With limited access to health care, women's health in villages like Grima is very precarious.

Communities across Sierra Leone face maternal health challenges. According to the United Nations Children's Fund (UNICEF), maternal deaths account for 36 per cent of all deaths (UNICEF, 2023). When a mother does safely give birth, the situation for her and her baby remains dire. One in eight children in Sierra Leone dies before they reach the age of five (Statistics Sierra Leone [STATS SL] and ICF, 2020), and most of these deaths are preventable if there are proper healthcare services (UNICEF, 2023). These deaths continue despite Sierra Leone receiving several billions of dollars in development assistance (World Bank, 2023). On top of this, the Sierra Leone government spends a comparatively high amount on health. In 2019, 8 per cent of government spending was on health care, double that of their neighbour Guinea (World Bank, 2020). Nevertheless, resources are hard to access in remote places like Grima. There are shortages of medicine, unreliable power connections, and little funding for general clinic maintenance. Of course, this made Fatmata's job difficult:

> I do a life-saving job. Imagine, it's late, I had no lights, and there were three pregnant women in the labour room, waiting for my service. There was no space to accommodate all of them. It was hard for me to do my job well under such conditions. I felt so bad and was so worried.

Why do maternal health challenges persist despite all the aid intended to prop up healthcare systems like Grima's clinic? The answers to this question have led to endless debates, but in the immediate term, people in Grima live with this tragedy. Ineffective aid has left communities feeling as though projects meant to benefit them are not theirs. When a drinking water well was constructed in Grima, people referred to it by the name of the NGO that built it. "People didn't feel like there was a place for them to make any decisions on projects," shared Moigua Bockarie, another community member from Grima (Rogers, 2022b). Processes that enable local decision-making and eventual ownership over development solutions can counteract the ineffectiveness of aid and, in the case of maternal health, resolve persistent challenges around service delivery and save lives.

OneVillage Partners implements community development programs that address the social and material challenges of multi-dimensional poverty – a measurement of poverty beyond monetary deprivations (World Bank, 2022). We[2] accomplish this through intensive collaboration and consensus-building practices to ensure that all community members are involved in all decisions on the project.

This community-led methodology is a more equitable, efficient, and targeted way of delivering aid. As we show in this chapter, some of the solutions to the poverty experienced in Grima and throughout Sierra Leone reside in building new community spaces where all development actors, including community members, develop a partnership within and between communities and services that strengthen societies and save lives. There's no better place to demonstrate this process's effectiveness than in Grima, "The Thinking Place."

Our chapter proceeds as follows: First, by briefly situating Sierra Leone's current public health realities within its colonial and post-colonial history, we contextualise the breakdown of social capital within rural communities. After pausing at Eisler's partnerism concept, we introduce OneVillage Partners' community-led programming, describing how it works towards cultivating collaboration within and between communities as well as with broader government structures. The last sections evidence the importance of community-led engagement and collaboration processes through two ethnographic and first-person narratives.

Humanitarianism, Imperialism, and the "Social Glue"

Grima's multidimensional poverty is rooted in Sierra Leone's unique modern history: Sierra Leone was colonised for "charitable" purposes. The settlement of Freetown was established as a community for formerly enslaved people from the Americas in the 1790s, with support from a British charity and facilitated by the British Empire. The colony was an early form of "Humanitarian Imperialism," where humanitarian rhetoric was used to justify war and empire-building (Bricmont 2006). Colonisation also manifested through "Indirect Rule"[3] that favoured inequality and rigid hierarchies in the colony (Jones 2020). "Indirect Rule" reshaped African societies by force to the economic benefit of the British Empire, where rules and social order were dictated to the colonies from afar. Once the Freetown colony began, it conquered the indigenous communities surrounding the settlement. Colonisers dehumanised indigenous communities in pursuit of resources, which often involved full-scale warfare (Ochai 2017). Eventually, the United Kingdom "gave" Sierra Leone independence in 1961, but the state apparatus was very fragile, and within 30 years, Sierra Leone descended into a civil war that was as brutal and dehumanising as anything societies in this new nation had experienced. Sierra Leone's interwoven history of charity, the dehumanising force of the British Empire, and the conquering and destruction of indigenous societies have implications for how services and economic development are delivered in Sierra Leone today.

When the West Africa Ebola outbreak began in 2014, millions of dollars of humanitarian aid poured in from abroad. Many Sierra Leoneans immediately attached cynical motives to this, accusing the government of exploiting the crisis and trying to get "more funding" (McCordic 2014). People's cynicism had devastating consequences for communities as they did not take proactive measures to protect themselves (McCordic 2015). At the same time, people's cynicism also signified that many did not see the benefit of humanitarian aid. They felt disassociated from it, and the oftentimes vital work it funds. Sadly, this also meant that many communities took no steps to address this crisis collectively. The Ebola Outbreak of 2014–2015 claimed more than 4,000 lives in Sierra Leone. Most of these deaths were in the early days of the outbreak, when mistrust was high, and communities were often violently split in how to respond to the crisis (McCordic 2015).

This alienation that bred the mistrust and the breakdown in connectedness between communities is a symptom of a loss of social capital, which is the tangible network of social interactions in a community. "Social capital refers to the norms and networks that enable people to act collectively…[they] constitute an important asset, one that can be called on in a crisis, enjoyed for its own sake, and leveraged for material gain" (Woolcock and Narayan 2000). Social capital has distinct forms, which we will explore further, but for now, we can think of social capital as the glue that holds a group together. Without it, a community's resilience in the face of challenges is at risk.

If we investigate where this breakdown of social capital started, we can see its origins in colonisation. Most of the world's poorest countries have had recent experiences with colonialism, and many authors and activists make the compelling case that these countries are poor *because* of colonisation (Ziltener 2013). Colonisation had lasting implications for people experiencing poverty in the Global South, and the implications extend to how the development sector and funders have tried to address poverty.

Aid has followed a top-down model, with foreign aid offices making decisions in home countries and dictating terms to local offices and national implementing agencies. This process is similar to the colonial system of "indirect rule" and has rightly been criticised. Most of the critiques, however, use an economic lens to discuss aid's failures and pay less attention to the human and social elements of aid's "ineffectiveness" or the multiple dimensions of poverty we mentioned before. To its credit, the aid industry has responded to these critiques and piloted programs to address social capital loss.

One such program was the 2005 World Bank-funded project "GoBifo" (which means "Move Forward" in *Krio*, the lingua franca). The World Bank designed the project to foster democratic engagement and deliver a community development project that would materially improve the quality of life in rural communities, like agriculture and livelihood investments, water and sanitation projects, and more. Community members would establish a coherent and unified vision for development, and the district government would implement them, with financial support from the World Bank, in untied block grants. Sierra Leone had just emerged from 10 years of civil war, where social capital was not just destroyed; entire villages were burned down. The GoBifo Project would rebuild these villages and strengthen the lost social capital. While there were immediate improvements in well-being, the project did not realise all social capital outcomes. "GoBifo created immediate positive benefits for the community, [but] it did not send the communities onto a stronger development trajectory that would continue to accrue benefits beyond the life of the project" (Casey, Glennerster and Miguel 2013). In other words, the impact remained within the project's scope, and the gains in social capital seemed not to be sustained.

In 2015, OneVillage Partners implemented a program similar to GoBifo, and we saw similar success in sustainable improvements in village infrastructure and quality of life. However, as we will show, we sustained the social capital in development projects. We did so by broadening the implementation beyond the traditional frameworks of community development projects and focusing on community engagement and consensus building throughout the project, even after completion.

Measuring Metrics Differently

OneVillage Partners' CLD process draws from Riane Eisler's ideas on "partnerism." Eisler's research considers how economies prioritised certain metrics over others, and these "flawed metrics" shaped our society into ones based on domination, where negative events like natural disasters (or, more recently, a global pandemic) are still recorded in terms of "economic growth." Eisler stated that "we need what we have not yet had. Economic systems that give visibility and value to the most essential human work: the work of caring for people and the work of caring for the earth" (Eisler, 2011). This led to her theory of partnerism, "a socio-economic system where all relationships, institutions, policies, and organisations are based on principles of equitable partnership that supports linking rather than ranking and hierarchies of actualisation rather than hierarchies of domination" (Partnerism, n.d.). Social groups based on partnerism exist in opposition to those based on "domination," where hierarchy is maintained by the decision-making of a few.

Colonisation is a perfect example of this "domination"-based society. It was, first and foremost, an *economic* system and a brutal system of extraction and dehumanisation. Partnerism's inclusive approach can be effective in addressing the existing inequalities in Sierra Leone and rebuilding social capital. What does partnerism look like in practice? Our experience in Grima can illustrate this.

"This is the first time anyone has asked us what *we* want!"

In 2015, OneVillage Partners began a CLD program in Grima. Philemon McSenesie was one of the 12 volunteer "Change Agents"[4] who joined the program. OneVillage Partners trained them in public speaking, meeting facilitation, and participatory tools that would assist the community in identifying their development needs. OneVillage Partners staff and the Change Agents consulted with the community on their development needs and vision for the future. On the final day of the consultations, more than a hundred people gathered in the village square to participate in voting for their development priority. Philemon led the community in publicly selecting what needed to be addressed.

As the voting unfolded, the community members chose two top priorities: education and public health. The boisterous event suddenly shifted in mood. The traditional women's leader called the women present to join her outside for a discussion. A serious conversation began on which immediate need members should choose: education or public health. One woman spoke of the deplorable physical condition of the primary school building. Another talked about how public health would mean something everyone needed, like water or sanitation. We were there as OneVillage Partners' representatives, but we knew this discussion wasn't about us, and it wasn't for us. Even those of us who spoke Mende, the indigenous language in the area, stayed outside the huddle. The women quickly reached a consensus. They dispersed and informed the men what they would be voting for. Traditionally, men make decisions in rural Sierra Leone, so we did not anticipate that gender hierarchies would be shifted in our CLD model, both explicitly and quickly. We called the vote again, and like a wave of humanity, hands shot up, establishing public health as the community's priority. Suddenly, the mood shifted again. This time, it was ecstatic. Someone brought out a pair of drums, and everyone there erupted into dance. When we had a chance, we asked Philemon why everyone was *this* happy. "We've had seven NGOs do projects here," he said. "This is the first time anyone has asked us what *we* want!" Then he went back to dancing.

When people actively participate in implementing their community projects, it holds great value. This is especially the case for marginalised members, such as women, who are given a chance to make choices they were unable to make previously. This aligns with Amartya Sen's Capability Approach (Robeyns and Byskov 2021), holding that the freedom to achieve well-being is of primary moral importance and that this freedom must be understood in terms of their capacity (Robeyns and Byskov 2021). The people of Grima danced that day because of their freedom to choose how to achieve their vision of well-being. Social capital is neither a reservoir nor something you can "deliver" to a community. OneVillage Partners' work, and other CLD approaches, help draw out social capital and direct it towards tangible improvements in well-being; even if drawing it out looks like a dance party.

After this meeting, Grima implemented community-led public health projects with OneVillage Partners. All households now have latrines, up from 40 per cent before. Additionally, 90 per cent of households reported improved hand-washing practices, and there was a 70 per cent reduction in diarrhoea. These projects targeted children's health, as diarrhoeal disease is a leading cause of death among children. Then the community participated in an agriculture training project and the construction of safe produce storage, which increased harvest yields for farming groups and 75 per cent of the community adopted more hygienic practices for storing their produce (OneVillage Partners 2018). These measurable improvements in health happened because of the work of many people, but it is hard to see this happening without the woman leader mobilising her community, in the village square, on that day in 2015, and prioritising public health. OneVillage Partners did not train her to do this; all we did was open up a space for her to use her leadership skills. We didn't "provide" the social capital; we just gave room for the woman leader to use her capabilities to draw it out.

Building Consensus and Bonding Capital – Between Communities

The power of CLD projects exists beyond the scope of an organisation's project frameworks, which are time-bound and evaluated based on external targets. To measure and sustain social capital, a broader view is necessary. This was shown in a second evaluation of the GoBifo program. The study took place soon after the Ebola outbreak ended and demonstrated that social capital was indeed forming. The reason the evidence of social capital was initially missed was the short time frame used to assess it. The authors wrote, "Programs are now 'ageing' into a stage where it is possible to assess longer-run effects" (Casey et al. 2021). In addition, the study

> provides suggestive evidence that the [GoBifo] program may have generated some benefits for villages during the Ebola crisis...This happened in the form of new by-laws around behaviours around Ebola Virus Disease and the establishment of local task forces who might identify and report cases.
>
> *(Casey et al. 2021)*

This evidence aligns with OneVillage Partners' experience. In our "Post-Ebola" household survey in 2015, we discovered that communities with "strong, unified leadership" and experience in "community mobilising" were the ones who managed the crisis better (McCordic 2015). In Grima, volunteers, including Philemon, were trained as Ebola educators and contact tracers by Médecins Sans Frontier (Doctors Without Borders). When the outbreak began, the number of cases developed fast in Grima, and soon there were 23 cases of Ebola Virus Disease there. Philemon said, "Even though people didn't believe [in the existence of Ebola], even as people became sick, they started to trust the education I was providing to them since I was one of them. I was a son of their soil." In the end, there were three deaths from the disease, a much lower death toll than other afflicted communities in the area (McCordic 2015).

This trust in "local" expertise on Ebola is another example of social capital contributing to social good. There are three types of social capital: Bonding, bridging, and linking, and each does exactly that: Bonds people together, bridges people across social divides, and links people to power. The trust those in Grima had for Philemon was "bonding social capital," which refers to "connections within a group or community" (Claridge 2018). One of the ways OneVillage Partners strengthens social bonds is through an intentional process of consensus building: engaging all community members, recognising and including all voices, visually mapping out issues, and, as we have seen, voting. Using consensus building in community-led development is essential as it creates a virtuous cycle of social capital growth. "As group members begin to experience the difference their consensus building can make…it builds the confidence and strength of the group" (Madden 2017). Working at a small scale allows our work to get immediate consensus built and ensures the community has evidence of a tangible improvement in their quality of life. Since the Change Agents are already well known, learning about the project becomes as easy as talking to your neighbour.

Our partners in the village of Kigbai have shown that consensus-building is an effective tool for community development. After the implementation of a water well project, OneVillage Partners facilitated a meeting with Kigbai community members to share data on the level of handwashing practice among children in the village. One section of the community had much lower reported rates of handwashing, and this caused a sudden commotion. With a few facilitation prompts and some active consensus building, an impromptu public health initiative took place: parents from households with high handwashing rates agreed to model proper handwashing to children in that area (OneVillage Partners 2018). In this example of community-led development, the community identified a public health need and devised a solution through consensus, with minimal involvement of the NGO present.

Building a New Community Space for Engagement and Collaboration

OneVillage Partners also works on developing linking social capital, which refers to "relations between individuals and groups in different social strata in a hierarchy in which power, social status and wealth are accessed by different groups" (Claridge 2018). This type of social capital can dictate the long-term success of projects through advocacy. We host meetings among community members, volunteers, and their elected representatives to discuss ways to sustain the gains they have made through projects supported by OneVillage Partners. Sometimes, we accompany community members to the government office so they can continue their advocacy. However, the best example of linking social capital is within the Leadership Engagement and Development (LEAD) program, where communities write self-help project proposals to be funded by OneVillage Partners.

In Sierra Leone, government officials are used to projects being presented to them with little room for input. However, the LEAD program aims to involve them more deeply, inviting them to provide input on project ideas and to decide which LEAD projects OneVillage Partners should fund. Convening traditional authorities (like paramount chiefs and women's leaders) as well as sub-national government officials, OneVillage Partners provides training on how to evaluate proposals based on specific criteria. The cohort interacts with the community and their proposal, then builds a consensus on which projects OneVillage Partners should fund. This process *links* the community directly to those in authority but also *bonds* the authorities themselves, reinforcing two forms of social capital within the program. Since colonial times, Sierra Leone has had both traditional and "modern" governing systems, but they have not always worked effectively together. OneVillage Partners is not interested in installing a new "system" of governance. Instead, it facilitates a new community space where authorities can interact with each other and community members in a purposeful way. This also shifts power, from decisions by external actors, like an NGO or funder, to making decisions openly with the community members and their leadership.

As we have seen in Grima, OneVillage Partners' projects make a measurable positive impact on people's lives. These gains are sustainable because of our community-led model, where enhancing social capital is explicitly baked into all projects. Of all our supported projects, 90 per cent are still in sustainable use, including those initiated by Grima community members back in 2015 (Jawara 2022). We have found that social capital is augmented and sustained as well. Out of over 300 Change Agents trained, half have secured formal leadership positions within their community or local government. With leaders experienced in intentional consensus building, a more inclusive style of leadership has the space to emerge, reinforcing all types of social capital. In communities we partner with, people talk about social improvements in the same breath as their material improvements, and they consistently report higher levels of social cohesion. One community leader called programs supported by OneVillage Partners "an ointment that can heal the pain from things that have divided us" (OneVillage Partners 2018). This indicates that community-led projects can address historical injustices while still improving well-being well into the future.

We believe these gains will be sustained in Grima because the community has developed social capital that extends beyond the scope of any individual project. Even without the direct intervention of OneVillage Partners, community members continue to work together. For example, farmers in Grima were involved in a business deal with a local palm oil company, which had leased an area of palm tree forest for exclusive extraction. However, the farmers realised that the established deal was not as beneficial to them as it should be. The deal had also been reached somewhat secretly between the company and a few chiefs, and the elite of the community. To address this issue, the community members facilitated a dialogue with all farmers in Grima affected by this deal, using what they called "The OneVillage Partners Method." They reached a consensus on a new deal with the palm oil company that would improve payment for their harvests. In essence, the community developed a new norm on how they would build consensus and make an action plan. With the support of traditional leaders, they then drafted a new proposal and presented it directly to the company. The company agreed to the new terms of remuneration and the more equitable use of the palm tree plantation (OneVillage Partners 2020). The consensus the farmers built together secured their social capital, which can sometimes be more valuable than the bottom line of a multinational palm oil company.

Of course, a methodology that critiques one size fits all will not be one size fits all, and will have unique drawbacks. Community-led development shows us that there is no single solution and that cultivating an experimental mindset and an adaptive framework is critical. Community-led approaches are time intensive, and the type of community engagement with the intensity of how OneVillage Partners practices it is not easy or cheap. Even though the power is centred on collaboration, there is still need for financial resources to fund this approach, which is hard when funders are used to specific plans with predetermined outcomes. Additionally, community-led development calls for a unique engagement with each type of community, and each has a different baseline of social capital and skills. For example, some villages might not have the necessary carpentry or masonry skills to build the needed infrastructure. Community-led development is also ill-suited for certain immediate emergency responses. However, as the GoBifo evaluation has shown, community-led development can be the basis for a more robust and long-term social response to these crises, specifically through peer-to-peer education and mobilisation. So, while community-led development has limits, it is also endlessly adaptable to improve all community development interventions. But the real question is the one we started with. Though it is effective at delivering certain forms of sustainable development, can CLD address a systemic issue as complex as poor child and maternal health in Sierra Leone?

"This is going to be one of the very important things I remember about my role here"

Grima's experience with the LEAD Program serves as an example of how community-led development can create systemic change while also improving the health of community members. In 2019, the Grima community identified maternal health as their top public health priority once again. Volunteer Change Agents wrote a proposal to improve the existing health clinic with the help of Fatmata, the clinic's lead nurse. The clinic, operating for nearly a decade, had deteriorated in the harsh tropical weather and needed more space to accommodate population growth. But Fatmata and the Change Agents' proposal also focused on the needs of pregnant women in Grima and surrounding communities. While the whole clinic was to get an upgrade, the project would completely rebuild the birthing room. It would provide running water, tiled floors, and solar-powered lights for late-night births, something Fatmata struggled with.

The project received financial support from OneVillage Partners, but Grima community members led all aspects of it, from the masonry to the monitoring and evaluation. Despite the pandemic and global shutdown, the Grima community kept working. As they neared the end of the project, the volunteer committee increased their engagement with the Ministry of Health's District Health Medical

Team (DHMT) to ensure the project received support and service improvements. OneVillage Partners also advocated for the project during our meetings with the Ministry of Health in the capital, Freetown. The Change Agents in Grima continued to interface with the DHMT independently, even after completing the clinic construction.

After Grima completed the project and people started using the clinic, OneVillage Partners coordinated several Focus Group Discussions and mixed-methods evaluations to assess the project's impact. We found that attendance had increased drastically because of the additional space. There was a 66 per cent increase in clinic attendance for children under five from 2019 to 2021, with most new attendance coming from mothers outside Grima. There was also an upward trend in safe deliveries from 96 in 2019 to 254 in 2021. Meanwhile, there was a significant downward trend in infant deaths. In 2018, Grima's community of 120 households recorded 23 deaths of children under five. In 2021, the year after the clinic renovation project was complete, there were only six deaths. In 2022, there were only four infants who died in Grima. These impressive results and the sustained advocacy led to the Ministry of Health changing the clinic's status to a Community Health Centre in 2022, ensuring it would receive more resources and financial support and house more qualified staff (Reisz 2022). Fatmata saw the improvement first-hand and recognised that this would not have happened without collaboration. She told us, "I want to praise the people for their cooperation with [the volunteers] and OneVillage Partners. We jointly saved lives working together. This is going to be one of the very important things I remember about my role here" (Rogers 2022a).

A Space to Come Together and Think

OneVillage Partners' model has evidence of success, but none of this would have been possible without a relentless amount of reflection and experimentation. There is no community-led development playbook, nor should there be one. Community-led approaches like OneVillage Partners' demonstrate the need for adaptation and flexibility to meet the specific needs that each community might have. Collaboration will look different depending on those collaborating, so to truly build a movement, this spirit of experimentation must continue, even as we gather new partners.

Even with this success, partnerism shows that our society still operates under norms of domination, and the aid industry continues to be shaped by the historical ramifications of colonialism. However, we believe that community-led development provides a relevant approach to decolonising humanitarian aid by creating new community spaces and ensuring immediate improvements in quality of life and social capital. This approach can benefit all development actors, from the national government to the smallest civil society groups. These new community spaces are crucibles for creative collaboration, and they are driven by the desire to shift power away from structures that have marginalised those living in poverty. To truly decolonise aid, we must build new community spaces based on partnerism; this means valuing and reflecting the voices of the most vulnerable and grounding our actions in the lived experience of those we are serving.

Philemon spent several years volunteering with OneVillage Partners as a Change Agent in Grima while he finished his distance-learning college courses. After he graduated, he applied for a job with OneVillage Partners and was hired. He managed CLD projects in a variety of communities in Sierra Leone, some far away from Grima, but when we asked about how his home village is now, he was confident. He says, "People are healthy, things are better. At this moment, people in Grima are proud of the work they've done, and they feel independent. Like, they can do the work themselves." Philemon sees this extending to the future too. "People here still come up with new ideas…they still think of new ways we can solve our problems." This was, after all, what Grima was named for: A place to come together and think.

Notes

1 All names and testimonies in this chapter were collected and are shared with the individual's expressed consent.
2 All authors and OneVillage Partners staff have experience implementing these development programs in Sierra Leone.
3 "The British conception of 'indirect rule' and the French idea of 'association', both emphasised in the 1920s, were attempts to put a positive light on colonial failure to remake African societies and to confine politics to tribal cages." (Cooper 2002).
4 Change Agents are a group of community members trained to take an active role facilitating development projects and the necessary community engagement around them. They continue to advocate for positive change in their own communities after the project.

References

Bricmont, Jean. 2006. *Humanitarian Imperialism; Using Human Rights to Sell War*. Aakar Books.

Casey, Katherine, Glennerster, Rachel and Miguel, Edward. 2013. "The GoBifo project evaluation report: Assessing the impacts of community-driven development in Sierra Leone". *3ie Impact Evaluation Report* no 3. New Delhi: International Initiative for Impact Evaluation (3ie) https://doi.org/10.7910/DVN/QXEZBN

Casey, Katherine, Glennerster, Rachel, Miguel, Edward and Voors, Maarten J.. 2021. "Long Run Effects of Aid: Forecasts and Evidence from Sierra Leone". NBER Working Paper No. 29079, July 2021. https://doi.org/10.3386/w29079

Claridge, Tristan. 2018. Institute for Social Capital: "What is Bonding Social Capital? What is Bridging Social Capital? What is Linking Social Capital?" www.socialcapitalresearch.com/what-is-bonding-social-capital/

Cooper, Frederick. 2002. *Africa since 1940: The Past of the Present (New Approaches to African History)* (p. 18). Cambridge University Press. Kindle Edition.

Eisler, Riane. 2011. "Building a Caring Economy." Filmed at TEDxSanta Cruz on June 11, Santa Cruz, CA. www.youtube.com/watch?v=f9cMcTWWDkU

Fiszbein, Ariel, and Lowden, Pamela, eds. 1999. *Working Together for a Change: Government, Business, and Civic Partnerships for Poverty Reduction in Latin America and the Caribbean.* World Bank Publications.

Jawara, Al-Haji. 2022. "OneVillage Partners: Project Sustainability Survey." Unpublished/Internal Document.

Jones, Alex. 2020. "Colonial Expansion from Freetown to Sierra Leone. 1800–1900." Accessed on January 03, 2023. https://alex-jones.medium.com/how-did-colonisation-spread-from-freetowns-coast-to-all-of-sierra-leone-85ed3698a30d

Madden, James. 2017 "A Practical Guide for Consensus-Based Decision Making". Accessed on January 03, 2023. www.tamarackcommunity.ca/latest/a-practical-guide-for-consensus-based-decision-making

McCordic, Chad. 2014. "Newsweek: Ebola Frontline: In Sierra Leone, Villagers Starting to Believe Ebola Is Real". *Newsweek.* August 6, 2014. Access on January 3, 2023. www.newsweek.com/ebola-frontline-sierra-leone-villagers-starting-believe-ebola-real-263216

McCordic, Chad. 2015. "Post-Ebola Survey. OneVillage Partners". Unpublished/Internal.

McCordic, Chad, Pardello, Renee, Artibello, Jennifer, and LaLonde, Jill. 2020. "Making Decisions, Not Bricks: Collaborative Decision Making in Community-Led Development Projects." *Interdisciplinary Journal of Partnership Studies* 7 (1), 6.

Ochiai, Takehiko. 2017. "In a Grove? Sierra Leone's 1898 Hut Tax War Reconsidered". *Asian Journal of African Studies*, 41, 58–62.

OneVillage Partners. 2018. "Most Significant Change Evaluation, 2018". Unpublished/Internal.

OneVillage Partners, 2020. Bristol-Stool Chart Report, Unpublished/Internal.

Partnerism. n.d. "What Is Partnerism". Accessed on January 3, 2022. www.partnerism.org/#partnerism-is-page

Reisz, Taylor. 2022. "Impact of the Grima Clinic Lead Project". Unpublished/Internal.

Robeyns, Ingrid and Morten, Fibieger Byskov. 2011. "The Capability Approach". *The Stanford Encyclopedia of Philosophy.* https://plato.stanford.edu/archives/win2021/entries/capability-approach/

Rogers, Nyangajia. " November 2022a. "Interview with Fatamata Moigua.

Rogers, Nyanganjia. November 2022b. "Interview with Community member Moigua Bockarie".

Statistics Sierra Leone (Stats SL) and ICF. 2020. *Sierra Leone Demographic and Health Survey 2019.* Stats SL and ICF.

UNICEF. 2023. Sierra Leone: "Maternal, neonatal and child health: Lack of quality and uninterrupted delivery of comprehensive life-saving services still deny children their right to life and survival". Accessed on January 3, 2023. www.unicef.org/sierraleone/maternal-neonatal-and-child-health

OneVillage Partners, 2020. "OneVillage Partners: Grima Monitoring and Evaluation Results Feedback". Unpublished/Internal.

Woolcock, Michael and Narayan, Deepa. (2000). "Social Capital: Implications for Development Theory, Research, and Policy". *The World Bank Research Observer*, 15 (2), 225–249. https://doi.org/10.1093/wbro/15.2.225

World Bank. 2020. "Data: Net Official Development Assistance Received (current USD) – Sierra Leone" Viewed on January 3, 2023. https://data.worldbank.org/indicator/DT.ODA.ODAT.CD?end=2020&locations=SL&start=1960&view=chart

World Bank. 2022. "Multidimensional Poverty Measure". Viewed 10 March 2023 www.worldbank.org/en/topic/poverty/brief/multidimensional-poverty-measure

World Bank. 2023. "Data: % of Government Expenditure on Health Expenditure". https://data.worldbank.org/indicator/SH.XPD.CHEX.GD.ZS?locations=SL

Ziltener, Patrick, and Kunzler, Daniel. 2013. "Impacts of Colonialism: A Research Survey". *Journal of World-Systems Research* 19 (2), 290–311. https://doi.org/10.5195/jwsr.2013.507

4

COMMUNAL LAND ORGANISATIONS AND PAYMENTS FOR ENVIRONMENTAL SERVICES IN THE HUASTECA POTOSINA REGION OF MEXICO

Aida Ramos Viera

Introduction

In this chapter, I introduce two case studies to focus on two dimensions of community-led development: first, local resources and knowledge, and second, interactions with local government. The case studies are part of a larger project in which I evaluated how communal land organisations have been impacted by neoliberal land reform and a payment for environmental services (PES) programme at the regional (Huasteca Potosina) and at community levels from 2011 to 2012. For this project, I created a multi-scale geographical information system (GIS) with a sample of 43 communities and *ejidos*[1] to spatially analyse forest cover, land tenure, socioeconomic marginality, and the implementation of PES. The data collection combined archival and bibliographic research about the region's history of land tenure, development programmes, environmental impacts, and forest conservation initiatives. I walked hundreds of miles of forest with community members, applied questionnaires at community assemblies, interviewed community leaders, and undertook participant observation at countless meetings related to the PES programme in communities and at government workshops.

In what follows, I describe the history of communal land organisations in Mexico and the region in which these two cases develop. Specifically, I will focus on how the communities have responded to land reforms and government programmes while trying to benefit from the PES programme. As background to the case studies, the next sections provide brief summaries of the history of community land titles in Mexico, the geographic and sociocultural context of the [Huasteca] region, and neoliberal policies with regard to land ownership. Before introducing the case studies, I also describe the governing structures inherent to indigenous communities and elaborate more on the PES programme. Thereafter,

DOI: 10.4324/9781003377917-6

I look at how the PES was implemented in the *ejidos* of La Concepción and El Cristiano and the lessons these two cases offer for the practice of community-led development in Mexico.

The *Ejido* and Indigenous Community Lands

Original indigenous community land titles in Mexico can often be traced back to the early colonial period (1519–1821), if not earlier. During the first half of the colonial period, as the population plummeted and more Spaniards came to settle, the invaders took some of the best indigenous lands. This trend accelerated in the 1700s despite an indigenous population rebound when Mestizos (mixed indigenous-Spanish) began invading indigenous lands. After Independence in 1821, Mexico privatised indigenous communal lands, and most communities could not pay for their titles. Expanding *haciendas* (large commercial estates) absorbed many communities as peons for cash crop production for the international market.

The Mexican Revolution (1910–1921) was essentially a reaction to unequal land redistribution, including many of the largest and most productive parcels in foreign hands. In the three subsequent decades, land redistribution involved expropriating from *haciendas*, often where petitioners had previously worked as peons. After that, particularly between 1958 and 1976, the state, pressured by rural unrest, essentially awarded uncultivated forests to petitioners (Mathews 2011, 37), who were, by and large, Mestizos. The redistributed land remained registered to the state as communally controlled land, or *ejidos*.

For indigenous people, formal recognition of communal lands and governing structures did not begin until the 1930s, but indigenous land recovery was perhaps the most active in the 1980s. Indigenous communities could reclaim ancestral land using colonial maps and taxation records. Some also purchased and incorporated former lands into their existing communal land-holding structure (Tiedje 2005). When indigenous groups found it hard to reclaim ancestral lands, they sometimes joined Mestizo *ejidos*. The National Agrarian Registry (RAN) refers to both indigenous communities and *ejidos* as *nucleos agrarios* (agrarian units).

The official cession of communal lands ended in the late 1990s. After over 70 years of revolutionary agrarian reform, Mexico redistributed about 50% of the nation's agricultural and livestock grazing lands and the majority of forests as *ejido* or indigenous community lands. These small-scale territorial jurisdictions are the core of Mexico's cultural diversity, biodiversity, and peasant organisation and development (Herlihy et al. 2022).

The Huasteca Potosina Region

The Huasteca Potosina is a multicultural and biodiverse region of 11,292 km^2 located in the Sierra Madre Oriental mountain range of San Luis Potosi (Map 4.1). It includes 20 counties (*municipios*) with a mixed mestizo and indigenous

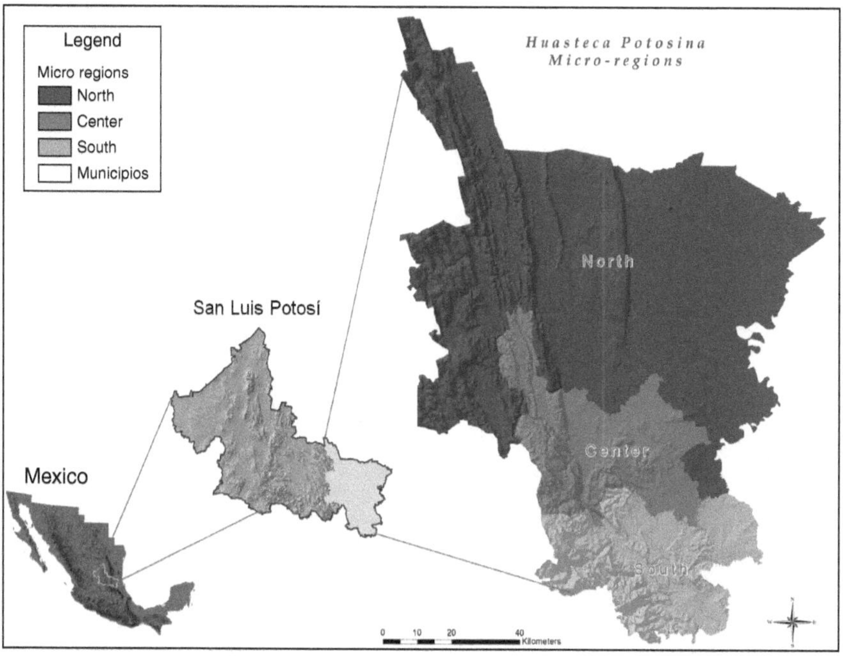

MAP 4.1 Huasteca Potosina Micro regions.

(Tenek 20%, Nahua 70%, Xiu 6%) population (Herlihy et al. 2022) inhabiting four major ecosystems: oak–pine forest, rainforest, semi-deciduous tropical forest, and deciduous tropical forest (Flores Mata et al. 1971, Puig 1976, Rzedowski 1978).

Within the 20 *municipios* are 613 *ejidos* and indigenous communities occupying 59% of the land, mainly in the rugged mountainous zones as opposed to the well-watered flat valleys dominated by large private commercial properties (Ramos Viera 2015). The distribution of *ejidos* and indigenous communities shown on the map below reveals how indigenous communities cluster in the south. In contrast, *ejidos*, composed mainly of Mestizos, are spread throughout the region (see map.4.2). Both types vary significantly in size, economy, culture, and population.

The Neoliberal Land Reform

In the 1980s, Mexico implemented neoliberal reforms as part of the World Bank's (WB) and International Monetary Fund's (IMF) structural adjustment programmes. These reforms aimed to reduce the government deficit by decreasing subsidies, privatising state-run firms, and the opening of local markets to foreign products and capital investment. The (counter) land reform that followed was intended to reinvigorate productivity and investment in rural areas as well as jumpstart the urban financial system and this was put into motion by enabling the buying and

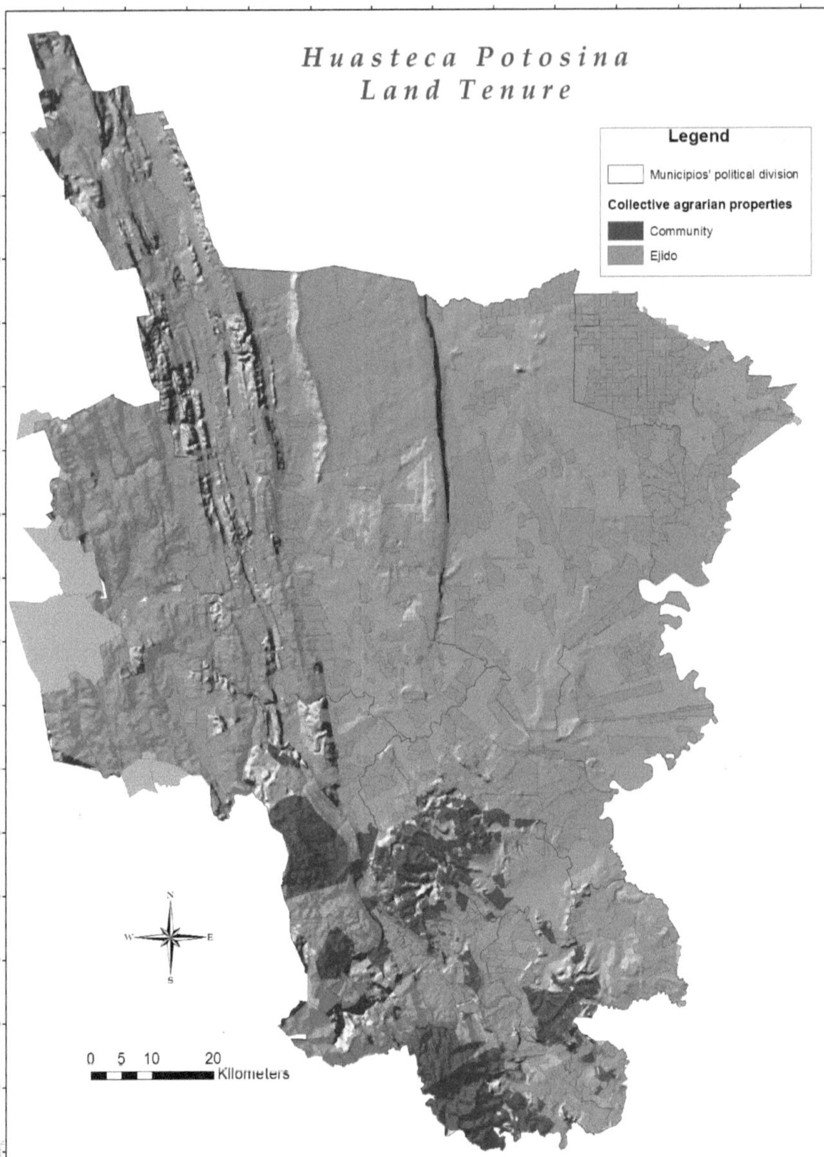

MAP 4.2 Huasteca Potosina land tenure.

selling of newly titled land (Fernandes 2002, Johnson 2001). The land certification and titling programme (PROCEDE) was implemented in 1992 to provide private individual land titles if *ejido* and indigenous community members so choose. By 2006 the vast majority of *ejidos* and indigenous communities had "voluntarily" recertified, (re)titled, or privatised their lands to varying degrees. Significantly, very few individuals chose to privatise completely and even fewer elected to abandon the communal governance structure. Mexico's peasants, particularly indigenous ones, have a strong tradition of communitarianism. While decisions to maintain communal property or privatise some have mainly depended on geographical location, local economy, and culture, almost all *ejidos* and indigenous communities have kept collective ownership over some land. Even when indigenous communities decide to assign parcels of land to individual families permanently, the families still unite to have sufficient land to qualify for PES programmes.

Social Organisation and Governance of Indigenous Communities and *Ejidos*

Despite the option to privatise, indigenous communities and *ejidos* have resisted disintegration and striven for community-led forms of development. Federal reforms in 2001 allowed states to establish the parameters of indigenous auto-denomination and autonomy, and several states, including San Luis Potosi, did so. The 2003 State Constitution of San Luis Potosí recognises that indigenous communities (a) are political, economic, social, and cultural entities, (b) have defined territories, and (c) practise their own legitimate traditional governments. Article 9 declares that such communities are legal entities with public authority, meaning their traditional leadership and judicial systems are recognised as official institutions (Artículo 9. Constitución Política del Estado de San Luis Potosi 2022, 3–5). The state's decision to recognise indigenous communities' legal authority was based on an internal analysis of 28 indigenous communities, including El Cristiano, one of the case studies here, demonstrating a history of solid and efficient organisation and auto-regulation (Ávila Mendez 2009).

With the new legislation, communities can now challenge outside authorities such as the county (*municipio*) government (Cisneros 2011b). Although the legislation was created with indigenous communities in mind, the state also recognises that Mestizo *ejidos* can claim the same rights as long as they have a comparable organisation (Article 9. State legislation of San Luis Potosi, 2003).

The internal organisation of indigenous communities and *ejidos* is quite complex and varies from community to community. Still, generally, it directly involves at least 10–15% of members in core governance.

The general assembly carries the most authority and finalises all community decisions. The commission that calls these assemblies serves for three-year terms, while the security council, auxiliary judge, and municipal delegate usually serve for one year. The security council is in charge of ensuring the acts of the commission follow the agrarian legislation and the general assembly agreements. Depending on the community's traditions and customs, members cannot serve consecutive terms, and service commitments are usually unpaid. A municipal delegate or auxiliary judge attends all legal disputes within the community. If the problem is minor, an extended group of authorities, like the assembly of residents, will deal with it. The general assembly also organises the communitarian work called *faenas* or *tequio* and the coordination of committees (Cisneros 2011a, Ávila Mendez 2009).

Communication between the municipal council and communities happens through committees that attend official county meetings. Depending on the subject, government agencies may also attend community assemblies to comply with community regulations. Committees are constantly created and dissolved according to the ebb and flow of government programmes. Still, some endure indefinitely, like those dealing with health clinics, senior citizens, utilities like electricity, the Integral Development of Families programme (DIF), schools, and PROCAMPO, which provides economic support from the government to rural producers. There are also committees dealing with natural resources management, such as communal forests and related government programmes like PES.

The complexity and extension of community governance vary according to factors like the size, origins (of recent creation or dating back to the colonial period), settlement pattern, and the level of assimilation or penetration of Western culture. The biggest communities are divided into neighbourhoods called *barrios* or *anexos*, each with a mayor and committee representatives, like the indigenous Nahua *ejido* of El Cristiano, which I will introduce shortly. Smaller communities might have some settlements dispersed from the centre without official representatives.

The Payment for Environmental Services (PES) Programme

PES emerged worldwide in the 1990s as a way to encourage local conservation and climate change mitigation, with great variation of reach, sources of financing, and services provided. One strength of this programme is its recognition of local dependency on and ownership over natural resources. In developing countries with PES programmes, like Nicaragua, Brazil, Bolivia, Guatemala, Mexico, the Philippines, and Uganda, land reforms have included the cession of forest rights to local people. In Latin America, Colombia (1990), Costa Rica (1997), and Mexico (2003) were the earliest to implement PES programmes at the national scale. By 2016 Mexico had the largest state-led PES programme in the world, with 11,114 rural communities and smallholders participating, mostly to provide hydrological services (Shapiro-Garza 2019, 199).

As mentioned, most communities and *ejidos* maintain Mexico's forest and natural resources. Forests are, therefore, communally owned, shelter biodiversity, and provide environmental services of regional and global importance (Toledo 2001, Boege 2008). Not unlike other areas in the world, in Mexico, population growth, land tenure insecurity, industry, poverty, and government policies contribute to natural resource degradation (Vandermeer and Perfecto 2005, Lambin et al. 2001, Boyer 2007, Merino and Martínez 2009, Kepleis 2003). Although customary peasant land use and tenure systems have successfully maintained healthy natural resources under communal stewardship (Herlihy 1992), neoliberal policymakers saw certification as necessary to halt deforestation due to land invasions and resource overexploitation. They also intended to incentivise communities to profit perpetually from their natural resources (Igoe and Brockington 2007). The Huasteca Potosina region's biodiversity has long been severely threatened by agricultural and cattle ranching expansion. PES was introduced as part of a national and international effort to protect the remaining forests.

The Mexican PES programme initially prioritised ecology, climate, and profit by aiming to prevent deforestation, reduce soil erosion, maintain biodiversity, improve air quality, and restore overexploited aquifers. The programme was initiated by the National Forestry Commission (CONAFOR) in 2003, focusing on hydrological services due to growing concerns about overexploited watersheds. These concerns were especially linked to cloud forests, which provide water quantity and quality to populations living below the forests (Muñoz-Piña et al. 2008). Eventually, however, the programme shifted its attention towards social elements like poverty reduction, equality, and social justice (Shapiro-Garza 2019).

CONAFOR used a prioritisation scheme of areas eligible for the PES programme that considers six categories related to the forest type. Categories I to IV originally focused on hydrological services, while V and VI emphasised biodiversity conservation (CONAFOR 2012). Categories I and II refer to cloud forests under very high and high risk of deforestation (INECC 2013), respectively, while III pertains to temperate and sub-deciduous tropical forests; IV concerns perennial and sub-perennial tropical forests under deforestation risk. Cloud forests receive higher payments (typically around 70 USD/ha per year), while dryer and disturbed forests with lower deforestation risk receive the lowest payments (around 55 USD/ha per year). In 2012, the PES moved the latter category from hydrological to agroforestry services, and payments reduced to 11 USD/ha, impacting the poor indigenous southern region the hardest. As of 2023, CONAFOR offers around 50 USD/ha per year for new participant communities, with no differentiation of payments between categories.

In San Luis Potosi, the programme's success in preventing deforestation while reducing poverty had a marked geographical variation between the more commercialised northern *mestizo* area dominated by scarcely used, large extensions of temperate forest and the impoverished southern indigenous areas dominated by tropical shade-grown coffee. Despite the different economic impacts, PES programmes proved sustainable where community organisation is strongest.

Overall, the neoliberalisation of environmental custodianship proved to have little impact, and privatisation seems to have decreased forest coverage. During the first decade of the land certification process from 1990 to 2000, forest coverage within the Huasteca region actually decreased by 7%, with those *nucleos* that completely privatised losing 24% of their forest and those that titled family plots losing 6% of their forests, while those that only certified the perimeter of their communal lands losing only 2% – the opposite of the "tragedy of the commons" (Hardin 1968) argument used to justify private land titling. Since the Mexican government started with their PES programme, deforestation rates decreased slightly for all types of landholdings. So far, land certification has had little impact on forest coverage (Aida 2015, 147), but the privatisation and disintegration of these *nucleos* agrarios remain a threat (Herlihy et al. 2022). Populations depending on subsistence agriculture are more vulnerable to climate change and more likely to migrate. Privatisation also weakens communities in the face of threats like destructive extraction by oil and gas companies. In contrast, those maintaining communal land and strong community organisations have managed to keep at bay the national oil company's (PEMEX) attempts to extract oil and gas through fracking in this highly populated region (Martínez Castro 2018).

The *Ejido* of "La Concepcion"

In many respects, La Concepción is a model PES community. My first visit to the *ejido* in 2013 was arranged when the head of the ecology department of the municipality provided me with a list of participant *ejidos* and the phone numbers of their heads of commissions. I usually introduced myself to the head of the commission and then had to wait until they had a scheduled assembly to present my research to the rest of the community, but here the entire PES committee agreed to meet with me ahead and were eager to tell me about their recent and scheduled work in the forest. My first impression was that they were very prepared to work in the PES programme and wanted to show it. The *ejido*, located in the northern mestizo region, was originally formed in 1963 with a land grant of 1,550 ha to 22 landowners (*ejidatarios*). In 1982 they received two more extensions totalling 2,766 ha for 45 of the original awardees' sons. They were certified in 1997 with 53 male heads of household registered as *ejidatarios* (PHINA 2023). By 2013, La Concepción had a total population of 293 people living in one settlement.

Ninety-three per cent of La Concepción's land, mostly temperate mountain forests, is of common use (4,051.28 ha), leaving only 261 ha in the valley as parcelled plots where sugarcane is the principal economic activity followed by some cattle grazing. La Concepción entered the PES programme in 2005, submitting 3,600 ha of their common forest for hydrological services. In 2010 CONAFOR renewed their PES programme after La Concepcion's success in maintaining and improving their forest. La Concepcion, as a locally based organisation, comprises the typical local authority system mentioned above, which functions as the direct connection between the PES programme and the local community. The community assembly charged the commission with receiving the PES money and distributing it according to a set of guidelines. The assembly decided to allocate 50% of the payments to fulfil the forest maintenance requirements, such as equipment and wages for constructing ditches and fences and demarcating the participating area. Another 20% of the funds go towards new community infrastructure, such as mountain shelters, paved roads, and a health clinic. The remaining 30% is distributed directly to landowners. The community assembly also let landowners decide whether to monopolise the maintenance activities and thus the payments for themselves or subcontract to landless members, with elders often preferring the latter. The assembly instituted a PES committee, on which the *Comisariado* (head of the community or *ejido* commission) always serves. As per PES requirements, participating communities must also select a trusted professional forestry technician from a list approved by CONAFOR. The technician teaches techniques for forest management, like clearing firebreaks, constructing washout barriers, and provisioning, organising, and coordinating firefighting crews with neighbouring *ejidos.*

At bimonthly regional CONAFOR forums, technicians teach participant communities how other *ejidos* successfully manage their forests. Thanks to La Concepción's accomplishments in managing their PES programme and their technician's initiative, their PES committee won an all-expenses-paid trip to attend a PES convention and visit a community in another part of Mexico renowned for its sustainable forestry. La Concepción delegation was pleasantly surprised to learn that PES could include extraction of forest resources instead of simple preservation.

La Concepción's forest has increased by 12% from 1980 to 2010, following the trend throughout the region, even in areas not participating in PES. Still, members value PES because of the acquired knowledge about the profitability of forests, new techniques to prevent washouts and fires, and its contribution to successfully sustaining their natural resources, diversifying their economy, and contributing to improve their community's infrastructure. Another valuable asset derived from the PES was the formation of a multi-community firefighter crew, in which La Concepcion took a leading organising role.

Nevertheless, even La Concepción experienced challenges working with the PES programme. Corruption has prevailed at all levels. Originally, the programme stipulated that the participant communities who hire the technicians should also pay them. However, after some time, the PES programme supervisors discovered that many participant communities nationwide did not pay their technicians regardless of performance. CONAFOR then decided to take over the payment of both communities and technicians.

La Concepcion selected a trusted technician who was well-known in the region and, therefore, also hired by other communities and private owners. This reduced the time he could commit to them. When CONAFOR began withholding payments to the *ejido*, the community surmised that it was due to the technician's insufficient community visits (2 per year) and tardiness in submitting required reports to CONAFOR, so they replaced him. This speaks to the incessant challenge of communication between the PES organisers, CONAFOR staff, different levels of government, and the community. Even the best-organised community groups cannot function optimally if their official counterparts do not communicate with them clearly.

Moreover, some members complained that CONAFOR had reduced the payments per hectare in the second contract (2010), but CONAFOR records, which are open to the public, actually showed an increase of USD 24 per hectare to USD

35. Someone was embezzling – a common occurrence. Gossip and accusations about the possible perpetrators were regular parts of community assemblies and meetings.

At an organisational level, despite approval and guidelines by the community assembly focused on participation and inclusion, such ideals fell short in practice. Even though the community might hire landless members to do maintenance work, many women, who are typically landless, were left out of direct payments. They were nevertheless always present in assemblies where community infrastructure projects were approved, which in the northern zone included the construction of assembly halls, furniture for those halls, and paved roads.

Another common problem in the northern region, which also impacted La Concepcion, is CONAFOR agents extracting illegal fees. Some *ejidos* simply resign themselves to paying these as the cost of participation, but in Concepción's case, the state PES administrator withheld their payments because he suspected them of being complicit in the corruption of a notorious CONAFOR regional administrator.

Nevertheless, the northern region showed several successful cases of PES among participant *ejidos*. Communities' previous experience managing government-led forestry projects and having an inter-community sugarcane mill facilitated the coordination of PES by neighbouring *ejidos*, including forming a regional fire crew. The deep involvement of municipal ecology departments and technicians' expertise was also key. Good technicians link communities to CONAFOR resources like travelling scholarships, workshops, and reforestation reserves. Effective heads of ecology departments spread the word about meetings and workshops, arrange for carpooling to meetings at CONAFOR headquarters, and ensure municipal matching funds for projects. The north also has the advantage of having valley lands amenable to sugarcane production, such that payments to maintain the mountain forests complement – not compete with – this primary source of income.

But it is La Concepción's unity as an *ejido* that ultimately accounts for its success. *Ejidos* neighbouring La Concepción were disqualified early on due to border disputes resulting in deforestation, unsuccessful reforestation, or refusal to prevent forest fires. La Concepción's organisation of neighbouring *ejidos* in firefighting crews, despite border problems with them, served not only to protect their own forests but to demonstrate their leadership when soliciting and acquiring approval for a second period of PES support. Being able to set aside property boundary issues speaks to their deep engagement with PES and sets an example for their neighbours.

After two five-year periods of PES with government payments, participants graduate to the "Market of Ecosystem Services", in which communities receive payments from private enterprises and organisations for environmental services they provide, like water and tourism. Originally, communities were expected to engage in agreements with beneficiaries of their environmental services, but it became evident that only a few possessed the necessary capabilities. Since the inception of this market for environmental services with concurrent funding in 2008, only 7% of the communities and *ejidos* engaged in PES have progressed to the next phase.[2] CONAFOR subsequently altered the approach, shifting the responsibility to companies and NGOs to propose their providers of environmental services for concurrent funding. In the region, the sugar mill has initiated this transition with El Sabinito, one of its surrounding *ejidos* that had been engaged in PES prior to this new five-year contract. However, La Concepcion has yet to embark on this phase. The primary partnership lies with the sugar mill, which relies on river water supplied by several surrounding *ejidos* for irrigation. However, communities' decision-making authority appears diminished now that beneficiaries decide who receives payment.

El Cristiano

The Nahua[3] *ejido* of El Cristiano is in the southern region, a multicultural area of indigenous Nahua and Tenek communities and mestizo *ejidos*. I first visited El Cristiano in 2012, after meeting with their assistant agronomist, who suggested that I introduce myself at their general assembly for their approval. Once they accepted my research in exchange for maps for their territorial planning project, their PES committee immediately arranged a series of visits to each of their 12 *barrios* to see their areas under PES and for meetings with each *barrio*. During the course of a year in which we walked virtually the entire *ejido*, I began to see them as an apt example of how government programmes and community organisations can reciprocally strengthen each other in community-led initiatives, particularly when officials respect the community. Established in 1929 with an additional land grant in 1980, the Nahua community has 3,124 ha. It was certified in 1997, entering all the territory as individually parcelled areas but maintaining the communal governance structure listed in Table 4.1 (PHINA 2023). By 2013, it had a population of 9,000

TABLE 4.1 Basic authority structure

Level	*Authority*
1	General assembly (including agrarian assembly, assembly of authorities, or assembly of residents)
2	The commission (president, secretary, treasurer, and substitutes) Security Council (president, secretary, treasurer, and substitutes)
3	Auxiliary judge (1st, 2nd, 3rd judge) Municipal delegate, its substitute, and secretary
4	Major, sub-major, and corporal
5	Police and rural guards
6	Neighbourhood representatives (*vocales*)
7	Committees

habitants with 706 *ejidatarios* (landowners with legal titles and rights over the common areas), 27 *avecindados* (people with only land rights over their parcels), and 837 *posesionario*s (landowners with legal titles over their parcels and other rights granted by the assembly, usually sons and daughters of *ejidatarios*) which is densely populated compared to La Concepcion with 293 habitants and more than 4,000 ha. Like many in the region, they practise self-subsistence horticulture complemented by coffee as a cash crop. Coffee was introduced to the area during the early nineteenth century (Stresser-Péan 2008, 118), and shade-grown coffee has been integrated into forest management since the 1980s to lay claim to the land and avoid expropriation (Alcorn 1984).

In 2007, Cristiano submitted 97% of its territory to the hydrological services programme (category II). During my research in 2012–2013, I met a group of ten formally educated community members of 16–24 year-old men and women who managed the PES programme along with other development programmes. The group was formed in 2010 as part of the *ejido's* idea to become a self-sufficient community by having its young people work as technicians and promoters in all kinds of development programmes. The youth group was under the supervision of the *ejido*'s committee and an agronomist who had been working with the community for several years. The agronomist served as a promoter of the indigenous reforms to the constitution in 2000. The reform process reinforced their already strong community organisation, indigenous pride, and self-governance, all of which were evident in their management of the PES programme. A regional NGO, Huastec Forum, which also managed other regional programmes, originally managed Cristiano's PES programme. But after two years, Cristiano decided to take over since the Huastec Forum began advocating for a political party. Since 2010, the youth group has operated out of a small office in the community centre equipped with a conference room and computers. They promoted and obtained resources for the *ejido's* development programmes, ranging from eco-tourism to income generation. The youth represented each of the *ejido's* 12 *barrios*, and all but two or three members rotated in and out of the office to provide other young people the opportunity to contribute. Despite CONAFOR's early resistance to this unique management style of the PES programme, the youth were eventually allowed to present their own reports with the assistance of the aforementioned agronomist in lieu of a technician. I witnessed how *ejido* members proudly watched them present their action plan and progress at CONAFOR workshops.

Their overall organisation was remarkable. The young crew organised a series of meetings and tours for me in each of their 12 *barrios* to observe different development initiatives, including their shade-grown coffee parcels under PES, a butterfly sanctuary, and a beehive project. In each *barrio*, a PES committee kept a list of members and their activities as part of their best practices programme, including annual five-year goals. Members of the youth group led each of the meetings and visits to the different areas under PES.

As community members explained during these meetings, it was very difficult to develop these plans because it required the agreement of all the parcel owners, and most did not want to do the collective work required by the PES programme. In the end, the community decided to work on individual parcels and report the work by *barrios*. The PES committee pointed out to me during one of our visits to a *barrio* that this arrangement was not perfect because not all *barrios* responded well, and many considered the payments inadequate for the required activities. This was a common conflict in the south, where indigenous communities tended to enter their lands into the PES programme as communally managed, even though they were parcelled individually. The hydrological services programme required reforestation and other activities unsuitable for individual shade-grown coffee parcels, putting parcel owners in a predicament about how to apply them. This was only partially resolved when the category of benefits changed from hydrological to agroforestry for biodiversity services. Despite the communities' choice to enter PES communally, payments were distributed to each individual landowner. So many landowners and little income meant that little could be set aside for communal infrastructure improvements.

The *ejido* was well connected to indigenous organisations and government agencies, but most important was their focus on self-sufficiency, avoiding outside corruption or unwanted political propaganda. Unlike La Concepcion in the northern region, the head of the municipal ecology department here was not so helpful, and several communities, including El Cristiano, and local technicians suspected him of corruption. With their own crew managing development projects, they could avoid compromising partnerships, something that few communities enjoyed. It was their self-determination and skilful organisation of their own affairs that was vital to their PES programme's success and became a model for other communities and local governments in implementing the state's indigenous reforms. The *ejido*'s youth crew also served as a model for inclusive participation, as they not only ensured the rotation of young members across the b*arrios* but also actively included women. Unlike the La Concepcion PES committee formed by landowners, El Cristiano's committee consisted of youth and landless men and women.

Community-Led Development with PES in the Huasteca

La Concepción's and Cristiano's engagement in Mexico's PES programme offers insights into how community-led development is possible within the uniqueness of the Mexican context. Following the Mexican Revolution, the Mexican state became heavily involved in community development, especially in *ejidos* and indigenous communities, which led to dependency. People in rural areas have come to expect and even demand state responsibility in controlling prices, augmenting production, alleviating poverty, and managing ecosystems, while the Institutional Revolutionary Party, in particular, has demanded loyalty at the ballot box. With neoliberal decentralisation and promotion of entrepreneurialism pushed by the

IMF, WB, and the United States, the state, regardless of political party, envisions communities becoming more involved in their development, including privatising their land and selling environmental services. The PES programme represents a development initiative that potentially serves both communities and the neoliberal state by redistributing income, halting ecological and climatological destruction, and fomenting economic growth (Sims et al. 2014). Success requires an ingredient often taken for granted: community unity and organisation. The two relatively successful cases I presented here have in common outstanding community organisations in the face of serious challenges. While many more cases of such successful community groups are active across Mexico, they are more exceptions than the rule. Strong community organisations can meet the challenges of a culture of corruption, distrust, and lack of knowledge about technical assistance, government bureaucracies, and the private sector. In La Concepción, strong community unity and a dependable organisation were enough to overcome corruption and problems with inadequate technical support. Ultimately they could better care for a vast expanse of forest that supports biodiversity, including black bears, pumas, and jaguars, and invest funds in community infrastructure. It is true that its success was enhanced by profits earned in the valleys from the sugarcane industry, but other communities shared similar features and failed in the PES programme. La Concepción was well organised before PES, which contributed to its decision to invest in community infrastructure and ultimately strengthen its unity.

Lest one thinks that community unity and organisation stem from timeless, essential traditions; in Cristiano, we see the invention of new structures to better engage with development opportunities. Conditions there were even more challenging because of poverty, structural inequalities, lack of common forest lands, and relatively meagre PES benefits. The newly educated youth, however, stirred by a strong sense of ethnic pride and instilled with confidence by a trusted agronomist, effectively created a new interface between their community and the government's development programming and that enabled the community to make more independent decisions and avoid compromising relationships. For the PES programme in particular, Cristiano's strategy of creating a youth committee was key for its appropriation, and management and reinforced communal pride overall. Using the youth's education, pride in leadership, vision, and devotion to the long-term future is not a common strategy in Mexican community development but one that should be encouraged. The youth group's success involved not only respecting traditional community authority but instituting more just practices, such as ensuring representation across all *barrios* and including and thereby empowering young women. In effect, it evidences more democratic and effective community-led development. To CONAFOR's credit, it overcame its reservations about allowing the youth team to serve as the official technician, and this was reciprocated with community trust. This shows, in turn, how government programming and community-led activities, organising, and initiatives can be mutually beneficial.

As for sustainability, the youth group is currently inactive because Cristiano has no current development projects. But it has not ended the former youth members' commitment to local development. A founding female member serves as a community representative for the municipal government and advocates for women's participation in politics, while other former members continue to advise the *ejido* commission.

In both case studies, constant willingness to adapt and adjust by both the communities and the PES programme administrators was critical. Regional PES offices reworked national requirements to local realities and received feedback to adjust the programme. Bimonthly regional meetings and workshops were crucial for community engagement, sharing information, dispelling rumours, and making programme adjustments.

Still, the community appropriation of PES has not been without problems. As mentioned, participation was not equitable in most cases; official *ejido* members and landowners were privileged, and both were overwhelmingly male. Even though the programme targets marginalised communities, the most marginalised within them – women and the landless – were given little opportunity to participate in the overall programme and payment distribution. In San Luis Potosí, women represent only 22% of the *ejido* and community landowners (RAN 2022), reflecting the marginalisation of indigenous women nationally, as they represent 52.7% of all the extremely impoverished (CONEVAL 2018, 114). CONAFOR's 2023 operational rules finally acknowledge this as a problem they should address (CONAFOR 2022). During my time with the communities, some did include the landless by paying for their labour in the PES activities; others allowed women to participate in community meetings, visit areas under PES, and attend workshops. Cristiano's unique assemblage of youth and gender-diverse committees highlights the possibilities of inclusiveness.

Communities also pushed back against the PES's restrictions on the use and management of forests, struggling to make the programme community-led. Forest communities understand their local ecosystems more intimately than distant bureaucracies do, but "official knowledge" still trumps traditional ecological knowledge in Mexican bureaucracy (Mathews 2011). Local populations have maintained their forests for generations without the dictates of outside scientists and bureaucrats, who impose obligations that contradict successful traditions. Indeed, as mentioned, most of the remaining forests and biodiversity in the country are maintained by communities and *ejidos*. Arguably, the principal benefit of the PES programme is that communities recognise not only the value of their natural resources but also the efficacy of their knowledge in managing them. If private entities, NGOs, and public utilities do not acknowledge these benefits, the PES programme is fundamentally flawed.

The neoliberal land titling of communal lands instilled great fear among peasant communities and scholars about community dissolution, greater land inequality, and degradation of ecosystems. Looking back 30 years later, we see nothing so dramatic happening, largely because communities like those of La Concepción and Cristiano insisted on leading their own development. As of 2020, the state and the majority of the peasant *nucleos* continue to respect communal landholdings, and development is still funnelled through communal organisations. Our two case studies' appropriation of the PES programme demonstrates that state-led development and community-led development are not necessarily opposed but can complement each other under the right conditions. Required are (a) communities' ability to organise and govern themselves in ways that work for them, (b) flexibility by international donors, state officials, and communities, (c) acknowledgement of the value of local resources and knowledge, and (d) collaboration across all sectors, including within *nucleos*. For communities and *ejidos* to actually sell their environmental services, knowledge of markets and an expansion of government, private sector, and NGO contacts is necessary.

Notes

1 *Ejidos* are communally owned land.
2 From personal communication with the head of the Department of Environmental Services Financing Strategies Monica Cardenas Lopez 03/11/2024.
3 Indigenous groups that arrived at the region in two different moments in the pre-Hispanic period: 800 BCE and during the Aztec expansion around 1400 CE (Valle-Esquivel 2003). They constitute 59% of the indigenous speakers in the Huasteca region.

References

Alcorn Janis, B. 1984 "Development Policy, Forest and Peasant Farms: Reflections on Huastec-Managed Forests' Contributions to Commercial Production and Resource Conservation." *Economic Botany* 38 (4):389–406.

Artículo 9. "Constitución Política del Estado Libre y Soberano de San Luis Potosí, 2022." Pp. 3–5. Available at www.congresoslp.gob.mx

Ávila Mendez, Agustín. 2009. "La reforma indígena potosina. Un reto al centralismo." In *Una década de reformas indígenas?: Multiculturalismo y derechos de los pueblos indios de México*. 1. reimpr. México: Cámara de Diputados, LX legsilatura, 2009.

Boege, Eckart S. 2008. *El patrimonio biocultural de los pueblos indígenas de México. Hacia la conservación insitu de la biodiversidad y agrodiversidad en los territorios indígenas.* México: INAH. Comisión Nacional para el Desarrollo de los Pueblos Indígenas.

Boyer, Christopher R. 2007. "Miguel Ángel de Quevedo y la política forestal en México 1929–1940." *Historia Mexicana* 57 (1):91–138.

Carlos, Muñoz-Piña, Guevara Alejandro, Torres Juan M. and Josefina Braña. 2008. "Paying for the Hydrological Services of Mexico's Forest: Analys, Negotiations and Results." *Ecological Economics* 65 (4):725–736.

Cisneros, Juan. 2011a. *Indigenous Communities, Social Organization and Governance*. San Luis Potosi.

Cisneros, Juan. 2011b. *Reforma del artículo 9 de la Constitución de San Luis Potosí*. San Luis Potosí.

CONAFOR 2012. Reglas de Operación del Programa Proárbol 2012. *Diario Oficial,* 21 de Diciembre 2011. Secretaria del Medio Ambiente y Recursos Naturales (SEMARNAT).

CONAFOR 2022. Reglas de Operación 2023 del Programa Desarrollo Forestal para el Bienestar. Available at www.conafor.gob.mx/apoyos//docs/adjuntos/c973f53fba23d9b486bd63939008b358.pdf

CONEVAL 2018, 114. La Pobreza en la Población Indígena de México, 2008- 2018. Available at www.coneval.org.mx/Medicion/MP/Paginas/AE_pobreza_2018.aspx

Fernandes, Edesio. 2002. "The Influence's of De Soto's The Mystery of Capital." *Land lines* 14 (1): 5–8.

Flores Mata,G. et al. 1971. Tipos de Vegetacion de la Republica Mexicana. Secretaria de Recursos Hidraulicos, Mexico.

Hardin, Garrett. 1968. "The Tragedy of the Commons: The Population Problem Has No Technical Solution; It Requires a Fundamental Extension in Morality." *Science* 162: 1243–1248.

Herlihy, Peter. 1992. "Wildlands Conservation in Central America during the 1980s: A Geographical Perspective." *Yearbook, Conference of Latin Americanist Geographers*, 17–18.

Herlihy, Peter H., John H. Kelly, Andrew M. Hilburn, Aida Ramos Viera, Derek A. Smith, Miguel Aguilar-Robledo and Jerome Dobson. 2022. "Losing Ground: Indigenous Territoriality and the Núcleo Agrario in Mexico." In *Invisible Borders in a Bordered World: Power, Mobility and Belonging*, Alexander C. Diener and Joshua Hagen (eds.). pp. 144–175. Routledge.

Igoe, Jim and Dan Brockington. 2007. "Neoliberal Conservation: A Brief Introduction" *Conservation and Society* 5 (4):432–449.

INECC 2013. Índice de riesgo de deforestación (INEIRDEF-2.0.1). www.inecc.gob.mx/irdef

Johnson, Nancy L. 2001. ""Tierra y Libertad:" Will Tenure Reform Improve Productivity in Mexico's "Ejido" Agriculture?" *Economic Development and Cultural Change* 49 (2):29–309.

Kepleis, Peter. 2003. "Neoliberal Policy and Deforestation in Southern Mexico: An Assessment of the PROCAMPO Program." *Economic Geography* 79 (3):223.

Lambin Eric, F., et al. 2001. "The Causes of Land-Use and Land-Cover Change: Moving beyond the Myths." *Global Environmental Change* 11 (4):261–269.

Martínez Castro, José L. 2018. "Fracking es una realidad, harán perforaciones en cinco municipios." El Sol De San Luis. (CD. Valles) July 27, 2018 www.elsoldesanluis.com.mx/local/valles/fracking-es-una-realidad-haran-perforaciones-en-cinco-municipios-1872471.html

Mathews, Andrew, S. 2011. *Instituting Nature. Authority, Expertise, and Power in Mexican Forests*. Massachusetts, London: The MIT Press Cambridge

Merino Leticia and Ana E. Martínez. 2009. "Rights, Pressures and Conservation in Forest Regions of Mexico. The Results of a Survey on the Conditions of Community Forest." Workshop of Political Theory and Policy Analysis. Indiana University.

PHINA 2023. Padrón e Historial de Núcleos Agrarios http://phina.ran.gob.mx

Puigh, H. 1967. "Vegetation de la Huasteca ou region de Tampico, Mexique." *Bull Sci Hist Nat Toulouse* 103:305–326.

Ramos Viera, Aida. 2015. "Forest Conservation Policies and the Neoliberal Land Reform in Mexico: A Cultural Ecology Approach to the Payments for Environmental Services in the Huasteca Potosina Region." PhD Diss, The University of Kansas.

RAN 2022. Estadística con Perspectiva de Género. Sujetos de núcleos agrarios certificados y no certificados. Resultados 2022. www.ran.gob.mx/ran/indic_gen/nucag-certynocert-avance-2022.pdf

Rzedowski, J. 1978. *Vegetación de México.* Editorial Limusa, Mexico.

Shapiro-Garza, Elizabeth. 2019. "An Alternative Theorization of Payments for Ecosystem Services from Mexico: Origins and Influence." *Development and Change* 51 (1):196–223.

Sims, Katharine, et al., 2014 "Improving Environmental and Social Targeting through Adaptative Management in Mexico's Payments for Hydrological Services Program." *Conservation Biology* 28 (5): 1151–1159.

Stresser-Péan, Guy. 2008 "Los Indios Huastecos." In *Viaje a la Huasteca con Guy Stresser-Péan,* Guilhem Oliver (ed.). pp 117–133. Mexico: Centro de estudios mexicanos y centroamericanos.

Tiedje, Kristina. 2005. "People, Place and Politics in the Huasteca, Mexico." *Anthropology Today* 21 (4):13–17.

Toledo, Victor M. 2001. "Indigenous Peoples and Biodiversity." In *Encyclopedia of Biodiversity*, Vol. 3, Levin, S. et al., (ed.) pp 451–466. San Diego, CA: Academic Press.

Valle-Esquivel, Julieta. 2003. *Nahuas de la Huasteca.* Edited by CDI:PNUD, *Pueblos indígenas del México contemporáneo.* México: CDI, PNUD.

Vandermeer, John and Ivette Perfecto. 2005. *Breakfast of Biodiversity. The Political Ecology of Rainforest Destruction.* 2nd ed. Oakland, CA: Food First Books.

5

THE POWER OF SYNERGY

Unlocking Sustainable Development through Collaboration in Uganda

Amani Initiative

Introduction

It's 10 am in Vurra Sub-County, located in northwestern Uganda, and the "Amani Driwala Ayia Ode Savings Group" is about to start their meeting. Many members are present. They are young mothers, ranging between the ages of 15 and 21, who got pregnant at a very young age – either as a result of violence, little knowledge about contraception, or coercion – had to leave school because of their pregnancies, faced familial scrutiny, and are currently raising their babies in precarious socioeconomic conditions. The young mothers never miss these meetings because they can contribute to their respective savings, see each other, discuss their challenges, and draw strength from their collective experiences. Of the 40 mothers in the group, 12 decided to return to school. They could make these decisions because they found caretakers for their babies and gained the necessary courage from peers in their Savings Group. They are devoted to helping their peers make more informed choices regarding relationships and pregnancies.

The young mothers are, however, not the only ones meeting today. Joining their conversations are representatives from the local boda-boda association – the motorbike transport service used across the country – local government representatives, an older mother, a cultural leader, a religious leader, a farmer, and a community journalist. As the meeting unfolds, all present share their roles, responsibilities, actions, and plans to prevent future teenage pregnancies while supporting new mothers.

This is not their first meeting. Instead, the group meets weekly. The group has been working for two years on strengthening their connections and identifying ways to prevent and respond to teenage pregnancies. And doing this work is crucial. Uganda faces a significant challenge with teenage pregnancies, with

DOI: 10.4324/9781003377917-7

severe health, social, and economic consequences. Actions at a local level are therefore essential in addressing this challenge. For the young mothers within this community self-support group in Vurra Sub-County, Arua District, their group and several community structures have provided the safe and trusting support needed to overcome such challenges.

As in the case of the group from Vurra, existing community structures provide invaluable support in addressing the often daunting effects of poverty. These structures comprise individuals with unique knowledge, experiences, and insights. By working together, they represent a key aspect of effective community-led development. Through them, interventions create and maintain support networks and cross-collaboration, which is essential for impactful change. In what follows, we consider what such collaboration entails, drawing from the community-led activities of Amani Initiative, a Ugandan grassroots nonprofit focused on preventing and responding to teenage pregnancy and child marriage through integrated community-led interventions. Through different voices, we describe how Amani's interventions purposefully engage social structures and institutions already present within the areas where they facilitate activities. However, the engagement does not end there. By participating in Amani's activities, local actors and the structures they represent also transform, evolving their worldviews to reflect the experiences they gained from participating in community-led initiatives.

The Amani Initiative, the different social structures contributing to the initiative, and their respective actors represent collaborations that reflect ongoing interactions between individuals and structures in response to changing needs in their immediate social, political, and cultural environments. We argue that such ongoing interaction is not only a process crucial to community-led development interventions but also a sought-after outcome. When existing structures within communities become activated towards supporting shared goals and objectives, the sustainability of any intervention is far more plausible.

This chapter comprises five sections. The first section discusses the issue of teenage pregnancy and child marriage as a global social, economic, and health concern. The second and third sections introduce the Amani Initiative through the lens of its founder. Here, Nixon Ochatre shares how and why Amani was initiated and then presents the community-centred solution it has developed to prevent and respond to unwanted pregnancies. The fourth section reflects on the importance of collaboration in community-led development, using the Amani Initiative as a case study. The section also briefly touches on the transformative potential of collaboration in community-led spaces while considering accompanying challenges. In the final section, various community actors involved in Amani share their experiences and collaborations in preventing and responding to teenage pregnancy and child marriage. This section preserves the community's voices and perspectives in their own language and ensures that the final word remains with the community and their change agents.

Teenage Pregnancy – A Global Concern

Teenage pregnancy is not unique to Vurra Sub-County. Annually, in the Majority World, about 21 million girls between the ages of 15 and 19 years become pregnant (Sully et al. 2020). According to the United Nations' 2022 world population prospect report, at 101 births per 1,000 women, sub-Saharan Africa had the most adolescent pregnancies in 2021, more than double the global average. In Uganda, more than one out of four teenagers become pregnant (Ochen et al. 2019). Studies show variation regarding household income, with girls from poorer backgrounds more likely to fall pregnant than their wealthier counterparts (41 versus 16 per cent). Where girls live also makes a difference, with the West Nile sub-region in Northern Uganda, where Vurra Sub-County is located, having the second highest national rate (29.6 per cent) (Gideon 2013).

From a health perspective and compared to older women, girls younger than 19 years are more likely to suffer from eclampsia, infections, and puerperal endometritis (Ganchimeg et al. 2014). In turn, babies from these pregnancies face preterm birth risks, neonatal conditions, and low birth weight. When born in dire economic conditions, the mother and baby will likely face acute malnutrition and impaired physical development (Fleming et al. 2015). But teenage pregnancy is as much a public health issue as a clinical health problem (Scally 2002). In addition to physical health risks, adolescent pregnancies have detrimental social and mental health impacts on the young mother, ranging from maladaptive coping abilities to possible substance abuse (Walker and Holtfreter 2021). Girls' education also comes to an abrupt halt when they fall pregnant, and without completing at least primary education, their chances of future employment decrease significantly (Ayamolowo et al. 2019; Gideon 2013). Furthermore, there is evidence linking teenage pregnancies to physical and mental abuse, with many young girls forced into abusive relationships that often result in further unplanned pregnancies (Nabugoomu et al. 2020). Many women experiencing these forms of abuse face a lifetime of mental illness and trauma.

Teenage pregnancy is linked to many cause factors and predictors. When considering sub-Saharan Africa, Gunawardena et al. (2019) identified 27 predictors, of which the most obvious include sexual coercion and pressure from male partners, low or incorrect use of contraceptives, and poor parenting or low paternal communication and support. These predictors align with those Nabugoomu et al. (2020) identified in Eastern Uganda. These include a lack of social skills, little to no knowledge of how to avoid pregnancy, low acceptance and use of contraceptives, parental neglect, sexual abuse, the pressure to contribute to family welfare, little community responsibility, peer pressure, and customs that promote early marriage.

Aware of the issue's scope and impact, the global development community and governments have prioritised addressing the challenges around teenage pregnancies through changes in policy and subsequent interventions. Such changes closely respond to teenage pregnancy predictors and thus consider, among others, sex education and reproductive health care programming, peer education, counselling, and youth-friendly clinics as possible interventions (Gunawardena et al. 2019). The Ugandan government has also taken monetary and legislative measures to address teen pregnancy. This includes a US$182 million budget on health care for teenage mothers and their children's education (UNFPA–UNICEF 2022), setting the legal marriage age at 18, and leading the African Union Campaign to end child marriage in 2015. Additionally, in partnership with several international organisations and agencies, the country has implemented sensitisation campaigns under the "Girls not Brides" partnership (Girls not Brides 2018).

The Constitution of Uganda (1995) recognises children's rights to health, education, and protection from exploitation under Article 34. The government should be responsible for ensuring that quality social services, such as education, health, child protection, justice, and social protection, are available at the national, district, and community levels. However, inadequate funding and prioritisation of security and construction projects often result in service delivery gaps. To tackle the issue of teenage pregnancy, it is necessary to involve local communities through locally led initiatives. This is because factors contributing to adolescent pregnancy are individual, economic, and social, requiring a collective responsibility and response (Nabugoomu et al. 2020). Therefore, interventions should involve as many community actors as possible and collectively foster a shared commitment towards addressing the challenge of teenage pregnancy. Amani Initiative and its community partners are an example of such an intervention.

The Amani Initiative

In 2009, at 19, I Nixon Ochatre took an 8-hour bus ride to Maracha District, a place I call home, and not too far away from Vurra, where the "Amani Driwala Ayia Ode Savings Group" meets weekly. During this trip, I interacted with three people whose stories and feedback ignited my passion for challenging teenage pregnancy and child marriage. The first person was a police officer at one of the police stations. When I asked about the crime rate within his jurisdiction, he only spoke about petty chicken thieves. He did not talk about the cases of defilement present within the community, with many girls below 15 years already pregnant, despite the Ugandan Penal Code Act making "unlawful sexual intercourse with a girl under eighteen years" punishable by death.

The second person I met was a headteacher at a prominent secondary school in Maracha District. He told me it is common for schools to do regular and unannounced pregnancy checks. Those girls whose pregnancy tests are positive have to leave school, and when they do, fellow learners will form two long lines up to the school's exit. The pregnant girls are told to walk through these two lines, with their classmates hurling insults at them. Apparently, this activity is a way of deterring fellow learners from engaging in sexual intercourse. But it happens without considering how this public shaming event can traumatise pregnant girls.

Without education, skills, experience and with social isolation, they become uncertain of the future for themselves and their unborn child. Additionally, the men or boys who impregnated these girls are absent and not exposed to any comparable forms of stigma and shame.

The third story was from a teenage mother who told me her peers advised her to have sex to avoid painful menstrual periods. Due to a lack of appropriate sexual and reproductive health information, she could not make an informed decision about her sexuality. Instead, she followed her peers' advice and decided to have sex with her boyfriend to escape the ordeal of monthly painful menstrual periods. She is now a child mother, responsible for a baby without any support or guidance. Her parents forced her to marry her boyfriend, who denied the pregnancy. He is also just a child with no financial ability to care for himself, let alone a baby.

These stories made me recognise the challenges within my community regarding prevention and response to teenage pregnancy, which denies girls and boys an opportunity for a better future. Because of teenage pregnancy, most girls from my village did not complete primary education. At the same time, the stories also pointed to several societal structures, organisations, and agencies being present within communities, but they are not necessarily functional. My friends and I were increasingly thinking about how to trigger such structures towards enabling positive change. For starters, child marriage and adolescent pregnancy is a local problem, with the perpetrators and victims usually members of the same community. Therefore, a solution for this problem might also be local. I also learned how most cases are linked to unequal decision-making processes. Commonly this would include somebody with either social or cultural power. Those most impacted by these decisions have no room to question or consider their options and little to no awareness of how they might be affected long term. For instance, a father deciding to marry off his teenage daughter, a boda-boda driver deciding to have sex with an underage school girl, and a teenager deciding to have unprotected sex. I felt that we could reverse these decisions. Such reversal should start with changing people's individual and collective mindsets.

I decided to look for and mobilise like-minded community members and peers: those who also recognise the challenges of teenage pregnancies and are aware of the impact of unequal and uninformed decisions concerning young girls and relationships. I started with people from the village where I was born, as they understood the context and were passionate about ending the problem.

We had community members who could either be the problem or the solution. We started responding to our initial motto, "Use what you have to get what you want," and decided to collaborate with rather than confront existing social structures. We saw such possibilities in collaboration with schools, health facilities, religious institutions, and community gatekeepers.

I was a teenager at the time with a vision to free my community from teenage pregnancy and child marriage. I had yet to learn how to navigate the power relations that often emerge from particular cultural norms and how we can address them.

I also needed to gain experience in project management. I did know how central local community structures and their practices were within our communities' daily existence. So, with little experience and technical knowledge, the most logical starting point was to leverage these structures and their actors towards making change.

Following suit, my peers and I connected with the leadership at three schools, a religious institution, and a health facility. They were our first set of collaborators, and alongside two community volunteers who oversaw the activities, we engaged directly with 109 adolescents as our first cohort in 2011. This cohort made up our maiden programme, "Our Time Is Yet To Come." We selected students with leadership, communication skills, and the ability to become Amani ambassadors. We referred to them as Amani scholars. We designed the programme so that the Amani scholars completed a six months training with content on self-awareness, teenage pregnancy, and child marriage. We then encouraged them to connect with at least five other students within their school or community through whom they would share the information they received, and in the process, the awareness training could be even more far-reaching.

That was the beginning. We started connecting with diverse community structures, expanded our volunteer network, and secured financial support. The latter came from our friends, families, and volunteers. We were passionate about the cause and put ourselves into it, which included, for some, personal savings. The funds were crucial in covering Amani's registration costs, and travel expenses.

Amani's first two years were significant for at least two reasons. We became more aware of the severity of issues like child marriage and teenage pregnancy, but, at the same time, we also saw the dedication of local communities to address them. We wanted to facilitate local involvement, recognising that when communities take ownership of their challenges and solutions, it leads to meaningful change.

Our first collaborators played a crucial role in establishing the foundation of our future operations. Between 2010 and 2012, we engaged with different social and cultural institutions and community members to devise a solution for the challenges around teenage pregnancy. We recognised that because the problem stems from many root causes, the solution must be diverse and embedded in different social, cultural, and economic institutions. For example, we recognised that a girl who is not in school has a higher chance of being married off or conceiving than one who is in school or stays longer in school. Low-income families often look to the dowry of their teenage daughters as a source of income. But then, even if a girl's family has the financial resources to support their schooling, she can still become pregnant because of little to no access to sexual and reproductive health services and information. Instead, they look to their peers for information, which is not always reliable. Additionally, this happens within a particular social and cultural context that strongly influences sexual practices. A girl child is referred to as "Za mva" in Lugbarati (the language of the Lugbara people who live in the West Nile region), where "za" means "meat" and "mva" means child. In Lugbara culture, once a girl has seen her menstrual period, she is considered ready for marriage.

Although laws exist to protect young girls from abusive practices, such as sexual abuse, they are often not enforced. Some local communities may not even be aware of these laws and instead rely on traditional courts led by cultural leaders. Even those who are aware, such as police officers, might use them to extort money from both abusers and victims. For example, suspected abusers are often asked to pay bribes to have reported defilement and child marriage cases dropped. Meanwhile, police might ask victims to cover the costs of case investigations, which can discourage them from reporting abuse altogether. This lack of justice has led many victims of defilement and child marriage to drop out of school, enter abusive marriages, and stay home after giving birth. Considering these realities, we formulated four thematic areas where we wanted to focus our attention: Education, Child Protection and Safeguarding, Socioeconomic Empowerment, and Health.

We initially registered Amani as a Community-Based Organization (CBO) in 2010. Our name means "ours" in Lugbarati. We chose this name because it captures our intentions to remain community-led while cultivating collective local ownership of our interventions. We started as a CBO in one sub-county in Maracha District but expanded to register as an NGO with a wider reach in 2012. As of 2023, we work with 12 health facilities, 3,000 low-cost schools, 15 community groups across 15 districts in Uganda, and over 250 community change agents. In the following section we share examples of how we collaborated with local structures across the four distinct thematic areas identified by Amani to not just address the issue of teenage pregnancy but also to bring to life the vision of change that had been co-created with the communities.

Collaborating with Local Structures

Thematic Area: Education

Uganda's Ministry of Education and Sports requires schools to have parent–teacher associations (PTAs) and appointed in-school Senior Teachers. The PTA platform allows school leaders and parents to share ideas and information on school improvement. Senior Teachers, already employed by their respective schools, offer guidance on social, physical, and emotional well-being. These structures are required, but they are sometimes not fully functional. This can cause friction between the PTA and School Management on funding allocation or, more often, limited direction and guidelines on the PTA's mandate.

Early on, Amani and its community partners recognised the value of these structures. Whereas PTAs have the potential to bridge the concerns of parents and teachers, developing in the process more impactful policy changes, Senior Teachers have the skills, background, and experience to become direct school-based liaisons between the information-sharing and awareness-raising activities Amani had in mind, and the learners directly impacted by teenage pregnancy. Amani, therefore, started engaging these structures to collaborate on the challenges around adolescent pregnancy.

PTAs have since proven valuable in developing policies on feeding programmes, re-entry processes for child mothers back into school, menstrual hygiene and management, and clean and hygienic water facilities. For instance, the school improvement plan prepared by the PTA of Ajono Primary School, a school within our network, includes constructing and renovating classrooms, electricity connections, a water pump, and regular staff meetings to track teacher performances. These resolutions have been included in the school budget for funding. In another area, a 15-year-old girl from Meki Primary School in Maracha District was asked to go home after the school heard about her pregnancy. However, because of the advocacy efforts of her school's PTA, she was allowed to return to complete her exams. The PTA also resolved to sensitise teachers and fellow learners not to stigmatise her so that she could return quickly. Through this engagement, the school has established a safe re-entry policy that is aligned with the revised guidelines on the Prevention and Management of Teenage Pregnancy in School settings by the Ministry of Education and Sports in Uganda.

The Senior Teachers, in turn, have become integral actors in Amani's in-school programming, including setting up and running school clubs for boys and girls. When starting these clubs as a safe and engaging platform for raising awareness and information sharing, Amani used a mapping exercise to consult directly with school administrators. During this exercise, they identified two teachers who can liaise with Amani. These are often one senior man and woman teacher who then play the role of patron to the school clubs. However, the Senior Teachers also voluntarily offer their time and expertise as counsellors, creating a vast support network within Amani's 3,000 partner schools. As part of their counselling, Senior Teachers hold both individual and group sessions with learners on career guidance, relationships, and sex education. In addition, Senior Teachers serve as the first contact point for learners who need to report abuse or domestic concerns.

Child Protection, Safeguarding, and the "Duty of Care"

Amani's second thematic area draws from the African proverb, "It takes a village to raise a child." To this end, communities and Amani mobilise specific members of the community, called Change Agents, to take responsibility for ensuring children's safety. This mobilisation starts during community dialogues that Amani facilitates when beginning their intervention in a particular community. During these dialogues, community members nominate any number of Change Agents who they believe would be valuable in helping address teenage pregnancy. Change Agents include, but are not limited to, a religious leader, cultural leader, community reporter, boda-boda rider, parent, and political leader or any other individuals active within the community. Their duties involve interacting with government structures, such as the Office of Community Development, the police, health workers, and community leaders. During these engagements, they represent community voices to the duty bearers but also collect data on cases of defilement reported to police or the number of teenage girls accessing antenatal services from health centres which are used for advocacy, programming, and community sensitisation by the community and Amani. Community Change Agents also lead community awareness efforts and report on and follow up on local teenage pregnancy cases. They have led efforts to conduct household support visits, deliver essential HIV-related drugs, distribute food, and provide counselling services for at-risk families.

Change Agents are valuable linkages between community members and larger agencies, including those from the government. But perhaps their most significant responsibility is to consider, question, and adjust particular practices related to teenage pregnancy. For example, religious leaders can use their influence to sensitise their congregations to the stigma often faced by young mothers. By doing so, Change Agents can save girls from being expelled from homes. Because communities nominate Change Agents, the religious leaders they identify represent the communities' religious diversity. Therefore, religious leaders within the Amani network of change agents can come from various faith-based groups.

Similarly, cultural leaders representing local cultural institutions can work with elders and other influential cultural decision-makers to identify and redress harmful customs and practices. For example, clan leaders tasked to lead in bride price negotiations can play an essential role in determining and condemning child and sexual abuse, often linked to teenage pregnancy.

Ugandan communities have come to associate motorbike taxi-riders (*Boda-Bodas*) as some of the leading perpetrators of sexual abuse and gender-based violence, which, in turn, are obvious factors contributing to teenage pregnancy. Therefore, many communities frequently nominate *Boda-boda* riders as Change Agents, hoping they would influence their colleagues against the often violent sexual practices associated with these riders. Ultimately the goal is to change potential perpetrators into allies. The *Boda-Boda* Change Agent's role is to mobilise their association's members to identify and report sexual abuse and condemn other members who engage in violence against women.

Engaging with community reporters as Change Agents provides communities with a platform to advocate and create awareness of teenage pregnancy and child marriage issues. Community reporters collect news from the community, which they transmit through daily bulletins on radio and newspapers, reaching a wider audience than what Amani or the communities themselves could have achieved. As nominated Change Agents, these information sharers become integral collaborators towards addressing teenage pregnancy.

Parents and guardians of teenagers represent another vital set of Change Agents. They should guide, protect, and provide for their children. The Constitution of Uganda also makes it a national priority. Onboarding some individual parents as Change Agents is critical in driving home the responsibility that starts at home.

Together with other nominated Change Agents, Amani seeks out model parents in communities who can instil positive parenting.

Child, Adolescent, and Maternal Health

The third thematic area Amani and community partners identified during their initial problem analysis pertains to health and community members' low levels of awareness regarding family planning and women's and maternal well-being. Collaboration should therefore involve access to and knowledge of services specific to sexual and reproductive health, including family planning, maternal and under-five health care, and HIV/AIDS.

Amani and community collaborators have strengthened connections between two existing health stakeholders, Public Health Centres and Village Health Teams, and established a crucial third element, Community Linkage Referral Assistants (LRAs).

Across Uganda, public health centres are government-managed, locally based clinics that provide essential public health services and consultancies. Nurses and community health workers typically staff them. Through these centres, the Ministry of Health also operationalises primary health care, ranging from vaccine provisioning to guiding parents on maternal health. While these services are available to communities, they are not always used or accessible. For starters, due to limited information sharing, teenagers and young mothers might not know what services are available at the clinics. If teenagers know the services available at health centres, these might not always be accessible. For example, nurses who can provide youth information on contraceptives do not always do this because of their biases against such usage. Similarly, they might shame pregnant teenagers during their first visit, stopping them from returning for follow-up consultancies.

Village Health Teams, in turn, comprise community members trained by the Ministry of Health in primary public health care services. They serve as a vital resource for community members seeking health information and services, making them the crucial link between the people and available services. Individuals can access well-trained and readily available resources for improved child, adolescent, and maternal health by engaging with Village Health Teams. However, like health facilities, community members often need to be made aware of who the Village Health Teams are, what they do, and how they can help. To bridge this gap, Amani has introduced LFAs who can connect community members, particularly young people seeking advice and services for reproductive and maternal health, with Village Health Teams members and Community Health Centres.

Socioeconomic Empowerment and Community Self-Support Groups

Amani and collaborators identified socioeconomic support as a fourth focus area to address teenage pregnancy. As a reactive measure, this support should aim at helping young mothers manage the financial challenges they might encounter while also providing them with training in leadership and capacity strengthening. Such training will enable them to pursue future employment, entrepreneurial activities, and other opportunities. To this end, Amani established community self-support groups in close collaboration with partner sub-county governments. They host self-help groups, providing young mothers with a venue to hold weekly meetings and participate in any activities they hold.

The self-help groups are for and by young mothers. They are established and registered as savings groups by the mothers themselves, and through these groups, the mothers also mobilise on issues and needs they collectively identify. They receive guidance from community Change Agents, especially during their initial formation, but eventually, such advice becomes need-based. Within the groups, the young mothers can save together, loan each other resources for business and social support, and access various social services such as family planning, business skills, and hands-on skills training. These groups are led by their constitution and leadership structures, providing young mothers with a collaborative space to learn, share, and grow.

Local Voices and Engaged Collaboration

Figure 5.1 includes the significant collaborators active within the Amani Initiative. They are all integral to Amani's operation. But perhaps even more important is how they are connected to and with each other. Arguably, they represent an integrated system of structures, always present within their communities but through community-led engagement activities towards collaboration.

Collaboration: Mutual Learning, Transformative Engagements

Over the Amani Initiative's ten-year engagement, we and our stakeholders, community collaborators, and participants have identified at least five key insights on the close connection between collaboration and community-led interventions.

First, there is great potential in existing structures, organisations, and institutions already present within community contexts. Such potential is especially productive when these communal entities are brought into decision-making processes from the start rather than being merely consulted sporadically throughout an intervention. Community-led interventions therefore work with what is already within communities rather than developing additional or alternative social infrastructure.

Second, community-led interventions not only acknowledge and collaborate with the existing social and cultural structures within communities but also engage directly with those individuals that represent such structures. In the case of Amani, establishing connections with particular individuals is the key. Recognising the institutions is one thing, but seeing and continuously collaborating with those individuals within such institutions is vital.

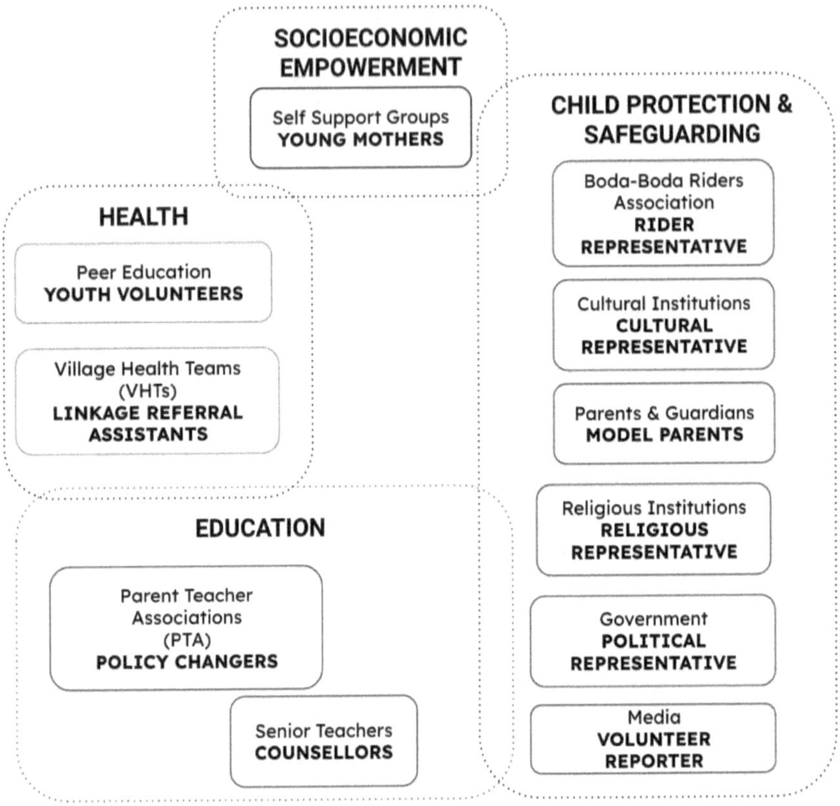

FIGURE 5.1 Collaboration facilitated and sustained within the Amani Initiative.

A third insight stems from how collaboration between different community structures towards addressing a shared concern can also impact individual actors' personal worldviews and actions. In the case of the Amani Initiatives, *Boda-Boda* Associations' involvement in the broader community collaboration not only contributed to a change in how people view *Boda-Boda* riders, but those riders involved in the collaboration are also adjusting their personal worldviews and norms. The same can be said of cultural leaders engaging in personal reflection on previously unquestioned norms and values.

A closely related fourth insight links to culture and social values. They are not static but ever-changing. And such change is possible if people from different and sometimes opposing cultural and social institutions talk with each other, and then through facilitated dialogue, in the case of Amani focused on teenage pregnancy, they also start to see the broader challenges. Worlds can change, and mindsets can alter. Through dialogues, shifts in such understanding and practices can happen, and such shifts can be further cemented through collaborations and shared responsibilities.

Finally, collaborating with local government structures such as the office of the Community Development Officer, Community Health Centers, and police stations is integral to the Amani Initiative's approach to preventing and responding to child marriage and teenage pregnancy through integrated community-led interventions. By working hand-in-hand with these entities, we not only cultivate community ownership of our initiatives through the legitimacy gained from aligning with government-backed interventions but also enhance their sustainability and scale while substantially reducing implementation costs. This partnership ensures that our interventions are effectively delivered and empowers communities to address these critical issues collectively, leveraging existing resources and structures for long-term impact.

Our Collective Action for Change

Thus far, we shared the story of Amani and our collaborative approach through the eyes of the organisation. Yet community-led development is about the community, its voices and choices. And no story about collaboration for collective action and change can be complete unless we hear the voices of the community, unfiltered. In what follows, representatives of community structures share their entry into the Amani Initiative and also their experience participating in the shared objective of addressing teenage pregnancy and child marriage. In the spirit of authenticity and community voice, the contributions have been translated into English, where needed, with minimum changes. We are sharing contributors' reflections in response to the questions: (1) What is your role in the community? (2) When and why did you start collaborating with Amani? (3) What was the situation before and after you started collaborating with Amani to prevent and respond to child marriage and teenage pregnancy? (4) Please share your role in collaborating to end child marriage. We list the contributions in the same order as Figure 5.1 earlier, starting with a reflection from a mother and ending with an Amani representative. We end with this segment because we believe that the community should have the final voice.

My name is Kitty, 23 years old, a mother of two children, six and one year. *I am currently the Chairperson for the Kijomoro Young Mothers Savings Group. The group was formed out of the collaboration between Amani Initiative, Kijomoro Sub-County, and 20 child mothers in 2020. We have been able to grow the group to 40 members now.*

There have always been many cases of young girls like me getting pregnant and sometimes being married off mainly because of the circumstances that surround us, like exposure to risky behaviours like discos, lack of parental care, etc. This usually causes girls to drop out of school, sometimes chased from home into abusive marriages they are not prepared for.

When Amani Initiative engaged with the sub-county chief on how best to create a safe self-support group for young mothers like myself, one of the community Change Agents reached out to me to mobilise my fellow peers. We formed and registered our Savings group. More girls and other at-risk girls are now joining the group … to be in a position to survive the socioeconomic impact of being a teenage mother as a child without any form of education and limited life opportunities.

My role as a chairperson is to lead the group and create awareness of the dangers of child marriage and teenage pregnancy through sharing my experience with group members and other people in the community. I also act as an example exemplary to the rest of the girls – even though I married early, I can still work hard and manage on my own.

***My name is Patrick, and my role as a Village Health Team member** is to provide health education to the community, including adolescents, parents, and different community members and leaders, on the dangers of child marriage, closely monitoring young girls; facilitate to have youth corners to discuss their issues; linking young children to family planning methods through Marie Stopes and to health facilities.*

Why are we collaborating with the Amani Initiative? Because they support us to do our work both materially and technically. They organise dialogues which provide a platform for us to engage with the community and also our capacities. Over the years, Amani Initiative has directly worked with me and my other Village Health Teams as a delivery channel for health-related information and services. This approach has been effective as we know the community and the community trusts us.

***My name is Geoffrey.** In 2011 as a Teacher at St. Mary's College Namugongo, Maracha Campus, I joined Amani Initiative as a **liaison teacher,** making me the first school teacher to collaborate in the fight against teenage pregnancy and child marriage in the district. I was motivated to be part of the vision and approach of putting members of the community at the centre of activities.*

My role was to link the school to the community in the prevention and response to teenage pregnancy and child marriage. I was a patron of the Amani Club at my school. The club was made up of 25 learners who met on a weekly basis and conducted activities within the school and surrounding communities. These activities included awareness of sexual and reproductive health, entrepreneurship, active citizenship, and child protection. Each of the 25 learners was directly attached to 5 others as part of the exponential learning process. During that time, the organisation did not have an address or office. My school was considered an address for the organisation. All files of the club activities were kept at the headteacher's office. In case of visitors or meetings of the organisation, they were done at the school.

Over the years, the organisation has spread across Uganda with strategic operation areas. I am excited to be part of this journey and still continue to volunteer with them despite my busy schedule as a teacher. I am happy that they have continued with their original approach of looking at members of the communities not as beneficiaries but as people who have a critical role to play in ending child marriage and teenage pregnancy as strategic partners.

***My name is Eunice, the Senior Woman Teacher** at Oyoo Primary School in Vurra Sub-County, Arua District. We currently have an enrolment of over 1,167 children of which 589 are girls. My responsibilities include regularly meeting with learners, receiving and reporting cases of abuse against learners, counselling learners, and guiding them on life choices.*

When Amani approached our headteacher in 2019 and proposed to work together in preventing and responding to the rampant cases of teenage pregnancy and child marriage within the school and surrounding community, I was selected as the School Liaison Officer with my role to directly link the school to the activities of Amani Initiative. This is a voluntary role that directly relates to my existing role as the Senior Woman Teacher.

My role in this collaboration is to offer counselling and guidance to the girls who are at school and child mothers who have returned back to school, household support visits to girls who have been challenged and talk to their parents, offer training on making reusable sanitary pads, offer referral linkages to girls who need further skills training, and also act as a patron to school clubs.

Before we started collaborating within the Amani Initiative, such activities were not there and we never used to follow up with these girls who have dropped out of school despite the roles we had as Senior Woman Teachers in the school structure. We used to not keep track and records of teenage pregnancy and child marriage in the school. The school clubs were not active, and the girls used to shy off from the obligations assigned to them. With the Amani Initiative, the girls can now better express themselves freely during debates, participate in essay writing competitions … They show interest whenever something comes up in the school. The learners have now become closer to us, the Senior Man Teacher and Senior Woman Teacher, which is making our roles functional. At the end of the day, the learners who are at the centre of these roles are greatly benefiting.

***My name is Solomon,** I was selected by the school administration of Opia Primary School in Vurra District to play the role of **Senior Man Teacher**. In this role, I am responsible for handling issues related to safety, career guidance, mental health, and any other social issues facing boys in the school. I am like a school counsellor for the boys. When Amani Initiative started working with my school in 2019, they asked the school administration to nominate two teachers who will directly collaborate with them as School Liaison Teachers which is how I started volunteering with Amani Initiative.*

My role as a School Liaison Teacher of Amani Initiative is to mobilise learners for activities on ending child marriage and teenage pregnancy such as school debates, school outreaches, health awareness sessions, and school essay writing competitions. I also represent issues affecting learners, particularly the boys, during the parent–teacher Association (PTA) meetings . These roles directly feed into my responsibilities as the school's Senior Man Teacher.

Before I started to collaborate with Amani Initiative my role as a Senior Man Teacher at the school was not active. A number of boys dropped out of school because there was no proper guidance from both the school and parents. The environment which these learners come from is full of discos; late market days affected these children so much, bad peer influences and the community mindset had affected these children's situation before the Amani Initiative collaboration.

Since our collaboration with Amani, we have realised that the number of school dropouts has reduced. Through the Community Development Officer who is also a Community Change Agent attached to our school, two girls who had dropped out of school came back and the learners can now participate in activities like essay writing, life skills, and debates. My fellow teachers envy me, thinking that Amani pays me for my services which is not the case. We are simply working together for the benefit of our children as I do the roles expected of me. With Amani, I just get the extra push, guidance, and motivation to perform these roles.

***I am Ronald**, a community **freelance journalist** associated with Arua One FM and Vision Group. I am also a Community Change Agent with Amani Initiative in Vurra Sub-County, Arua District. Before the Amani Initiative became active in Vurra Sub-County in 2018, many teenage girls who got married or pregnant were always left unattended and in the hands of the man responsible for the marriage/pregnancy. In most cases, the said "husband" is also underage, hence, child producing child, and the end result is to leave the baby with the parents which, at most times, becomes a burden on the parents. Through the savings group initiated by teenage mothers, under the umbrella of the Amani Initiative three to four years ago, where the participants teach one another economically, educationally, motherly, and socially, we have seen improvements in the livelihoods and confidence of the child mothers which has given most hope for a better future. As a Freelancer Journalist, I also played a great role in educating the public on teenage marriage and pregnancy through sharing issues of the community on the local radios as captured by the community hence amplifying their efforts to the broader community at no cost.*

***My name is Reverend Candia.** I lead a congregation in my local church every Sunday and I have also been volunteering as a Community Change Agent with Amani Initiative since 2019. My current position and age in the community give me the mandate to end child marriage which is affecting many girls in my community. Working with Amani Initiative gives me the opportunity to fulfil this mandate.*

Before Amani Initiative became active in my community, parents did not take child marriage as a bad thing but instead regarded it as a source of wealth. Since Amani Initiative trained some community Change Agents like me as a part of a strategy to work together in addressing the issue of the challenge, we have seen some change in the community. This was important because the Change Agents who were trained were respected in the community and also had people who followed them. The Change Agents went out and sensitised the communities about the danger of child marriage. Some Change Agents like us who regularly talk to gatherings have used these opportunities to always talk to parents about the dangers of child marriage and its legal implications.

My name is Hon. Bako Judith; I am the former ***Secretary for Social Services for Maracha Local Government*** *from 2016 to 2021. I would also wish to consider myself one of the Senior Champions of Amani in the fight against teenage pregnancy and child marriage. In the absence of international and national NGOs in Maracha District, Amani in Lugbara means "ours". They have stood with us as a district, region, and whole country in the fight against child marriage and teenage pregnancies since 2012.*

It was not easy in the beginning to convince a parent of a girl child who conceived because in our Lugbara culture, once a girl has seen her menstrual period and has had sexual intercourse that resulted in teenage pregnancy, this eventually became a child marriage.

At whatever age, mostly between 12 and 16, the culture allowed her to be married off and she deserved no second chance even to return to school after giving birth. Culture alone had eroded our community and though it was taboo to give a girl child in exchange for wealth, girls were exchanged with five goats.

When Amani started working with my office and empowered me who was already in the struggle to fight the vice, communities' mindset towards marrying off their teenage daughters began to change as a result of the community outreaches and radio talk shows I participated in. I also started partnering with both police and magistrate court in following up on cases of defilement which were reported through the community Change Agents from Amani.

In 2018, through collaborating with Amani Initiative and Community Change Agents, we mobilised over 300 signatures from members of the community to petition the district to allocate funds towards ending teenage pregnancy within the district. Through this, we successfully pushed for the Education and the Sexual Gender-Based Violence ordinances that became policy documents that greatly helped to reduce teenage pregnancy and child marriage within the district.

My name is Eric. *I am* ***Parish Chief*** *of Ajono Parish, Vurra Sub-County. Many programmes in the sub-county fail because the local people are not involved, this includes even some of the government programmes since it is a top-down approach where at the ministry level all things look to be okay, but at the village level, it is* *not. They dictate enterprise or activities on the people without people's interest and yet mindset change is essential. I am happy with Amani Initiative's approach of community-led, grassroots solutions which has given a leeway for the community members to participate and they are part of the change process right from the beginning, before even implementation kicks off.*

***My name is Abaru Stella, the Community Development Officer** of Oluffe Sub-County in Maracha District. Community Development was established in 2007 following the restructuring of the Ministry of Gender, Labour, and Social Development and became active on 1 July 2008.*

My key role in ending child marriage and teenage pregnancy in the community is to create awareness of the dangers of child marriage through community dialogues, reporting cases of child abuse like rape and defilement to police, and following up the issues to prosecution. I am also directly engaging with Amani Initiative as a community Change Agent to support their community activities.

Before we started collaborating with Amani in 2014, many parents were not giving chances for child mothers to go back to school. Child marriage was seen as a regular and normal occurrence by most people mainly due to the limited functionality of community structures such as my office whose role is to prevent and respond to issues related to teenage pregnancy and child marriage.

As a sub-county, we got interested in directly collaborating with Amani because it is a grassroots organisation that works in the community and works to address real community problems. Amani works with all the existing structures in the community such as schools, police, health centres, and local leaders which makes involvement easy. They work with children, girls, and women who are directly or indirectly affected by the issues of child marriage and teenage pregnancy. Their community-led, human-centred, and grassroots approach made it easy for us to directly collaborate with them as we take the organisation as belonging to the community, not the founders or staff like the case with many organisations. We are okay to invest our time and even resources without expecting anything else apart from services to our people.

I have directly been involved to share with parents and members of the community key issues around child marriage, defilement, and teenage pregnancy across the sub-county through Amani through which we are seeing change in community attitudes to accept the fact that child marriage and defilement are a violation of the rights of children punishable in the courts of law.

***I am Joel.** I am the **Chairperson of the Okokoro Market Stage Boda Boda Association** where I am responsible for leading, guiding, and representing my fellow boda-boda riders at the stage [taxi stand]. I started collaborating with Amani Initiative in 2020 during the Covid-19 period as a Community Change Agent with Amani Initiative [connected] to Kijomoro Young Mother's Village Savings and Livelihood Activities (VSLA) group and four government schools around the* *sub-county. My current role is to sensitise my peers and also young people within my stage about the dangers of teenage pregnancy and child marriage. I not only sensitise but report to the authorities in case of such cases. I also act exemplary so that my colleagues can learn from me as their leader.*

As a person who has spent most of his life around Okokoro Market which is a business centre with lots of activities such as growing and using of mairungi,[1] *disco, and late markets, I have seen many girls below 16 years being defiled or married off with no structures and organisations committed to helping them. Since the Amani Initiative actively started its operations here in 2018, I have seen change within the people, local leaders, and young people themselves. Through community dialogues, communities have been made aware of the dangers of teenage pregnancy and child marriage and also the related laws which have led to increased reporting of cases, unlike the previous time where cases of defilement were sorted out of court. Under the Kijomoro Young Mother's VSLA group started by the Kijomoro Sub-County through collaboration with Amani Initiative, a saving culture has developed among the child mothers. They have also been empowered and can freely speak and share with others. This positive change process is being directly led by the members of the groups and my fellow community Change Agents.*

Because of Amani, I have seen value in educating children and also giving second chances for girls which opens their minds to go back to school, empowering them economically and socially. I am happy to share this message with my fellow boda-boda riders who elected me to lead and represent them.

My name is Patrick. *I started the journey with Amani Initiative in 2011 basically to be part of the transformation the organisation intended to bring to the community and being born in Maracha where Amani was founded, I wanted and still want to give back to the community I come from since they (community) have contributed a lot in my being today.*

I joined the organisation in the year 2011 as a volunteer field officer but am now the Head of Programs. Even though funds were not available, we kept moving with the skills and little resources we had because we knew we were transforming our own people and the exciting thing was our approach of directly working with members of the community to carry out the organisation's activities. This made the community consider the organisation as their own. Together with the community, we achieved a lot despite the limited financial resources. What the community provided in terms of time, space, and local knowledge was more significant than what money would do to prevent and respond to teenage pregnancy and child marriage.

Cases of teenage pregnancy and child marriage have significantly reduced, the youth knowledge of SRHR (sexual and reproductive health rights) has improved, and the socioeconomic status of the communities we work with has greatly improved compared to before the Amani initiative. I'm so grateful for the Amani' initiative because it has also positively impacted and enriched my career journey.

Note

1 Mairungi is the local name for Khat, an evergreen scrub often abused as stimulant.

References

Ayamolowo, Sunday Joseph, Aanuoluwapo Omobolanle Olajubu, and Funke Elizabeth Akintola. 2019. "Perceived social support and depression among pregnant and child-rearing teenagers in Ile-Ife, Southwest Nigeria." *African Journal of Midwifery and Women's Health* 13, no. 4: 1–9.

Constitution of Uganda. 1995. Article 34. URL: www.lawglobalhub.com/article-34-uganda-constitution-1995/

Fleming, Nathalie, Teresa O'Driscoll, Gisela Becker, Rachel F. Spitzer, Lisa Allen, Debra Millar, Philippa Brain et al. 2015. "Adolescent pregnancy guidelines." *Journal of Obstetrics and Gynaecology Canada* 37, no. 8: 740–756.

Ganchimeg, Togoobaatar, E. Ota, Nea Morisaki, M. Laopaiboon, P. Lumbiganon, J. Zhang, B. Yamdamsuren et al. 2014. "Pregnancy and childbirth outcomes among adolescent mothers: a World Health Organization multicountry study." *BJOG: An International Journal of Obstetrics & Gynaecology* 121: 40–48.

Gideon, Rutaremwa. 2023. "Factors associated with adolescent pregnancy and fertility in Uganda: analysis of the 2011 demographic and health survey data." *American Journal of Sociological Research* 3, no. 2: 30–35.

Girls not Brides. 2018. At what cost? A Policy Brief on the Economic Impact of Child Marriage in Uganda. Policy Brief. www.icrw.org/publications/at-what-cost-policy-brief-on-child-marriage-in-uganda/

Gunawardena, Nathali, Arone Wondwossen Fantaye, and Sanni Yaya. 2019. "Predictors of pregnancy among young people in sub-Saharan Africa: a systematic review and narrative synthesis." *BMJ Global Health* 4, no. 3: e001499.

Nabugoomu, Josephine, Gloria K. Seruwagi, and Rhona Hanning. 2020. "What can be done to reduce the prevalence of teen pregnancy in rural Eastern Uganda?: multi-stakeholder perceptions." *Reproductive Health* 17, no. 1: 1–12.

Ochen, Anthony Mark, Primus Che Chi, and Stephen Lawoko. 2019. "Predictors of teenage pregnancy among girls aged 13–19 years in Uganda: a community-based case-control study." *BMC Pregnancy and Childbirth* 19, no. 1: 1–14.

Scally, Gabriel. 2002. "Too much too young? Teenage pregnancy is a public health, not a clinical, problem." *International Journal of Epidemiology* 31, no. 3: 554–555.

Sully, Elizabeth A., Ann Biddlecom, Jacqueline E. Darroch, Taylor Riley, Lori S. Ashford, Naomi Lince-Deroche, Lauren Firestein, and Rachel Murro. 2020. "Adding it up: investing in sexual and reproductive health 2019." New York: Guttmacher Institute.

UNFPA–UNICEF. 2022. *Teenage Pregnancy in Uganda: The Cost of Inaction*. Kampala.

Walker, D'Andre, and Kristy Holtfreter. 2021. "Teen pregnancy, depression, and substance abuse: the conditioning effect of deviant peers." *Deviant Behavior* 42, no. 3: 297–312.

6

TO TRANSFORM SYSTEMS, START WITH THE HEART

CLD-Benin's Story of Collective Power and Collective Impact

CLD-Benin

Introduction

You may wonder about the authorship of this article. We at Community-Led Development Benin (CLD-Benin), know that to sustain a collaboration, we need to leave our egos and logos behind. We are all working individually in different communities and with different groups of people on different issues on a day-to-day basis. But in our collaborative space, we come together for values that cut across our work. That is why, when it comes to decision-making or authorship, we do it together. Our story does not belong to any one of us. It is a coming together of many individual stories and was scripted by all of us, together. So we have chosen to tell it together. Throughout this chapter, you will hear the voices of our members. Through the interplay of their experiences, we share a story of how collaboration is not just a principle but an intentional process. And because it is our story, we narrate it in first person.

But first, let us introduce ourselves. CLD-Benin is a network of over 1,000 civil society organisations nationwide and embodies the spirit of grassroots empowerment, championing the voices of its diverse members. We are a part of the Movement for Community-Led Development (MCLD or the Movement), a Majority World-led network of networks committed to putting communities front and centre in development. There is a saying in Fongbé, a Beninese language spoken in the southern part of the country "*Hêfoun-mè wê hê non sou dé*" (A bird's plumage provides the best conditions for it to grow). This is why we embrace community-led development. And we choose to be a movement because "Movements 'open up peoples' hearts and minds to new possibilities,' 'create the receptive climate for new ideas to take hold,' and 'embolden policymakers' and

DOI: 10.4324/9781003377917-8

system leaders. Movements change the ground on which everyday political life and management occur" (Cabaj & Weaver 2016, 4).

Until 2023 CLD-Benin had no formal institutional structure and was hosted by The Hunger Project (THP) Benin, the country office of an International Non-Government Organisation (INGO) that housed the global secretariat for MCLD. In 2023, we embarked on the next step in our journey and became a locally registered organisation with its own Board, strategy and constitution. We recognise the value of collaboration not just within communities but between groups in a country and networks internationally. So, we have remained an active association with the global MCLD network.

This chapter describes CLD-Benin's journey to demonstrate how we can unleash the power of collective action for transformative change by mobilising networks and organisations on common values and, more importantly, how we can sustain this mobilisation. In the first section, we delve into the launch of CLD-Benin and how it built and strengthened the trust necessary for any collaboration. In the second section, we speak about how we decided to practise inclusion in our collaborative space through the creation of a youth network. The third section delves into our collective action practices and unpacks two specific examples that emerged from our collaboration. It highlights not just how collaboration leads to collective action but also how collective action is itself the glue that sustains a collaboration over a period of time, particularly a collaboration that is not based on funding partnerships. The fourth section brings together our experience and learning with collaboration and situates it within the community-led worldview of systems change that has emerged from our experience (Djohossou et al 2023). We conclude with the most important lesson that has emerged from our work on systems transformation in Benin: start with the heart.

The Launch of a Movement

> It was in March 2017 that we launched CLD-Benin – it was called MCLD Benin then – with 19 youth and women's groups. At that time, I had been leading the Benin office of The Hunger Project (THP). I had heard about the launch of MCLD in 2015, first in Malawi and then at the sidelines of the UN General Assembly in New York, by John Coonrod, the Executive Vice President of THP,

recalls Pascal Djohossou, who launched the Movement in Benin and serves as our coordinator.

MCLD started as an initiative of 18 INGOs to transform the current development and humanitarian systems and ensure that every person has a voice in decisions that affect their lives (Veda 2023). Soon after its launch, Movement members realised that this transformation requires vibrant local ecosystems comprising strong, healthy, local and community-based organisations, participatory local governments and adequate community finance. All of this work needs to happen in countries and has to be led by local organisations. Thus MCLD began to transform itself into a space for collective action and advocacy by local and community-based organisations, with the support of their INGO allies. It encouraged local organisations to come together to create what was then called National Chapters to promote community-led development in every country. These chapters were to be self-organised, self-directed and self-governed entities with their own strategies and advocacy agendas, often hosted by an INGO which had the office and human resources to support the group.

Coonrod, who co-founded MCLD, began by reaching out to the country offices of THP, the INGO that hosted the Secretariat for the Movement, to support local organisations in forming these Chapters. Djohossou was at that time the Country Director of THP Benin.

He recalls:

> When John first came to me about launching a movement in Benin, I knew this was the opportunity for Benin's civil society to come together to realise the vision of our people. My experience with THP's programmes, including nutritional interventions, had taught me the importance of inclusion, particularly of women and youth. Working through THP's community-led programming had also led me to understand the critical role of relational capital. It is this relational capital that I chose to build on. Instead of going organisation by organisation, I began by reaching out to existing networks in Benin that already had relationships with a wide range of community-based organisations. Each of them had a specific area of focus, but I knew that if we could all come together on shared values, then our collective strength could truly transform our country.

Therefore, instead of competing with existing networks for membership, Djohossou began to build on the strength of those networks. He realised that transforming systems required collaboration and collective action focussing on strengths, not competition arising from a scarcity mindset.

"I began by tapping into my own relational capital," says Djohossou.

He called the heads of The House of Civil Society, a nationwide network of community-based organisations, along with the Chair of PASCiB (Patforme des Acteurs de la Socité Civile au Bénin), which comprises 16 national Civil Society Organisation (CSO) networks, including *Réseau d'Intégration des Femmes des ONG et Associations Africaines* (RIFONGA), a network of women's groups. He described to them the objectives of MCLD and sought their support in reaching out to their members. These leaders recognised the importance of coming together and began to spread the message through their own networks. Armand Vignon, Executive Director, The House of Civil Society (Maison de la Société Civile), explains, "We wanted to create a vibrant, inclusive and powerful network of diverse stakeholders (government CSO, private sector) who are implementing the

MCLD approach and who are proud to share evidence on resilient communities in Benin." Thus even though CLD-Benin started as a group of 19 organisations and networks, both formal and informal, it connected with hundreds of CBOs all across the country.

MCLD in Benin began with a high-profile launch event in Cotonou on March 24, 2017, with a keynote address delivered by a government minister. Representatives from ministries, embassies and UN agencies were invited alongside many local and community-based organisations. We wanted them to understand what we meant by community-led development and why it is important. That is also how CLD-Benin began building partnerships right from the beginning. We knew that for progress to be sustainable, we would need to work with all parts of the local ecosystem.

Sènami Chrystelle Dakpogan Houngbedji is the Executive Director of Organisation pour le Développement Durable et la Biodiversité (ODDB), an initiative of young Beninese people convinced that there cannot be sustainable development without the involvement and empowerment of local communities in natural resource management. She recalls,

> I trusted a colleague who enthusiastically shared the information about the launch of CLD-Bénin with me. The audience at the launch comprised officials, ministers representing the Government, United Nations representatives, many CBO leaders and a couple of INGOs. Youth and women's associations were impressively also part of the audience. I decided to become a member of CLD-Bénin with the dream and the commitment that we, together, could make a difference in terms of changing the prevailing paradigm and truly supporting communities in Bénin towards the well-being they deserve and need to have access to.

Building Trust and Connection

After the launch, we began holding meetings to strengthen the connections among us, and to learn and share views and practices about how each organisation is supporting communities to make social transformation and sustainable development happen. We discussed what was missing and what CLD-Benin should do to leverage our collaborative effort for improved results and impacts. Visits by our national coordinator to member organisations to strengthen connections and mutual learning were an important part of our work during those initial years. We call it our mobilisation phase. In the beginning, we did not decide on any frequency for our meetings. This, however, changed quickly, and we began to meet every two weeks. During the COVID-19 pandemic, we met weekly to identify quick action plans to support the communities we were a part of and to advocate with the government.

Right from the outset, we have intentionally invited organisations outside our network to our meetings and events so that they could understand our work and explore synergies. When we have conversations with such organisations, we ask them if they are satisfied with existing NGO projects. They often say: "No. When the money stops, everything disappears." So we ask them to think about why this happens. The answer: "People are not involved in designing the projects. Local assets are not valued. And so nothing lasts beyond the money." And we say,

> Now imagine the opposite – imagine starting with the people, their knowledge, their assets. That is community-led development. At CLD-Benin, we believe that community-led development with a focus on partnership, dignity, voice, and agency for all is the best way to end poverty. We strengthen the resilience of communities and address the sustainability conundrum through a social platform that focuses on co-creating a way forward and journeying together using systems practices. Would you like to come on board?

Almost always, they respond with a resounding yes.

A large part of being a member of CLD-Benin is about reflection and introspection into our own practices and work. As John Kania and his colleagues (2018) point out, mindset transformation is where it all begins. We need to understand the existing power dynamics and the mindset that underpins and sustains it in order to create the partnerships we need to truly shift the power as reflected through the policies, practices and budgets. And we need a safe space to do so – what Cabaj and Weaver call the "container for change" (2016). CLD-Benin functions as this container for change. All new members participate in an introductory conversation on the six conditions of systems change (Kania et al 2018). We keep it short – we know our members are volunteers who are undertaking important work in their communities, and we value their time. This first conversation takes about 90 minutes.

We also recognise that local and community-based organisations might not necessarily practise community-led development. We are all part of the same system, after all, and have embraced many of its failures, including the top-down approaches that value colonial knowledge and devalue the knowledge of communities. As Svieby (1997) points out, since knowledge is contextual, its application can lead to reproducing the context in which it was originally generated. Introspection allows us to identify these contextual reproductions. As a result, our members enthusiastically embraced the Participatory CLD Assessment Tool when it was launched in 2021. We use it to reflect on our own practices and work. For instance, are we truly including women in our work? What about the youth? Who else is missing? These moments of reflection, alongside the tools that allow us to have them and equip us with skills to make our own work more community-led, have served as a glue for our association. In these moments of collective learning and reflection, interconnectedness is strengthened, and trust begins to grow.

We found that by applying the principles of community-led development to our own work, starting with local knowledge and resources, we could actually sustain the momentum within the movement. We do not wait for funding to undertake our collective activities. When we decided to organise events to support the transformation of food systems and promote local superfoods (described in the third section), members like GRABE-Benin and JINUKUN began to mobilise their own resources for these campaigns.

When the COVID-19 pandemic came in 2020, the power of our approach was proven. The first weekend after COVID-19 was declared a pandemic, we mobilised CLD-Benin members to establish approximately 3,000 hand-washing stations across the country. Our collective strength and focus on partnerships enabled us to work with the government and influence its response to the pandemic, successfully urging them to include social determinants of health such as nutrition and proper rest.

Practising Inclusion: Creating a Platform for Youth

Inclusion has been a key part of CLD-Benin's agenda from the outset. We knew the importance of engaging youth and women's organisations for social transformation. Our strategy has always been to mobilise existing networks for maximum reach and impact. But when we started out, there was no active nationwide network for youth groups that we could work with. So we supported the formation of one.

The creation of this youth platform once again reflects how we leveraged existing relationships and connections, one of the key conditions for systems change (Kania et al 2018).

> In 2015, THP Benin started a thematic partnership initiative with youth and women's associations in the country to implement activities under the Her Choice Project. This partnership aimed to strengthen the capacities of the associations involved. Thus when CLD-Benin was launched, it already had access to youth and women's organisations through its host organisation, THP Benin,

explains Beranger Tossou of Youth Service Africa, a youth-led organisation that joined CLD-Benin when it was first founded in 2017.

> We had already been in conversation with THP Benin about the need for a platform for youth groups. When we heard about the Movement, we liked the idea of coming together to centre communities and strengthen their resilience in Benin. So we became one of the eight women and youth-led organisations that was part of the launch of CLD-Benin. Subsequently, we set out to co-create a credible platform that enabled us to work together,

he adds. Thus the Platform of Youth Organizations for the Sustainable Development of Communities (POJDDC) was created and registered on March 28, 2018.

> We received much help from CLD-Benin in terms of strategic orientation and drafting of founding documents. The POJDDC focuses its efforts on gender, leadership and governance in community development. We have learned a lot

> and continue to benefit from the opportunities offered by CLD-Benin. These include connecting with other platforms like the International Network of Young Francophone Leaders (RJLF) and ProEnvironnement and having access to various tools and trainings,

says Justiana Ahouansou, Executive Director of AFUD (Association des Femmes Unies pour le Développement), a women's organisation in Benin.

Today, the POJDDC is a vibrant platform with 20 youth and women's organisations. It has leveraged the tools offered by CLD-Benin to get grants for projects from funders, including the Swiss Cooperation.

Collective Action to Sustain Collaboration

Deciding on a course for collective action with such a diverse group of members is not easy. Identifying our priorities tested both our connection with each other and our own principles. We knew that any advocacy we undertake has to be evidence-based and we could not do this for all the sustainable development goals. So we identified five thematic areas where impact can be the highest for communities: (1) governance, (2) agriculture and nutrition, (3) environment and climate change, (4) well-being of the community and (5) local economic development.

We had a real debate on how to set these priorities – should we first go to the communities and ask them? But when we tried to do that, people focussed on the immediate challenges they faced individually. We also recognised that in order to bring about sustainable change, we had to understand and, where possible, build on what was available from the government. In the end, we arrived at these thematic areas through a three-step process. First, we studied the existing reports and data on the situation in Benin and spoke with government officials. Next, we shared these findings with our members and sought their perspectives to see if these matched their experience of the community's aspirations. Finally, we took this information and presented it directly to small groups in the communities where our members worked. We undertook sense-making workshops with these groups to arrive at areas of maximum impact that the community wanted us to focus on.

Eventually, for us in CLD-Benin all five of these thematic areas come together in the food system. Since 2019, we have been focusing on food systems transformation for climate resilience and food sovereignty in Benin through the promotion of local superfoods like Moringa, building on the experience of many stakeholders in Benin, including THP.

Moringa is readily available in Benin. The elders in villages knew of its value and power, but it was ignored by the "modern" sectors of society who promoted expensive processed foods from outside. Thus despite its health benefits, Moringa became known as a poor person's food. CLD-Benin leveraged the existing Moringa campaign's impacts in the country and moved further by launching a powerful campaign on "Fruits and vegetables in the daily diet". That campaign is going on since 2023. We ensured people had access to vegetable seeds for home gardening. We worked with chefs from popular restaurants to develop recipes that would make it taste better and attract youngsters. We brought the elders of the communities to talk about the nutritional value of Moringa and other local vegetables.

We did not have the resources to reach each and every organisation individually. This is where we once again reap the benefits of collaboration. When we want to launch an action campaign such as the one to reclaim Indigenous "SuperFoods" or to respond to COVID we communicate through the member networks and ask who wants to participate. We usually call the network leadership directly on the phone and then communicate more widely through WhatsApp or email.

We always start with community knowledge and resources first. For instance, in the local SuperFoods campaign, we collected traditional recipes like peanut Djongoli, Agnan (mashed sweet potato), Zankpiti (made from beans) and Mangnignan (made from smoked or fried fish) from the communities. However, we also recognise the value of integrating relevant knowledge and resources from outside the community to supplement what we already know. So we used research findings from the University of Abomey-Calavi and the University of Wageningen to evidence the wisdom of community elders around nutritious local foods. This mix of knowledge and resources enabled us to appeal to different segments of the population and to enhance the existing recipes. Through events and exhibitions, we introduced people to over 50 varieties of Indigenous seeds and 30 local recipes. Planning and working together with our pooled resources enabled our members to experience the strength of our collaboration and develop connections amongst themselves.

Another example of our collective action was in our response to the COVID-19 pandemic. We had hoped to work directly with the government, but they were moving very slowly. So we came up with the idea of creating posters about habits to prevent the spread of the virus and distributing them nationwide. We designed the poster and brought it to the government, and they immediately took it up. Like the Participatory CLD Assessment Tool that we have adopted widely, these posters became a tool to create awareness and initiate conversations. Both these tools gained popularity across the country very rapidly. This is why we firmly believe that "Tools Matter for systems change," particularly when such tools are co-created directly with those closest to the problem. The process of co-creation of these tools and their dissemination enhances mutual trust, as we have experienced time and again at CLD-Benin. And as a bonus, these tools get rapidly adopted unlike the thousands of other tools and toolkits created by INGOs. This is not just because these tools are demand-driven, but because in being involved in their development, people understand and trust them.

These tools, the process of co-creating them, mutual sharing and our collective action projects have kept network fatigue at bay. Members who came together to launch CLD-Benin remain active and engaged even today. PASCiB (Plateforme des Acteurs de la Société Civile au Bénin) was among the first networks that Djohossou had approached to create MCLD. Yécy Peggy Tohinlo, the Program Manager at PASCiB sums up their reasons for staying in CLD-Benin:

> It means a lot to me to be a member of CLD-Benin. It has broadened my horizons to diverse stakeholder views and experiences of working in communities and taught me valuable lessons about building equitable partnerships based on the principle of dignity and respect for local knowledge(being taken into account). I have gained tools and frameworks to enhance our partnership with the community and found a space to share and learn from common challenges. Being a part of CLD-Benin is a continuous journey of learning. As we expand our own network at PASCiB, we are confident that the community-led development approach is putting us on the right track to achieve the SDGs.

Seven years of working together in CLD-Benin has taught us many lessons about systems change, collaboration and sustainability. From the outset, we realised the value of collaboration with different parts of the local ecosystem, particularly with the government, both local and national. We are already working with the Ministry of Health, the Ministry of Environment, The Benin Nutrition Society and the National Association of the Communes – our system of local government. These partnerships not only reinforce our momentum but they enable us to carry out collective action at scale. For instance, our campaigns to fight COVID-19 and improve nutrition have reached every part of the country because of our collaboration with the government, the private sector (chefs) and research partners.

"When the youth begin to participate in conversations with government officials, they become highly motivated. They feel that their voice truly matters," explains Tossou. These partnerships also build credibility for the network. "Whenever we speak to someone, they want to know who is supporting us," he adds.

The second lesson we learnt at CLD-Benin is the importance of inclusion, particularly of women and youth, who are the driving forces of change. We also realised that transparency and sharing information are vital to developing and maintaining trust. As our network grew in influence and reach, we began to find more ways to engage our members and co-create with them. We began to set in place democratic processes that would help us to maintain our values even as we grew and transitioned to a more formal organisational structure. In July 2021, we held our first annual general meeting (AGM). Thirty members came together in person to review our collective work from the first half of the year and to plan activities for the rest of the year and for 2022. Our experience at CLD-Benin has taught us that while virtual collaboration spaces are helpful, it is during in-person interactions that bonds are truly formed. It is here that we engage with one another beyond predetermined topics. The importance of the energy that emerges during these meetings and the impact of the process of collective action and planning cannot be overstated. As Afiavi Sehonou, the chair of the Board of CLD-Benin says:

> I cannot overstate how crucial the AGM is in terms of sharing what is going on at CLD-Bénin related to plans, budgets and other strategic issues with its members. Indeed our Constitution stated clearly what the AGM is meant for.

> The deliberations in the AGM are important to sustain trust, solidarity and the relational work within CLD-Bénin as it is also for any other network. Indeed, accountability and transparency are core ingredients to continuously hold together people who join CLD-Benin and who contribute their time, their commitment, their experience, their knowledge… on a voluntary basis. To further emphasise the importance of the AGM, let me share this african proverb, "If you want to go fast, go alone. If you want to go far, go together."

The AGM, alongside the thematic working groups and a Board, are the backbone of our newly registered organisation. It is in the AGM that members will vote on policies and the work plan proposed by the Board and the CLD-Benin Secretariat.

The most important lesson for us, however, has been that collaboration for systems transformation requires intentional investment. While speaking of Collective Impact, Kania and Kramer wisely noted that "Coordination takes time, and none of the participating organizations has any to spare. The expectation that collaboration can occur without a supporting infrastructure is one of the most frequent reasons why it fails" (2011, 40). At CLD-Benin, we have seen that our members have successfully mobilised their own resources for collective action campaigns like Moringa. However, getting them to the point where they trust the Movement and each other enough to do so required dedicated time and resources.

> When we started out, I had a small budget. It was enough for me to visit member organisations in the communities where they worked, to sit with them and understand their ways of working. We were also able to organise some events to bring people together. These visits and time spent together strengthened trust and interconnectedness. I also serve as the West Africa coordinator for MCLD, and I have seen how difficult it is to mobilise organisations and maintain the momentum when National Associations do not have a dedicated coordinator to engage with members, facilitate collective action and build trust, says Djohossou.

Arriving at a Community-Led View of Systems Change

In their seminal work on the Water of Systems Change, John Kania and colleagues (2018) identify six interdependent conditions that hold a system in place and are, therefore, important for systems change. These are *Policies* which refer to the government or institutional rules and regulations; *Practices* that encompass procedures, informal shared habits and activities to improve social and environmental progress; *Resource Flows* which refers to how money, knowledge and other assets are allocated and distributed; *Relationships and connections* between actors in a system; *Power Dynamics* which refers to the distribution of decision-making power, authority and influence between actors, and *Mental Models*. The last refers to "Habits of thought – deeply held beliefs and assumptions and taken-for-granted ways of operating that influence how we think, what we do, and how we talk" (Kania et al 2018, 4). They point out that while most funders and, consequently, programmes focus on policies, practices and resource flows, it is the less explicit conditions i.e., relationships, power dynamics and most importantly, mindsets, that are the drivers of activity in any system. Thus an introspection of mental models is invaluable for systems transformation.

At CLD-Benin, we have been using this framework as a tool for reflecting on our individual and collective work. Yet, over time we realised the limitations of this framing, which is geared towards funders. So we began a long process of working with over 300 colleagues within our national association, in the MCLD Global Secretariat, across other MCLD National Associations and John Kania himself to reimagine what this model would look like from a community-led perspective. This is a work in progress that was first published in 2023 (Djohossou et al 2023). Here is how we believe we should approach systems transformation from a community-led perspective. It all starts with local knowledge and worldviews.

> Local knowledge and worldviews are the basis of mindset, which then enable actions that leverage mutuality, relationships, and networks and proactively modified power dynamics. This flows into successful advocacy for improved policies, practices, and resource generation that support inclusive, authentic community aspirations, both tangible and intangible, at multiple levels, e.g. local, middle, national, and even international. The loop of transformation is complex and continuous.
>
> *(Djohossou et al 2023, 96–97)*

This model explicitly, as captured in Figure 6.1, defines the mental models that Kania et al. speak about as collective and individual mindsets rooted in community knowledge. Instead of using the original framing of a mindset shift, which is often an external and colonial exercise, the community-led worldview of systems change places a growth mindset, both at the individual and collective level, as the starting point for systems transformation. Recognising the truth behind Martin Luther King's "inescapable network of mutuality" that binds us all and the wisdom behind the African philosophy of Ubuntu, the model places mutuality alongside power dynamics and relationships at the centre. Finally, Djohossou et al's model recognises that systems change is not linear but entails a continuous transformational loop, starting with the implicit intangibles (like mindsets and consciousness), moving to the explicit tangibles (like policies, practices and resource flows) and then back again to the intangibles.

At CLD-Benin, we bear witness to this model in practice every day. As Djohossou et al. note,

> When we clear the air of colonial fog and come together in solidarity, we have seen that a vibrant civil society can cause amazing things to happen – in

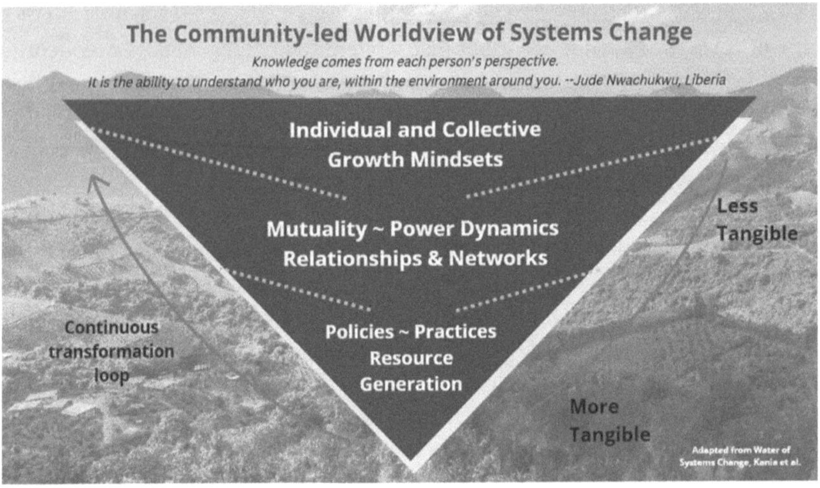

FIGURE 6.1 The community-led worldview of systems change.
Source: Djohossou et al. (2023).

> partnership with governments and many other stakeholders – to all of us, by all of us, for all of us.
>
> *(2023, 90)*

Conclusion: Start with the Heart

Over the years, we at CLD-Benin have learnt that just like inclusion, collaboration requires intentionality. It is anchored in shared values, a shared vision and mutual trust. Collective action that is born from collaboration further reinforces trust and mutuality when it follows the principles of equity, human dignity and respect for all. It fosters interconnectedness and enables us to better leverage our resources. This, in turn, strengthens the collaboration and makes it self-refuelling. Organisations and networks continue to participate voluntarily in CLD-Benin because they want to transform the current system. Working together not only amplifies their knowledge, resources and voice, it enables them to partner with powerful actors like the government. This partnership enhances their individual and collective agency as it further attracts new organisations to the network creating a virtuous cycle of collaboration.

An exciting new phase for CLD-Benin started in 2024. Even though we dropped the word Movement from our name, we have taken measures to ensure that the essential values that underpin a social movement continue to guide us as an organisation. We have already co-created a strategic plan which spells out our priorities and our path towards systems transformation. We have identified ways to continue our collaboration with the government, other sister networks and academia in Benin. We have created avenues to ensure that information is shared equitably and members have an opportunity to work together because collective action keeps the momentum alive. We know that systems transformation is not easy and that sustaining a network of voluntary participants is hard work. As Peter Senge notes, "You cannot force commitment. What you can do is nudge a little here, inspire a little there, and provide a role model. Your primary influence is the environment you create" (in Cabaj & Weaver 2016, 11). We know that translating our vision into reality will require effort from each one of us, and yet the last seven years have shown us that it is possible. We conclude with these words from our colleague Djohossou:

> Transformation of a system fundamentally requires a transformation of the heart that sustains the status quo. Once the heart resonates in harmony with the transformation we are envisioning, transformation becomes a reality. A *growth mindset* that encapsulates solidarity, leadership, ownership and partnership on an equity basis, along with the *policies, strategies, and processes* that support localised actions, all fueling into broader amplified collective actions through networking are the *heart* that makes social transformation happen in communities. Systems change refers then to the heart of individuals, collectives and systems. *Start with the heart of the system, from the heart of the individual.*
>
> *(MCLD 2024)*

References

Cabaj, Mark, and Liz Weaver. 2016. Collective Impact 3.0: An Evolving Framework for Community Change. www.tamarackcommunity.ca/library/collective-impact-3.0-an-evolving-framework-for-community-change

Djohossou, Pascal, Sera Bulbul, and Ann Hendrix-Jenkins. 2023. "The Community-Led Worldview of Systems Change: A Framework Centering Local Knowledge and Aspirations in Pursuit of Transformational Sustainability and Resilience. Part 1." *Knowledge Management for Development Journal* 17, no. 1/2. Special Issue on 'Uncomfortable truths in international development: approaches to the decolonization of knowledge from development practice, policy and research.' 86–106. www.km4djournal.org/index.php/km4dj/article/view/539/647

Kania, John, and Mark Kramer. "Collective Impact." *Stanford Social Innovation Review* 9, no. 1 (Winter 2011): 36–41.

Kania, John, Mark Kramer, and Peter Senge. 2018. The Water of Systems Change, June 2018. www.fsg.org/wp-content/uploads/2021/08/The-Water-of-Systems-Change_rc.pdf

Sveiby, Karl. 1997. *The New Organizational Wealth: Managing & Measuring Knowledge-Based Assets*. San Francisco: Berrett-Koehler Publishers.

MCLD. 2024. CLD-Benin: A Civil Society Network for Sustainable Development. The Movement for Community-led Development. April 3, 2024. https://mcld.org/2024/04/03/introduction-to-cld-benin/

Veda, Gunjan. 2023. "Chronicles of a Transformative Movement: Strengthening Our Interconnectedness." *Interdisciplinary Journal of Partnership Studies* 10, no. 1). Article 4. https://doi.org/10.24926/ijps.v10i1.5458

PART II

Responsiveness to Local Context

Elene Cloete and Gunjan Veda

The chapters included in this section illustrate the symbiotic relationship between context and community-led programming. When considering its etymology, context refers to "weaving or knitting together" and "making connections between a phenomenon and what is relevant for understanding it" (Meier and Dopson 2019, 1). It is frequently used, showing up in daily conversations and in phrases like "don't take it out of context" or "context matters." The concept's common usage makes sense because, as Bate (2014, 3) insists, "nothing exists and therefore can be understood, in isolation from its context, for it is the context that gives meaning to what we think and do." A close connection, therefore, exists between context and meaning, because "to situate something within a context is already to make it meaningful, while to grapple something as meaningful is also to grapple its situation within a context" (Malpas 2002, 411). Context is thus a crucial element of people's daily lives. And since community-led development programming is directly involved in and focused on people's daily lives, context is also an undeniable component of such programming. Stated differently, understanding context and valuing its role in people's social worlds should be part and parcel of community development interventions. And that is why it is prioritised by community-led interventions.

But what is context, and how does it show up in community-led development? Before introducing Howlett and Bolton's chapter, and also Reeves' account of the Aga Khan Foundation and their work across different geographical, social, and cultural locations, the following section briefly pauses to reflect on features of context as captured within the social and evaluation sciences.

DOI: 10.4324/9781003377917-9

What Is Context?

Even though it's a commonly used term, context is a complex concept. It is ever-changing and unbounded at its core, making it challenging to analyse, control for, or measure (Meier and Dopson 2019). Additionally, the omnipresence of context is natural, even evasive, with people using context, drawing from it, and shaping it without thinking about it (Akman and Bazzanella 2003, 322). At the same time, these characteristics of contexts and therefore the undeniable role it plays in making, shaping, and altering society, makes it crucial for researchers, implementers, and practitioners to understand context and consider its role in development activities. Context can either make or break interventions. Knowing how and where it functions can, in the best-case scenario, further strengthen interventions or, in the worst-case scenario, explain programme failure.

Meier and Dopson's (2019) definition is a productive starting point to describe what context is and how it functions. They describe context as

> a relational construct that specifies what is at any given point considered the background for understanding a phenomenon or event. This background/foreground relationship is continually constructed by people, as they make sense of their experiences and the social worlds in which they engage.
>
> *(p. 3)*

The definition includes features of context worthy of a quick pause: *background*, people's *relationships* to and with such a background, including their direct involvement in constructing this background, and the ongoing sensemaking of their social worlds and experiences.

Context as Background

We first pause at Meier and Dopson's reference to *background* and the assumption that this refers to context as time, place, and accompanying sociocultural and political dynamics. Arguably, both time and place are interconnected to how, why, and with whom people establish relationships, participate in activities, and so on (Zapf 2010; Flouris et al. 2016). As far as time is concerned, Bate (2014) emphasises how history and time "leave a permanent and ongoing imprint," which captures the features and contextual factors contributing to a particular situation or outcome at a particular moment in time. From a development and programming perspective, implementers need to continuously look and learn backwards because "the temporal perspective and the 'weight of history' should not be forgotten in future research and practice" (Bate 2014, 7). In this section, the chapter of Howlett and Bolton takes such a historical view to describe how Outreach International's (OI's) community-led methodology has evolved. The authors trace the historic confluence of ideas, funding opportunities, and then subsequent action of the organisation and its community-led interventions. But as the authors illustrate, OI's history is also closely linked to place.

Drawing from the works of Lefebvre (1974) and Cresswell (2004), Butler and Sinclair (2020) describe *place* as a "meaningful location," thoroughly and thickly embroiled with "social relationships, cultural characteristics, history, natural and geographical landscapes, and built environment" (p. 66). Additionally, *place* can also come with particular political connotations and power hierarchies that can contribute to discrimination and systemic inequality. However, just as *place* can be linked to oppression, it can also become a site of resistance – "they can function as a setting for people from marginalised backgrounds to escape and resist oppression" (p. 64). Throughout this volume, such practices of oppression, resistance, and corresponding empowerment have provided the contextual background to different community-led practices. For example, in their respective chapters in the third section of this volume, Metz and Behal describe challenges to and manifestations of meaningful participation, inclusion, and voice against the historical and political backdrop of particular places and social spaces – in this case, Guatemala and India's northeastern corridor. However, Metz and Behal's chapters also illustrate how community-led practices are shaped around and by such contexts in order to provide locally specific solutions to people's poverty-related challenges. Similarly, the chapter by Reeves in this section reflects in even more detail the varied nature of the Aga Khan Foundation's interventions across different geographic locations and thus places community-led development, as these cases confirm, is *place* specific and thus contextually responsive.

Another feature that can be labelled as *background* is the cultural elements associated with a particular place, phenomenon, or event. Such elements include, but are not limited to, certain norms, values, patterns of behaviours, and beliefs shared among a particular group of people. Culture can dictate people's behaviours and shape their worldview. But, at the same time, culture is also responsive to and subject to change. It is in constant flux, changing and evolving. The same goes for context. It is a process that is "dynamic, fluid and constantly moving, not lumpen, material or static" (Bate 2014). Community-led interventions take cultural dynamics within a particular context seriously, respecting how they shape local contexts and inform human interaction. But they are also not beholden to it, remaining attentive to the evolving nature of culture and broader contextual factors. Arguably, community-led interventions lean into this fluid nature of culture and context. For example, through community-led activities, the Amani Initiative (Chapter 5 of this volume) has engaged with local groups such as local taxi drivers, cultural leaders, and religious entities to critically reflect on existing patterns of behaviour, norms, and values, particularly regarding child marriage. Since Amani's activities are community-led – including stimulating meaningful and inclusive participation and activating collaboration across different social structures – local community members have come to acknowledge a need for cultural change when it comes to child marriage. They have actively participated in shifting local perspectives, cultural norms, and behaviour patterns so that young women in their communities can engage directly in decisions pertaining to their lives and their futures.

Context as Relations and Interaction

A second element in Meier and Dopson's definition is the relational element of context. From an interactionist perspective, contexts and those people directly involved in them have a symbiotic relationship, with context not only shaping, informing, even dictating people's behaviours but people also informing and shaping their contexts. Context, therefore, constitutes social action and is also the result of it. It is both a generative principle and a resulting outcome. The definition and deployment of context is part of actors' strategies, as individual participants can actively attempt to shape context in ways that serve their own interests (Duranti and Goodwin 1992). But in addition to context shaping people and people shaping context, researchers also point to two additional interactions: the relationship and interactions between different types of contexts (i.e. the environmental, political, cultural, temporal, and historical) and also how contextual interaction can occur on different levels and at different scales. For example, Pettigrew's (1987) seminal work on how context operates within organisations differentiates between "inner" and "outer" contexts. Whereas inner contexts can include structure, culture, power, and political characteristics and can therefore be linked to aspects like organisational and divisional norms and internal political processes, outer contexts pertain to external factors often outside the immediate control of organisations. Outer levels of context influence inner levels, but the opposite can also be true (Pye and Pettigrew 2005). Social movements, for example, that at one point might have started at a microlevel, are perhaps an obvious example of how inner momentum around a particular issue can lead to broader structural change at an outer and thus, macro level. When it comes to different layers of contexts, Pawson's (2013) classification system, typically referenced within realist evaluations, is especially productive in emphasising the varied levels worthy of consideration while both describing and analysing context. Pawson's classification operationalises context by classifying it as individuals, interpersonal relationships, institutional settings, and infrastructure (cultural, economic, and social aspects) (Greenhalgh and Manzano 2022, 591).

Who Defines What Context Is?

Context comprises multiple layers of complexity. Additionally, many of these layers are also subjectively defined and interpreted by people living within and experiencing a particular context. From a subjective perspective, and when defining and also analysing context, it is important to pay attention to "how people (selectively) attend to, interpret, and attach significance and relevance to what they perceive as being out there and external to themselves (the reified world), and how that feeds into their behaviour and interactions with others" (Bate 2014, 8). People's perceptions of their environments, place, histories, and culture ultimately contribute to the way they are impacted by their context.

The subjective side of context, combined with its dynamic, ever-changing, and layered nature, brings interesting challenges to the community development sector. When it comes to evaluating success, evaluators face the predicament of controlling for context or incorporating contextual analysis into their work. Theory-driven evaluations have taken the latter approach seriously, considering context's dynamic, ever-changing, but undeniable role in any intervention. In these evaluations, evaluators do not control for different contextual factors or features but instead consider these, in combination with programmatic mechanisms, as integral to the success or failure of interventions (Greenhalgh and Manzano 2022; Paparini et al. 2021). From a programmatic perspective, context directly impacts planning, implementation, and management processes, sometimes unexpectedly. For example, those planning a particular intervention might think it will work, but some contextual factors can, on the one hand, derail its success or, on the other, contribute to unexpected successes.

Within a community-led approach, context is integral to the programme life cycle. Implementers and practitioners acknowledge and then work with, rather than against, context, being flexible to how it can influence outcomes and impact. They are also conscious of how their methodologies and approaches continue to evolve as a result of being responsive to local contexts. Howlett and Bolton's chapter illustrates such openness when describing how OI's community-led methodology has absorbed the nuances present in its different geographic and political contexts to be adequately responsive to local contexts.

But as mentioned before, community-led development approaches are also critically attentive to contexts that might strengthen rather than address inequalities, discrimination, and oppression. Facilitating such attentiveness, are community-led practices that intentionally emphasise meaningful and inclusive participation of all stakeholders, including people often excluded from decision-making activities because of particular contextual factors. The same can be said of community-led accountability practices that can bring into question the status quo, and therefore normalised contextual factors.

References

Akman, Varol and Carla Bazzanella. 2003. "The complexity of context: guest editors' introduction." *Journal of Pragmatics* 35, no. 3: 321–329.

Bate, Paul. 2014. "Context is everything." In *Perspectives on Context: A Collection of Essays considering the Role of Context in Successful Quality Improvement*." London: The Health Foundation.

Butler, Alisha, and Kristin A. Sinclair. 2020. "Place matters: A critical review of place inquiry and spatial methods in education research." *Review of Research in Education* 44, no. 1: 64–96.

Cresswell, Tim. 2004. *Place: A Short Introduction.* Malden, MA: Blackwell Publishing.

Flouris, Anna, Phil Crane, and Melissa A. Lindeman. 2016. "Youth programmes in remote indigenous communities: Context matters." *Rural Society* 25, no. 1: 37–54.

Lefebvre, Henri. 1974. *The Production of Space.* Oxford: Blackwell Publishing.

Malpas, Jeff. 2002. "The weave of meaning: holism and contextuality." *Language & Communication* 22, no. 4: 403–419.

Meier, Ninna, and Sue Dopson. 2019. *Context in Action and How to Study It: Illustrations from Health Care*. Oxford: Oxford University Press.

Paparini, Sara, Chrysanthi Papoutsi, Jamie Murdoch, Judith Green, Mark Petticrew, Trisha Greenhalgh, and Sara E. Shaw. 2021. "Evaluating complex interventions in context: systematic, meta-narrative review of case study approaches." *BMC Medical Research Methodology* 21: 1–22.

Pettigrew, Andrew M. 1987. *The Awakening giant: Continuity and Change in Imperial Chemical Industries.* Chichester: Wiley-Blackwell.

Pye, Annie, and Andrew Pettigrew. 2005. "Studying board context, process and dynamics: some challenges for the future." *British Journal of Management* 16: S27–S38.

Zapf, Michael Kim. 2010. "Social work and the environment: understanding people and place." *Critical Social Work* 11, no. 3: 30–46.

7

WHEN THE HELPED HELP THE HELPERS HELP

The Global Diffusion and Transformation of Community-Led Development Practices in an American INGO

David J. Howlett and Matthew Breay Bolton

Introduction

Matthew, one of the authors of this chapter, started his career at Outreach International (OI) in the early 2000s, inspired by its then slogan of "helping people help themselves." The staff of Outreach, a small, faith-based NGO based at the time in Independence, Missouri, USA, saw themselves as different from traditional humanitarian organisations. Rather than direct assistance to the communities where it worked in Latin America, Asia, and Africa, Outreach recruited, trained, and managed teams of "facilitators" who worked at the grassroots to catalyse a process of community-led development (CLD) called "Participatory Human Development" or PHD. Many Outreach staff saw their method as a unique invention and had an almost mystical belief in its power to engender liberation from poverty. When leaving an assignment in the Philippines, a local staff member gave Matthew a gift with an earnest message of blessing: "May the [PHD] Process be with you." However, in that same visit to the Philippines, Matthew began to trace the history of the PHD idea, interviewing local staff and reading through organisational archives, learning that PHD had a complex global genealogy, emerging in Outreach's Philippines programme in the late 1980s and drawing on influences from urban organising in the USA to liberation theology in Latin America. Shortly thereafter, Matthew also came across the scholarly Development Studies literature questioning whether the discourse of "participation" in development occluded its power dynamics (e.g., Cooke and Kothari 2001). There is a hubris implicit in the idea that one can help another help themselves. Even as it suggests a less directive approach to aid than traditional humanitarianism, helping others help themselves implies a one-way relationship – the helper remains unchanged. However, by the early 2000s, Filipino field staff had transformed the very organisation that had

DOI: 10.4324/9781003377917-10

hired them, as Outreach headquarters increasingly adopted their PHD model – developed in marginalised communities in the Philippines – as the standard field methodology. Counterintuitively, the Filipino communities Outreach aimed to help themselves were helping Outreach help itself.

While participatory and community-led development focuses on local people's internal capacity to change their own situation, Development Studies scholars have observed such discourses can obscure the role of external actors – the state, aid agencies, donors, consultants – that position themselves up as "facilitators" of the process. But aid agencies themselves may be transformed as they encounter communities that they seek to help/support. "Powerful" actors intervening in the global periphery can find themselves transformed, unsettled by the encounter. Ideas, discourses, and practices originating in one setting go through a process of "translation" and "hybridisation" as they travel, diffusing in complex feedback loops worldwide. This essay uses OI as a case study of CLD to illustrate this very process. We draw on multiple qualitative methods in our research, including Matthew's participant observation as a researcher, trainer, and manager at OI from 2000 to 2012; David's fieldwork and key informant interviews with Outreach staff and communities in the Philippines in 2015; and research in archives related to the history of Outreach's sponsoring church, the Community of Christ.

Faith-Based NGOs and Community-Led Development in Post-Colonial Perspective

Like many influential terms, the meaning and use of the words "faith-based NGO" or the more widely used term, faith-based organisation (FBO), is contested, variable, and pervasive (Tomalin 2012). For pragmatic purposes, we define a faith-based NGO as a group with a significant tie to a specific organised religious body (i.e. the affiliation of the majority of its board members or funders). In doing so, we recognise that, as Smith and Sosin noted, the "faith" in faith-based might be more implicit than explicit. Thus, they argue "agencies most closely aligned with faith must act in the secular world, while agencies with a strongly secular orientation might be influenced to some degree by their religiosities" (Smith and Sosin 2001, 653). For example, OI, the organisation that we analyse in this chapter, does not self-consciously characterise itself as a "faith-based NGO." However, it is officially affiliated with an American-based Christian denomination – the Community of Christ – and received a considerable share of its budget directly from church tithing in the first decades of its existence. A mass email in early 2023, to Outreach's supporters, invited "our wonderful Community of Christ partners" to an "open house" at the denomination's 2023 World Conference. A significant proportion of donors, board members, staff, and volunteers continue to have ties to the Community of Christ, though their influence has diminished since OI's founding. Furthermore, its methodologies, as will be seen, have their roots in liberation theology and radical pedagogies created by radical Christians in the

1970s. Thus, following Sider and Unruh (2004), we argue that faith-based NGOs, like the particular case study we analyse, may be better thought of as organisations falling on a spectrum between "faith-permeated" to "secular." From where we stand, OI falls squarely in the middle of this spectrum. Finally, we use the term "faith-based NGO" to characterise OI due to the term's legibility – it places us in conversation with other studies of organisations that are not dissimilar to Outreach in terms of shared methods (community organising [CO]) or origins (a sponsoring church whose donor-base provides economic support for the NGO).

In the past decade, a growing number of scholars have produced studies of faith-based NGOs. Some scholars have offered sweeping accounts of the rise of NGOs in the 1960s through the 1980s (Davies 2014; O'Sullivan 2019), mentioning faith-based NGOs in passing. Others have offered synthetic accounts of faith-based NGOs, ranging from the suspicious and critical ("Introduction" in Barnett and Stein, 2012) to the sympathetic and pragmatic (Tomalin 2013; Welty 2014). Still, other scholars have used extended case studies to offer larger insights. Recent notable works have included a study of World Vision, a global NGO with links to evangelical Christianity, and the reorientation of the conservative politics of compassion (King 2019); a study of the multi-billion dollar child sponsorship sector and conservative Christian global imaginaries (Kaell 2020); or a study of Lutheran development NGOs in Minnesota and Madagascar and the revivification of colonial linkages in a post-colonial world through material exchange (Halvorson 2018). With a few notable exceptions (Barnett and Stein, 2012; Tomalin, 2015; Halvorson, 2018), scholarship on NGOs, and faith-based NGOs in particular, has overwhelmingly studied American organisations (or, more daringly, Irish, Canadian, and British organisations, i.e. O'Sullivan 2019), and their attendant policies, with little attention to how individuals in the Majority World have reshaped these institutions or created their own.

Within the wider field of Development Studies (which has significant overlaps with the study of faith-based NGOs), the American-centric, top-down story of "development," and of the NGOs producing development discourse, has begun to shift in a new direction. As historian Joseph Morgan Hodge noted in 2016, "scholars are beginning to explore the viewpoints of local communities and players and to reassess their roles not only as recipients of aid but as advocates and producers of development knowledge" (2016, p. 155). Our own work follows this turn by leveraging the perspectives of Post-Colonial Theory to understand faith-based development NGOs, their methods, and the transnational relationships that produce them. In particular, we consider how the politics of the Philippines and the radical development theories of Filipino community organisers reshaped the development methodologies of the American faith-based NGO for which they worked. First, though, we offer a bit more explanation of what we take from Post-Colonial Theory.

Post-Colonial Theory suggests that the dynamics between people in highly unequal power relations are not fixed or determined (Ngũgĩ 2012). Colonial contact not only transforms the people colonised but also the societies of the colonisers, which are shaped by processes of hybridisation through resistance, appropriation, migration, creolisation, and cultural exchange (Orwell 1936; Pratt 1992; Shih and Lionet 2011). Hollinger (2019, 1, 3), for example, shows how American Protestant missionaries in Asia embarked expecting "to make the world look more like the United States" but instead "encounter with peoples beyond the Christian West…led missionaries to question many cherished beliefs of the folks back home." Interaction with local people moulded "missionary cosmopolitans" who came to embrace ideas of multiculturalism, cultural relativism, and decolonisation that undermined the very project that had sent them overseas. Thus "powerful" actors intervening in the global periphery can find themselves transformed, unsettled by the encounter. Ideas, discourses, and practices originating in one setting go through a process of "translation" as they travel, diffusing in complex feedback loops around the world (Shih and Lionet 2011, 30). Similarly, Post-Colonial Development Studies thinkers have highlighted the agency of people framed as passive beneficiaries, who may use dominant institutions and discourses to pursue their own goals, even as they remain constrained by the existing systems (Kapoor 2008). Escobar (2011) shows how pursuing "development" is a project of meaning-making that enables the "helper" to shape and perform a more "civilised" and "developed" identity in comparison with the "helped."

Post-Colonial Theory thus provides us with an overarching theory to think about and think with CLD. Another source directly applicable to our topic provides a generative conversation partner – both generative in the sense of thinking *with* and thinking *against.* In the celebrated intellectual history, *Thinking Small*, Daniel Immerwahr (2015) argues that CLD, once mainstream in the so-called Third World in the 1950s, was widely regarded in these same places as a project that failed to deliver its promises by the mid-1960s. Yet, he also points to the appeal of "community" and the power of the local in movements that went beyond this era, such as the community-organising movement by the New Left in the late 1960s or feminist consciousness-raising groups in the early 1970s. He goes on to highlight how community development came back in vogue in the 1990s. What he fails to explain is how it migrated from one era to another.

The story of OI helps bridge these gaps, but it also highlights other sources for development philosophy, namely radical Filipino community organisers who gestated their ideas in their experiences with groups like the Philippine Ecumenical Council for Community Organization (PECCO) or Community Organization of the Philippines Enterprise (COPE). Both groups organised to resist the Marcos regime and Filipino Outreach employees had worked for or alongside both. In contrast, Immerwahr focuses on larger organisations more directly connected to American neo-imperial projects, like the International Volunteer Services, USAID, or the International Institute of Rural Reconstruction (IIRR), an NGO founded by anti-Communist Chinese emigre, Dr. Y.C. James Yen. Even so, he does not interrogate if the official philosophies of such organisations and the actions and intents of their employees matched. Furthermore, Immerwahr fails to consider if or how communities receiving community development projects themselves affected the philosophies, practices, and programmes of CLD, other than to note mismatches between the two parties. Thus, by focusing on the big, he ironically neglects the small.

Filipino Community Organizers and the Origins of Outreach International

OI was founded in 1979 as the successor to NGOs started by members of the midwestern-American-based Reorganized Church of Jesus Christ of Latter Day Saints (RLDS), now the Community of Christ, in the late 1960s and early 1970s. In 1972, RLDS Apostle Charles Neff, whose ministerial field included the Philippines, visited IIRR in Silang, Cavite, Philippines where an old college friend was on staff as a researcher. Neff's visit was no coincidence. Key RLDS leaders, most of them American, had begun to take an interest in "development" discourse. Across the 1970s, several apostles (administrators over global regions) attended graduate programmes in development anthropology and global public health.

Nevertheless, as career missionaries and church administrators, none of these individuals had practical experience in running NGOs. For this, they relied on the expertise of individuals already in the field. In 1974, for example, Neff recruited several Filipino IIRR employees to staff a nascent RLDS NGO, charged with resettling a Filipino RLDS congregation that had been displaced by counterinsurgency in the highlands of Luzon. In 1979, Neff recruited Filipino IIRR staff once again when he helped found Outreach, giving the Filipino staff control of the field operations and working philosophy. These same Filipino staff helped organise a week-long 1981 conference on development philosophy at IIRR headquarters, attended by Outreach board members, key donors, and global RLDS leaders (Tyree 1981). Matthew, co-author of this article, attended a second conference at IIRR in 1983 as a toddler, when his parents, RLDS missionaries in Japan, were invited to attend, as the church looked for people to work at the nexus of mission and development. This pattern – hiring Filipino NGO professionals from IIRR to staff and shape RLDS-sponsored NGOs – would continue well into the 1980s and beyond, too.

While IIRR might be described as a creation of Cold War trans-Pacific liberalism (Immerwahr 2015, 101–128), favouring localised development projects and neoliberalism, its Filipino staff often held more subversive aspirations. In places like Metro Manila and Cabanatuan City, Nueva Ecija, Philippines, these IIRR staff members worked in proximity to other NGOs, some of whom had more radical origins in the Filipino Community Organising (CO) movement in the early 1970s. Such was the case with Dr. Dennis Labayen, a charismatic IIRR employee hired by Outreach in 1982. Labayen was a graduate of a prestigious medical college in the Philippines and the nephew of the Catholic Bishop Julio Xavier Labayen, one of the "magnificent seven" bishops who publicly opposed Marcos's imposition of martial law. As an IIRR employee, Dennis Labayen had encountered the CO movement and saw its potential to enhance the implementation of the IIRR's Four-Fold Approach to development emphases (education, livelihood, health, and self-government). To this end, Labayen headed up an IIRR research team that sought to synthesise CO and development strategies, and, when he was hired by OI, Labayen continued on the IIRR research team as a consultant (Labayen et al. 1983).

While working for Outreach in Cabanatuan City (a centre for NGOs in the Philippines), Labayen networked among other NGO workers and befriended Eduardo "Toto" Delfin, then an employee of the CO group ACES (Agency for Community Education Services). If Labayen came from a patrician family, Delfin came from a humbler socio-economic background and had a different route into CO. An excursus into his career as an organiser, contextualised within the history of Filipino NGOs, is helpful for understanding Outreach's evolving CO philosophy.

Toto Delfin grew up in an impoverished Catholic family in Mindanao but, through academic merit, had attended a private Catholic high school and later earned a BA in agriculture and development communication from Xavier University –Ateneo de Cagayan (1975–1980), a Jesuit university known at the time for its radicalism. Delfin, like many of his classmates, was attracted to join the CO movement springing up among student activists eager to resist Marcos's martial law regime. At the time there was funding available for CO movements from a variety of transnational sources.

Delfin witnessed first-hand the transformation of the NGO sector in the Philippines at a moment when select NGOs became radicalised in the global justice movement (cf. O'Sullivan 2019, 57–77). Before the 1970s, welfare agencies had dominated Filipino non-profit organisations (Bankoff 2007). Government community development programmes, at first premised on ground-up solutions to local problems, had been co-opted by the Marcos regime as bases for localised political power (Immerwahr 2015). By contrast, CO promised a more democratic path, organising ordinary people for their own interests. Like other global justice-oriented NGOs, Filipino CO NGOs in the 1970s combined Marxist structural analysis with the pedagogical theories of Paulo Freire and Catholic liberation theology, as well as Alinskyite organising techniques (Savaris et al. 2019, 10; O'Sullivan 2019, 64–65; Constantino-David 1995, 157).

Reacting to the tendency of the Catholic Church in Latin America and the Philippines to side with the elite and justify the oppression of the poor, liberation theologians argued that God is a partisan on the side of the poor and oppressed in their struggles for freedom. Contending that traditional theology and philosophy had been formed in isolation from society, liberation theologians said true theology could only be formed in dialogue and interaction with the world through the process of praxis – the continual cycle of action and reflection (Gutierrez 1988; Boff and Boff 1987). Liberation theologians drew upon the work of Brazilian educationalist Paulo Freire (1999) who argued that gaining literacy should not be perceived as a value-free process, in which elites "deposited" knowledge into the poor. Rather, education should be a process of "conscientisation", in which people reflect critically on their situation and solve their problems independently from a dependence on the elite. Community development workers in the Philippines and beyond drew on these ideas to focus their efforts not on an expansion of market relations, but rather working in solidarity with those most marginalised to build organisations capable of advancing their interests.

Nevertheless, in conversations with the authors, Filipino activists and NGO workers reflected that they found it initially difficult to operationalise the abstract and theoretical insights of Freire and liberation theology. For a methodology to guide their work, they turned to strategies and tactics developed by community organisers in American cities, documented by the progressive sociologist and activist Saul Alinsky. Working in Chicago during the 1950s and 1960s, Alinsky explored whether the lessons of union organising could be applied to poor and marginalised communities as a whole. A protege of John L. Lewis (one the most prominent early twentieth-century American union leaders, who coincidentally grew up RLDS [Roberts, 1991]), Alinsky felt the unions' weakness lay in their exclusive focus on workers and labour issues. He decided to experiment with using labour organising tactics of collective bargaining and collective problem-solving to a whole impoverished community. Alinsky believed that though people in a community may distrust each other, they had common problems like poor sanitation, failing schools, and unresponsive public institutions. If they could be agitated to feel the urgency of their problems and begin to act on small but concrete problems, they would build up a collective experience of victories and failures that would eventually unify and solidify the community into a formal organisation that could hold the government accountable, build community solidarity, and address local concerns. Alinsky was critical of the traditional welfare and social work activities of the government and charities providing services to the poor. He felt they failed to ask people what they really needed or bring about a genuine systemic change. Instead, he called for interest-driven mobilisation of the poor, using confrontational, creative, and even humorous tactics. Central to the process was the "Organizer," modelled after union organisers, who integrated themselves into community life, becoming familiar with people's problems, hopes, and dreams. Once established, known, and acquainted with the local situation, the Organizer "agitated" people to acknowledge and act on their collective problems (Alinsky 1989; Horwitt 1992; Rubin and Rubin 2007).

Ostensibly, CO itself had been transplanted to the Philippines by way of two American Presbyterians, Herbert and Margaret White, who worked as training directors at the PECCO from 1970 to 1972 (Constantino-David 1995, 156; Savaris et al. 2019, 10). Before arriving in the Philippines, the Whites had lived in Rochester, New York, where they had participated in local efforts led by Alinsky's Industrial Areas Foundation (Horwitt 1992, 456). Shortly before Alinsky's death he visited the Philippines to meet with community organisers and came "away very impressed with their courage, resourcefulness, and imagination in the face of police-state harassment, imprisonment, and torture" (Horwitt 1992, 537–538).

PECCO was initially a broad-based coalition including individuals affiliated with the Communist Party of the Philippines (CPP) and "social-democratic groups to church-based and non-aligned individuals" (Constantino-David 1995, 117). With the Marcos regime's imposition of martial law in September 1972, though, the government raided PECCO's offices and arrested some of its leaders. In the next five years, ongoing tensions increased between PECCO and the CPP, as many non-CPP PECCO organisers felt that the latter was using their organisation to recruit individuals in poor communities, rather than contribute to CLD. These disagreements resulted in the dissolution of any cooperation between PECCO and the CPP, and after 1977, CO groups began to proliferate in the Philippines beyond PECCO (Constantino-David 1995, 158). For example, Denis Murphy, a former Jesuit priest and veteran of PECCO, helped co-found COPE, a group that would take CO beyond the Philippines into other Asian countries, too. It was this latter organisation that Delfin joined once he graduated from college in 1980.

Delfin entered the field of CO at a moment that looked both promising and perilous for activists like himself. On January 17, 1981, Filipino dictator Ferdinand Marcos officially lifted martial law in the Philippines. As an upshot, "organising efforts multiplied and innovative approaches and tools were developed and replicated all over the country" (Savaris et al. 2019, 10). Constantino-David also described the era between 1977 and 1983 as an era of creative experimentation with new organising methods. However, the end to martial law was in name only, and Marcos effectively retained all of the powers he had accrued in the previous years. His regime continued its extra-judicial killings of those perceived to be its enemies, making CO a dangerous act of resistance.

Within this context, Delfin was sent by COPE to organise Christian and Muslim villages (*barangays*) in a mining region of Zamboanga del Sur, Mindanao. Without direct funding, he and his organising partner were given a plot of land, a small house, and some rice to plant and use for food. As an organiser, he experienced the constant threat of violence by forces benefiting from the exploitation of the poor communities. In 1982, unknown assailants (presumably, forces connected to the government) murdered Delfin's organising partner at the home where the two organisers lived. Delfin arrived at the house just moments after the assassination. Thus, his partner likely became one of the more than 10,000 individuals killed by the regime before its ultimate overthrow in the People Power Revolution in 1986.

After the death of his organising partner, Delfin was pulled out of the project by COPE. Corazon Juliano-Soliman, then a community organiser, invited him to work in Cabanatuan City, Nueva Ecija for another CO group, ACES. There, and in association with other NGOs whose offices were in close proximity, Delfin met his spouse, Felina or "Felee", and Dennis Labayen and his spouse, Dr. Lorna Labayen (also a medical doctor who worked at IIRR). In 1986, Dennis hired Delfin to work with him in the local RLDS NGO Community One Resources Development (CORD) and later for OI in 1988. Together, the Delfins and the Labayens refined their own CO methodology that they called PHD, or Participatory Human Development, and this methodology would become the central organising vision for the work of OI.

Innovating and Disseminating a Methodology – Participatory Human Development

The PHD method focuses on first building small issue-based groups at the very grassroots level. Outreach field workers, called Human Development Facilitators, convene local dialogue, agitate and conscientise people through Socratic questioning and try to encourage participation of all people in the community in processes of development and social development. Starting with modest, apolitical problems, Facilitators aim to reduce the potential for political polarisation in the community and build the experience necessary to tackle bigger, structural problems. Outreach argues effective local leaders can eventually guide the process themselves, as they emerge through successful community mobilisation and project management.

The Labayens and the Delfins saw the PHD method as having both significant resonances with and divergences from other CO methods used in the Philippines by the 1980s. First, unlike some groups involved in electoral politics, individuals deploying the PHD method did not primarily engage in the politics of confrontation. Second, unlike Alinsky's method, individuals using the PHD method did not immediately identify community leaders who would take charge of the PHD process or its resultant projects. Based upon their observations of varied CO groups, the Labayens and the Delfins found that identifying local leaders at the outset of the PHD process more often than not entrenched pre-existing local elites (one of Immerwahr's [2015] primary critiques of community development). Third, influenced by Freirean pedagogy, the Labayens and the Delfins saw PHD organisers as not the vanguard of a local development movement but instead as facilitators. Vanguardism, in their opinion, resulted in the dependency of local people on NGO workers as leaders, and, in the end, made the development project itself an "outside" project imposed on local people.

By the late 1990s, OI was implementing and refining its PHD method in communities around the Philippines and beyond. OI populated its literature with continual references to "Participatory Human Development," too. In 1994, an article in the official RLDS magazine detailed the history of Outreach on its 15th anniversary and highlighted the group's method. The then Executive Director of Outreach, Russell Fletcher, enthusiastically stated, "The whole process of PHD is a revelation… The main emphasis is the process. It's a radical approach to go in 'agenda-less.' And it works!" (in Monsees 1994, 152). The writer then highlighted a variety of "success" stories from around the world – the Philippines, the Dominican Republic, and the USA – where PHD had been applied. Furthermore, OI staff wanted to expand the reach of their organisation within the USA and "hoped to share the PHD process with other organisations" (Monsees 1994, 154).

Fletcher even claimed to have applied the PHD method to the running of the OI headquarters, then in Independence, Missouri.

Thus, while OI has developed out of more traditional humanitarian, health, and education programmes associated with RLDS missions, PHD became the organisation's primary conceptual framework. By the early 2000s, Outreach's Filipino staff members were responsible for managing its field programmes at the global level. Dr. Dennis Labayen had moved to Outreach headquarters, appointed the Director of Field Operations. Along with Felee and Toto Delfin, and with occasional consultancies from Dr. Lorna Labayen, Dennis was training staff in the PHD method – and measuring their performance by its standards – not only in the Philippines but also in Nicaragua, Dominican Republic, Bolivia, Zambia, Malawi, Democratic Republic of the Congo. Headquarters' staff were also expected to attend PHD trainings, which were increasingly attended by RLDS ministers in countries where Outreach worked. Legacy projects supporting RLDS parochial schools were also increasingly evaluated according to PHD's underlying principles of empowerment and self-help. The organisation had undergone a kind of conversion process, in which PHD, a method innovated by Filipino field staff in conversations with the communities where they worked, became the predominant discourse of an American NGO.

In a 2015 interview, Toto Delfin expressed confidence in the PHD method – a conviction that people "can improve their life if they have the opportunity." "It is God-given to know their situation," he continued, "to decide about their situation, act on their situation … and learn from their experience." This has been a "basic human function – from the first man and woman made by God – knowing, deciding, acting, effecting, and learning." He asserted that, if you gathered a hundred development professionals in a room, "everyone would agree that PHD is the method, even government people." For him, there was no doubt about the efficacy of the PHD method, if applied properly.

At times, the diversity of Outreach's field contexts posed challenges to the Filipino staff who had to adapt to divergent political and cultural contexts. Some of PHD's Marxist influences, for example, had to be tempered in training of staff in Nicaragua, who were politically polarised in the aftermath of the 1980s proxy war between the Sandinistas and Contras. In conversations with Outreach's Filipino trainers, some expressed frustration with the expectations in African states that religious institutions should directly perform social services neglected by colonial and post-colonial governments, not just "facilitate" change. While some of Outreach's more radical staff have grumbled about ongoing support to RLDS parochial schools, such as in Haiti and India, they are important to many Community of Christ donors. In conversations with Outreach staff who were more steeped in the Filipino CO tradition, Matthew found they made peace with this compromise by using a proverb associated with IIRR, often attributed to Dr. Yen: "Start with what they know, build on what they have." In other words, they sought to facilitate Outreach's gradual transition to PHD, rather than demand a wholesale and sudden jolt away from existing obligations. They were treating Outreach's headquarters, donors, and schoolteachers as another community needing "conscientisation."

While its projects and organising philosophy reflected some of the radical aspirations of its Filipino field staff, Outreach appealed to a wide range of donors in the USA and Canada, most affiliated with the then RLDS Church (now Community of Christ), who saw it as their church's official human development NGO. These included socially prominent individuals like the Canadian radio and cable television magnate, James "JR" Shaw (Tyree 1981); the politically neo-conservative U.S. Ambassador John K. Menzies (Menzies 1994, 191); as well as more rank-and-file RLDS members who spanned the conservative/liberal North American cultural divides. For example, in the late 1990s and early 2000s, Outreach ran PHD programmes in the mid-south region of the USA, funded by the Walton Family Foundation, the philanthropic arm of the founders of Walmart. Thus, OI's programmes and philosophy could be adopted and co-opted by a surprisingly diverse array of boosters.

By the later 2000s and 2010s, Outreach's donors and headquarters managers increasingly sought to measure and document the changes that resulted from PHD processes. There was pressure to "scale up" Outreach's impact and administrators sought grant funding from more mainstream development donors, including the UN, US government, and large foundations. Field staff were now expected to write up regular reports on their work and measure the success of their facilitation according to indicators common to all Outreach PHD programmes. The Outreach International (2022) website now features a dashboard of its "Current Scope of Impact," including "504 issues addressed" and "84,066 people benefitting." It boasts of a 4/4 Charity Navigator rating (which rates nonprofits largely according to standards of financial transparency and accountability to donors) and a 20/20 rating with the Better Business Bureau. PHD – which emerged out of a leftist "power to the people" mystique – has thus been retrofitted into the discourses of neo-liberal audit culture.

As a result, Filipino field staff transformed the very organisation that had hired them, as Outreach increasingly adopted a PHD model developed by communities in the Philippines as the standard global field methodology. But the model has been further transformed by encountering donor and managerial expectations, as well as divergent contexts in communities in the Americas, Asia, and Africa.

Conclusions

OI was formed out of efforts by North American missionaries and humanitarians to transform Filipino communities that they saw as "in need." But Outreach's founders were religious leaders, not development workers, and so they borrowed ideas and staff from the local context in which they worked. This meant that the development projects they sponsored were not one-way transmissions of change from the Global North to the Global South. Rather they germinated the growth of transnational networks of ideas, practices, and discourses that changed Outreach's headquarters too.

In dominant global policymaking, the concept of "Development" has troubling echoes of colonial notions of a "standard of civilisation" that ranked societies according to European rubrics of social and economic progress. Hence a division between societies that are supposedly "developing" and those that are already "developed." This idea was embedded in the UN's Millennium Development Goals (MDGs), that set benchmarks for developing countries to meet between 2000 and 2015 and called on "donor countries" to support them. CLD is framed in opposition to this dominant, government-led, and technocratic discourse, in which local communities lead their own processes of development, rather than following prescriptions from international and national policymakers. But CLD discourse still often replicates a distinction between the "the community" that is developing itself and the outsiders who may facilitate or support change.

The UN's Sustainable Development Goals (SDGs), adopted in 2015, have many of the same top-down problems as the MDGs they replaced. But in one key respect they have moved away from the underlying assumptions of a "standard of civilisation" – the SDGs obligate all UN Member States to pursue sustainable development. No one is above the need to develop a more prosperous, equitable, peaceful, just, and environmentally sound global economy. Sustainable development discourse has enabled "developing countries" to point out the ways the economies and societies of "developed countries" also have problems. The concept of development has turned back on itself, transforming what we can expect of those who claim to be developed.

Similarly, our case study of OI shows that processes of CLD may transform not only the communities where development was planned to happen but the very organisation that initiated the process. The "beneficiary" community leading the process of its own development may also change the "donors" involved, who in turn reuse and retool ideas, discourses, and practices for their own purposes. We hope our case study can help reconsideration of development as a complex field of social relations that affects both the supposed "helper" and "helped" in unexpected ways. Surely development organisations have a stake in this academic reconsideration of the field of development.

More directly linked to the narrative of this essay, development organisations might also benefit from reflecting on some of the more radical strands – CO, radical pedagogy, and resistance to autocracy – that formed the methods of OI. In doing so, they may find more participatory, more grassroots, and more radically democratic strands in the many-braided cord that constitutes their understanding of CLD.

Bibliography

Alinksy, Saul. (1989) *Rules for Radicals*. New York, Vintage Books.

Bankoff, Greg. (2007) "Dangers to Going It Alone: Social Capital and the Origins of Community Resilience in the Philippines," *Continuity and Change* , 22(2), pp. 327–355, Cambridge University Press.

Barnett, Michael and Janice Stein (Eds.). (2012) *Sacred Aid: Faith and Humanitarianism.* Oxford, Oxford University Press.

Boff, Leonardo and Clodovis Boff. (1987) "A Concise History of Liberation Theology." Available from https://liberationtheology.org/library/a-concise-history-of-liberation-theology.pdf Accessed 28 January 2023.

Constantino-David, Karina. (1995) "Community Organizing in the Philippines: The Experience of Development NGOs." In: Gary Graid and Marjorie Mayo (Eds.). *Community Empowerment: A Reader in Participation and Development.* London, Zed Books, pp. 154–167.

Cooke, Bill and Uma Kothari (Eds.). (2001) *Participation: The New Tyranny?* London, Zed Books.

Davies, Thomas. (2014) *NGOs: A New History of Transnational Civil Society*. Oxford, Oxford University Press.

Duranti, Alessandro and Charles Goodwin. (Eds.). (1992). *Rethinking Context: Language as an Interactive Phenomenon.* No. 11. Cambridge, Cambridge University Press.

Escobar, Arturo. (2011) *Encountering Development: The Making and Unmaking of the Third World.* Princeton, Princeton University Press.

Freire, Paulo. (1999) *Pedagogy of the Oppressed.* New Rvsd Ed. Myra Bergman Ramos (Trans.). New York, Continuum.

Greenhalgh, Joanne and Ana Manzano. (2022). "Understanding 'Context' in Realist Evaluation and Synthesis." *International Journal of Social Research Methodology* 25 (5): 583–595.

Gutierrez, Gustavo. (1988) *A Theology of Liberation: History, Politics, and Salvation.* Rvsd Ed. Maryknoll, New York, Orbis Books.

Halvorson, Britt. (2018) *Conversionary Sites: Transforming Medical Aid and Global Christianity from Madagascar to Minnesota.* Chicago, University of Chicago Press.

Hodge, Joseph Morgan. (2016) "Writing the History of Development (Part 2: Longer, Deeper, Wider)," *Humanity: An International Journal of Human Rights, Humanitarianism and Development*, 7(1), pp. 125–174.

Hollinger, David A. (2019) *Protestants Abroad: How Missionaries Tried to Change the World but Changed America.* Princeton, Princeton University Press.

Horwitt, Sanford D. (1992) *Let Them Call Me Rebel: Saul Alinsky: His Life and Legacy.* New York, Vintage Books.

Immerwahr, Daniel. (2015) *Thinking Small: The United States and the Lure of Community Development.* Cambridge, Harvard University Press.

Kaell, Hillary. (2020) *Christian Globalism at Home: Child Sponsorship in the United States.* Princeton, Princeton University Press.

Kapoor, Ilan. (2008) *The Postcolonial Politics of Development.* New York, Routledge.

King, David P. (2019) *God's Internationalists: World Vision and the Age of Evangelical Humanitarianism.* Philadelphia, University of Pennsylvania Press.

Labayen, Dennis, Henry Mercaida, and Eva Dueñas. (1983) "Learning from and Working with the Rural Poor." *Rural Reconstruction Review*, 5, pp. 56–68.

Menzies, John K. (1994) "An Instrument of Hope and Change." *Saints Herald*, 141(7), pp. 289–293, Herald Publishing House.

Monsees, Laurie. (1994) "Outreach Celebrates 15 Years." *Saints Herald*, 141(4), pp. 151–154, Herald Publishing House.

Orwell, George. (1936) "Shooting an Elephant." *New Writing*, pp. 1–7. Available from www.orwellfoundation.com/the-orwell-foundation/orwell/essays-and-other-works/shooting-an-elephant

O'Sullivan, Kevin. (2019) *The NGO Moment: The Globalisation of Compassion from Biafra to Live Aid.* Cambridge: Cambridge University Press.

Outreach International. (2022) "Impact." Available from https://outreach-international.org/our-work/impact/ (Accessed 1 November 2022).

Pawson, Ray. (2013). *The Science of Evaluation: A Realist Manifesto.* London, Sage.

Pratt, Mary-Louise. (1992) *Imperial Eyes: Travel Writing and Transculturation.* New York, Routledge.

Roberts, Ron. (1991) "A Waystation from Babylon: Nineteenth-Century Saints in Lucas, Iowa." *John Whitmer Historical Association Journal*, 11(1991), pp. 60–70.

Rubin, Herbert J. and Irene S. Rubin. (2007) *Community Organizing and Development.* 4th Ed. Needham Heights, MA, Allyn & Bacon.

Savaris, J. P., D. G. Dequito, and R. L. Golbeque. (2021). *Manual on Community Organizing for Sustainable Development.* Bonn, Federal Ministry for the Environment, Conservation, and Nuclear Safety of the Federal Republic of Germany.

Shih, Shu-mei and Françoise Lionet. (2011) "The Creolization of Theory." In Shu-mei Shih and Françoise Lionet (Eds.). *The Creolization of Theory*. Durham, Duke University Press, pp. 1–36.

Sider, Ronald J. and Heidi Rolland Unruh. (2004) "Typology of Religious Characteristics of Social Service and Educational Organisations and Programs." *Nonprofit and Voluntary Sector Quarterly* 33 (1): 109–134.

Smith, Steven Rathgeb and Michael R. Sosin. (2001) "The Varieties of Faith-Related Agencies." *Public Administration Review* 61(6), pp. 651–70.

Thiong'o, Ngũgĩ wa. (2012) *In the House of the Interpreter: A Memoir.* New York, Anchor Books.

Tomalin, Emma. (2012) "Thinking about Faith-Based Organisations in Development: Where Have We Got to and What Next?" *Development in Practice* 22(5/6), pp. 689–703.

Tomalin, Emma. (2013) *Religions and Development.* New York, Routledge.

Tomalin, Emma. (Ed.). (2015) *The Routledge Handbook of Religious and Global Development.* New York, Routledge.

Tyree, Alan D. (1981) "Outreach International Goes to School." *Saints Herald* 128, p. 136.

Welty, Emily E. (2014) "Faith-Based Peacebuilding and Development: An Analysis of the Mennonite Central Committee in Uganda and Kenya." *Journal of Peacebuilding and Development*, 9(2), pp. 65–70.

8

AGA KHAN FOUNDATION

Adapting Community-Led Development to Diverse Contexts

Matt Reeves

> *"Through a great variety of village and community organisations, we encourage people to overcome their antagonisms, and work together to find solutions to common problems in the search for a better life."*[1]
>
> His Highness the Aga Khan

Introduction

Keynote Address to the Annual Conference of German Ambassadors, Berlin, Germany, September 6, 2004.

The Aga Khan Foundation (AKF) was established in 1967 with the intention to integrate professional management and technical skills with genuine participation by local people to explore innovative approaches to development challenges across Asia and Africa. Initially, AKF's primary role was to support and enhance the social development infrastructure of the broader Aga Khan Development Network (AKDN) encompassing schools, universities, health centres and cultural programmes.

In the early 1980s, the AKF took a strategic decision to expand its efforts to support holistic community-led development in priority geographical areas. This decision built upon the significant experience that AKF had accumulated in its early years and was aligned with a foundational belief, articulated in the above quote, that for development interventions to be successfully implemented, relevant to local stakeholders, and sustained over the longer-term, communities needed to be at the heart of decision-making processes.

Our initial investments, in the 1980s, were in the mountainous regions of Gilgit-Baltistan and Chitral in northern Pakistan, and on the plains and coast of Gujarat state in western India. Central to our strategy was the mobilisation and formation of

DOI: 10.4324/9781003377917-11

broad-based citizen-led organisations at the village level. Leadership of the village organisations was determined through a democratic process. Organisations were supported to meet frequently and to engage in inclusive processes that identified community development needs, opportunities, and challenges. These became the focus of solutions, designed, implemented, and monitored by village organisations. Our initial model also included the establishment of community-based savings groups within every village organisation to mitigate against shocks and ensure local contributions towards community-led development. Where solutions and resources were not locally available, AKF sought to connect external resources to local development needs.

This holistic community-led development approach – delivered through the Aga Khan Rural Support Programmes (AKRSP) – resulted in tangible improvements in incomes, welfare, and overall quality of life (World Bank OED Summer 2002). The AKRSP in Pakistan was evaluated four times by the World Bank's Operations Evaluation Department (World Bank OED, 1987, 1990, 1996, 2002), which described it as "a development effort that has become a model for rural programmes throughout the country and across the globe" (World Bank OED, 2002, p. XI).

Bolstered by initial successes in Pakistan and India, AKF took its community-led development efforts further afield: to mountainous areas of northern Afghanistan; to the mangroves of the Swahili Coast in Mozambique; to the banks of the Nile in Aswan, Egypt; and to the Portuguese capital, Lisbon. In each of these countries, AKF began implementation at the invitation of the national government. Over the past 30 years, we have learnt that community-led development can work at scale. In 2020, for example, AKF worked with over 30,000 community-led organisations that, in turn, reached 9.7 million individuals.

We have also learnt many lessons along the way, both from our successes and from our failures. This chapter will explore, through a series of vignettes, some of the adaptations that we have made to our community-led development approach, as we have adapted to new contexts, and as the contexts where we work have changed over time.

Following the vignettes, we will analyse our adaptations, identifying aspects of AKF's approach that are core, as well as those that are flexible. We will end by sharing learnings from AKF's country teams, from their experiences of implementing and adapting community-led development.

This chapter emerged through a series of open-ended conversations with AKF country teams that took place in January and February 2023. All the colleagues I spoke with are national staff, many are from the communities in which we work, and most have been engaged in community-led development for over a decade. Draft vignettes were shared back with the country teams to check for accuracy and gather additional details. We are indebted to our wonderful colleagues for these contributions, as well as for the incredible work that they are doing on a day-to-day basis.

Adapting Community-Led Development to New Contexts

Since the early 2000s, AKF has brought our focus on community-led development to several additional countries. The following vignettes describe our experiences in Afghanistan, Egypt, Syria, Portugal, and Mozambique.

Afghanistan – Adapting to an Evolving Political Context

The agencies of the AKDN began working in Afghanistan on a humanitarian basis in 1996, with a transition towards community-led development beginning in 2003. Since then, AKF has mobilised and supported hundreds of Community Development Councils (CDCs) across the north-eastern and central highlands of Afghanistan. A series of World Bank funding mechanisms (the National Solidarity Programme (Beath, Fotini, & Enikolopov, September 2015) and Citizen's Charter (The World Bank, October 20, 2020) resourced the creation of CDCs, elected village decision-making bodies positioned as the last-mile of government in Afghanistan.

The achievements of CDCs during this time were significant and included strengthening social cohesion in diverse communities, generating revolving funds for community health, supporting the food security of the poorest and most marginalised families, and introducing community-based early childhood development centres. As they developed, CDCs were gradually federalised into Cluster Community Development Councils (CCDCs) and District Development Agencies (DDAs) to influence local government policy and planning and support resource flows to the community level.

The situation in Afghanistan changed beyond recognition in August 2021 when the Taliban took control, forming a de facto governing authority and precipitating a funding crisis that has impacted the operations and activities of most international development agencies and non-governmental organisations.

Initially, AKF did not know what would become of the CDCs. We discovered that the groups, many of which had 15 or 20 years of history, continued to be active, meeting and working for the benefit of their communities. The AKF team in Afghanistan revisited our support to CDCs, replacing our approach based on small grant funding with a focus on asset-based community development (ABCD). Our Afghan colleague explained, "ABCD encourages a shift in focus from needs to assets, and supports communities to leverage the resources – the individuals, institutions, associations and physical infrastructure – that have been developed over the past two decades with the help of international donors" (email correspondence, April 27, 2023).

In May 2024, CDCs were officially abolished by the de facto governing authority in favour of a system led by handpicked village headmen (Afghanistan Analysts Network, 2024). Despite this uncertainty, AKF remains confident that the need for village-level collaboration to address immediate problems will continue to bring people together. To this end, AKF is prioritising values over institutions and broadening its focus to engage other community-based groups focused on savings, natural resource management, and regenerative farming.

Aswan Governorate, Egypt – Patiently Evolving Existing Structures

In the Aswan Governorate, Egypt, AKF works through the Om Habibeh Foundation (OHF), which was established in 1991 by His Highness the Aga Khan's late step-grandmother. When OHF began its community-led development activities in the early 2000s, we found that there were already Community Development Associations, known locally as *Gameyas*, in every community.

Gameyas are a form of communal savings group codified in law by Egypt's socialist government in the 1960s. *Gameyas* brought together key decision makers from within the community, and the foundation of trust and respect that they held was an essential ingredient for community mobilisation. However, some of the values and approaches of *Gameyas* did not fully align with OHF's values. Decision-making was controlled by elite male elders, and where women were listed among *Gameya* leadership, they were frequently wives and family members of male elders.

Our OHF colleague explained the dilemma they faced. "The *Gameyas* had trust and respect from the community. If you create a new organisation there is going to be competition. Imagine that you are in a small village, and you are causing a conflict" (interview, January 17, 2023).

Ultimately, OHF decided to harness the trust and legitimacy held by existing *Gameyas* as the foundation of our community-led development work. Since that time, we have worked with them, supporting participatory village planning and making small grants available for community initiatives.

Through our support, OHF has sought to carefully influence the structure and direction of the *Gameyas*. Women were initially engaged in community-led development as volunteers within early childhood development and kitchen gardening activities. Through their volunteer work, several women learnt more about the work of *Gameyas* and demonstrated their potential to existing leadership.

Today, all the groups that OHF works with have begun to incorporate and value the voices of women in their leadership structures. In collaboration with women leaders, OHF has been able to bring gender equality training to *Gameyas*. Following the training, OHF team members work with *Gameya* leadership to brainstorm ways to make women's involvement safer. This has led to some *Gameya* buildings designating gender-segregated toilets and others improving lighting in and around their buildings, all of which enhance women's participation in activities.

There is still a long way to go towards shifting societal norms that limit opportunities for women in Aswan. However, by working alongside and slowly influencing the *Gameyas*, we are beginning to see signs of progress in the roles that women are playing, and conversations around gender-based violence and sexual reproductive health are becoming more acceptable. As our OHF colleague says, "we must be patient, some of these bigger changes take a long time" (interview, January 17, 2023).

Hama Governorate, Syria – Adapting to a Humanitarian Crisis

AKF has operated in Syria since 2003, with a mandate to support social and economic development. However, our support to community-led development began in earnest in 2016 with the formation of 30 Village Committees in a mixture of rural and urban locations.

The backdrop to the formation of these groups was the Syrian Crisis, which began in 2011, and, at that time, there was frequent shelling across Hama Governorate. AKF's Civil Society Programme Manager in Syria remembers that "community members were looking for ways to come together in solidarity at a very difficult time. They were scared" (interview, February 8, 2023).

Village Committees are informal and not legally registered as NGOs. This gives them some freedom to operate in coordination with local authorities, but it also makes it challenging for them to seek resources independent of AKF.

AKF has supported Village Committees in Syria through village development planning and small grants for priority initiatives. In 2017, for example, AKF provided the Jadoua'h Village Committee with a small grant to establish a hall for the village's social, cultural, and economic activities. Following a participatory assessment, the Village Committee developed a proposal for the hall, with support from the AKF team in Syria. The committee was able to mobilise most of the 450 families in the village to contribute volunteer time, cash, and in-kind resources towards the building of the hall. In total, the local community contributed around 30% of the cost of the hall.

Today, the hall is a place where the community meets for social events, various trainings are delivered, and sometimes condolences are shared. The village hall in Jadoua'h has become a model which has been replicated in five other villages. And from our team's perspective, the experience "enhanced civic contribution, collective work, communication, a sense of ownership, belonging, trust, solidarity, helpfulness, and confidence" (email correspondence, April 24, 2023). Between 2020 and 2023, price inflation in Syria exceeded 100 per cent each year, reaching a point where most families are no longer able to afford basic food items. In response to these dire needs, the AKF team in Syria worked with humanitarian donors to deliver food baskets to communities.

AKF worked through Village Committees, both to identify which families had the greatest need of support and to distribute food baskets. However, due to fluctuating humanitarian budgets, the number of food baskets available changed frequently. This tested the trust that AKF had built with communities over the years.

In response, we maintained open and frequent dialogue with Village Committees. We also shifted our focus away from humanitarian aid and towards self-reliance by supporting alternative livelihoods through the formation of farmer cooperatives and provision of vocational training.

Portugal – Supporting Immigrants and Minorities in an Urban Setting

AKF has operated in Portugal since 1983 with a mandate to improve the quality of life of migrant communities in urban contexts through social and economic support. This was our first community-led development initiative in a western European country and, unlike our predominantly rural focus elsewhere, was targeted towards underserved migrant communities living in the Greater Lisbon area.

In Pakistan, India, Central Asia, and East Africa, the Aga Khan's initiatives are well recognised and come with an element of trust and legitimacy. Community members are aware of and have benefitted from Aga Khan schools or health clinics. This was not the case in Portugal, where, in many cases, immigrants were from countries with no AKF presence.

With this in mind, the first priority was to build relationships of trust with community members. To do this, the team spent many days in the communities talking and engaging with people and understanding their lives, challenges, and opportunities. We wanted to begin with an activity that brought people together and showed our commitment to them (see Figure 8.1).

The immediate priority that community members identified was support for an information technology training centre to allow them to access new job opportunities. People attending training at the centre began to share and discuss other ideas for community initiatives. As some of these ideas gained traction, AKF supported them as Community Innovation Projects.

Over time, the Community Innovation Project concept has evolved from informal suggestions into an intentional competition of community-led ideas. AKF works through community groups to solicit and develop ideas, bringing together local stakeholders from government, business, and civil society to review, improve, and recommend initiatives.

Our AKF colleague in Portugal explained, "the competition element is important, because it brings people together around the project ideas, creating a network of groups that can support implementation and build common ground for shared governance" (interview, January 31, 2023).

One Community Innovation Project, which began in 2019 with seed funding of 5000 Euros, has evolved into Bandim. Today, Bandim is a collective of 18 small businesses, bringing together 300 participants (88% women) of 29 different nationalities who have united with the common goal of activating their creativity and developing high-quality handcrafted products for the contemporary market (https://bandim.pt/).

Colleagues credit the success of Bandim and other Community Innovation Projects to AKF's incremental approach, slowly bringing together supporters and funding around initiatives while learning from what works and what doesn't.

AKF community-led development initiatives in Portugal take advantage of reliable funding sources at the municipal level. In Lisbon, for example, the municipality has created neighbourhood funds that communities can draw upon. These funds allow communities to seed pilot initiatives that can build local leadership, foster social cohesion, and attract additional resources over time.

Local government funding can also create power dynamics where groups try to second guess the interests of the government rather than the needs of their community members. However, we seek to limit this through transparent processes that involve diverse stakeholders in reviewing and recommending initiatives.

Northern Mozambique – Adapting to a Fragile and Low Resource Context

At the time AKF began its community-led development programme in Mozambique, in 2000, there was a commitment that decentralisation would bring each district government an annual pool of a minimum of 7 million Meticais (around US$500 at that time) to support community projects. It quickly became clear, however, that in an environment of significant economic uncertainty, communities would need to be largely self-reliant, mobilising their own resources for initiatives.

AKF has facilitated the establishment of a network of over 100 Village Development Organisations in Cabo Delgado and Nampula Provinces in Northern Mozambique. Because of resource scarcity, the focus of these groups has been on maximising existing community resources to meet community needs. AKF's community mobilisers support VDO members to develop Dream Maps[2] (ActionAid International, November 17, 2014, p. 37) of their aspirations and then match aspirations to locally available resources. In Ilha, for example, VDOs have mobilised community volunteers for regular cleaning of the island rainwater drainage channels to prevent floodings and water-borne diseases in communities. Elsewhere, community members have used local materials and expertise to construct meeting halls, started sports teams for youth, carried out regular cholera prevention campaigns, mobilised parents to enrol their girl children in school, and convened singing groups at community events.

Between 2015 and 2019, AKF did not have resources available to support and mentor the VDOs in Cabo Delgado. Our teams did check in with them occasionally and found that several groups were still meeting regularly and sustaining their efforts in our absence. This was particularly true in communities where VDO leadership had remained consistent, and where community members had seen the positive impacts of organising. Where this was the case, it was much easier to reengage with communities once resources did become available again.

Since 2017, Cabo Delgado has been the focus of an insurgency which has led to the displacement of over a million people from their home communities and has resulted in an influx of NGOs and humanitarian aid to the region (ACAPS, July 7, 2023).

As a result of the insurgency, internally displaced people (IDPs) began arriving in AKF-supported villages in huge numbers. And today, more IDPs are housed within existing communities than in humanitarian camps. IDP integration has become a major focus of adaptation for the VDOs. Humanitarian aid provides for the urgent needs of food and shelter. VDOs have taken a longer-term, holistic perspective, wanting to understand who is arriving in their village, what professional skills IDPs bring, how many classrooms would be needed for arriving children, and how to ensure clean water access for all. To foster social cohesion between existing community members and new arrivals, IDPs were integrated into savings groups and sports teams, and included in community rituals such as maintaining the cemetery. As our colleague in Mozambique pointed out, "these are dimensions of inclusion that only residents could bring to the table" (interview, February 1, 2023).

The influx of NGOs to Cabo Delgado has brought with it new operating models and significant new resources. There is a concern that new actors and resources will build dependency and reduce the relevance and resilience of community structures, leaving communities weaker once humanitarian support pulls out. In the communities where AKF works, we are trying to ensure that these resources maximise long-term benefits to communities. VDOs are being supported to play a coordination role that reduces duplication of effort and ensures that resources are directed towards community priorities (see Figure 8.2).

Adaptations over Time in Pakistan and India

Even as AKF has brought its community-led development approach to new contexts over the past 20 years, life has continued to evolve in our original geographies in India and Pakistan. As the political, social, and environmental context has shifted over time, we have continued to adapt our approaches. The following vignettes share examples of adaptation over time in our original geographies (see Figures 8.3 and 8.4).

Pakistan – Adapting to Funding Shifts and Engaging Youth

Adaptation of our approach to community-led development began early in AKRSP's 40-year journey. We realised early on that the Village Organisations we had set up were dominated by men and therefore decided to set up corresponding Women's Organisations in each village. Not only did these groups provide a vehicle for engaging and supporting women, but today Women's Organisations are frequently more active with larger savings pools than their Village Organisation counterparts.

By the mid-1990s, in Gilgit-Baltistan, communities were beginning to organically federate Village Organisations, clustering around initiatives that served multiple villages and coming together to influence local government at the Union Council level. At the same time, AKRSP Pakistan was experiencing shifts in funding that made it harder to direct small grants support to every village in our focal geographies.

These shifts suggested the potential for federations of Village Organisations and Women's Organisations at the Union Council level, and in the early 2000s, AKRSP began supporting the development of Local Support Organisations (LSOs). LSOs included representation from each Village Organisation and Women's Organisation in the Union Council. The LSO mandate was to (i) support villages to identify shared opportunities and challenges, (ii) facilitate collaboration in identifying solutions and external resources, (iii) be accountable for funding and other resources secured across multiple villages, and (iv) represent the interests of villages with the Union Council government.

Today, many LSOs are highly effective, bringing in funding from multiple sources, and enabling Village and Women's Organisations to meet a much wider array of needs than they did initially with AKRSP. These LSOs are often deeply engaged with the communities they support, interacting with them more frequently than AKRSP would ever have been able to. Other LSOs, however, remain dependent completely upon AKRSP and have been unsuccessful in mobilising support from alternate sources. In some cases, these organisations have lost their connection to the communities they exist to serve and are perceived as "just another non-governmental organisation."

LSOs that move towards independence tend to have leaders that are better connected, more highly educated, and more energetic. These are often also LSOs that are based within or close to urban centres and able to access resources and networks that their rural counterparts are not. In fact, our AKRSP colleague says, "some rural organisations are registering offices in urban centres precisely to take advantage of the available resources and networks" (interview, February 21, 2023).

Another trend that arose in the early 2000s related to the dynamics of youth engagement in community-led development. Older community members who had participated in Village and Women's Organisations since their inception remained highly committed but these groups were not attracting interest and engagement from the emerging youth population.

We are finding limitations to engaging young people in long-term, place-based community-led development. Younger people engage with the world differently than older generations. They are much more mobile, wanting to support their communities but rarely being able to join in-person meetings. They also use information technology to communicate and mobilise people and resources in different ways than previous generations.

Two of the more promising approaches have been the creation of Adolescent Friendly Spaces and Youth Communication Forums that are designed by young people to meet their own needs as they emerge as active citizens.

Adolescent Friendly Spaces (AFSs) are physical spaces within community halls designed by and for teenagers. They are places where young people come together with mentors outside of an academic environment to explore their aspirations for themselves and society. They are also inclusive spaces which welcome out of school and disabled adolescents. AKRSP has created over 250 AFSs in villages across Gilgit-Baltistan and Chitral.

Youth Communication Forums (YCFs) bring older youth together to discuss, promote, and act on priorities. Members of the YCF in Hunza District arranged a Youth Convention in the fall of 2022, in which they presented a charter of 16 requests to local government departments. Twelve of the 16 requests were accepted by government, including requests for digital skills training, dedicated buses for female students, and psychosocial support for youth. Where requests were not prioritised by government, YCF members are taking action together with local CSOs to create youth societies and clubs at village level and initiate a hostel for female students.

India – Promoting Gender Inclusion in Community Institutions and Local Government Systems

During the early 2000s in India, AKRSP observed civil society organisations experimenting with the creation of Women's Federations. The women's organisations that AKRSP had been working with for the previous 15 years were doing important work, but on a small and isolated scale at the village level. By federating these groups at the district level, they could tap into the full potential of women's ideas and leadership.

Today, some of the Women's Federations that AKRSP convened include thousands of women. They are influencing a wide range of issues, including land rights, water rights, financial literacy, organic farming, and women's rights. Because of their scale, Women's Federations are able to capture the attention of other stakeholders in government and the banking sector, which would not have been possible had these groups remained at the village level.

Take the Balwadi Women's Federation in Maharashtra, whose president is a landless woman named Sumli Didi. In her role, Sumli has supported 1200 women to access a government backyard poultry scheme, enhanced access to financial products for income-generating activities, created open spaces for villages to discuss issues related to gender equality, and promoted vaccination against Covid-19.

Simultaneously, over the past two decades in India, local self-government (Panchayat Raj) institutions have started playing a key role in community development. In 2010, AKRSP started collaborating directly with village Panchayats. In some communities, this has meant linking Village Organisations to the Panchayat for collaborative action. In other communities, this has meant disbanding Village Organisations and incorporating their responsibilities into the mandate of the village Panchayat.

Working through village Panchayat structures has enabled AKRSP India to connect community members to the government services and benefits they are entitled to. It also ensures government buy-in and support for a wide range of community initiatives. To ensure the active participation of women in these local self-government institutions, AKF and AKRSP invest in building the capacity of elected women representatives to voice the needs and priorities of women in the Panchayat planning and budgeting processes. These efforts require significant interventions in building the understanding of elected women representatives on their roles and responsibilities and in engaging with women's groups to ensure that women's voices are heard within the institutions of local self-government.

Globally – The Emerging Challenge of Climate Resilience

The geographies in which AKF operates are among the most vulnerable to climate change. This includes the mountain areas of Afghanistan, Pakistan, and Central Asia, and coastal areas of India and Eastern Africa. These communities are experiencing more frequent catastrophic landslides, floods, and changing weather patterns.

AKF has long worked through community groups to support the management of watersheds, forests, and pastureland. Today, we are building upon this work to incorporate climate analysis into the community planning process and to incorporate climate change adaptation and mitigation approaches into activities. For example, over 400 communities have been supported to plant and manage micro forests that play an important role in environmental restoration and carbon sequestration as well as provide communities with plants for food, animal feed, and medicines.

Analysing Our Adaptations

Speaking with colleagues from around the world, it was clear that several features of AKF's approach to community-led development vary with context.

First, we work with appropriate and flexible institutional designs. In some contexts, gender equality is advanced by working through separate men's and women's groups, while in others, it is advanced by bringing men and women together. In many places, we find active and trusted civil society organisations already in place, while in others, we need to mobilise communities and nurture organisations from scratch. In certain political contexts, community-led development organisations must be formalised and registered with authorities, while in others, it is appropriate for organisations to remain informal and unregistered. And, in some contexts, there is a strong rationale for the formal federation of community organisations, while in others, interaction among community groups might remain informal.

Second, we experiment with different community-led methods and approaches. Historically, we drew heavily from participatory rural appraisal (Narayanasamy,

2009), including village transect walks and dream mapping, while today we are integrating elements of human centred design,[3] including empathy interviewing and rapid prototyping. In some countries, we have embedded community-based savings groups into community organisations to support sustainable engagement. While elsewhere, we separate savings components so as not to burden savings groups with multiple complex mandates. Information and communication technology has advanced beyond recognition since we began our community-led development work. And today, there are opportunities to connect people via messaging applications, organise data in management information systems, share successes on social media, and raise resources through crowdfunding applications. Opportunities for technology use vary significantly across our operating contexts, from urban Lisbon where access is universal to remote communities in Afghanistan, which remain off the grid.

Third, our support teams are structured differently in different contexts. In some geographies, our community support officers are staff of AKF. In others, they are staff of a local partner organisation or even community volunteers who are paid a stipend. In some contexts, it is culturally appropriate for female staff to support Women's Organisations and male staff to support Men's Organisations. While, in others, anyone can cross gender lines to support any organisation. In some contexts, we always work directly with local communities. In others, we engage local NGOs to play a role in supporting communities.

However, there are also features of our approach that transcend context and apply across time and geography.

We always begin by spending time in communities, listening to the needs, frustrations, and aspirations of diverse community members. By actively listening to everybody in the community, we build rapport and a foundation of trust.

We mobilise communities into formal and informal groups with inclusive participation and democratically determined leadership. Together with those groups, we facilitate processes that support communities to surface their needs and identify their priorities for action.

We support communities to mobilise resources in support of their goals. The first place that we look for resources is within the communities themselves. Even if communities don't have their own financial resources, they often have in-kind resources and volunteer time that they can bring. Only once we have exhausted internal options do we look externally for support.

Communities take leadership of the process, prioritising needs, identifying and implementing solutions, contributing financial, in-kind, and volunteer resources, monitoring change, and creating the conditions for sustainability. We use our convening power to link communities to relevant partners in government, civil society, and private sector, to support access to financial and technical resources.

Throughout the process, we look for ways to step back and put the community at the centre of their own development. Our intention is to provide long-term support and mentorship to groups while avoiding dependency.

Beyond approaches, AKF's community-led development is founded upon a set of core values that transcend time and geography and precede conversations around structures and approaches:

- Mutual respect: We value communities and treat them with transparency and respect. We are accountable to them, and they are accountable to us.
- Equity and pluralism: We believe that everybody in the community has something to contribute, especially women, youth, and vulnerable people, who have been traditionally excluded. The best results are achieved when we recognise and value the ways in which we are different and seek to meet the needs of all.
- Optimism: We believe in the potential of communities. We believe that most change comes from within. And we believe that, with the right conditions and support, all communities have the potential to flourish.
- Proximity: Our community organisers are from the communities in which we are working. They know the issues, speak the language, spend time there, and are trusted.
- Long-termism: We take a long-term approach to community development. In our experience, it takes five to ten years before an institution is fully embedded within a community.
- Place-based: We are focused on all the people, issues, and opportunities in the community, not just on a single theme or challenge.

We believe that it is this focus on core values that has enabled AKF to adapt our work in community-led development to diverse and changing contexts. Our long-term focus in specific geographies means that we are less tied to specific outcomes, funding streams, and short-term results. Our proximity to communities and the mutual respect that we build enable us to keep our finger on the pulse of what is changing and what really matters to people. Our commitment to equity and pluralism builds a broad base for community support. And our optimistic outlook means that we are always seeking opportunities for communities, regardless of the challenges in any given context.

Although we have had much success, we do not always get it right, and the communities that we work with do not consistently thrive. But we are always there alongside them, working together to find solutions to common problems in the search for a better quality of life. Moreover, we have seen that investments in community mobilisation are never lost in their entirety. Community groups may lie dormant for several years, before new opportunities arise to harness our initial investment in social capital. We have witnessed old institutions taking on new forms, and once dormant institutions experience a resurgence as opportunities and circumstances shift.

Learning from Our Teams

We asked our teams what advice they would give to someone looking to begin a new community-led development initiative. Here's what they had to say:

1. Before you do anything else, spend time in the community, doing things together with community members. Listen to the issues that are preoccupying people. Come to understand local norms and customs. In this way, you will begin to gain trust and respect. (Egypt)
2. Build a support team from the talent, creativity, and expertise that exists locally, rather than bringing in external expertise. (Portugal)
3. Engage with the full diversity of the community, women, men, the youth, the elderly, the differently abled, religious, and ethnic minorities. Work with them to understand the community from every possible angle. (India)
4. Ensure you understand the legal context. Do the organisations you are working with need to be registered? Might registration of community organisations lead to their co-optation? (Egypt)
5. Maintain good relations with local government. Seek local government agreement before setting up community led development organisations, keep them informed of progress, and find ways to develop mutually supportive and respectful relations between community institutions and local government. (Mozambique)
6. Think hard before creating and formalising a new organisation. Are there already trusted local organisations within the community? If no organisation currently exists, is a formal and permanent structure necessary to mobilise community members? (Pakistan)
7. Where you do create or support an institution, avoid that organisation being perceived as belonging to you. Don't put your logo on their banners or t-shirts. Help them create their own logo instead. Support them by creating connections to other stakeholders that might support or work alongside them. (Mozambique)
8. At every stage, empowering processes are more important than efficient processes. Anything that you do, the community will not own, and if the community does not own something, they will not sustain it. (India)
9. Be realistic. Community-led development is a powerful and inclusive approach, but it has constant challenges, and change is frequently slow. (Syria)
10. Remember people live complex and holistic lives. Even if your organisation comes into community-led development with a particular agenda around livelihoods, food security, or climate resilience, always create opportunities for community interests to emerge. (Portugal)

FIGURE 8.1 A community meeting in Bihar, India. Credit: Aga Khan Foundation.

FIGURE 8.2 Village Development Organisation members engage in a dream mapping activity in Cabo Delgado, Mozambique. Credit: Aga Khan Foundation/ Lucas Moura.

FIGURE 8.3 Youth participate in a life skills session organised by the Aga Khan Youth and Sports Board in Chitral, Pakistan. Credit: Aga Khan Foundation.

FIGURE 8.4 A community festival in Serra das Minas, Portugal. Credit: Aga Khan Foundation Portugal/Rui Gouveia.

Notes

1 AKDN (September 6, 2004) *Annual Conference of German Ambassadors. Speech by His Highness the Aga Khan*. AKDN. https://the.akdn/en/resources-media/resources/speeches/annual-conference-german-ambassadors
2 A Dream Map is a map of the village onto which community members draw images that describe their hopes for the future. Dream Mapping is an approach to building consensus around community goals and actions.
3 IDEO.org. (2015) *The Field Guide to Human-Centered Design*. IDEO.org. Available for free download at https://www.designkit.org/resources/1.html.

References

ACAPS. (July 7, 2023). *Thematic Report. Mozambique: Impact of the Five-Year Conflict in Cabo Delgado*. www.acaps.org/fileadmin/Data_Product/Main_media/20230707_ACAPS_Thematic_report_Mozambique_impact_of_the_five-year_conflict_in_Cabo_Delgado.pdf

ActionAid International. (November 17, 2014). *Village Book Training Manual: Community Led and Planning Process*. ActionAid International. https://actionaid.org/publications/2014/village-book-training-manual-community-led-and-planning-process#:~:text=The%20Village%20Book%20provides%20micro,according%20to%20people's%20expressed%20needs

Afghanistan Analysts Network. (June 2024) *The Fate of Village Councils: The Emirate's effort to institute hegemony over rural Afghanistan*. Afghanistan Analysts Network.

Beath, A., Fotini, C., & Enikolopov, R. (September 2015). *The National Solidarity Program: Assessing the Effects of Community-Driven Development in Afghanistan. Policy Research Working Paper 7415*. World Bank Group. East Asia and the Pacific Region. https://documents1.worldbank.org/curated/en/671121468190777792/pdf/WPS7415.pdf.

Narayanasamy, N. (2009). *Participatory Rural Appraisal: Principles, Methods and Application*. 10.4135/9788132108382

OED (Operations Evaluation Department). (1987). *AKRSP: Interim Evaluation. A World Bank Operations Evaluation Study*. Washington, DC: World Bank.

OED (Operations Evaluation Department). (1990). *The Aga Khan Rural Support Program in Pakistan: A Second Interim Evaluation. A World Bank Operations Evaluation Study*. Washington, D.C.: World Bank.

OED (Operations Evaluation Department). (1996). *The Aga Khan Rural Support Program. A Third Evaluation. A World Bank Operations Evaluation Study*. Washington, DC: World Bank.

OED (Operations Evaluation Department). (2002). *The Next Ascent: An Evaluation of the Aga Khan Rural Support Program, Pakistan. A World Bank Operations Evaluation Study*. Washington, DC: World Bank. https://documents.worldbank.org/en/publication/documents-reports/documentdetail/147641468759321609/the-next-ascent-an-evaluation-of-the-aga-khan-rural-support-program-pakistan

OED (Operations Evaluation Department). (Summer 2002). *Précis. The Next Ascent: An Evaluation of the Aga Khan Rural Support Program*. Washington, DC: World Bank.

https://ieg.worldbankgroup.org/sites/default/files/Data/reports/precis_226_aga_khan.pdf

The World Bank. (October 20, 2020). *Results Briefs: Afghanistan's Citizens' Charter Program: Empowering Communities for Better Services*. www.worldbank.org/en/results/2020/10/20/afghanistans-citizens-charter-program-empowering-communities-for-better-services

PART III

Participation, Inclusion and Voice/Local Knowledge and Resources

Elene Cloete and Gunjan Veda

This section includes three chapters that capture, in diverse ways, how the principles of participation, inclusion, and voice and local knowledge and resources manifest in the community-led development context. Representing three diverse locations, Guatemala, South Africa, and India, these chapters also illustrate how these principles reinforce each other. This should come as no surprise, considering how participatory development and local knowledge emerged almost in tandem as alternatives to mainstream development in the 1970s (Sillitoe and Marzano 2009; Smith 2011).

What Is Participation?

Participation is a "development orthodoxy" (Cornwall 2003). Viewed as both an ideology and a methodology that incorporates local perspectives into development (Sillitoe and Marzano 2009), participation is prominent in the work and discourse of a range of institutions and organisations, from radical NGOs to large-scale multilateral agencies (Cornwall 2008). It can be a means to an end but also an end in itself (Hayward et al. 2004). The former pertains to participation as a development tool, involving people in activities such as decision-making processes, project implementation, and overall management (Trivelli and Morel 2021). Participation as the end goal is more focused on personal and social development. The latter include different levels of participation, and they are often presented in a linear or hierarchical way (see, for example, Arnstein 1969, Pretty 1995, and White 1996).[1] Here, participation takes on various types, ranging from non-participation to full participation, with the latter also linked to goals of transformation and empowerment (Cornwall 2003).

DOI: 10.4324/9781003377917-12

Whether as a means, or an end in itself, participation was not a priority for the development sector in the immediate post-World War period. Top-down decision-making, technocratic and modernisation ideologies were the norm. In the 1970s, "popular participation" emerged (Cornwall 2000). It was informed by populist movements from the 1960s to 1970s, the perceived failure of top-down development models, and subsequent high-level commitments towards the "basic needs" of people, with participation seen as one of such needs (Sillitoe and Marzano 2009; Biggs 2008; Cornwall 2000). And for the next two decades, more participatory approaches started to emerge across different institutions, contexts and practices (Hickey and Mohan 2004; Cornwall and Scoones 2022). In the late 1990s, large-scale multilateral agencies, including the World Bank, started to include participatory methods in funding requirements. Participation became mainstream and has remained mainstream ever since. A recent example is the inclusion of participatory decision-making in the 2030 Agenda for Sustainable Development (Jiménez et al. 2019).

Not all references or use of participation are, however, equal, particularly when considering quality, meaning, and impact. When it comes to quality, some early concerns were linked to large-scale funders, such as the World Bank, and intentions of scale (Cornwall and Scoones 2022). Participatory development advocates cautioned these funders to "go slow," but driven by large-scale objectives, timelines and other funder requirements, going slow was not always an option (Cornwall and Scoones 2022). Participation in these cases can then easily become tokenistic, taking on the form of consultations with local communities or implementing organisations providing information on planned activities.

Scholars and practitioners were also noticing participatory approaches' limiting engagement with structural issues and political contexts, particularly within the early days of formalised participatory practices (Cooke and Kothari 2001; Sillitoe and Marzano 2009; Cornwall 2008). Additionally, as participation emerged increasingly more as discourse and method, so did an awareness of the concept's multiple and often conflicting meanings. Such meanings have come to include a full range – "window-dressing," outsider-directed and manipulated interaction, self-mobilisation, genuine collaboration and collegiate interaction (Sillitoe and Marzano 2009, citing Chambers 1997). These sentiments are unfortunate, considering the promise participation holds for "creating spaces for the less vocal and powerful to exercise voice and gain more choices" (Cornwall 2003). Participation spaces should therefore be inclusive, and practitioners should be diligent in ensuring such spaces are inclusive and enabling. But what do such spaces look like?

The chapters of Behal and Metz represent case studies of participation from two geographically diverse community-led contexts. In both cases and captured through ethnographic methods, the authors' chapters focus on indigenous communities that not only deal with violent colonial pasts but also with persistent systemic political, social and economic inequalities. Both chapters also capture the dynamic and ever-changing nature of participation through first-person experiences. In combination,

Behal and Metz's chapters include descriptions of who participates, why they participate and how they participate. Their chapters also point to how practitioners and their organisations can align with and adjust to these elements of participation, enabling inclusive invited spaces for participation. Considering both these chapters, three themes are especially relevant to community-led development practice. If we are serious about transforming power relations, we need to understand who is participating and who is not (inclusion), understand why some people are not participating, and to what extent people have a voice when participating.

Who Participates?

Critique, especially during the late 1990s and early 2000s, raised concerns about how participatory practices often overlook power hierarchies within communities (Cooke and Kothari 2001). Power structures exclude, dominate and discriminate. It can include hereditary and political power, some of which are still drawing on colonial governing systems, to socio-cultural power asymmetries associated with gender, ethnic, or religious expectations. These power structures also intersect to create "further exclusions within as well as between groups" (Bharadwaj et al. 2021, 3). The, by now seminal ethnographies of Mosse (2005) and Ferguson (1994) draw out the impact of unrecognised power asymmetries on development. The warning is that if practitioners and their organisations do not find ways to deal with and potentially diffuse such power differences, elite capture and perpetual power asymmetries are inevitable. We see examples of these power hierarchies active within Behal and Metz's chapters. Both chapters describe how indigenous people, their opinions and voices, are typically excluded from decision-making processes. Behal draws further attention to women within Naga society.

If community-led development practitioners are committed to shifting the power and localising ownership, then they have to pay close attention to local power structures and devise ways of negating their exclusionary impact. If not, programmes with goals of empowerment and greater representative civil and civic engagement will undoubtedly fail. To avoid this, organisations and their practitioners have to design and facilitate what Cornwall (2008) calls "invited spaces of participation." In designing these spaces, practitioners must first gain an expansive understanding of a particular place's cultural and political landscapes, and second, develop trusting relationships with all groups within a particular community (Mansuri and Rao 2013; Mubita 2017; Bell and Reed 2022). We see this in the chapters of Metz and Behal where they describe how participant observation, ongoing integration and perpetual returns to Nagaland and eastern Guatemala exposed them to different power dynamics and enabled trusting relationships. Within community-led development these relationships and the insights they unveil are crucial. They provide practitioners with a well-informed understanding of the power structures so that they can locate different sub-groups and recognise how they are embedded in and impacted by power hierarchies (Cameron et al. 2016).

One group that has received much attention as far as participation and inclusion in development is concerned is women,[2] with participation in community activities in India being no exception (Cornwall 2003; Kanji 2004; Batliwala and Dhanraj 2007). For example, the work of Agarwal (2001) describes how women are excluded from community forestry but navigate such exclusion through bargaining with the state, their community, and family. With a focus on Nagaland in particular, Behal's chapter adds to this scholarship, showing how women are subjected to deeply entrenched gender norms that automatically limits or even discredits their participation in civil and civic activities. Bringing women into participatory activities, finding ways to elevate their voices and cultivating moments of engagement for them is therefore a priority of many international and national organisations, and the North East Network (NEN), featured in Behal's chapter, is one such organisation.

But merely having women included in participatory activities does not fully qualify as inclusion. Because, as Cornwall (2000) reminds us, women are not a homogenous group. By treating them as such, we obscure the differences among women and their diverse livelihood options. Moreover, among women, as indigenous knowledge scholars would argue, resides a diverse set of local knowledge. Thus, seeing women as a single group with a single objective and a single set of knowledge might be more exclusionary than inclusionary.

And yet, inclusion is also an iterative process that requires intentionally seeking the most invisibilised within communities. It necessitates a critical process of self-reflection among different sub-groups, particularly the most powerful ones in a community. And also awareness that power shifts are possible, potentially moving some people onto the periphery. It requires time and trust. Therefore, often practitioners and organisations seeking to develop the trust that is essential for participatory approaches start with community leaders as demonstrated in Behal and Metz's chapters. Over a period of time, they channelise this trust to gradually chip away at hegemonic structures. In the case of NEN, it took years to bring women into governance structures.

But What about Non-Participation?

People often do not participate, regardless of time spent or trust built. But such non-participation is not necessarily linked to social exclusion (Entigar 2021, Hayward et al. 2004). In fact, Switzer (2020) advises against seeing non-participation in binary terms, where non-participation is the same as disengagement, deviant of or acting outside their community's best interest. Instead, we should see non-participation as a heuristic tool to better understand why people are not participating, including the costs and constraints of participating. This might even require reflection on the part of the practitioner and implementing organisation to understand how local communities not only view them as individuals and organisations but also what they represent. As Metz's chapter shows, because of years of development "failures" and broken promises, indigenous groups in eastern Guatemala are reluctant to engage in new initiatives. Their non-participation is, therefore, more a form of self-protection. It deters them from having to invest their time and resources into something that has already been a time, resources, and also, emotional drain.

Voice

The concepts of participation and inclusion are intrinsically linked with voice. Often participation is viewed as an exercise to unearth the "voices of the poor" (Goetz and Jenkins 2002). But, as Tacchi (2016) holds, voice is more than that. For the most historically marginalised, for example, invisibility and lack of formal listening can be a necessary condition for survival. Thus, "having a voice, in a way that matters, requires attention to both processes of voice and the valuing of voice" (p.117), including how it is performed and reflecting on how we think of and value voice. Additionally, voice gains additional meaning if it results in change. It is therefore also important that organisations and practitioners have practices in place that can effectively include the opinions, thoughts and ideas shared by people who use their voice, regardless of how they choose to practise their voice. Equally so, the invited participatory spaces in which voice becomes activated must be a safe space so that the marginalised can share their knowledge in a place of respect, without fear of any repercussions.

Voice becomes audible through participation. Behal's chapter traces the journey of women in a patriarchal community from types of participation that, according to Pretty (1995), moves from passive participation (where they participate because they are asked to) to interactive, even self-mobilisation participation (where they participate because they wish to). Behal's chapter shows how women started to recognise that their voice matters, their ideas and knowledge will be valued and therefore invest time and effort into exercising their voice.

Local Knowledge and Resources

Misperceptions and biases inform people's understanding of local resources and knowledge, particularly when it comes to poverty and community development. For example, there is a common misperception that people facing poverty-related challenges do not have any resources. This perception needs checking. While they might experience poverty brought on by political and financial restraints, resulting in little to no resources such as land, clean water or housing, people living in poverty still have access to different forms of cultural, social and emotional resources. Not recognising these and people's resourcefulness in deploying their own resources, Cammarota (2011) argues, "exonerates social or economic structures from any culpability in reproducing poverty and oppression generation after generation."

When it comes to knowledge, public perceptions often reflect a bias towards Western-based and scientific knowledge as the more legitimate and formal kind of knowledge. When compared to "legitimate knowledge," other ways of knowing that are based on local and regional community expression are subjugated and pushed to the side as less valid and trustworthy (Chouinard 2013). The distinction between scientific knowledge and other forms of knowing, as Sillitoe (2006, 3) remarks considering the work of Agrawal (1995), "has an unpleasant political edge, with connotations of superiority and inferiority." Therefore, knowledge's value, quality and usefulness are often measured against Western-based and scientific forms of knowledge, perceived as more rigorous, legitimate and impactful.

These perceptions do not inform community-led interventions. On the contrary, community-led and owned activities seek out ways to (re)discover and bring attention to local resources and knowledge, raising awareness of their value and their possible contribution towards change. And such awareness-raising does not only extend to community members, who, because of colonised mindsets, see their resources as less valuable than external ones, but also to programme practitioners and implementing organisations themselves (Matthews 2019).

Similarly, community-led development advocates denounce practices that pit knowledge systems against each other, in most cases prioritising Western-based and scientific knowledge over other forms of knowledge. Instead, they encourage the coexistence, integration and usage of multiple knowledge systems that can yield positive change. We see examples of such integration, with positive results, within agriculture, disaster risk management and climate change resilience (Khalil et al. 2016; Limpo et al. 2022; Magni 2017). Such integration also happened in Nagaland, as Behal's chapter describes, when local women leaders started to participate in exchange visits with other farmers, learned about millet and then also joined the Millet Network of India. By doing so, NEN's women leaders recognised the value of this ancient grain, then started to create awareness of the grain among local farmers and through farmer-to-farmer knowledge sharing, more people started to plant millet. As an ancient grain with deep origins in India (Veerabadhran et al. 2023), millet has seen a recent revival, not only because of its high nutritional value but also climate-resilient nature. These benefits now extend to Nagaland, because of NEN's investment in ancient agricultural practices and varieties, their curiosity on how to improve such production and their facilitation of peer-learning.

In addition to the recognition, usage and co-sharing of knowledge on millet, the NEN example exemplifies two more manifestations of local resources: Social capital and local leadership. It is because of active connecting, networking and thus enabling social capital that NEN's women leaders gained insights into resources they could then share back to their communities. But none of that would have been possible without active and engaged leadership. Both social capital and leadership are examples of intangible, human resources or "soft infrastructure" that can contribute to the strengthening of community agency and cohesion (Barraket et al. 2019).

The chapter by Nel further illustrates how local resources and knowledge[3] functions within community contexts. Nel draws from asset-based community development (ABCD) to describe how communities across both urban and rural South Africa are participating in different activities that make visible what they have. Drawing from positive psychology and positive enquiry traditions, ABCD "starts with what the people have" and builds on their resources rather than placing emphasis on that which they do not have and where their deficiencies are (Mathie et al. 2017). The process of identifying local resources rather than problems, Mathie et al. (2017) argue, prompts a change in subjectivity among participants. They begin to see themselves not as powerless with nothing to give but instead as subjects able to act with others on their shared challenges. They experience "a shift in their subject position – from done to, to doer" (p.5). Nel describes how this shift happened for women from the rural Eastern Cape province.

The Challenges

Local resources and knowledge are not magic bullets to solve development challenges. Equally so, we should guard against romanticising local resources and local knowledge as perfect alternatives. Local knowledge is not homogeneous, meaning multiple forms of knowledge can coexist in a particular social setting. And with such a multitude comes the potential of power asymmetries, with the knowledge of some groups regarded as better than others. Examples can include the knowledge of women versus men, or youth versus adults. A further challenge comes with local knowledge's dynamic and procedural quality. It is ever-evolving which means establishing consensus among local communities on meanings, practices and histories might be challenging (Sillitoe 2006; Sillitoe and Marzano 2009). Potential responses to these challenges reside with authentic and meaningful participation, as discussed earlier, seeing knowledge production as iterative and from a holistic rather than individual perspective, and by intentionally breaking down the misleading science versus knowledge distinction (Sillitoe and Marzano 2009). If we facilitate inclusive participation, mindful of who is included and who is not, whose voices are heard and whose not, then tensions around whose knowledge gets included and who's not can be diffused. The same can be said about whose knowledge counts, making explicit that knowledge systems can complement or even reinforce each other.

Local resources are not infinite. When people are placed under more than usual pressure, because of environmental, political or other constraints and for an extended time, they eventually exhaust their intangible resources, particularly their social ties and networks. Perhaps to the point of no recovery. Therefore, local resources used and deployed within development initiatives should come with the necessary protection and accountability to safeguard against exploitation.

Notes

1 For a detailed discussion on participation typologies, see Cornwall (2008) and Fursova (2020).
2 Women in development discourse, including mainstreaming of women as development priority, have seen several changes, adjustments and corresponding debates. For more on these conversations, see Moghadam et al. (2011).
3 Local knowledge is often used interchangeably with indigenous knowledge. Both are place-based, contextual and experiential, with information often shared through social learning (Khalil et al. 2016). But whereas local knowledge can be linked to any community's relationship with its environment and social contexts, indigenous knowledge is connected with communities that have long-term cultural ties with a particular place and its natural environment (Agrawal 1995). For the purpose of this volume, we use local knowledge to include indigenous knowledge.

References

Agrawal, Arun. 1995. "Dismantling the divide between indigenous and scientific knowledge." *Development and Change* 26, no. 3: 413–439.
Arnstein, Sherry. 1969. "A ladder of citizen participation." *AIP Journal* 35, no. 4: 216–214.
Barraket, Jo, Robyn Eversole, Belinda Luke, and Sharine Barth. 2019. "Resourcefulness of locally-oriented social enterprises: Implications for rural community development." *Journal of Rural Studies* 70: 188–197.
Bharadwaj, Sowmyaa, Jo Howard, and Pradeep Narayanan. 2021. "Using participatory action research methodologies for engaging and researching with religious minorities in contexts of intersecting inequalities." *CREID Working Paper*, Volume 2021, number 5.
Batliwala, Srilatha, and Deepa Dhanraj. 2007. "Gender myths that instrumentalize women: A view from the Indian front line." *Feminisms in development: Contradictions, contestations and challenges* 35, no.. 4: 11–18.
Bell, Karen, and Mark Reed. 2022. "The tree of participation: A new model for inclusive decision-making." *Community Development Journal* 57, no. 4: 595–614.
Biggs, Stephen. 2008. "The lost 1990s? Personal reflections on a history of participatory technology development." *Development in Practice* 18, no. 45: 489–505. doi:10.1080/09614520802181228
Cameron, Jenny, Paul Hodge, Amanda Howard, and Graeme Stuart. 2016. "Navigating dilemmas of community development: Practitioner reflections on working with Aboriginal communities." *Community Development* 47, no. 4: 546–561.
Cammarota, Julio. 2011. "Blindsided by the avatar: White saviors and allies out of Hollywood and in education." *Review of Education, Pedagogy, and Cultural Studies* 33, no. 3: 242–259.
Chouinard, Jill Anne. 2013. "The case for participatory evaluation in an era of accountability." *American Journal of Evaluation* 34, no. 2: 237–253.
Cooke, Bill, and Uma Kothari, eds. 2001. *Participation: The new tyranny?*. Zed Books.
Cornwall, Andrea. 2008. "Unpacking 'Participation': Models, meanings and practices." *Community Development Journal* 43, no. 3: 269–283.
Cornwall, Andrea. 2003. "Whose voices? Whose choices? Reflections on gender and participatory development." *World Development* 31, no. 8: 1325–1342.
Cornwall, Andrea. 2000. *Beneficiary, consumer, citizen*. Swedish International Development Cooperation Agency.

Cornwall, Andrea, and Ian Scoones. 2022. *Revolutionizing development: Reflections on the work of Robert Chambers*. Taylor & Francis.

Entigar, Katherine E. 2021. "To choose not to be included: Critical perspectives on practices of inclusion with adult immigrant students." *International Review of Education* 67, no. 6: 833–849.

Ferguson, James. 1994. *The anti-politics machine:" development," depoliticization, and bureaucratic power in Lesotho*. University of Minnesota Press.

Fursova, Julia. 2020. "Stepping up the ladder: Reflecting on the role of non-profit organisations in supporting community participation." *Research handbook on community development*. Edward Elgar Publishing, 76–92.

Goetz, Anne Marie, and Rob Jenkins. 2002. *Voice, accountability and human development: The emergence of a new agenda*. No. HDOCPA-2002-04. Human Development Report Office (HDRO), United Nations Development Programme (UNDP).

Hayward, Chris, Lyn Simpson, and Leanne Wood. 2004. "Still left out in the cold: Problematising participatory research and development." *Sociologia Ruralis* 44, no. 1: 95–108.

Hickey, Samuel and Giles Mohan. 2004. *Participation: from tyranny to transformation: exploring new approaches to participation in development*. Zed Books.

Jiménez, Alejandro, Hélène LeDeunff, Ricard Giné, Johanna Sjödin, Ryan Cronk, Sofia Murad, Marina Takane, and Jamie Bartram. 2019. "The enabling environment for participation in water and sanitation: A conceptual framework." *Water* 11, no. 2: 308.

Khalil, Momtaj Bintay, Brent C. Jacobs, and Natasha Kuruppu. 2016. "Grassroots technologies and community trust in climate change adaptation: Learning from coastal settlements of Bangladesh." In Leal Filho, W. (ed.). *Innovation in climate change adaptation: Climate change management* (pp. 297–311). Springer, Cham. https://doi.org/10.1007/978-3-319-25814-0_21

Kanji, Nazneen. 2004. "Reflections on gender and participatory development." *Participatory learning and action: Critical reflections, future directions*. International Institute for Environment and Development, 53–62.

Limpo, Syahrul Yasin, Imam Mujahidin Fahmid, Abdul Fattah, Abdul Wahid Rauf, Elza Surmaini, Muslimin, Saptana, Haris Syahbuddin, and Kuntoro Boga Andri. 2022. "Integrating Indigenous and scientific knowledge for decision making of rice farming in South Sulawesi, Indonesia." *Sustainability* 14, no. 5: 2952.

Magni, Giorgia. 2017. "Indigenous knowledge and implications for the sustainable development agenda." *European Journal of Education* 52, no. 4: 437–447.

Matthews, Sally. 2019. "Colonised minds? Post-development theory and the desirability of development in Africa." In *The Development Dictionary@ 25*, Routledge, pp. 104–117. www.taylorfrancis.com/chapters/edit/10.4324/9780429451386-8/colonised-minds-post-development-theory-desirability-development-africa-sally-matthews

Moghadam, Valentine, Chandra Talpade Mohanty, Sarah White, Diana L. Wolf, Deepa Shankaran, Lourdes Beneria, Aysan Sev'er et al. 2011. *The women, gender and development reader*. Bloomsbury Publishing.

Mosse, David. 2005. *Cultivating development: An ethnography of aid policy and practice*. Pluto Press.

Pretty, Jules N. 1995. "Participatory learning for sustainable agriculture." *World Development* 23, no. 8: 1247–1263.

Mubita, Aurick, Mundia Libati, and Munalula Mulonda. 2017. "The importance and limitations of participation in development projects and programmes." *European Scientific Journal* 13, no. 5: 238–251.

Mansuri, Ghazala, and Vijayendra Rao. 2013. "Can participation be induced? Some evidence from developing countries." *Critical Review of International Social and Political Philosophy* 16, no. 2: 284–304.

Sillitoe, Paul, and Mariella Marzano. 2009. "Future of indigenous knowledge research in development." *Futures* 41, no. 1: 13–23.

Sillitoe, Paul. 2006. "Indigenous knowledge in development." *Anthropology in Action* 13, no. 3: 1–12.

Smith, Thomas Aneurin. 2011. "Local knowledge in development (geography)." *Geography Compass* 5, no. 8: 595–609.

Switzer, Sarah. 2020. ""People give and take a lot in order to participate in things:" Youth talk back–making a case for non-participation." *Curriculum Inquiry* 50, no. 2: 168–193.

Tacchi, Jo. 2016. "When and how does voice matter? And how do we know?" In Tufte, Thomas and Oscar Hemer (eds). Voice & Matter: Communication, development and the cultural return. Goteborg: Nordicom.

Trivelli, Carolina, and Jorge Morel. 2021. "Rural youth inclusion, empowerment, and participation." *The Journal of Development Studies* 57, no. 4: 635–649.

Veerabadhran, Vijayalakshmi, Hema Raju Palakuru, Goli Penchala Pratap, Bommidi Rajeshwari, Goli Penchala Prasad, Narayanam Srikanth, and Rabinarayan Acharya. "A critical review of the history and practices of millets in India." *Journal of Drug Research in Ayurvedic Sciences* 8, no. Suppl 1 (2023): S18–S25.

White, Sarah C. 1996. "Depoliticising development: The uses and abuses of participation." *Development in Practice*, 6, no. 1, 6–15.

9

THE CHRONICLES OF CHIZAMI

How Women from a Small Naga Village Built the Road to Resilience

Monisha Behal

The Road to Chizami

The year was 1994. It was my first visit to Nagaland, a state in the Northeastern frontier of India. Over five days, I visited a few districts in the state to assess women's role in environmental activities on behalf of CIDA (Canadian International Development Agency, which has now become Global Affairs Canada). Being originally from Assam, a neighbouring state, I was aware of the political unrest in the region and people's call for self-determination against the country's central government. Yet, this initial trip to the state incited a curiosity within me.

I began to find ways to go back. The opportunity arose the following year, in 1995, through the MacArthur Fellowship. This time I visited as an individual researcher to study the health status of women in different Naga communities – there are 16 major Naga tribes and many sub-tribes across the state. As someone involved in the wider debate on women's development and rights, I was interested in understanding women's lives in these remote areas, their health issues and the mechanisms they used to respond to challenges, alone or together.

Nagaland was under-studied compared to other regions of India primarily because of its geographic and cultural isolation from the rest of the country. In addition, situations of conflict led to continuation of restrictions on entry into the region. The Northeast region is connected to the rest of India through a narrow strip of land, making communication and access weak. The distance between mainland India and the Northeast is not just cultural and psychological but also physical. I remember when Gunjan, one of the co-editors of this volume, told me about a survey she had conducted in the year 2000 among the educated, middle-class, mostly college going population in New Delhi, India's capital. Most respondents were unable to name the seven states of the Northeast region and many did not

DOI: 10.4324/9781003377917-13

know Nagaland was a part of India. This was not an uncommon occurrence in India of the 1990s and 2000s. The history and culture of this very distinct region still do not form any part of the school curricula in the country.

Along with the lack of information and development, access into the region was also restricted for researchers and tourists. The lack of records, archival material, libraries and institutions made it difficult for scholars to study the region. Language was also a barrier, particularly as many communities depended heavily on oral traditions. Documentation was therefore limited to ethnographic work of colonial-era government officers and 20th-century anthropologists writing about Naga life and customs (von Furer Haimendorf 1939; Elwin, 1959, 1964). This has changed somewhat in the last decade with works like *A Terrible Matriarchy* (Easterine 2007), *Highway 39* (Chakravarti 2012) and *Christianity and Politics of Tribal India* (Chophy 2021).

I was convinced we had much to learn from and about this neighbouring society. So one September morning, I boarded a bus that would take me from the plains of Assam to the hills of Nagaland.

I clearly remember the journey of uncanny silence as we wound our way upwards through the forested highways. Instead of birds, there were soldiers perched on top of trees along the highway to check on the insurgents, as well as every vehicle passing by. We were stopped by the army who checked our luggage and found nothing, allowing us to continue. This was normal for 1995. What irked the Nagas was the aggression demonstrated by the armed forces against the local Nagas, majority of whom were rural. House searches, rape and murder of villagers by armed forces had churned out stories of annihilation and torture, some of which became a part of oral narratives. Language was the biggest barrier between the people and the security forces who came mostly from mainland India. This exacerbated the fear and the distance between the Nagas and the army. All that persisted were memories of conflict, domestic turmoil and vulnerability, felt by the people of Nagaland. Women, as is typically the case in conflict, felt such vulnerabilities most.

This chapter is an autoethnographic account of my work in Nagaland over 30 years, independently and then through the North East Network (NEN), a small non-profit I co-founded. Here, I have reflected on my own experiences, corroborated, at times, by secondary sources. My entry point into the state was through a research project on the status of women's health in Nagaland which I started in Chizami village of Phek district.

Chizami is a small village of about 600 households and a population of 2592 (Census of India, 2011), over 3 hours by car from Kohima and 6 hours from Dimapur, the closest air and rail line. Today, government officials and staff from local and international development organisations regard Chizami as a model village for Nagaland. People from Nagaland and neighbouring states visit it to understand how a community and its women can bring about transformational change. It is this story that I tell in this chapter through six sections: Section one provides a background of Nagaland and its historical context, which has a strong bearing on its present realities. Section two discusses community entry through my experience in Chizami. In Section three, I lay out how we sought to build and strengthen women's position in a highly patriarchal society. Section four outlines the partnership between NEN and the community. Section five specifically unpacks the "how" of participation and voice. The concluding section includes reflections on the "secret sauce" needed for something as complex and intense as participation.

Nagaland over Time: A Quick Overview

Nagaland is a small hilly state, approximately 16,600 square kilometres in area, in the Northeast of India, bordering Myanmar. During the 1990s, it had a population of just 1.2 million (Census of India 1991).

The Naga people are a group of heterogeneous tribes of Mongoloid and Indo-Burman origin and significantly differ from people from other parts of mainland India in appearance, language, customs and religion. On December 1, 1963, Nagaland became the 16th state of India to provide to the Naga people what the then Prime Minister Jawaharlal Nehru termed "the fullest opportunity for self-expression" (Elwin 1959). This was way less than the calls for independence issued by the people of the state. But alongside Article 371A of the Indian constitution, adopted in 1962, this guaranteed a high degree of autonomy and self-governance to the Naga people, including the right to preserve their own customs, culture, values and administrative systems.

The calls for autonomy for the Naga people can be traced back to the formation of the Naga Club in 1918 and were deeply rooted in the British administration system for the region (Misra 1978; Chasie and Hazarika 2009). Two significant shifts occurred in the Naga Hills between the late 19th and 20th centuries. In 1872, Christianity arrived in Mokokchung district, a region inhabited by the Ao tribe. This led to a spread of education but also the loss of many traditional beliefs and institutions (Horam 1977; Eaton 1984; Imtimangyang 2017). Second, in 1881, after fierce resistance from the Nagas, the British occupied the Naga Hills. On these densely forested Hills, they initiated a new model of administration, which soon spread to other areas in the region.

Those were difficult years with multiple rebellions. The bureaucracy experienced much hostility. So, the British left the Naga tribes to govern themselves per their traditional systems, which ranged from democratic village councils (VCs) in some communities to autocratic chieftains in others (Devi, 2015). They introduced an inner line permit (ILP) system in the Naga Hills region regulating the entry of people who were not inhabitants of Nagaland. This kept the people in the state isolated and disconnected from the rest of India (Misra 1978; Chasie and Hazarika 2009). The ILP system continues to date. Even I, as a native of a neighbouring state, required a permit to enter Nagaland and conduct research.

In 1946, the Naga National Conference (NNC) was created and on August 14, 1947, the eve of Indian Independence, it declared independence. In 1951, the NNC conducted a "referendum" in which over 99% of the Naga supported an independent Nagaland. The Government of India never recognised this referendum and thus began a period of protracted armed conflict with the NNC creating an underground government and an army. Nagaland thereby earned the "dubious distinction of being home to Asia's longest-running insurgency" (Loitongbam in Chasie and Hazarika 2009, p.viii).

The Indian government retaliated by sending paramilitary forces, colloquially called the army, to combat underground activities of the young rebels, commonly named the UG, an abbreviation of "underground boys." Violence between the two was unabated. In 1958, the government enacted the Armed Forces Special Powers Act (AFSPA). This Act not just transferred "civil power to deal with a political challenge" to the army and paramilitary forces (Chasie and Hazarika 2009, p. 11), it also allowed the armed forces to search, arrest or even kill someone on mere suspicion without fear of prosecution, except by the central government. The Act led to intense militarisation of the region. There is a record of sexual violence, torture and rape against women in the region by the security forces shielded by the AFSPA. Protests have been expressed through poetry, music, confrontation by human rights groups, particularly women, all over the Northeast region (Veda 2001).

The activism of the UGs in Nagaland was intense, characterised by holdups, roadblocks, extortion, siphoning of public funds and "taxing" public servants. This led to disruption of the governance systems and people lived in fear of attacks and cross-firings. Yet, there was another side to rural Nagaland, one that was seldom noted in the rare mentions of the state – pristine hills, strikingly green terraced fields of rice and maize with verdant forests and people hard at work. The forest-based economy was gradually giving way to an agro-based one. Members of each community lived together by carrying out agricultural work, reeling and twining their own yarn, weaving their own clothes, storing indigenous seeds and hunting birds and animals for their food. But the Naga Hills were bereft of support. Characterised by the absence of cash income and food security, low productivity, absence of technical, institutional and infrastructure development, they "lagged behind" with poor access to electricity, safe drinking water, roads and health services (NFHS 2 1999).

This was the state I was travelling to on that September morning in 1995, when I boarded the bus to Kohima. When I first arrived in Chizami in 1995, it was like the rest of Nagaland (and indeed much of India), highly patriarchal. Given the conflict and political situation in the state, I adopted the "health" approach; it would keep away from identity and related political discussions. Indeed, my being in Nagaland showed me what rural inhabitants experienced daily – fear and mental turmoil. I also studied the contemporary situation of governance regarding women, the changing policies towards women's "welfare"[1] at the national level and whether they influenced the state. My question, as someone involved in the wider debate on women's development and their voices in a strong patriarchal society, was where do women stand in this domain of rural governance?

Community Entry: From Consent to Confidence

My first entry into Chizami was with Keweii Y Kenye, a District Social Welfare Officer who I had met earlier in 1994, at Zunheboto, a district in the centre of Nagaland. Stimulated by our conversations on women's development, she had urged me to start work in her village – Chizami in Phek district. She arranged a meeting between me and members of the VC in Chizami, headed by its Chairman, Mr. K.Z Mero.

Traditional village governance systems have long been present in all the Naga communities – for example, the Hangvanao among the Tangkhul (Ukhrul, Manipur), Putu Menden among the Ao. These structures preceded and also continued throughout the colonial period and then were formalised as VCs and given statutory recognition under the Nagaland Village and Area Council Act, 1978 (Devi, 2015). These Councils comprise members of a village who take care of law and order, development, natural resources management and the administration of justice per their own customs. Historically, women were debarred from these Councils and members were required to be married, preventing the youth from participating (Devi, 2015). Since the Act sought to preserve the traditional structures, no modifications were made to challenge these exclusionary practices.

The gradual formalisation of VCs and empowering village elders with roles and responsibilities gave them a sense of authority. The Act also authorised every VC to create a Village Development Board (VDB), which would formulate development priorities for the village and prepare and execute action plans for development, notably communications and transportation with administrative and community resources.

At that first meeting with the Chizami VC, I explained the purpose of my visit, and the Council members approved my long-term plan of working with the women of Nagaland. The meeting was attended by members of the VC, the VDB and the Chizami Women's Society (CWS). The attendance of the CWS pleased me immensely. They were the women who would be my entry point, whom I would talk to and depend on for organising meetings and activities. At the meeting, I volunteered to talk to a wider audience so that every individual in that village would know the purpose of my work. I knew this would be the first step towards not just overcoming suspicion but also getting the community's consent for my work.

The meeting to gain community buy-in was organised at the local church the next day. Close to 150 people attended. "Nagamese," a colloquial mix of Assamese and Hindi, is used popularly across the state, because there are over 60 dialects spoken among the 16 major tribes of Nagaland. The Phek district is inhabited primarily by the Chakhesang community who speak four dialects: Khezha, Chokri, Poula and Sumi. The village of Chizami speaks Khezha. That morning, the man who served as my interpreter noted, “This woman is from India and has come to our village to work with women.” His remarks were not meant to be derogatory – people from the plains are termed Indians in Nagaland! I, of course, replied that I am from Assam and know Nagamese. “Borderline case!” he gleefully exclaimed. During my first three years of travel in Nagaland, I witnessed this sense of humour among many of my colleagues, new acquaintances and even district-level officers. I also experienced a code of conduct towards visitors – people were civil, but the interaction was socially controlled and formal.

Once I had shared my plans with the gathering, I requested for two young women volunteers. The village elders asked the CWS to select the two women. That was perhaps the beginning of legitimacy given to the CWS. Neizokou Thopi and Kezuteu Wetsah joined my team. I gave them a short orientation on the importance of “correct” data and how this data would help keep the entire village informed about its health status and support self-assessment of one’s own health. We started our survey in October 1995. The first day was long – we took time interacting with one woman per household. We not only asked questions but also sought to build relationships, to understand the lives of the Chakhesang community. We covered only three houses that day.

During these house visits, I approached the subject of health in ways that would not alarm my hosts. I knew that my visit and the nature of questions would assure the community that I was not a central government spy. Through the months, the UGs tracked my work. Fortunately, no questions were asked, though three “encounters” assured them that I am “okay,” my work was “women’s stuff” and not a threat.

Every trip I made to Nagaland, I had to ask different questions, especially in areas where there was anxiety because of the drug use by the youth or where the militants had a substantial presence. Gradually I began to understand that the methodology had to be flexible, free from an academic research framework. Instead of relying on theoretical paradigms, I used simple language and focused on building community consensus. But before that, I had to gain social acceptance and trust.

As my objective was to study the health status of women, the first intervention was in the form of household surveys, which I conducted alongside local women who knew the people, customs and local issues. In Chizami, in sharp contrast to the rest of India, husbands helped their spouse during childbirth either by using a fine thread of bamboo to cut the umbilical cord or supporting their wives while being in labour. Some, however, admitted that they preferred preparing food for the new mother, while the women of the household performed a home delivery. This caregiving by the husband is no longer the norm in Chizami because of the Primary Health Centre which has been upgraded to a Community Health Centre since August 2021. At the time of my research, women bore six children on average. Infant mortality was low and Chizami village, like many others in the state, had large families with 10–13 children, most of whom accompanied the parents to the field.

After the surveys in Chizami, I met with groups of women to conduct Focus Group Discussions (FGDs) about women's role in society, the rights they enjoy or the limitations they face. I had noticed the general "meekness" of women, the quiet atmosphere and their polite nods of acknowledgement to me. Meetings with women's groups from different *khels* (homesteads), as well as the women's wing of the Church, showed me how much I had to learn not just about them but from them.

I can never forget their gestures of welcome, accompanied by a short prayer to bless the meeting, the meal or even a traveller. The time spent in conversations and leisure activities during my visits gradually created openness and trust between us. Such activities are usually deemed unproductive in research but are the basis of community-led work. Between peals of laughter, remarks and curiosity, a bond was forged between us. That bond was what I cherished most. My intention had not been to just get data. I sought to undertake participatory, action-oriented research leading to informed community development. Therefore, the community's support, trust and goodwill were of primary importance.

Strengthening Women's Participation and Voice

My time with the communities in different parts of Nagaland helped me to understand that the women of rural Naga society were essentially homemakers in a patriarchal set-up. They were also household managers, caregivers, weavers and indigenous farmers (North East Network 2016). Women carried out all farming-related activities from ploughing, sowing, weeding, binding, and transplanting to harvesting and husking in the terraced rice fields. Men did the ploughing too, but they focused on the *jhum* fields (slash and burn agriculture).

As early as 1995, I noticed the absence of men in several Naga households. With militancy raging high in the state, most men would seek opportunities in the plain areas of Dimapur (the economic hub of Nagaland) as church workers, construction workers, sharecroppers or as labourers. Male cultivators were rare as they feared being apprehended by the army and, for the same reason, both men and women farmers had to hurry back home from their fields after completing their day's work. If they were from different nearby villages or *Khels*, women preferred to go in groups for fear of assault from the security forces. Fewer hours in the field had a direct impact on their productivity leading to serious food security issues. With the men engaged elsewhere, the onus of managing the home and outside work fell squarely on women.

Women, especially those in their 60s and above, carried out agricultural work out of compulsion – a majority of rural Nagas live in a subsistence economy. The health status of women was determined by the hours of work, their intake of food and the mental load that goes into adjusting between the household and the field. Women grew and continue to grow local and seasonal crops; their seed saving processes protected the biodiversity and sustained yield of maize, millets and grains.

Though women carried out a bulk of the agricultural labour, their contribution to household food security went unrecognised (North East Network 2016). Moreover, the inability of rural Nagas to communicate with people outside their villages, due to language barriers, could be terribly isolating and eventually affect people's voice and agency. During my time in Nagaland, I was struck by the absence of discussion and debate in the villages. While interviewing an elder, I remarked that nobody asked me questions during a training I had conducted or at a talk. She explained that not questioning a village elder or a Chief was tradition. Nobody could speak up or pose a question during a meeting. People not asking anything was a mark of respect. I also believe that the relationship with the church in Naga society may have contributed to the culture of silence. People were accustomed to sermonised preaching, being told what to do and how.

Having spent time with the women and men in Chizami, I understood that it was important for the men to comprehend the worth of women's participation in rural governance. Community-led development would require long months of engagement with women alongside the men. And it had to be based on a participatory approach, which gives people an incentive to make decisions collectively once a problem is identified. I gradually introduced participatory exercises and tools from Robert Chambers' Participatory Rural Appraisal (PRA) approach. These included Chapati or Venn diagramming, where community members would identify the institutions and individuals important in and for their community, and their relationships (Chambers 2002). These methods that used local materials and resources caught the attention of respondents and sessions were often filled with smart quips and laughter! They strengthened the confidence between the grassroots women and me.

I realised that investing time and attention with men and women in Chizami would not just strengthen their community consciousness, it could also lead to women voicing their needs. I identified six key steps for this process: (a) goodwill; (b) organisational work; (c) training for women so that they could realise and demand their rights; (d) documentation, building networks for learning, (e) accountability and transparency; and (f) exposure trips for Chizami women to meet with groups outside Nagaland. This last action, engaging with women's groups from other cultures, was critical for encouraging interaction between the rest of India and the state, and developing a common understanding around issues of food security and domestic violence. This would enable women to learn from each other even as they retained their own indigenous farming methods and knowledge. It would also encourage them to question existing traditional norms.

Institutional Support to Enable Community-Led Development

The 1980s were a time of intense activism on women's rights in India. The United Nations' Decade for Women in 1976 influenced many governments, including that of India, to promote equal rights and opportunities for women. The academic and intellectual interest in feminism instilled widespread consciousness over women's rights and their subordination in a patriarchal society. Numerous studies and micro-analysis opened the path towards activism. Research organisations like the Centre for Women's Development Studies, New Delhi, of which I was a part, taught me to decipher the inherent patriarchal culture that shaped and controlled the lives of women in India.

Pursuing various action-research projects in Assam and Northern India, I learnt why and how we should work with women in India. I began to understand the need for grassroots activism by and for women to enable them to take advantage of the government's efforts that for the first time sought to integrate women's perspective into the socio-economic development of the country. All this led me towards community-led development.

My work on the health of women in Nagaland led to the setting up of a Women's Health Centre in Chizami, with support from the Chizami Women's Society. Yet, more was needed – we had to dig deeper to transform the mindsets of men and women on gender. Women had to be sensitised about their selfhood, recognise their collective voice on rural governance and seek equity in all domains. And this work had to be inclusive of women across religions, age groups, economic backgrounds and ethnicities. This was not easy. Particularly, as it required not just working across differences among women but also the tacit approval of the men of the village. The different levels of intervention required concerted action through broad-based organisational support. Thus, in 1995, I along with Roshmi Goswami, another activist from the Northeast region, established the North East Network (NEN), a women's organisation that sought to address inequalities that women experienced. We believed that women had the right to participate in local governance, at par with men, and sought to shift their perspective from a "needs to a rights" approach. To begin with, we focused on the states of Meghalaya, Assam and Nagaland. The year 1995 was also the year of the landmark Beijing Women's Conference. NEN, through Assam's Tezpur District Mahila Samiti, utilised the opportunity presented by the consultations to the Beijing platform, to train rural women from the Northeast on feminist thinking and involve them through local languages and participatory methods in the broader regional and national conversations.

The Process of Participation: How to Do It

Through NEN, we began to take concerted steps towards the inclusion of all women in our work, be they farmers, weavers, homemakers, street vendors, single or married. Our meetings, open discussions and interactive methods engaged women. Our workshops used participatory tools that enabled women to recognise the discrimination and the continuous vulnerabilities they faced. Instead of giving lectures on patriarchy, we asked women to map out the work done by men and women in their community and the time spent on it.

We also collectively looked at schemes being offered by the State government and examined whether basic amenities like water supply and medicines were reaching the villages. In the workshops, we encouraged women to work in groups and discuss one topic at a time. This enabled them not just to recognise their rights but also to collectively think about what was missing and what needed to be done. We used advocacy tools to provoke ideas to influence the group of men or the VC. This, however, can happen only if people in the seat of power are democratic and have the empathy to share information, listen to others and decide that the end output will be an enriching one. At the same time, it was important to understand how familiar women were with local issues to address their collective concerns. We involved both women and men in several of our workshops, knowing that our method of participatory discussion would be strange to them. Yet the men were surprisingly receptive to what was being said and empathetic to the issues highlighted. Collective thinking contributed to self-esteem and hope among women. Moreover, if women addressed a local issue, the community was most likely to agree to their participation and also start interacting with them on the subject. Meanwhile the women would gain confidence and understand the power of their collective. Remembering those early days, Akhale, a woman from Chizami Village, recently told me, "I experienced something unique when you first exposed us to things like healthcare and hygiene… It made a difference…."

Workshops and exposure tours encouraged fresh thoughts, new perspectives and initiatives among people who, until then, had limited exposure and had been taught not to exercise their own wisdom. A co-fellow of the MacArthur Foundation, Abhijit Das, sensitised communities in Zunheboto and Phek districts about reproductive and sexual health. This was a great eye opener for the men. Feminists like Nalini Nayak and Gabriele Deitrich shared ideas about sustainable development and unionisation of the unorganised sector women workers using biblical references and social analysis tools. This ensured that the diverse group of participants – village leaders, youth, church leaders, women's groups and unorganised sector workers – could instantly connect with the messages. Akole, (formally called Wekoweu Tsuhah) a member of NEN, was the link between Nayak and informal sector women workers, i.e. farmers, home-based workers, vendors, and ultimately formed SEWA Nagaland[2] to secure full employment and self-reliance for all its members in 2013. Through sheer persistence of the NEN team, the SEWA initiative took off with vendors and home-based workers; today SEWA Nagaland has over 3,000 members from six districts (Chümoukedima, Dimapur, Kohima, Phek, Shamator, Tuensang).

Gradually women began to speak out against discrimination, violence, subordination and patriarchy. Their interaction with women from other parts of the Northeast and India, through exposure visits to Tezpur and Guwahati in Assam, Shillong in Meghalaya and New Delhi, also strengthened their understanding of the feminist ideology and gave them a network of friends and peers to consult, confide in and collaborate with.

As noted earlier, even in the 1990s, women were excluded from governance structures in Nagaland. The 73rd and 74th Constitutional Amendments which reserved one-third of the seats in all local bodies for women did not apply in the state due to the protection offered by Article 371A to customary laws. The adoption of the 73rd and 74th Amendments could only happen through a resolution of the Legislative Assembly, which was men's domain. And the men of Nagaland would not hear of women being a part of the governance structure or in the electoral rolls, be it the local Municipal elections, or any Assembly seat.[3] Because our work was in the rural areas, we knew that participants in our workshops were not going to immediately question the ban on women's participation in the VCs and the VDBs. Instead, the issue was discussed gradually and subtly in our workshops and in discussions with the VC. We never confronted the VC members – we knew that we could work in the community only as long as we had their consent. Instead, we focused on continuously sharing the possibility of women's participation and examples of the changes this could bring.

Over time and after years of continued engagement, attitudes began to change in the male-dominated VDC in Chizami. In 2002, for the first time, it nominated two rural women into the Council. K.Z Mero, the first person I met in Chizami in 1995 and the Chair of the Council, explained the reason behind this change: "This space was allocated so that women can raise their concerns and views and also take equal part in contributing toward community development…" (Report of the Chizami Women Society 2009).

At that time, many felt that the admittance of women was simply tokenism. Yet slowly and steadily these women claimed their place, bringing in oft-neglected yet necessary issues to the VDB. They raised the issue of harnessing the water flow for equitable distribution across the village. However, it took another 20 years for the number of women in the Chizami VDB to increase to four. In September 2020, the Chizami Village Development Board inducted 6 women out of a total of 23 members, ensuring that 25% of its members were women. The tokenism from earlier has also given way to parity.

> The process of mindset transformation in a community, particularly on entrenched issues like gender, is gradual. Organisationally we continuously engaged with people and managed to take a few steps forward, but each small win was accompanied by a backlash. The back and forth continued. The important thing is to keep the engagement going; to not give up,

explains Seno Tsuhah, who was among the first women from Chizami to join NEN.

As women from Chizami began to attend trainings and meetings and join NEN, they began to understand their rights and carried forward the baton for change. Despite women doing most of the work in Nagaland, they were seldom paid and never at par with men.

> After joining NEN and understanding the importance of equal wages, in 1998 I began trying to convince the village elders on the need for equal wages.

> I would weave it into different conversations with them and yet, year after year my efforts were met with jokes about the strength of men. The village elders would point out how men being on top was the natural order of things. Even for procreation men have to be at the top, they would guffaw,

recalls Seno. But Seno understood that any change requires tenacity, and finally on January 4, 2014, the Chief of Chizami announced equal wages for men and women. This proclamation, like the induction of the two women into the council, bore testimony to the strength of women once they decided to claim their agency. It also served as an example to the community, particularly the youth. They saw women participating in our training workshops alongside village men and church leaders and bringing about change. This created an inspiring and self-reinforcing cycle of change and growth.

Two stories illustrate just how impactful this change was. The first is the story of how NEN began agroecology projects in Chizami and its impact on the community. The second, of Chizami Weaves.

NEN and Agroecology

During one of NEN's exchange visits, Seno met representatives from the Deccan Development Society, an organisation based out of Hyderabad in Southern India, that dealt with millets, among other crops. She was immediately hooked, and the NEN team from Chizami started meaningful dialogue with the Deccan Development Society in 2009. They undertook a study on the climate crisis using PRA exercises in six villages to understand the kind of climate change that people were experiencing. Being a part of this study enabled NEN to become a member of the Millet Network of India in 2010. Thereafter the team engaged in raising awareness on millets to link it with local foods of the past, present and future.

Why did we engage so deeply with the community on millets? Because a community leader like Seno, belonging to Chizami, saw an opportunity and recognised how it could revive sustainable traditional practices in her community, even as it facilitated an inter-generational transfer of knowledge. She and Akole, along with their team, produced booklets with stories and recipes and developed audio-visual material to create awareness.

Seno also attended the Conference on Climate Change (CoP 15) in 2015 in Copenhagen. This reinforced her belief that local networks and grassroots organising could be used to promote indigenous ways of sustaining biodiversity, which also has direct interface with the global concerns of climate change. Our underlying emphasis was on creating local farmers to cater to local markets with local distribution and sales. Because of its high nutritional value, we hoped that millets would be brought in under the public distribution system[4] run by the government. That never happened, but facilitating farmer-to-farmer knowledge sharing, providing on-farm support to revive millets, training on value addition, and marketing opportunities have led to increased production and consumption among several communities of Nagaland. Millet farmers were able to increase their income through the NEN farmer market. The *Millet Festivals and Biodiversity Festivals* initiated by NEN in 2010 brought together diverse communities from within and outside Nagaland. This facilitated the sharing and exchange of knowledge on local seeds and food, including uncultivated and cultivated diversity. It fostered solidarity amongst diverse communities practising ecological farming. For example, in Pathso Nokeng village of Noklak district, the local community which participated in one of NEN's biodiversity festivals returned to their village and established a Community Seed Bank to protect their traditional seeds.

Community Seed Banks were initiated by NEN with the local women groups in ten villages to revive and enhance traditional social seed networks in rural Nagaland, which include seed saving, seed exchanges, seed sharing, etc., to enhance the traditional knowledge on seed management, secure food and seed sovereignty for local communities. As of 2023, they are operational in Kohima, Noklak and Phek districts. The Community Seed Banks have generated awareness and understanding of the importance of indigenous food systems amongst local communities. They are also reviving lost seeds and community-led documentation of indigenous seed varieties in the region.

In order to encourage young people, we initiated short courses called Chizami Farm schools in the village. The NEN farm school began in 2016 to tackle the dwindling interest in agriculture among young urban-based students, both boys and girls. Seno and her team of young activists initiated the programme to create awareness on food, nutrition and ecological security issues. Young Naga students often travel to metropolises to earn money to send home. The initiative tried to reconnect these young people to their local culture, and sustainable and indigenous farming systems so that they become responsible consumers and citizens. Each of these agroecology initiatives, that attract visitors from all over to Nagaland, began with the efforts of the women of Chizami and their vision for their community. That is what makes them successful.

Weaving Empowerment

The second initiative that transformed Chizami also built on local cultural practices. In 2008, we began to think about generating income for women through their traditional weaving, which is a non-commercial household activity. I requested a young designer from the National Institute of Design to come to Chizami to understand the patterns and weaving techniques of the Chakhesang community, and to assist seven women weavers in designing household products. This initiative pooled the weaving expertise of the women with the market savviness of the designer to create livelihood opportunities for over 900 weavers from Phek, Kohima and Tuensang Districts. Today Chizami Weaves is a brand of NENterprise, an entrepreneurial venture, starting initially as the economic wing of NEN. In 2017, NENterprise became a separate entity.

It is a decentralised economic model where women weave at home alongside farming and other economic activities. It promotes livelihoods whilst preserving the art of traditional waist loom weaving and economic empowerment of rural women. Women and girls are trained in product design, development and diversification. Currently there is an effort to revive natural fibres such as stinging nettle fibre and traditional cotton. This has led to the revival of cotton cultivation among women artisans in Meluri, Khumiasu and Chizami. It has also facilitated inter-generational skill transfer through workshops on cotton processing and weaving.

More importantly, Chizami Weaves has enabled women to exercise their agency. During workshops with weavers, the team would bring up discussions around gender justice. Weavers articulated their views around health, food security, environment, rights and entitlements while supporting their families. A weaver, Kotele, shared,

> This weaving project has helped us in different ways. Because we take work home, we can weave in our own homes, at our own time, without pressure, and I enjoy this freedom. My earnings are always paid on time. My public speaking and leadership skills also started from here. I became aware of women's rights and women's role in society through their meetings and training workshops.
>
> *(NEN Annual Report 2015–16)*

The impact of Chizami Weaves can be understood from this simple statement from a weaver, Neikhrolou, as early as 2014. By then, she had been part of the project for six years.

> Besides agricultural wage work that is seasonal, we have no other regular employment options available throughout the year, and NEN has provided that… Today, I have a [sic] regular income with which I am supporting my siblings' education and meeting household needs. Also, because of participating in training workshops, meetings, discussions, and interaction with people, I have become more aware of social issues such as domestic violence, biodiversity and health, and I have gained more confidence to speak in front of people.
>
> *(NEN Annual Report 2013–14)*

This agency also led to a marked improvement in gender relations between weavers and their spouses. Said Aneile Kapfo,

> We weave in order to earn our living. Agriculture requires hard labour so we prefer weaving. Earlier, my husband used to tell me not to weave, but I

> continued weaving …Later he started to help me in turning hanks of yarn into tightly bound yarn-balls. He also looks after the livestock while I weave. With the income I am earning, I have gained more respect from my family members. My children now look after the household work too.
>
> *(NEN Annual Report 2015–16)*

Even as the women continued to transform the patriarchal society in which they lived, we realised the importance of them being able to tell their own stories. InsightShare, a UK-based organisation, trained NEN staff and community volunteers in handling the camera and telling their stories. The participatory videos (PV) made by the women of Chizami have been generating awareness about the importance of indigenous cultural values and local food systems and have influenced community attitudes, decisions, and actions. They have also received several awards for their films.

Concluding Reflections

What does the Chizami story mean for civil society organisations and community-led development practitioners? Chizami shows us how the participation of women and youth paved the way towards sustainability and improved the quality of life for the community. No two places are the same, but I do believe the intentional process of building community leadership, centring community knowledge and always ensuring the inclusion of all community members (however long the process may take) that we followed offers valuable lessons.

Here are some pointers:

- Seek community consent and collaboration: Explain what you would like to do and why to not just the leaders but all the community members. Start by seeking their input, their permission, and their partnership.
- Listen: Work with and through community members. Listen to them throughout the process. They carry local knowledge, and they understand local customs. Let them guide you.
- Build mutual trust and respect: Trust and relationships are built through seemingly non-productive activities – cooking a meal together, sitting around the fire, and laughing with each other, singing together, gently teasing each other. It is in these activities that we begin to see, hear, appreciate, and respect one another
- Create opportunities for people to share knowledge: When people believe they are being heard and their knowledge is valued, they have an incentive to participate.
- Initiate new ideas around inclusion: Once people begin to trust and respect you, they will listen more. Introduce ideas of inclusion, gender equality, and the power and agency of women through participatory action. Do not preach

or confront. Instead, engage. And remember that shifting centuries-old power dynamics to encourage participation takes time. Be patient. Participation is a process.

- Take a multi-pronged approach: Participation and inclusion of marginalised groups require two parallel conditions – the participants must be willing to participate and the powerholders and community members need to recognise the value of including these marginalised groups. For the latter, you need to supplement training and sensitisation with efforts that showcase the value of inclusion by, for example, paying women equal wages, improving household standard of living of women in the governance structures, and ensuring access to water. And for the former, design specific activities that enable collective learning, engagement and action. Here one has to get to the root cause of the problem, even if it is to do with patriarchy. So we initiated advocacy, which for me literally means lobbying, persuading or convincing the power structure. We also listened to the women. Gradually sharing each other's experiences became a process-oriented approach, sowing seeds of collective expression to form a pathway to their progress.
- Let community members lead: NEN's highly successful millet programme was initiated because a woman from Chizami recognised how the crop offered an opportunity not just to strengthen livelihoods in her community, but also to protect the ecology and ensure an inter-generational transfer of knowledge. No outsider would have been able to design this. Including local community members in your team increases their self-esteem and ensures that the programmes are well-suited to the community.
- Connect the dots: Even as you initiate the process of mindset change to ensure participation and voice for historically marginalised groups like women and youth, remember connecting them to their peers from other regions not only strengthens their confidence and offers a support system, it also sparks new ideas. After all, an exposure visit sparked NEN's agroecology programme.
- Enable communities to tell their story: The best stories are told by those who have lived them. Equip the community to tell their own stories, internally and externally. Reiterating democratic values is the only pathway to empowerment. Change takes place through learning that is participatory, not top down.

As I write this chapter, a crisis is unfolding in Chizami. In 2002, the community contributed land and pooled resources to set up the NEN Resource Centre. A young terrace architect and friend, Vrinda Makwana, came in several times to Chizami, and built the NEN Resource Centre which was completed in 2005.

At this centre, the participatory discussions on agroecology, photography and training were conducted. The emphasis was on innovative learning and also showcasing what Chizami offered to its young people – wild life conservation, seed saving mechanisms including variety of indigenous seeds/grains. Along with this women's meetings were held, and Chizami Weaves was created. It was in this attractive building, sitting on a steep hill on a piece of land donated by a community member, that the youth of Chizami acquired new skills and showcased them through plays, music, dance and their cameras. It was here that the media and others flocked to witness the power of communities.

In 2021, the government started building a two-lane highway near the centre. This caused irreparable damage to the structure, and despite multiple efforts by the community and NEN, no compensation has been provided thus far. Yet I write this chapter with hope in my heart. In the summer of 2022, I visited Chizami and asked the people what we should do. The men suggested we speak to the chief minister. A colleague stood up to suggest that we make a mini replica of our Centre in memory for all to see. The women decided that for their own safety the building had to be dismantled. And we did so, saving whatever we could of the materials. Now the people of Chizami are working together to find an alternate site for collective action and innovation. It has been 28 years since I first entered Chizami. In that time I have seen the women, the youth, and the community members come together, nudge at age-old patriarchal systems, protect their environment, improve their standard of living, and become ambassadors for community-led development. I know that together they will handle this challenge as well, with goodwill, congeniality, and their ever-present sense of humour.

Notes

1 The use of the term welfare here is intentional. That is how the government at that time looked at the issue – it was about women's welfare not rights, agency or empowerment. Those concepts and language were introduced later by feminists.

2 The Self Employed Women's Association (SEWA) is a women's trade union that was born out of the Textile Labor Association (TLA), India's oldest and largest union of textile workers. Started in 1972 by women workers in the state of Gujarat under the guidance of Ela Bhat, by 2023 it had over 2.9 million members across 18 states of India.

3 The year 2006–7 was particularly painful with public violence against women aspirants in several districts of the State.

4 The public distribution system is a food security mechanism established by the Government of India wherein food and non-food items are made available to people living in poverty at subsidised rates.

References

Agarwal, Bina. 2001. "Participatory Exclusions, Community Forestry, and Gender: An Analysis for South Asia and a Conceptual Framework." *World Development* 29, no. 10: 1623–1648.

Census of India. 1991. Office of the Registrar General & Census Commissioner, India. Population Census 1991. Table C-1:Age Sex And Marital Status, Nagaland.

Census of India. 2011. Office of the Registrar General & Census Commissioner, India. India. Web Archive www.census2011.co.in/data/village/267886-chizami-vill-nagaland.html

Chambers, Robert. 2002. *Participatory Workshops: A Sourcebook of 21 Sets of Ideas and Activities*. London: Routledge.

Chasie, Charles and Sanjoy Hazarika. 2009. *The State Strikes Back: India and the Naga Insurgency*. Washington, DC: East-West Center Washington. www.eastwestcenter.org/publications/state-strikes-back-india-and-naga-insurgency

Chakravarti, Sudeep. 2012. *Highway 39: Journeys through a Fractured Land*. Noida: Fourth Estate.

Chizami Women Society. December 9, 1999. *Silver Jubilee Report*. Nagaland: Chizami Women Society.

Devi, Jonali. 2015. "Traditional Village Government and Village Council in Nagaland." *Man in India* 95, no. 2: 261–74. Retrieved from www.serialsjournals.com/abstract/93020_10.pdf

Easterine, Kire. 2007. *A Terrible Matriarchy: A Novel*. New Delhi: Zubaan.

Eaton, Richard M. 1984. "Conversion to Christianity among the Nagas, 1876–1971." *The Indian Economic & Social History Review* 21, no. 1: 1–44.

Elwin, Verrier. 1959. *The Art of the North-East Frontier of India*. Shillong: North-East Frontier Agency.

Elwin, Verrier. 1964. *The Tribal World of Verrier Elwin; an Autobiography*. Bombay: Indian Branch Oxford University Press.

Horam, M. 1977. *Social and Cultural Life of Nagas (the Tangkhul Nagas)*. Delhi: B. R Publishing Corporation. Retrieved from https://aptribes.ap.gov.in/pdfViewer.jsp?pdf=1052&id=digital

Imtimangyang. September 2017. "A Brief Historical Account: Christianity among the Ao Nagas of North-East India." *National Journal of Multidisciplinary Research and Development* 2, no. 3: 77–82. https://doi.org/10.22271/njmrd

Kanato Chophy, G. 2021. *Christianity and Politics in Tribal India: Baptist Missionaries and Naga Nationalism* First SUNY Press ed. Delhi: State University of New York Press.

Mathie, Alison, Jenny Cameron, and Katherine Gibson. 2017. "Asset-Based and Citizen-Led Development: Using a Diffracted Power Lens to Analyze the Possibilities and Challenges." *Progress in Development Studies* 17, no. 1: 54–66.

Misra, Udayon. 1978. "The Naga National Question." *Economic and Political Weekly*, 618–24. www.jstor.org/stable/4366506

National Family Health Survey (NFHS-2). 1999. Mumbai: International Institute for Population Sciences (IIPS) and ORC Macro. https://www.dhsprogram.com/pubs/pdf/FRIND2/FRIND2.pdf

North East Network. 2016. *Enquiry into the Status of Women in Nagaland*. Guwahati: North East Network.

von Fürer-Haimendorf, Christoph. 1939. *The Naked Nagas*. London: Methuen.

Veda, Gunjan. 2001. *Tailoring Peace: The Citizens' Roundtable on Manipur and beyond*. New Delhi: North East Network.

10

WHAT PARTICIPATION MEANS IN A DIVIDED INDIGENOUS COMMUNITY

The Case of an Engineers without Borders Water Project among the Ch'orti' Maya of Eastern Guatemala

Brent Metz

"Community" and an Engineers without Borders Project among the Ch'orti' Maya

In 2011, after an exploratory trip by Kansas engineers and me to Ch'orti' Maya villages in eastern Guatemala, where I had conducted research since 1990, we formed an Engineers Without Borders (EWB) project to partner with a community needing significant improvements in its gravity-fed water system. We were led to the community by a human rights NGO that knew it well. What seemed like a simple community-EWB five-year project turned into a decade of dancing forwards and backwards. Rumours abounded. Some would purportedly get more water than others. Some leaders were supposedly embezzling funds. Chlorination would poison everyone. Why should water users have to pay fees if water comes from God? EWB is making promises it will not keep. These were just some of the rumours and criticisms that would emerge whenever we returned to the US. Every time progress was made in community buy-in and organisation to implement and sustain the project, suspicions, rumours, misunderstandings, and community divisions spread like mould. The community requested more water but could not overcome their distrust of each other and outsiders. A more regular presence of EWB in the community became necessary.

Calls for collaboration and participation are not new. One might even argue that participation has long become a dominant ideological paradigm, although not necessarily put to impactful and meaningful practice (Cooke and Kothari 2001). When participation emerges as a key component of an organisation's work, it might reflect goals of *efficiency* or *equity*, or even both. Whereas the former refers to

DOI: 10.4324/9781003377917-14

participation as a tool for better project outcomes, the latter considers participation as "a process that enhances the capacity of individuals to improve or change their own lives" (Cleaver 2001, 37). In Guatemala, NGOs, aid agencies, and the government often tout participation and other locally led processes, and communities have indeed expanded their power and ability for self-driven development. Nevertheless, development, including intentions around participation, continues to be primarily top-down and technical in nature, and the structure of the development industry often invites competition, not collaboration (Sánchez 2016; e.g., Dickens 2007; cf. Olivier de Sardan 2005). Major international donors still prefer projects designed and led by professionals, while the rare bottom-up or grassroots development by those most in need of assistance is praised but underfunded.

As we have learned in the EWB project, when communities are indigenous, facilitating meaningful participation requires additional consideration. Prior colonisation, ongoing cultural and identity differences, and a systemic sense of marginality and inferiority continue to be the reality of many rural indigenous Guatemalans. It is commonly assumed in the participatory paradigm that indigenous groups want autonomy. However, in practice, they may, out of necessity, doubt, or previous disappointment, choose the easy route of receiving "fish" rather than the neoliberal ideal of "learning how to fish." Community leaders and social scientists are often key actors in community-led development. They are the tireless cross-cultural brokers and arbiters who are often critical in projects with several hundred or thousand participants because decisions by consensus, including among outside agents, cannot easily be achieved. The challenge is to garner and represent everyone's perspectives and interests.

As a social scientist for an EWB initiative in Guatemala, with the role of a cross-cultural interpreter, I describe the dynamics of participation in community-led development in the context of one poor, marginalised, indigenous community and a small, targeted project. The small scale of the project within the large community, without an established governing structure, made plain why participation is easier said than done. Social organisation – not technical support – was the greatest challenge as it cannot be resolved with one-size-fits-all formulae. All localities are unique, and so development must be as well. For impactful community-led development, participation that is active, intentional, and inclusive is key. Such participation also needs to happen on different levels: sustained engagement within communities, between communities and development professionals, and between professionals with different professional cultures.

The chapter proceeds as follows: first, I provide a brief overview of the Ch'orti' Maya, including the historical processes that have led to systematic discrimination and inequalities. Here I also share more on my entry into their contexts as a cultural anthropologist. The next section introduces the EWB project, followed by a section that summarises key takeaways with regard to the possibilities and challenges of participation within rural, marginalised communities.

Hesitancy to Participate: The Historical Roots of Marginalisation and Distrust

The Ch'orti' Maya are semi-subsistence farmers, poor, and marginalised by Central American standards. They exhibit some of the lowest health indices in Guatemala, which are also the lowest in Central America (Figeroa Ibarra 2017, 11; INE 2013, 7, 13–23). They grow corn, beans, squash, and sorghum on steep mountain slopes with digging sticks, hoes, and machetes. In the 1930s, when Wisdom (1940) undertook the first ethnographic study among them, their diet was a cornucopia that regularly included wild meat and fish. Since the 1960s, the growing population has meant forests have been slashed and rivers filled with topsoil. For at least two generations, few households have grown enough to feed their families year-round (Dary, Elias, and Reyna 1998; López García and Metz 2002; Metz 2006). Severe droughts since the 1910s have led to starvation and emigration. Today, the Ch'orti' depend heavily on chemical fertilisers and pesticides. Since the 1950s, they have been seasonally migrating to pick coffee and cotton and cut sugarcane for low wages to buy food. Malnutrition and stunted growth are widespread.

Perceptions of poverty are reinforced by juxtaposition to the local town-dwellings and modernised Ladinos (Hispanics), who have long had electricity, piped water, cars, paved roads, televisions, refrigeration, and means to travel; luxuries of which the Ch'orti' can only dream. The civil war with roots in ethnic oppression and forced labour in the 1930s reinforced the sense of marginalisation. Hope arose between 1944 and 1954, with emerging conversations about the possibility of democracy, only to be dashed again by the US-backed counter-revolution in 1954. Soon after, the civil war (1961–1996) began in earnest. The Ch'orti' faced mass torture and massacres by racist paramilitary vigilantes and the Guatemalan army, again with steady, if ambivalent, US support. The Ch'orti' were treated as nothing, at best, and vermin, at worst (Metz 2006).

When I first undertook fieldwork here in the early 1990s, the elders interpreted the cataclysmic changes as the end of an epoch. They had gone from God's chosen to God's abandoned. They blamed the "new generation" for refusing to follow the elaborate sacrifices of fowl, corn gruel, candles, and other prized items, logically resulting in God's refusal to provide rain and fertility. On the other hand, Catholic and Protestant missionaries, who stepped up their activities in the 1950s, blamed the Maya traditionalists for either naivete or Satan worship, resulting in the assassinations of traditional spiritual leaders.

The Ch'orti's sense of inferiority in the modern world is not total. They are proud and defensive when insulted. They are hypersensitive to disrespect. Their sentiments towards modern outsiders living in excess are mixed and complicated. Outsiders offer prized resources, opportunities, and genuine concern along with paternalism, denigration, contempt, shallowness, and unreliability. An outsider who knows the Ch'orti' well will appreciate their fortitude, generosity, devotion to family, sensibility, and intricate knowledge of subsistence agriculture and craft-making accumulated over millennia. Such acknowledgement opens the door to friendship and collaboration. Even a little recognition of the Ch'orti's abilities, fortitude, morality, language, and life, works wonders.

The development industry has complicated this complex social, cultural, and emotional transformation. The first orchestrated efforts at modernisation came with the 1944–1954 democratic opening, when the state expanded voting rights, introduced rural education, distributed "improved" agricultural produce like maguey and cattle, and protected the right to unionise and form cooperatives. While the 1954 counter-revolution reversed these advances, Catholic and Protestant missionaries brought their grassroots projects in the form of cooperatives, beekeeping, vegetable crops, roads, low-interest loans for chemical fertilisers, new settlements in the virgin forests of northern Guatemala, and more. Programmes by USAID and other foreign development agencies followed in the 1960s and 1970s. However, even these projects were considered subversive by a reactionary army and elite class that wanted to keep everyone in their place. Cooperatives were viciously repressed, especially if they were indigenous (Comisión para el Esclarecimiento Histórico 1999; ODHAG 1998). The state instituted its own rural development programmes at the end of the 1980s when the war was dying down. Some Ch'orti' took advantage, while many others cautiously refrained. From 1989 to 1994 the UN's International Fund for Agricultural Development (IFAD) attempted to transform the eastern corner of Guatemala with every tool in their toolbox, including milking goats, tilapia ponds, improved vegetable seeds for the market, rural roads, new craft designs, partnerships with transnational companies, and community centres ("Proyecto Desarrollo Rural para Pequeños Productores en Zacapa y Chiquimula" 1991). The administrators felt that the multi-million-dollar effort was a failure. Yet the Ch'orti's used many of these inputs, just not how the top-down planners had intended.

When I began fieldwork in 1991–1993, living in three Ch'orti' communities and learning the language, project administrators often called me to consult or meditate on community development projects. I conducted surveys of over 445 households in three communities of two *municipios* (small counties), where I found communities divided over modernisation. A minority but growing number of households were willing to take risks in development and exhibited greater education, land and cattle ownership, selling in the market economy, home improvements, ownership of radios, legal marriages, use of biomedicine and health clinics, and use of agrochemicals. Others shunned any activity that potentially interfered with maize and bean subsistence agriculture, such as using their land as collateral for loans or interrupting agricultural tasks. Subsistence farming has kept many alive when the market economy, the state, and international aid would not, including during the recent COVID-19 pandemic. Today, the divide between impoverished households reluctant to engage in development and wealthier households who take advantage of projects is dissolving due to pressure on a weakening land base, attraction to modern amenities, and cultural ideas introduced by schools, organised religions, the army, development projects, and migration to the US. In some communities, US wages have entirely broken the millennia-old tradition of growing corn and beans.

One source of ongoing hesitancy among the Ch'orti's about whether to participate in development interventions or not is the industry itself. When the neoliberal state largely abandoned development after the civil war, a growing number of INGOs and local NGOs with international funding began trying to fill the gaps, including in water provision (Ruano et al. 2011). Even in central and western Guatemala, where most of the country's 15,000 NGOs operate because communities are more accessible, scenic, demographically and culturally indigenous, and perceived to be more impacted by the civil war, the NGO patchwork has many holes (Rohloff et al. 2011). Yet at least in these regions, the industry is more stable, dominated by credit-based institutions and newly formed cooperatives (Beck 2017; Lyon 2013).

Sánchez Díaz (2016), who volunteered for an NGO in 2013 and conducted an ethnographic study of eastern Guatemalan development professionals in 2015, documented how in eastern Guatemala development is characterised by boom-and-bust cycles of disaster relief aid, such as after the 1992 cholera epidemic, Hurricane Mitch in 1998, and a famine in 2001. NGOs, consulting firms, and professionals within them compete for short-term grants to address basic water, sanitation, nutrition, health, construction, human rights, and marketing needs. Long-term development plans are either lacking or not carried out, and consulting firms and NGOs frequently sprout and wither. The most enduring projects are child-sponsorship programmes by agencies like World Vision and CARE or those carried out by the firmly rooted Catholic Church. Contradictions, corruption, and suspicions of corruption pose pervasive challenges. While neoliberalism has meant dispersing more tax dollars to local municipalities, the supposed bottom-up approach has proven to be easily corruptible and underfunded. Mayors often appoint rural development representatives (COCODEs) when they are supposed to be elected; they routinely embezzle public funds and distribute projects only to the communities who support their political rallies (Metz 2006; Sánchez Díaz 2016; see also Grant 2001).

Sánchez (2016) discovered that mainly due to the volatility and inadequacy of foreign funding, local NGOs and consulting firms see each other as rivals rather than collaborators. They spend much of their time competing for grants. Smaller operations are often outcompeted by larger ones in an economy of scale because the former cannot manage the range of projects or endure periods without funding. Donors prefer to fund NGOs that have managed numerous project participants and large budgets, assuming without merit that they have been effective and more accountable (Nolan 2002, 41–42). NGOs also compete for project participants, further complicating participation quality and nature. Rather than pool efforts, which the state half-heartedly attempted in the 2000s, they sometimes provide the same benefits to the same communities, resulting in duplication. Projects that offer the most benefits with the least Ch'orti' effort recruit the most participants.

Inequalities in aid can exacerbate community divisions and fan the flames of misunderstandings and rumours (cf. Clouser 2018).

Most professionals do not recognise the Ch'orti's talents, knowledge, and morality and thus do not gain their complete confidence. Instead, we have witnessed professionals chastising Ch'orti' adults as if they were errant children. These professionals typically view subsistence farming as a problem and the market as the solution. For example, development project administrators lamented that the earnings hardly offset production costs in one egg project, whereas the protein-starved Ch'orti's prize egg consumption. Other urgent needs are considered taboo by all and thus left unaddressed, such as family planning (which contradicts God's design), leveraging migrant remittances (which legitimises undocumented migration in the face of US pressure), and terracing and canals (which would direct attention to subsistence agriculture rather than payments for carbon sequestration). Many professionals are frustrated by their lack of success and blame the Ch'orti's for being "backwards Indians," even when the "handout culture" has admittedly been created by the development itself. They also aim their frustration at donors for their inflexibility and at each other for their lack of cooperative spirit (Sánchez 2016; cf. Rohloff et al. 2011).

The EWB Water Project

The EWB project began in 2011 when engineers with unsatisfying experiences in other EWB projects asked me to serve as a cultural liaison for a new, more socially and culturally sensitive project among the Ch'orti's. Their engineering expertise was water and sanitation, so they were keen to find communities that needed assistance in these areas. Many Ch'orti' communities indeed do. EWB projects must have institutional partners in the countries where they are carried out, so I led them to three ethnic-rights-oriented non-profits I know pretty well.

When I conducted fieldwork in the early 1990s, I collaborated with the emerging Maya Movement and witnessed how ethnic revitalisation created a new space for a proud Ch'orti' identity under modernisation. However, this was an inauspicious time to work with indigenous rights NGOs because they had been involved in a rebellion the year before that resulted in at least ten deaths and the burning of the mayor's office in Jocotán in the heart of the Ch'orti'-speaking area of eastern Guatemala. The root of the discontent was the municipal governments' approval of megaprojects, like a superhighway connecting the Pacific and Caribbean, that would displace subsistence farmers with no remuneration (Casolo 2011; Metz and Francesch 2015). The municipal government responded to the rebellion by cutting off all services to the participating communities and partnerships with the NGOs. This was when our support entered the scene. After the NGOs ushered us to several communities needing water, the engineers chose one with an existing water committee but a crumbling gravitational water system running from a source seven kilometres up in the mountain. The water committee's depiction of the situation was incomplete and inaccurate, making it seem like the renovations would be quick.

EWB carried out a household census replete with *Escherichia coli* water testing and a photovoice exercise among women to gauge their recognition of *E. coli* contamination and perceptions of broader community needs. Our survey found that the community had 470 households with nearly 3,000 people, not the 300 households and 1,600 people as represented initially. Since EWB projects typically occur in communities of under 100 households, we realised we were in over our heads but could not back out of our commitment. Their water was indeed contaminated by *E. coli*, likely because of cattle grazing above the water catchment dam, which had once been within a large mountain forest but was now surrounded by pasture and coffee orchards. The women, who are rarely recognised as community leaders or invited to formal positions and only occasionally critique the male leaders, essentially took the contamination and associated illnesses for granted, so much so that they only saw the quantity and regularity of water as the problem, not the quality. EWB also discovered that the NGO that had guided them to the community did not intend to invest any effort in the project. They had just begun to move into the economic development realm while still devoting most of their efforts to ethnic rights. This sent EWB scrambling to partner with one of the other 80 NGOs and consulting firms in the region. However, these organisations, including the official government development office, required money up front for collaboration, which EWB had yet to raise.

Some engineers also made fatal errors like banking on promises by large US funders and offering to pay for the Ch'orti's labour to install the new piping and buy their tools. The money was harder to procure than anticipated. So EWB returned to the common practice in Guatemala of having the development organisation pay for the materials and the community donate the labour. Many in the community were furious with the broken promise and began to wonder whether they were being swindled. Behind the scenes, competing factions argued whether they could trust EWB or not. Only after holding a community assembly were apologies accepted and a vote taken to continue.

The linkage of funding and professional commitment is often a conundrum, not only in the impoverished and marginalised rural mountains of the Ch'orti' area but also in community development more generally. Communities might prefer compensation for their time and effort when participating in development projects, but funding may not be enough. They may co-design projects with outside professionals, but the ability to fulfil the design may depend on funding that is not always easy to procure. When funding is insufficient, and promises around compensation fall through the cracks, community trust in development professionals can erode, endangering their commitment to the project and partnership. Therefore, at the start of the partnership and during project design, those facilitating interventions should clearly articulate the realities of precarious funding, and challenges in accessing such funding, so that all stakeholders can be prepared for changes in project design and funding adjustments.

Another challenge was the community organisation, in this case, the water committee. The community consisted of five competing neighbourhoods. The neighbourhoods were divided by kinship, the ability to speak Ch'orti', religion, inclusion in a World Vision project, and participation in the ethnic rights NGO. The water "committee" was an ad hoc volunteer group of male leaders who simply fixed the old system's pipes whenever it had major leaks or blockages. Not all community members recognised the water committee. They did not meet regularly or take regular fees to pay for repairs. They did not compensate themselves for their time on the water system, and when they needed funds for repairs, they would literally pass the sombrero (hat) to collect money. For the engineers, who regularly worked with township, city, and county utility commissions in the US Great Plains, this was not an "organisation" at all. They insisted on a US-type organisational framework with elections for a water board representing all neighbourhoods, monthly meetings, monthly household fees, and a bank account. The community never complied, either out of intention or lack of leadership. It had such a water committee in the 1980s and 1990s for its first water project provided by the Catholic Church's local development programme. However, accusations of embezzlement resulted in the dissolution of the entire structure. After that, few dared to serve on such a committee and expose themselves to rumours, accusations, and death threats. At the same time, less than half the households contributed to the sombrero when repairs were necessary. Some also pushed back on a single fee for each household because some were greedier and more wasteful with water than others. Water meters could solve this problem, but they were prohibitively expensive, and some surmised that high users would destroy them. Some households were too poor to contribute anything. Others argued that since the water comes from God, no one should have to pay monthly fees.

From an anthropological perspective, a major underlying problem was rapid population growth. Like many indigenous communities, the Ch'orti' prefer to make decisions by consensus, which they do remarkably well when their neighbourhoods or communities are small. Decision-making beyond consensus is necessary when communities expand beyond a few hundred individuals, yet the Ch'orti' have little trust in representative democracy (50+% rule) or, less, hierarchical rule. This posed challenges because, at the time of our project, in their community, one neighbourhood alone had over 2,000 residents, and the neighbourhoods were often at odds with each other.

The community and EWB made advances every time EWB representatives visited (once or twice per year for one to two weeks at a time), including finding new water sources and getting permissions to use them, mapping the existing and planned water systems, and overcoming the community's distrust of chlorination. However, lacking a reliable local development partner meant that when EWB returned to the US, rumours, innuendos, and gossip reversed understanding and progress. EWB attempted to partner with no less than five local NGOs, but none followed through with their tasks, including one that was paid upfront. Neither the Ch'orti' nor some in EWB completely fulfilled their obligations. EWB assigned the Ch'orti' simple tasks for designing the new water system, such as seasonally checking overflow from their existing catchment dam and measuring water pressure entering their pre-existing storage tanks. However, due to a lack of leadership, they failed to fulfil their commitment. When the going got tough, some EWB volunteers blamed the Ch'orti' and NGOs and quit. At one point, everyone thought that the problems would be resolved when a Honduran NGO specialising in rural water procurement and purification agreed to take on the implementation. Its lightning approach, though, did more damage than good. It preferred to carry out projects quickly to the point of failing to communicate expectations or facilitate the community organising needed for projects to be successful. Its engineer arrived in the community unannounced and immediately requested that it submit 20% of the material costs as buy-in for the project. While community leaders were aware of the new partnership, the community was taken aback by the abrupt arrival and request for money. Not only did many reject the demand, but also, according to the NGO, they threatened their lives. That was the last EWB heard from the NGO.

What eventually led to success was a partnership with the Catholic Church's development office, the opening of an EWB outreach office in Guatemala City, and a change in the EWB funding structure. Previously, all EWB chapters had to finance their own projects, including materials, travel, and lodging, with their own funds and donations. The new structure has large funders giving directly to the EWB central office, which then distributes those funds to chapter projects, usually covering 35–50% of costs. A new EWB outreach office in Guatemala City also provided an experienced project manager who visited the community with me and gained its trust. He was available in person or by phone to answer questions about implementation. The Catholic Church is the most trusted organisation in the region, even among the Protestant Ch'orti's. While their communication was not always reliable, as they had many projects, the ability of the Ch'orti' to walk to town and clear up any doubts with the Church was critical. Within a year of these changes, the project was implemented speedily, with hundreds of men doing the digging. The community now had double the water than before.

Several months after implementation, I returned to the community. While the water system was working as planned, the Church had not fulfilled its job of installing the water purification system. Some community members had backslid in their confidence that chlorination was not meant to poison them, and the Church seemed content to forego the chlorination system until the community unanimously demanded it. Besides, a chlorination system requires a community organisation that could collect regular fees from community members to buy chlorine. The Church was reluctant to attempt to train on chlorination in a divided community. Those community leaders who had kept the project alive by continuing to interact with EWB despite all the setbacks were falsely accused of hoarding much of the water for themselves and being paid by EWB. Their lives were being threatened. With community leaders, we had to facilitate a community assembly to dispel these rumours. Amid the recriminations and laments coming from community members themselves, we considered what they did accomplish: hundreds of men digging seven kilometres of ditch and burying 4-inch PVC pipe over very rugged and rocky mountainous terrain in only two days. The community agreed that no group of *Gringos* (foreigners) could have ever done this with only picks and shovels.

On the other hand, a permanent and respected water committee with a fee structure was a much harder sell. For such a committee to work, subcommittees must be established in each neighbourhood and report to an umbrella committee of the entire community. Also, regular full-community assemblies would have to be held. EWB needed more time, money, and partners for this. Community members who dared to be leaders were back to passing the sombrero. At the end of the assembly, the leaders urged the youth to take on the effort and risks of running an organisation, but the young men and women all stood silently with their heads down.

Discussion

This EWB project is a limited case, but the experiences of others lead us to believe that some lessons are generalisable. The first lesson is that participation, within the context of community-led development, means more than just people being part of projects designed by others. On the contrary, meaningful participation involves all stakeholders engaged in all project-related activities, eventually enabling ownership, agency, and ongoing collective action. When considering Cornwall's (2008) typology of participation, adopted from White (1996), participation in community-led development should be more than just *nominal* and *instrumental*. It should be *representative* to avoid dependency while also cultivating ownership, and *transformative* to strengthen people's agency in making and acting upon their own decisions.

Meaningful participation in indigenous contexts is no different. As Gray (1997) pointed out, especially for indigenous people, participatory approaches should be more than the indigenous people participating in projects directed towards them but that the outside professionals support them in such programming. Through cultivating such ownership, local communities can regain their collective efficacy and agency. Few would dispute this ideal, but we have seen only rare cases of the Ch'orti' communities having their own development agendas. When so, it is usually at the neighbourhood level. In most cases, communities look to outside projects for initial support, partly due to funding constraints, a shortage of available community leadership, and a lack of information about development options. Thus, many Ch'orti's either seek assistance or wait for it to arrive, including assistance running a community organisation. In a small indigenous project similar to ours, Smith, Loder, Xiquin, and Garcia (2016) present how their bottom-up approach led to success, in this case, project sustainability. Similar to our project, their project included external actors, i.e., four US volunteer groups providing funding, leadership, and technical training. However, it was the bottom-up and collaborative nature of their project, enabling the community to decide on the options the non-profits presented and how they would be carried out, that brought meaningful participation to life. Therefore, development led by local communities is always a matter of degree. For projects requiring outside assistance, participation implies collaboration in all directions – amongst community members, between members and professionals, and among project-related professionals.

Second, if participation implies collaboration, and collaboration implies unity, then everyone should have a voice. Women, the poorest, children, the disabled, and the most distant are often left out (Chambers 2008, 25–48). Our EWB project and community leaders attempted to confront this through our Photovoice[1] exercise, having regular community assemblies, and suggesting a women's oversight board, an innovation that some distant communities with successful projects had instituted. The lack of water impacted women the most, interfering with their daily cooking, washing, and cleaning chores. Some had to walk down a dangerous canyon on one-hour round trips to bring back filthy water for their households. Indeed, respect for women's labour and children's health helped unify and motivate the community to undergo the gruelling social and physical labour of overcoming distrust and organising. However, women shun leadership not only because of the risks but also because men still denigrate them in public. Men traditionally work outside the home and travel more than women, giving them an edge over women in public. If the Ch'orti' are publicly embarrassed by their marginalisation, women are doubly so. Some do voice their opinions, and women, in general, have indeed been participating more in development projects thanks to concerted efforts by development personnel, schoolteachers, and healthcare workers doggedly encouraging it. Still, project personnel must intentionally bring marginalised voices into decision-making without embarrassing them.

A third takeaway is that the history of colonisation and violence against indigenous communities presents additional challenges to participatory practices. Dispossessed of material, intellectual, and emotional resources to the point of no longer respecting themselves, they often have difficulty trusting anyone and organising. As Bodley (2007, 372) explains,

> (t)ribal peoples feel deprivation not only when the economic goals they have been encouraged to seek fail to materialise, but also when they discover that they are powerless, second-class citizens who are discriminated against and exploited by the dominant society.

Multidirectional collaboration among the indigenous is therefore often gruelling. Outside partners cannot take for granted that indigenous communities exist in some sort of cosmic harmony with a singular functional culture as if colonisation never happened (Keene 2007; Olivier de Sardan 2005, 74–74). The long-term effects of colonisation on the hesitancy to trust must be confronted. Olivier de Sardan (2005, 185–92) even counsels to expect conflict in all peasant communities, indigenous or not, and to start by searching for the competing factions.

This obstacle can be approached as an opportunity, however. By reversing colonial dispossession and re-instilling proud identities, projects can go beyond providing material benefits and impact the overall quality of life. Optimism, joy, self-esteem, collective strength, vitality, self-affirmation, and grounding, in turn, can overcome paralysing shame and give people the motivation and courage for greater community-led development (Kleymeyer 1994). Tuhiwai Smith (1999) and Kleymeyer (1994) point to methodologies or approaches by which this can be achieved: recovering one's history, recovering one's knowledge, celebrating what people have been able to maintain, revitalising language and culture by incorporating them in modern media, (re)naming colonised places, healing the social, psychological, and physical wounds of colonialism, engaging with policies and institutions that affect them rather than fatalistically accept them, expanding participation outward from colonially appointed leaders, and deliberately envisioning and creating the future, including new inventions with technology appropriated from others. If indigenous communities recover their history, know from where many (not all) of their problems come, and address them, they will no longer blame themselves for the sense of inferiority instilled in them by their colonisers. The measure of success for a CLD project can and should be more than just counting pipes installed, wells dug, or products sold; it should be about the quality of life. Therefore, facilitating processes that revitalise, energise, and engage people about their knowledge and resources can be a powerful means of initiating meaningful participation for all stakeholders.

Such holistic development is what the EWB project had hoped for. However, this required a partnership with an indigenous NGO that was not forthcoming. The NGO with which we started did not represent the entire community and was at odds with a small faction aligned with the mayor. When the mayor lost the next election, other projects and our own advanced in the community. The cultural revitalisation approach has worked in other areas of Guatemala, where indigenous peasants lead their own development initiatives. They first train members in indigenous history and rights and then seek outside support (Einbinder and Morales 2020; Lyon 2013; MacNeill 2014). The approach need not always come from within, as some communities experience identity transformations when initiated by outside patrons or clients (e.g., Dickens 2007). Part of community-led development is acknowledging that development partners bring their own values – good and bad – into the work that we do. A successful intervention requires a trust-based partnership where development partners recognise the "problematic" values they may be bringing in, and community members recognise the "good" values around inclusion and equity, which are being introduced. A prerequisite of meaningful participation is, therefore, to acknowledge and appreciate the value of different value systems. And through such acknowledgement, stakeholders can build trust in their partnership, collaboratively working towards equitable decision-making processes.

NGO partners lead us to the development industry itself. As Olivier de Sardan (2005, 70–71; see also Keene 2007) points out, someone engaging in development will be sorely disappointed if they believe development is principally about modernisation and improving the lives of others. It is a competitive market for funding and "beneficiaries" driven by the ideology of improving others' lives. Thus, development tends to divide, not unify. The development arena winners are those with the most countable results, which typically equates to large operations with well-established formulas that work quickly in a top-down fashion. The collaborative ethnographic approach advocated here is customarily considered too slow, too experimental, too unpredictable, too hard to measure, and an overall pain in the posterior (Nolan 2002, 98–103). Expecting social divisions, acknowledging local cultural diversity, and nurturing respect rather than commanding it are hardly recipes for accumulating fast and quick measurables. With this latter approach, the anthropologists, sociologists, psychologists, and social workers are the actors that become key partners, not the engineers and economists, the opposite of how the industry normally operates (Gow 2002; Nolan 2002, 105–113). This is where projects can often cause more harm than good if the industry is not paying attention. For example, with the rapid, shallow approach to development, the easiest route to measurables is simply "giving" benefits rather than painstakingly strengthening the community's existing capacities to realise its own vision for development. This contributes to a handout culture. Many Ch'orti''s would rather have gifts than self-reliance, contrary to indigenous stereotypes (Olivier de Sardan 2005, 147–48). "Sustainability" among some Guatemalan Mayas means the ability to perpetually attract projects, not autonomy (Dickens 2007). In a sense, this can be seen as a successful dependency created by the colonial – development complex. However, as other chapters in this volume show, a systematic process of decolonisation and shifting power to communities can go a long way in mitigating these harmful impacts.

Conclusion

Implementing a successful project with a large, poor indigenous community takes time, patience, and hard work. Consensus decision-making in indigenous communities is often favoured, but with communities of thousands of people, the odds are against it. Social divisions should be expected, as should psychological obstacles like shame and envy. Understanding local history and identity is critical. The EWB project partially succeeded when we overcame historically ingrained distrust exacerbated by past development failures, our own and our NGO partners' mistakes, the ethnic and competitive structure of the local NGO industry, and extreme poverty. Mistakes and obstacles should be expected and not become the cause of project abandonment. The project's partial success necessitated finding a trusted NGO partner, having experienced professionals on the ground more regularly, and gaining more funding. At a more general level, partial success required genuine respect and concern for the Ch'orti', especially the women and children, and determination by community leaders and EWB. The EWB project in Guatemala failed to unite and organise the community to sustain its project, as the sombrero continued to be passed, and no one volunteered to oversee chlorination. Building leadership representing entire communities would be necessary to overcome this failure while recognising that leaders sacrifice their time and safety in divided communities. For this reason, regular community assemblies are needed to dispel rumours and enhance community buy-in. From the development partner side, social scientists who know the background of, respect, and communicate well with the people can provide mediation support.

None of this is to say that community-led development is impossible among people like the Ch'orti's, who have many cards stacked against them. Some Ch'orti' communities and many other Maya ones as well have organised themselves to carry out their development, including their own water projects, but scaling beyond hundreds of households has been especially challenging (e.g., DeHart 2009; MacNeill 2014; Smith et al. 2016).

Finally, with the interactive model of development (Nolan 2002) that EWB ultimately used, success and sustainability are ephemeral, relative, and a matter of degree. It is not limited to materiality but social and emotional improvements, which are difficult to measure and thus regularly disregarded in development. We want people to appropriate the resources we offer, but in community-led development, it is up to them to determine how.

Note

1 Photovoice is a development exercise in which marginalised people are given cameras to document their perspectives. They are then interviewed as to why they took each photo, and fora and exhibitions are held for group consciousness-raising. For a fuller treatment and a review of our own photovoice exercise, see Gentry and Metz (2017).

References

Beck, Erin. 2017. *How Development Projects Persist: Everyday Negotiations with Guatemalan NGOs*. Durham: Duke University Press.

Bodley, John. 2007. "The Price of Progress." In *Faces of Anthropology*, edited by Kevin A. Rafferty and Dorothy Chin we Ukaegbu, 364–273. Upper Saddle River, NJ: Pearson/Prentice Hall.

Casolo, Jennifer. 2011. "Unthinkable Rebellion and the Praxis of the Possible: Ch'orti" Campesin@ Struggles in Guatemala's Eastern Highlands." PhD diss., Department of Geography, University of California, Berkeley. ProQuest Dissertations & Theses Global.

Chambers, Robert. 2008. *Revolutions in Development Inquiry*. London: Earthscan.

Cleaver, Francis. 2001. "Institutions, Agency, and the limitations of Participatory Approaches to Development." In *Participation: The New Tyranny?*, edited by Bill Cooke and Uma Kothari. London: Zed Books, pp. 36–55.

Clouser, Rebecca. 2018. "Reality and Rumour: The Grey Areas of International Development in Guatemala." *Third World Quarterly 39*(4): 769–785.

COMISIÓN PARA EL ESCLARECIMIENTO HISTÓRICO (CEH). 1999. *Guatemala: Memoria del silencio. Vol II. Las violaciones de los derechos humanos y los hechos de violencia.* Guatemala: Office of Services for United Nations Projects.

Cooke, Bill, and Uma Kothari (eds.) 2001. *Participation: The New Tyranny?* London: Zed Books.

Cornwall, Andrea. 2008. "Unpacking 'Participation': Models, Meanings, and Practices." *Community Development Journal* 43(3): 269–283.

Dary, Claudia, Silvel Elías, and Violeta Reyna. 1998. *Estrategias de sobrevivencia campesina en ecosistemas frágiles*. Guatemala City: FLACSO.

Dehart, Monica. 2009. "Fried Chicken or *Pop*? Redefining Development and Ethnicity in Totonicapán." *Bulletin of Latin American Research* 28(1): 63–82.

Dickins, Avery. 2007. "El Otro Lado: Local Ends and Development in a Q'eqchi' Maya Community." *Social Analysis* 51(2): 167–184.

Einbinder, Nathan Brian, and Helda Morales. 2020. "Development from Within: Agroecology and the Quest for Utziil K'asleem in the Maya-Achí Territory of Guatemala." *Journal of Latin American Geography* 19: 133–158.

Figueroa Ibarra, Carlos. 2017. "Los acuerdos de paz en Guatemala, veinte años después." *LASA Forum* 48(1): 9–12.

Gentry, Jodi, and Brent Metz. 2017. "Adapting Photovoice to the Marginal Indigenous Ch'orti'' Maya." *Human Organization* 76(3): 251–63.

Gow, David D. 2002. "Anthropology and Development: Evil Twin or Moral Narrative?" *Human Organization* 61(4): 299–313.

Grant, Emma. 2001. "Social Capital and Community Strategies: Neighbourhood Development in Guatemala City." *Development and Change* 32(5): 975–997. doi: 10.1111/1467-7660.00234.

Gray, Andrew. 1997. "Development Practice and Indigenous Peoples." In *Indigenous Peoples, Environment, and Development*, edited by Sylvia Buchi, Christian Erni, Luzia Jurt, and Christoph Ruegg, pp.287–305. Copenhagen: International Work Group for Indigenous Affairs and Department of Social Anthropology, University of Zurich.

INE (Instituto Nacional de Estadística). 2013. *Mapas de pobreza rural en Guatemala 2011: Resumen ejecutivo*. Guatemala City: Instituto Nacional de Estadística.

Keene, Courtney. 2007. "Development Projects That Didn't Work: The Perils of Narrow Approaches to Complex Situations." *Globalhood Research Paper*, October.

Kleymeyer, Charles David (ed.) 1994. *Cultural Expression and Grassroots Development: Cases from Latin America and the Caribbean*. Boulder: Lynne Rienner.

López García, Julián, and Brent Metz. 2002. *Primero Dios: Etnografía y cambio social entre los mayas Ch'orti's del oriente de Guatemala*. Guatemala City: FLACSO.

Lyon, Sarah. 2013. "Coffee Tourism and Community Development in Guatemala." *Human Organization* 72(3): 188–198.

MacNeill, Tim. 2014. "Culturally Sustainable Development: Maya Culture, Indigenous Institutions, and Alternative Development in Guatemala." *Cultural Dynamics* 26: 299–325.

Metz, Brent E. 2006. *Ch'orti" Maya Survival in Eastern Guatemala: Indigeneity in Transition*. Albuquerque: University of New Mexico Press.

Metz, Brent, and Alfredo Francesch. 2015. "Llamas de inseguridad en el oriente de Guatemala: Megaproyectos y la quema de la municipalidad de Jocotán." In *Dinosaurio reloaded: Violencias actuales en Guatemala*, edited by Manuela Camus, Santiago Bastos, and Julián López, 247–69. Guatemala: FLACSO and Universidad de Córdoba.

Nolan, Riall. 2002. *Anthropology and Development: Encounters in the Real World*. Boulder: Westview.

Oficina de Derechos Humanos del Arzobispado de Guatemala (ODHAG). 1998. *Guatemala: Nunca más*, 3 volumes. Guatemala: Proyecto Interdiocesano de Recuperación de la Memoria Histórica (REMHI).

Olivier de Sardan, Jean-Pierre. 2005. *Anthropology and Development: Understanding Contemporary Social Change*. London: Zed Books.

Proyecto Desarrollo Rural para Pequeños Productores en Zacapa y Chiquimula. 1991. Informe final del sondeo. Documento 003, Ministerio de Agricultura, Ganadería, y Alimentación/FIDA/Gobierno de los Países Bajos/OPEP/PMA/Gobierno de Guatemala.

Rohloff, Peter, Anne Díaz, and Shom Dasgupta. 2011. "Beyond Development: A Critical Appraisal of the Emergence of Small Health Care Non-Governmental Organizations in Rural Guatemala. *Human Organization* 70(4): 427–437.

Ruano, Ana Lorena, Kjerstin Dahlblom, Ana Karen Hurtig, and Miguel San Sebastián. 2011. "'If No One Else Stands Up, You Have to': A Story of Community Participation and Water in Rural Guatemala." *Global Health Action* 4.

Sánchez Díaz, Silvia María. 2016. "Failing to Address Structural Causes of Food Scarcity: The Politics of Development Funding, Competition, and Corruption in the Ch'orti" Maya Area." Masters thesis, University of Kansas. ProQuest Dissertations & Theses Global.

Smith, Jeffrey S., Rachel J. Loder, Sonia Xiquin, and Ana Adela Garcia. 2016. "How a Strong Sense of Community Led to Improvements in Rural Health Care: The Case of Patanatic, Guatemala." *Journal of International Development* 28: 631–639.

Tuhiwai Smith, Linda. 1999. *Decolonizing Methodologies: Research and Indigenous Peoples*. London: Zed Books.

White, Sarah C. 1996. "Depoliticising Development: The Uses and Abuses of Participation." *Development in Practice* 6(1): 6–15. doi: 10.1080/0961452961000157564

Wisdom, Charles. 1940. *The Chorti Indians of Guatamala*. Chicago: University of Chicago Press.

11

LOCAL KNOWLEDGE AND RESOURCES FOR COMMUNITY-LED DEVELOPMENT IN SOUTH AFRICA

Looking through an Asset-Based Lens

Hanna Nel

Introduction

Community development is embedded in the rights-based development approach of South Africa (Republic of South Africa (RSA) 1997) and has been seen as one of the most appropriate ways to address the country's unique history of human rights violation, underdevelopment, and inequality (Patel 2015). Although South Africa has undergone major changes since the end of apartheid, poverty has unfortunately increased. Community development interventions have not been sufficient in addressing the poverty-related challenges communities face. Within South Africa, community development has traditionally relied mostly on a deficit problem-based approach, both before and after 1994. In this case, community practitioners focus on "what they do not have and not what they have" (Nel, Louw, Schenck & Skhosana 2021, 19), which can easily lead community members to feel helpless, and reliant on outside assistance. Community-led development includes problem-solving cases but then also approaches that prioritise the recognition and appreciation of local resources and knowledge as an interventions' start-off point, one such being Asset-Based Community-Driven Development (ABCD).

As a community-led methodology, ABCD has gained momentum over the last ten years in South Africa (Nel & Pretorius 2012; Pretorius & Nel 2012; Nel 2018a, 2020). It has contributed to a shift that emphasises that community members have knowledge and resources valuable to their well-being. This shift in thinking, focusing on what people have and can do, addresses the internalised powerlessness and dependency of many South Africans caused by colonialism and apartheid. Furthermore, awareness of local knowledge and resources can prevent future exploitation, restore people's power, pride, and independence, and raise their consciousness about taking control of their future. Additionally, the

DOI: 10.4324/9781003377917-15

approach leverages local knowledge and resources and reinforces local organic leadership, accentuating the notion of civic duty in relation to rights. Recognising local knowledge and resources is important, but the mobilisation of communities towards the appreciation and utilisation of these resources towards sustainable development is crucial (Mathie & Cunningham 2003).

ABCD is the theoretical framework underlying this chapter and the focus of the chapter's first section. Sections two and three respectively outline the guiding principles of ABCD and a typology of assets typically explored and emphasised during interventions. Section four introduces some tools and methods community practitioners can use to make people aware of what they have and how they can use it, drawing from South African examples. Section five reflects on the issue of engagement with outside stakeholders within the ABCD framework. Section six outlines a case study from the Eastern Cape Province to show how community practitioners can use the tools discussed in the previous sections to play a role in people's recognition and appreciation of their own knowledge and resources. Section seven delves into the limitations and challenges of the ABCD approach. Section eight offers concluding remarks.

ABCD as a conceptual framework

To begin, let me clarify some of the key terms used in this chapter. The two most common distinctions of the term "community" are community as a place and community as a social construct which echoes shared interests and a sense of belonging (Block 2009; Preece 2017). Development can refer to either or both a process or an outcome. For the purposes of this chapter, community development is seen as a participatory process with an end goal of agency, i.e., "the capacity of people to order their world, the capacity to create, reproduce, change and live according to their own meaning systems, to have the powers to define themselves as opposed to being defined by others" (Bhattacharyya 2004, 12). Community-led development is the process of enabling the above (Preece 2017). It is a participatory, collective approach to enhancing individual as well as collective human agency while also providing people the support they need to address their material needs.

Community-led practice, on the other hand, is how community-led development takes place. It is "a managed change process facilitated with the community to build collective agency in meeting their needs to enhance their wellbeing and the quality of their own lives and those of the wider community of which they are part" (Nel et al., 2021, XVIII). In community-led development, facilitation is not restricted to only practitioners. Instead, community members are also instrumental in facilitating activities, meetings, and mobilisations.

ABCD is a community-led development approach that focuses on what communities have, what is strong, and what works, and then builds on from there (Mathie & Cunningham 2003, 2005; Kramer, Amos, Lazarus & Seedat 2012;

Pretorius & Nel 2012; Nel & Pretorius 2012; Nel 2018a, 2020). This approach guides community members in developing "new eyes about themselves and their surroundings," and for professionals "it shifts the conversation from thinking of citizens as objects to fix, to assets to tap" (Morse 2011, 10). The intention is to surface hidden local knowledge, resources, assets, gifts, and capabilities and grow a shared vision and appreciation from which to move forward. The intervention of ABCD always starts with a participatory synopsis of local resources and knowledge. Community-led development approaches, in general, value local knowledge and resources, but others may not start with this kind of analysis that centres on local assets. Within the ABCD framework, practitioners and scholars talk about assets but it comes down to the same as knowledge and resources within the community-led development context.

Kretzmann and McKnight (1993) coined the ABCD approach as an alternative to the deficit, problem-based approach to community development. What differentiates the ABCD approach from the problem-focused or the needs-based approach is the attention on strengths, capabilities, and assets, stimulating community-level organising and action, and the role of different stakeholders as responsive co-investors and co-creators in community-level action. This potentially also points to shared responsibility, keeping all stakeholders accountable. By using existing local knowledge and resources, strengths and capacities of communities (social, natural, cultural, financial, physical, human) as the starting point, the approach acknowledges citizens' contributions that have often been unnoticed or undervalued by development actors (Ashford & Patkar 2001; Braun 2005; Homan 2011; Landry & Peters 2018; Nel et al. 2021). The strength of ABCD is that community resources and knowledge are always used, in some way or another, and in all community initiatives.

The ABCD approach believes that community change should come from within. When using their own resources, communities realise they can build their future without depending on outside help. They experience success, build their confidence, and take ownership of their future. They become empowered and independent citizens by using their own knowledge and resources. ABCD is thus citizen-driven, where residents are both experts and drivers of change, using their capacities, abilities, and gifts in their development endeavours. In turn, by focusing on their internal existing assets and strengths as resources for change, communities feel a sense of agency and become owners of their destinies. They also decide how outside organisations can best support them in the process (Eliasov 2013; Frediani 2010; Preece 2017).

Principles of ABCD

Drawing on the discussion above, we can identify seven main principles of ABCD that also align with broader community-led development objectives. These principles emphasise the importance of recognising, making visible, and centring local resources and knowledge in community-led efforts. (1) Change comes from within the community; it is an endogenous inside-out approach. (2) Any engagement should focus on recognising what already exists in a community in terms of its knowledge and resources. (3) Development goals should be community-led, with communities using their resources and then leveraging outside support. This ensures the development aligns with their needs and priorities. (4) Change should be relationship-driven because relationships between people are needed to reveal and galvanise different kinds of resources. (5) The development process should be participatory and collaborative to ensure community ownership of decision-making. In ABCD interventions, participation is both a process and outcome. (6) Internal and external stakeholders, such as community-based organisations, government, and businesses, need to be involved in a collective way, supplementing resources already used by the community and on the terms determined by the community members. Internal stakeholders, such as a women's sewing group that makes uniforms for children in the secondary school, a women's support group focusing on gender-based violence, priests, and traditional healers, should be approached first before reaching out to external stakeholders. (7) Citizen power is the end goal for ABCD. All interventions should therefore strengthen community members' agency to address structural inequities (Ashford & Patkar 2001; Kretzmann & McKnight 1993; Nel 2018a, 2018b; Nel et al. 2021).

Phases of ABCD implementation

While keeping the principles in mind, change agents apply the following phases of ABCD, namely, connecting and discovering, dreaming/visioning, designing, delivery, and disconnecting and departing (Nel et al. 2021). The process begins with a period to connect and build relationships with community members and different stakeholders in the community, and to discover in collaboration with the community, "what works well." Based on the connecting and discovery phase where assets, strengths, and capabilities were discovered the group discusses how they can build on their strengths to better their community based on the discoveries made in the discovery phase.

Community visioning, the second phase of the process, is a collaborative process of giving the people who live, work, and play in a place the opportunity to have a say about what they want their community to be like in the future. They construct a vision of "what their community might be like if they build on and improve the best of what is and strengths they have become aware of" (Nel et al. 2021, 173).

Designing or planning, the third phase, is a pro-active process where the participants take control by making decisions about the design. It is the beginning of the transformation process from stories, ideas, visions, and feelings to actions and projects.

The delivery phase happens when the community implements the plan by mobilising their own and external assets (Yeneabat & Butterfield 2012; Eliasov

2013; Nel et al. 2021). External resources can be more effectively utilised if the community has already mobilised its own resources and knows what is needed from external resources. This potentially transforms the community into an active participant in development leading towards sustainability (Demeshane & Nel 2018; Nel 2018a, 2018b).

When sustainability is reached the community practitioner could disconnect and depart. This phase is not a one-off event but a process which consists of preparation for disconnecting and departing, evaluation, disconnecting, the stabilisation of achievements, and building sustainability and departing. People who are participating in the community interventions are introduced to participatory monitoring and evaluation (PM&E) from the initiation of the community interventions. PM&E is to track implementation and outputs systematically and to see to which degree the intervention is achieving its objectives and where changes may be needed. The importance is that the community members must be involved so that they can recognise the progress made and strengthen the sustainability of activities (Nel et al. 2021).

A local knowledge and resources typology

ABCD, as a community-led development approach, was designed to bring recognition to local, existing resources, challenging the misperceptions that external assets are better. Therefore, the community practitioner's focus is to facilitate community members to appreciate their resources, strengths, and capabilities, and enable them to see opportunities for collaboration to create the interventions they envision. Recognition of knowledge and resources is thus a condition for collaboration.

In community-led development, local resources and knowledge belong to everybody in the community and should therefore be beneficial to all. ABCD interventions, therefore, cultivate inclusivity by recognising the assets and capacities of individuals and the collective, and finding opportunities for collaboration that benefit everyone (Mathie & Cunningham 2003). These benefits should extend beyond those involved in the activities. Community-led interventions often have a ripple effect beyond the immediate participants, so even those who do not participate can still benefit. Emphasising local resources and knowledge is therefore not only about equity but also about generosity.

Assets are tangible and intangible resources available for people to use towards their shared and individual needs. The literature on ABCD identifies five types of assets: personal and human, physical, natural, financial, and social (Kretzmann & McKnight 1993; Mathie & Cunningham 2003; Ife & Tesoriero 2006; Green & Haines 2008; McKnight & Block 2010).

The first type of asset is human assets, which refers to human capacities, talents, knowledge, experience, and skills. To simplify, human assets can be divided into head, heart, and hands skills. Head skills refer to knowledge people have, e.g., strategic planning and knowledge of gardening. Assets of the heart refer to the passion people have, for example, the elderly, children, and animals, and hands skills refer to skills a person has gained at home, work, or in the community, e.g., hair-cutting, carpentry, sewing, beadwork, and baking. People often forget they have this kind of asset within themselves and focus only on external ones. Energised and motivated, strong, positive, and ethical leadership in informal leaders are also talents situated in people but are not always recognised.

Physical man-made assets such as buildings, institutions, and infrastructure, e.g., roads, water, and electricity, are the second type of asset. Examples of physical assets include higher education institutions, public schools, health care services, clinics, police stations, and banks. Institutions are often overlooked, but they provide valuable resources for communities. By identifying these institutions, community members can access resources such as meeting venues or the Department of Agriculture that could provide resources for community vegetable gardens.

The third kind of asset includes natural resources such as land, parks, rivers, and mountains. To raise awareness about these resources, participants often map them out in a participatory exercise. This helps people realise that they may not be using their land responsibly, not preserving clean water, not growing healthy food, and not utilising natural energy sources. It is common for community members to be surprised by the abundance of natural resources in their areas (Kretzmann & McKnight 1993; Nel et al. 2021).

The fourth kind of asset is the economic assets, such as wages, salaries, burial societies, and savings groups (called "stokvels" in South Africa) (Mathie & Cunningham 2008). Community members in poverty-stricken communities usually think they have no finances. Becoming aware of the above types of financial assets can be motivational, as it helps people recognise what they already possess (Alcock 2016, 2018; Nel 2018a, 2018b, 2020).

As within broader community-led conversations, there is also a strong emphasis on social capital in ABCD (Mathie & Cunningham 2003; Ife & Tesoriero 2006; Green & Haines 2008). The fifth typology of assets, social assets, refers to the networks, connectedness, and relationships of trust and reciprocity that people depend on to make a living. Social assets are also inherent to collaborative community-building (Green & Haines 2008; Ife & Tesoriero 2006), and the glue that not only keeps people together but also provides them access to all other assets (Mathie & Cunningham 2003). In addition, social assets encompass the philanthropy of the community, which in turn, highlights the horizontal relations among people, a key principle of "Ubuntu." This African philosophy emphasises the idea "I am because we are" and therefore "I cannot be if you are not." Ubuntu is thus about social networks and connections and views individuals in the context of their collective rather than separate entities, because personhood is expressed in terms of relationship, caring, sharing, and group solidarity (Preece 2017). Real social capital includes spiritual capital as well, as "no other kind of capital really works without an underlying base of spiritual capital" (Zohar & Marshall 2004, 3).

Community associations, both formal and informal, seen as social assets, are one of the main features of the ABCD approach, especially within the South African context. These voluntary organisations operate based on consent and play a vital role in building strong communities while facilitating the development and strengthening of social capital (Mathie & Cunningham 2003; Green & Haines 2008). In South Africa, various types of associations exist, including informal burial societies, "stokvels," church groups, women's groups, and groups formed around sports, arts, and culture or social issues, for example, gender-based violence – a pressing problem in South Africa. Citizen-driven development happens spontaneously when community members organise themselves and establish associations that strengthen communities. Many associations can expand beyond their original purposes by collaborating with public and private sector institutions (Mathie & Cunningham 2003, 2005).

Practices of recognition and appreciation: Methods and tools

ABCD has developed tools and methods practitioners can use to support communities in identifying their resources and knowledge. These tools and methods often also address the internalised powerlessness and dependency of many South Africans by engaging them in an in-depth way, conscientising them on what they have, and in the process strengthening local ownership (Nel 2018a, 2018b; Nel et al. 2021). I share examples of some of these methods and tools below.

The practice of *storytelling* is rooted in Appreciative Inquiry, developed by Cooperrider and Srivastva in the 1980s, and widely applied in the South African context (Whitney, Trosten-Bloom & Rader 2010; Nel 2011). Storytelling is usually the first point of entry when the community practitioner enters a community. Its purpose is to discover the best of the past with a particular group of people. Through these stories, they can then uncover assets, strengths, and resources to address their challenges and to build on to sustain their communities. Storytelling is also a way to interact and build relationships, a prominent value in South African culture, as expressed through Ubuntu (Pretorius & Nel 2012; Nel & Pretorius 2012; Nel et al. 2021). Through storytelling, people discover their local knowledge, resources, strengths, and networks of friends and relationships while also identifying what they care about as a collective, motivating them to take action (Block 2009; Ssewamala, Sperber, Zimmerman & Karimili 2010; Nel 2011; Eliasov 2013).

In Appreciative Inquiry, community practitioners encourage people to share their positive stories and listen to one another. They start by asking people to share more about themselves. They may ask: "Share about an event in the last three months where you experienced success, or tell a story about a time in the last three months when you felt very good about yourself." Then they explore the community's history and interventions, either self-initiated or externally organised, that have been successful, focusing on the strengths and successes. Probing questions can include: "What can you tell me about the people involved? What characteristics

TABLE 11.1 Head, heart, hand tool, used with a group of unemployed women from Soweto in 2018

Head/Knowledge	*Hands/Labour*	*Heart/Passion/Interest*
Strategic planning	Sewing	Passion for elderly people
Ideas/innovations	Washing Laundry	Taking care of children
Decision-making abilities	Gardening/Farming	Heart for gardening
Knowledge of beadwork	Cleaning	Heart for vulnerable children
Know how to do marketing	Ironing	Love singing
Budgeting	Needlework	Working with animals

did they have that helped make it successful? What was it about you that made it successful?" The community practitioner then helps community members draw themes from the stories beginning to understand why the process unfolded as it did and see the connections between the various assets, strengths, and capabilities (Mathie & Cunningham 2008).

In Nel et al. (2021), Erasmus describes how storytelling helped a community in Riemvasmaak, in the Northern Province of South Africa, grapple with the past and how to move forward. The community was forcefully removed from their land in 1984 by the apartheid government. After the end of apartheid in 1994, some community members could return to Riemvasmaak. Through storytelling, people were allowed to talk about their past and have their experiences heard. Their stories included not only negative experiences but also experiences of coping, adapting, and surviving, of what they are proud of, their successes and failures. In these stories lie the seeds of dreams, visions, and energy for the future. Highlighting personal successes and coping mechanisms can lead to a better understanding of oneself and the community.

Another tool ABCD facilitators use is the *Head, Heart, and Hand (HHH)* exercise. We use this tool to help communities identify their human assets, including talents and skills. Table 11.1 is an example of the "head, heart and hand" tool used by a graduate student with a group of unemployed women in Soweto, Johannesburg in 2018. During this exercise, several women discovered some "hidden gifts," became energised, and started identifying opportunities for income generation initiatives.

Typically after community members participate in a *transect walk* through their community, they map their physical and natural assets (see Figure 11.1). Transect walks and mapping are often used in community development practice, most notably in Participatory Rural Appraisal (PRA) (Chambers 1994). Transect walks are encouraged by facilitators to deepen people's awareness of these resources, physically seeing and experiencing them with new appreciation. The energy levels usually rise during these exercises. Community members start thinking about how to include these assets in the community-building endeavours. The

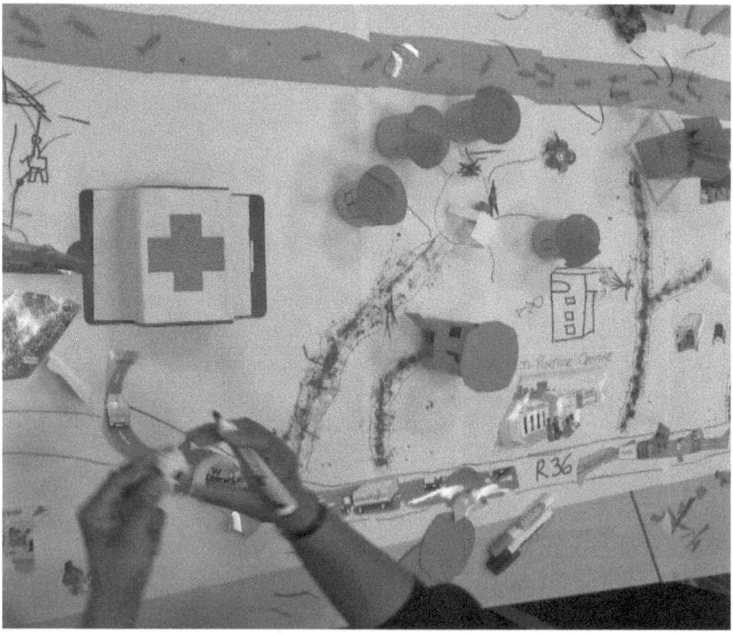

FIGURE 11.1 Mapping of physical and natural assets facilitated by a student in an informal township in South Africa in 2021.

mapping exercise in Figure 11.1 was facilitated by a Community Development and Leadership graduate student with a group of eight unemployed community members in an informal township in 2021. They drew the map collaboratively and were inspired to realise they have physical and natural assets despite their disadvantaged circumstances.

Another useful tool for mapping a community's economic assets is the *leaky bucket* exercise (see Figure 11.2).

It can help community members understand the local economy and their role within it (for example, sources of income, how people spend their income, and how well local resources are maximised for local benefit). The leaky bucket demystifies community economics (Mathie & Cunningham 2008). People realise that they have different income sources, can exchange goods and services, and buy and sell locally instead of outside the community. By participating in this exercise, community members also discover how they could build wealth by pooling their small wages and savings together instead of relying solely on individual means. For example, a group of community members in the Peddie community in the Eastern Cape Province noticed they were spending a lot of money and time buying vegetables outside their community. But when using the leaky bucket to understand their economic situation, they discovered they had access to open land, and some members had both passion and skills for gardening. They used their own resources

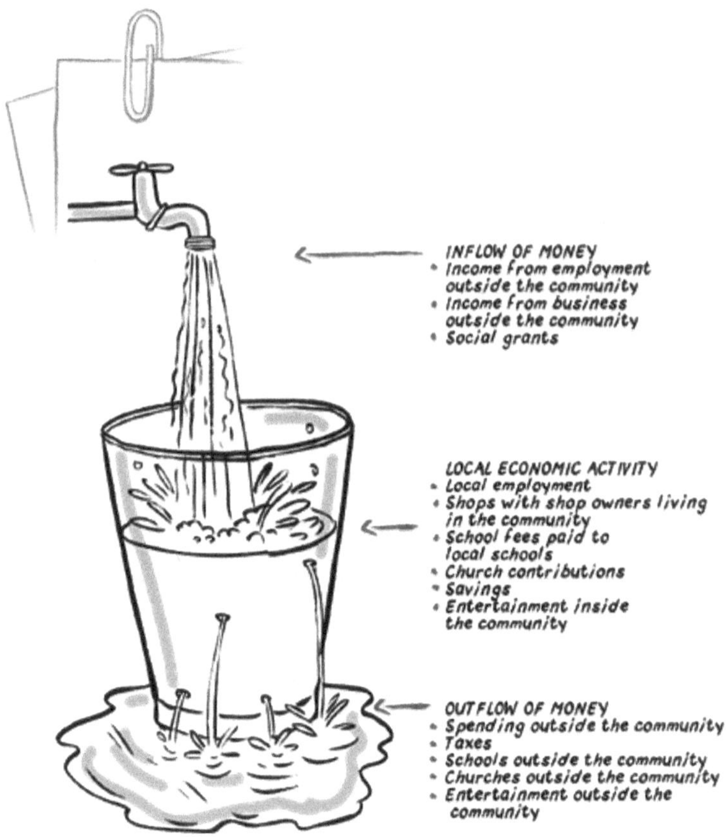

FIGURE 11.2 Economic activities in the community: Leaky bucket.
Source: Nel et al. (2021, 168).

in a collaborative manner to start the project, e.g., seeds, compost, and utensils, to start a vegetable garden on municipal property. They initially provided vegetables to their own households and later began selling them to the larger community.

Venn diagrams are usually used to enable citizens to discover their associations and community-based organisations (Mathie & Cunningham 2005; Nel & Pretorius 2012). Through this exercise people usually discover the strength of these associations and community-based organisations and their positive role in building communities. Often community members focus only on the conflict and negative relationships and networks in a community, but when they start mapping out their social assets, people recognise the positive relationships in small informal associations and community groups, such as a women's prayer group, community groups focusing on substance abuse, and gender-based violence. People discover the unity and partnerships in the community. For

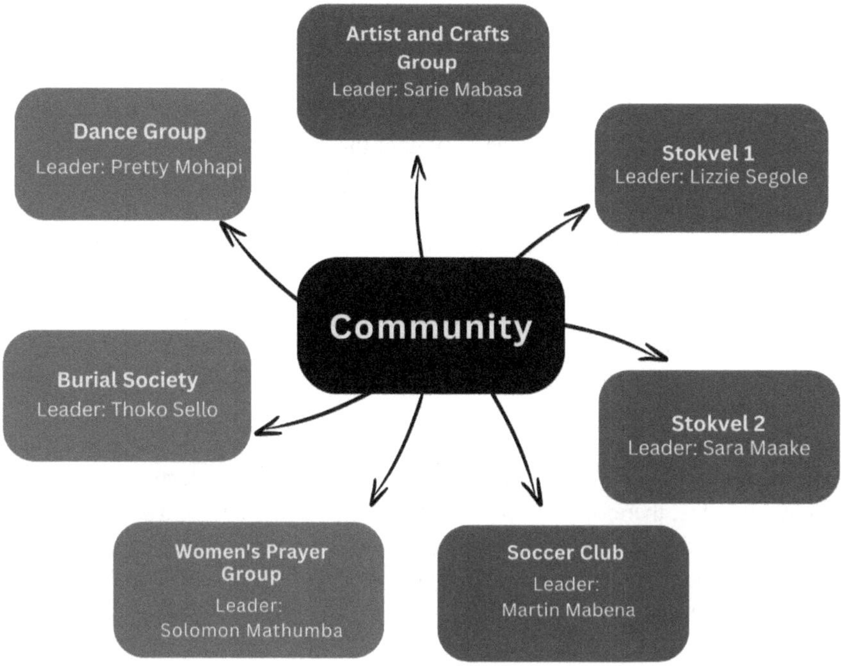

FIGURE 11.3 Venn diagram of associations done by students.

example, (see Figure 11.3) a community group in an informal community in Soweto, Johannesburg, in South Africa, discovered various associations and institutions inside and outside the community. The largest circle in the figure represents the community.

Outside stakeholder engagement in ABCD

The mobilisation and application of local knowledge and resources can increase the internal capabilities and capital of communities, which can be leveraged to attract investments from various "outside" stakeholders (Frediani 2010; Whitney, Trosten-Bloom & Rader 2010). In such cases external assistance from funders and the government will not have the power to dictate, but they will work together with the communities on their (communities') terms. The communities are the masters and experts of their situations, and livelihoods are better understood by the communities themselves. Outsiders can only learn in those situations and provide assistance in terms of knowledge and resources communicated by the communities (Nel 2018a, 2018b, 2020). Focus on local knowledge and resources will strengthen indigenous knowledge systems and cultural practices, which will lead to self-reliance and ownership (Nel 2020).

In the emerging literature on ABCD and stakeholder engagement, Landry and Peters (2018) mention the importance of building both horizontal and vertical forms of citizenship and accountability. For sustainability, collective agency within communities and stakeholder engagement need to be emphasised (Demeshane & Nel 2018; Nel 2018a, 2018b). It is important that communities form partnerships with relevant stakeholders on terms determined by the communities and not the stakeholders. However, this is often not the case. The community members as a partner are often informed, or at best consulted, about project designs and budgets. There is often a lack of transparency. These projects may be described as "locally owned," but often community members have little experience or power in the process. This could be a reason why many externally driven programmes and projects are unsuccessful (Ashford & Patkar 2001; Ife & Tesoriero 2006; Kramer et al. 2012; Mansvelt 2018).

This is not to question the participation of external stakeholders in ABCD initiatives. That is essential, albeit carried out on terms determined by the community. It is, therefore, important for the community members and partners to be clear about the types of engagements they wish to create. Building cooperative relationships between individuals, associations, and institutions will enable them to build their communities (Nel 2020).

Case study: The beekeepers of Gcinizwe: Turning local resources into hopeful futures

In this section, I share a case study of 12 women from the rural Eastern Cape community of Peddie who identified and then built on their local resources and knowledge to ensure better lives for themselves and their families using the five phases discussed above to implement ABCD (Nel et al. 2021). These are: (1) connecting and discovering assets, (2) creating a shared vision, (3) designing a plan, (4) implementing/delivering the plan by mobilising assets and connecting with outside resources, and (5) disconnecting and departing.

South Africa's rural Eastern Cape Province has some of the highest poverty numbers in the country, comparable to some of the poorest rural areas in sub-Saharan Africa (Crais 2011). In addition to poverty, people face unemployment, gender-based violence, HIV/AIDS, and crime. The 12 women approached a community practitioner in a nearby town. The practitioner met with the women individually and informally to get to know them better and build rapport. Thereafter she met with them in a group and applied storytelling to uncover their successes and achievements. When they did their transact walk to map their community's natural and physical assets, the women realised they had huge plantations where bees lived, high rainfall, fertile soil, and a river nearby. Additionally, they also identified physical assets such as a tarred road, houses (both built and informal houses), a school, a clinic, the Department of Agriculture offices close by, an NGO – Family South Africa (FAMSA), local municipality, and a satellite office of the Walter Sisulu University. When doing their head, heart, and hands exercises, they discovered skills such as baking, cooking, vegetable growing, and how they care for vulnerable children and their mothers. They also identified several associations, including a woman's beading work group, and a church choir group, and appreciated the positive and trusting relationships in the community. Regarding financial assets, the women listed various saving clubs and burial societies and shared that, however small, they receive unemployment, pension, and disability grants from the government.

Together these unemployed women decided to start a beekeeping project. They cleaned the bush and ordered bee hives from a carpenter in the community, sponsored by the NGO, FAMSA that they had identified. FAMSA also provided the group with R2,000.00 start-up capital. The women then used their social grant money to fence the beehives, and then, together, started to visit the beehives every day. They also decided to meet weekly to catch up on any and all other business. They decided to call the beekeeping project "Gcinizwe," or "supporting the nation" in amaXhosa, the local language. It took three years before the women and their families started benefitting from the bee project. First, they started selling honey in the nearby town of Peddie and later expanded their sales to other towns. As this area is popular among tourists, the sale of honey was successful. The group also started to network with other beekeeping projects, sharing resources and gaining advice in the process. With the income, they were now able to send their children to school and ensure they received an education.

But the women did not only focus on bees. Because the beekeeping project took some time to produce an income, they devised additional plans to address their basic subsistence needs. After securing access to a municipal plot, they started a big garden with mostly their own resources. And this garden, they shared "keeps us busy, and we are not hungry anymore." After negotiations, the Department of Agriculture also donated potato seedlings for their garden. As their vegetable garden project gained traction, more people in the community took notice and started their own vegetable gardens. Thus the women's project had a positive impact on the broader community, resulting in not only more vegetable gardens but also people offering advice and sharing vegetables with each other.

By participating in the ABCD approach, the group of 12 women and later the wider community were able to identify and appreciate the assets within themselves and their surroundings. They discovered trees and flowers as natural resources for the bees and became aware of the fertile soil, high rainfall, and the nearby river's consistent water supply. In addition, they discovered the physical assets in their community, such as the Department of Agriculture, the municipality, the clinic, and the tarred road connecting them to various towns, markets, and shop owners where they can sell their produce. They also discovered their human assets, including a local carpenter who assists them in maintaining their beehives. Most important, perhaps, is how they discovered and expanded on their social connections and built trust, camaraderie, and interdependence, especially among group members.

As they shared, “None of us just makes decisions for the group; there is no way that one person can decide for the twelve of us. We always decide in meetings, and everyone is free to come up with their views.”

As of 2016, the local government continues to support the women because of their commitment and the potential of the project. The municipality has pledged additional bee boxes, and the Department of Agriculture provided more seedlings and training. A local councillor has also shown support by putting up a billboard to advertise the project to passing drivers. While not providing big signposts, other formal and traditional community leaders have also pledged their support to the women and their initiatives. The women’s group has also grabbed the attention of the Walter Sisulu University, that is sending students from the university to “learn from the community women.” Overall, this case study demonstrates how a small group of women turned a problem into an opportunity by leveraging community assets.

Limitations and challenges of the ABCD development model

As with all approaches, ABCD, and community-led development more broadly defined, are confronted with limitations and challenges. Firstly, there is a danger that community-led development over-emphasises the contributions of community members and associations in terms of community-building endeavours. This could divert attention from the roles and responsibilities of external stakeholders such as government and businesses in community development endeavours and let these stakeholders “off the hook” (Friedli 2011; Foot 2012; MacLeod & Emejulu 2014). This scenario is changing in South Africa as community practitioners make an effort to engage external stakeholders on various levels, such as local government and businesses, and constantly remind them of the important role external stakeholders play in community-building initiatives.

Secondly, community-led development and ABCD have been interpreted as “neoliberalism with a community face,” meaning that the model encourages a free-market system and thus hostility towards government-sponsored social welfare (MacLeod & Emejulu 2014). Mathie and Cunningham (2008) are of the opinion that ABCD practitioners train communities to survive within Western societies that are driven by neo-liberal models instead of challenging, for example, the economic system. However, cases are emerging in South Africa where community-led development and ABCD practitioners, alongside the communities they work with, are challenging the economic system. They are doing so by enhancing informal township economies (KasiNomics) that are embedded in decolonised African culture and practices (see, for example, Alcock 2016, 2018).

Thirdly, while ABCD, in particular, has some opportunity for creating a dialogue with the macro-level structures that impact communities, for example, government, municipality, and businesses, the approach and model have been criticised for ignoring issues related to power and oppression (Mathie & Cunningham 2003). For practitioners and, most importantly, the communities they serve, the ideological foundations of the unjust macro issues might be not only difficult to accept but also difficult to challenge. However, in South Africa, attempts are being made to address power issues and oppression by establishing dialogues between government officials and residents of communities.

A major criticism of ABCD has been that written descriptive reports by the ABCD practitioners mainly focus on reporting about the capacity strengthening of community members and associations (internal-looking) without reporting on structural changes (external-looking) brought about by the approach (Mathie, Cameron & Gibson 2017). However, ABCD makes progress in enabling communities to work closely with local stakeholders such as the government.

In addition to this, South African ABCD facilitators face the following challenges at the community level. Community members have trouble moving from a poverty-stricken mindset and dependency syndrome, focusing on their problems and waiting for hand-outs and services to be delivered towards a mindset where they realise that they can make a living based on their personal and community assets. Community members tend to move back to needs and problems and struggle to focus on their assets. Development organisations are also not community-led and asset orientated but service-orientated (Demeshane & Nel 2018; Nel 2018a, 2018b, 2020).

Applying the ABCD approach is a slow process and practitioners need to move at the pace of the community and not the pace of the organisation and sponsors managing the process. People are often driven by what they can receive from the government and development organisations in terms of tangible resources and money. However, money and tangible resources are not at the centre of the ABCD approach. Instead, they focus on communities galvanising and leveraging their assets alongside assets from outside stakeholders even as they continue to retain control (Nel 2018a, 2018b, 2020; Nel et al. 2021).

Concluding remarks

The recognition and appreciation of assets is a bottom-up, inside-out approach which takes place in an engaged and participatory manner at the grassroots. It can lead to community members driving their own development by using their own assets and then leveraging activities, resources, and investments from outside the community to support locally defined development while retaining control over the process (Nel 2011, 2018a, 2018b;Yeneabat & Butterfield 2012). To make the most of external assets, it is important for communities to first use their internal assets, define their own priorities, and set the agenda for obtaining and using additional resources.

Community-led development, therefore, campaigns for a partnership with, rather than dependency on external experts. It advocates that external stakeholders recognise the value of local communities' knowledge and resources and how these can be as impactful, if not more so, than those coming from external stakeholders.

Sustainable development includes building from within the community, with the local community members recognising their individual roles, as well as their contribution towards positive change. Facilitating such recognition increases local ownership. Most importantly, such an internal focus, also implies that it is not external development organisations and their practitioners but rather community members themselves who identify and address the concerns that need to be resolved.

The discovery, appreciation, galvanising, and application of local knowledge and resources are crucial for sustainable development. The facilitation of community members towards the realisation that they (the community) have resources is a challenge in South Africa as people have a mindset of powerlessness and dependency and think their problems could only be solved by outside stakeholders. However, the community-led development approach, using ABCD as a model, can move communities from a sense of entitlement and dependency on outside assistance to a realisation that they have the assets and resources which could be utilised in building their own future.

References

Alcock, G.G. 2016. *KasiNomics; African informal economics and the people who inhabit them*. Johannesburg: Tracey Mcdonald Publishers.

Alcock, G.G. 2018. *KasiNomic revolution; the rise of African informal economies*. Johannesburg: Tracey Mcdonald Publishers.

Ashford, G., & Patkar, S. 2001. *The positive path, using appreciative inquiry in rural Indian communities*. Myrada: Department for International Development (DFID), International Institute for Sustainable Development (IISD).

Bhattacharyya, J. 2004. Theorising community development. *Journal of Community Development Society*, 34 (2): 5–34.

Block, P. 2009. *Community, the structure of belonging*. San Francisco: Berrett Koehler Publishers.

Braun, A.R. 2005. Beyond the problem-solving approach to sustainable rural development. In: Gonsalves, J., Becker, T., Braun, A., Campilan, D., De Chaves, H., Rivaca-Caminade, J., & Vernooy, R. (Eds.). *Participatory research and development for sustainable agricultural and natural resource management a sourcebook. Volume 1: Understanding participatory research and development*. Ottawa: International Potato Center-Users' Perspectives with Agricultural Research and Development and International Development Research Centre, 129–135.

Chambers, R. 1994. The origins and practice of participatory rural appraisal. *World Development*, 22 (7): 953–969.

Crais, C. 2011. *Poverty, war, and violence in South Africa*. Cambridge: Cambridge University Press.

Demeshane, J., & Nel, H. 2018. An application of the process of appreciative inquiry in community development: an example from Soweto, South Africa. *Southern African Journal of Social Work and Social Development*, 30 (3): 1–17. SA accredited journal. https://doi.org/10.25159/2415- 5829/3599

Eliasov, N. 2013. *Asset based and citizen led development (ABCD), ABCD training of trainers' toolkit*. Canada: Zanolele Inspiritual Creations.

Foot, J. 2012. What makes us healthy? The asset approach in action: Evidence, action, evaluation. www.scdc.org.uk/media/resources/assets-alliance/What%20us%20healthy.pdf

Frediani, A.A. 2010. Sen's capability approach as a framework to the practice of development. *Development in Practice Journal*, 20 (2): 173–187.

Friedli, L. 2011. *Always look on the bright side of life: The rise of asset approaches in Scotland. Scottish Anti-Poverty Review*. Glasgow: The Poverty Alliance. https://povertyalliance.org/newspubs/sapr/saprwinter20112012

Green, G.P., & Haines, A. 2008. *Asset building and community development*. Thousand Oaks: Sage Publications.

Homan, M.S. 2011. *Promoting community change, making it happen in the real world*. Australia: Brooks/Cole, Cengage Learning.

Ife, J., & Tesoriero, F. 2006. *Community development, community-based alternatives in an age of globalization* (3rd ed). Australia: Pearson.

Kramer, S., Amos, T., Lazarus, S., & Seedat, M. 2012. The philosophical assumptions, utility and challenges of asset mapping approaches to community engagement. *Journal of Psychology in Africa*, 22 (4): 537–546.

Kretzmann, J.P., & McKnight, J.L. 1993. *Building communities from the inside out, a path toward finding and mobilizing a community's assets*. Evanston: Center for Urban Affairs and Policy Research.

Landry, J., & Peters, B. 2018. *Assets on the right(s) track? Reflections at the intersection of human rights-based approaches and asset-based and citizen-led development. Innovation Series No. 19*. Antigonish: Coady International Institute.

MacLeod, M.A., & Emejulu, A. 2014. Neoliberalism with a community face? A critical analysis of asset-based community development in Scotland. *Journal of Community Practice*, 22 (4): 430–450. doi:10.1080/10705422.2014.959147

Mansvelt, N. 2018. Implementing ABCD tools and processes in the context of social work student practice. *Social Work/Maatskaplike Werk*, 54 (1):132–143.

Mathie, A., & Cunningham, G. 2003. From clients to citizens: asset-based community development as a strategy for community-driven development. *Development in Practice*, 13 (5): 474–486.

Mathie, A., & Cunningham, G. 2005. Who is driving development? Reflections on the transformative potential of asset-based community development. *Canadian Journal of Development Studies*, 26 (1): 175–186.

Mathie, A., & Cunningham, G. 2008. (Eds.). *From clients to citizens, communities changing the course of their own development*. Warwickshire: Practical Action Publishing.

Mathie, A., Cameron, J., & Gibson, K. 2017. *Asset-based and citizen-led development: Using a diffracted power lens to analyze the possibilities and challenges*, January 1. https://doi.org/10.1177/1464993416674302

Mcknight, J., & Block, P. 2010. *The abundant community*. Illinois: Berrett-Koehler Publishers.

Morse, S. 2011. *Communities revisited; the best ideas of the last hundred years*. Published online in Wiley Online Library (wileyonlinelibrary.com).

Nel, J.B.S. 2011. An application of appreciative inquiry in community development in South Africa. *The Social Work Practitioner-Researcher, Die Maatskaplikewerk Navorser-Praktisyn*, 23 (3): 343–362.

Nel, H. 2018a. A comparison between the asset-oriented and needs-based community development approaches in terms of systems changes. *Practice: Social Work in*

Action, 30 (1): 33–52. Taylor & Francis. IBSS journal. https://doi.org/10.1080/09503153.2017.1360474

Nel, H. 2018b. Community leadership: a comparison between asset-based community-led development (ABCD) versus the traditional needs-based approach. *Development Southern Africa*, 35 (6): 839–851, https://doi.org/10.1080/0376835X.2018.1502075

Nel, H. 2020. Stakeholder engagement: asset-based community-led development (ABCD) versus the traditional needs-based approach to community development. *Social Work/Maatskaplike Werk*, 56 (3): 264–278. http://socialwork.journals.ac.za/pub doi:http://dx.doi.org/10.15270/52-2-857

Nel, H., Louw, H., Schenck, R., & Skhosana, R. 2021. *Introduction to participatory community practice*. Pretoria: Unisa Press.

Nel, H., & Pretorius, E. 2012. Applying appreciative inquiry in building capacity in a non-governmental organisation for youth: an example from Soweto, Gauteng, South Africa. *Social Development Issues*, 34 (1): 37–55.

Patel, L. 2015. *Social welfare and social development in South Africa* (2nd ed). Cape Town: Oxford University Press.

Preece, J. 2017. *Community engagement and lifelong learning; the porous university*. Durban: Palgrave/Macmillan.

Pretorius, E., & Nel, H. 2012. Reflections on the problem-based approach and the asset-based approach to community development. *The Social Work Practitioner-Researcher/Die Maatskaplike werk Navorser-Praktisyn*, 24 (2): 266–87.

Republic of South Africa (RSA).1997. Ministry of Welfare and Population. *White Paper for Social Welfare*. Notice 1008 of 1997. Government Gazette, 368, (18166). Pretoria: Government Printer.

Ssewamala, F.M., Sperber, E., Zimmerman, J.M., & Karimli, L. 2010. The potential of asset-based development strategies for poverty alleviation in Sub-Saharan Africa. *International Journal of Social Welfare*, 19: 433–443.

Whitney, D., Trosten-Bloom, A., & Rader, K. 2010. *Appreciative leadership*. New York: McGraw Hill.

Yeneabat, M., & Butterfield, A.K. 2012. Part 3: Practice; "We can't eat a road:" asset-based community development and the Gedam Sefer community partnership in Ethiopia. *Journal of Community Practice*, 20: 134–153.

Zohar, D., & Marshall, I. 2004. *Spiritual capital – Wealth we can live by*. San Francisco: Berrett-Khoeler Publishers.

PART IV
Accountability/Sustainability, and Exit Strategies

Elene Cloete and Gunjan Veda

The chapters in this section illustrate how accountability, exit strategies, and sustainability work within the context of community-led development. Whereas colleagues from the Nuru Collective describe different accountability processes within their programming, Bissonnette and Robillard reflect on processes of transition. They showcase how two organisations, one with roots in the United States and another formed and established in Haiti worked together to plan, implement, and then realise an exit strategy and subsequent sustained action. This section briefly situates accountability, exit strategy, and sustainability within broader scholarly and international development conversations. We pause at what these concepts mean and how they have been operationalised across different organisational and focus areas.

Accountability

Accountability cuts across many disciplines and global settings, including international community development and humanitarian contexts (Gaventa et al. 2023; Denney et al. 2023). Interest in the concept has evolved into global networks and collaborations, including the Global Partnership for Social Accountability (GPSA), the Transparency and Accountability Initiative (TAI), and the Accountability Research Center at American University, with leading accountability scholar Jonathan Fox. While some scholars label accountability as a buzzword (Schnable et al. 2021), the concept would not have created momentum if it did not have potential. It is a concept that is "desirable" (Bovens 2007) and the Über-concept of the current century (Flinders 2014). Interests in accountability stem perhaps from the promises it holds with regard to good governance (Newell and Wheeler 2006) and increasing the effectiveness of service providers (Kaba

DOI: 10.4324/9781003377917-16

2021). When it works, people can make demands to power holders, ensure that such demands are met, and gain access to resources they are entitled to (Newell and Wheeler 2006).

But What Is Accountability?[1]

Accountability is about relationships between people and organisations across different dimensions and directions (Ebrahim 2003a; Fox 2022). *Vertical accountability* that is upwards and downwards accountability, includes NGOs' typical downwards accountability to project participants and upwards accountability to donors and funders (Ebrahim 2003b; Van Zyl and Claeye 2019). *Horizontal accountability*, which resembles a form of external accountability, can come from peer relationships with other NGOs and networks and emerging standards, best practices, and charters (O'Dwyer and Boomsma 2015). Examples here can include the Movement for Community-led Development's Participatory CLD Assessment Tool (See Annex) and the Community Development Society's Principles of Good Practice. *Internal and inward accountability* includes organisations' relationships to their mission and identity (Ebrahim 2003b). It can also include relationships between co-workers, staff, and the board of directors (Ebrahim 2003b), over not only broader strategic concerns but also day-to-day activities and priorities.

Accountability scholarship also identifies sets of accountability actions – *answerability*, insisting on getting a response, and *enforceability*, the capacity and action to redress when accountability fails (Newell et al. 2006). Answerability loses its effectiveness if there are no consequences (Fox 2007, 667). It, therefore, requires certain sanctions so that those needing answers get their responses and those who need to provide the answers are doing so appropriately and sufficiently.

The different accountability relationships and actions confirm the relational aspect of accountability and underscore the multiplicity of such relationships. However, they also conjure questions about the direction of such relationships, including project participants' role in accountability practices. What is perhaps typical is funders holding NGOs accountable for funds received. But less typical are accountability practices that involve project participants holding organisations and funders accountable. *Reverse accountability* is perhaps a response to such questions (Newcomer et al. 2013). In this case, accountability pressure comes from "below," with project participants holding funders and implementers to account for their involvement and actions through NGO activities. While there is always room for improvement in development practice, there is especially an opportunity to increase, strengthen, and empower accountability from below or reverse accountability. If organisations, funders, and practitioners want to understand how accountability works, where it works, and for whom it works, they need to include the voices and opinions of *all* stakeholders, project participants being no exception.

Opinions differ across programme areas and socio-economic and cultural contexts (Kaba 2021). Therefore, from a programming and operational standpoint, including programme and project participants in accountability frameworks can significantly support NGOs in realising their purpose, improving their interventions, and, if need be, making the necessary course corrections (O'Dwyer and Unerman 2010).

The multidirectional nature of accountability becomes explicit through the chapter by Eli et al. on the Nuru Collective. Eli et al. describe how these relationships function, are structured, and are sustained through different accountability practices. As they argue, these relationships are complex, creating a web of accountability connections and associations, across different socio-economic and geographic landscapes. Relationships include those between members of the different nonprofit organisations spread across different locations (horizontal accountability), between the nonprofits and the cooperatives they support, but then also between the cooperatives, Nuru Collective organisations, and government structures (vertical accountability). Additionally, Eli et al. describe how inward accountability practices take shape, specifically how the respective Nuru Collective organisations have principles, processes, and activities in place to strengthen their accountability to their mission. The authors also highlight that accountability practices are context-specific or *endemic*. Variations in how the different Nuru Collective organisations practise and maintain accountability are therefore crucial. This emphasises the need to avoid a one-size-fits-all model of accountability, as Kaba (2021) reminds us.

But What about Trust?

Discussions around accountability often use the term interchangeably with transparency, representation, or trustworthiness. However, this can make accountability a catch-all phrase and diminish its practicality, as Kaba's (2021) review points out. In the case of trust, even though trust and trustworthiness are closely related to accountability, the two concepts have an arguably linear relationship. If accountability practices are correctly implemented, they can strengthen trust. Conversely, if there is little or no trust in authorities, increased and effective accountability practices can help regain people's trust in their government officials, activities, and intentions (Bovens 2007).

The relationship between trust and accountability is foundational in community-led development. In this volume, Eli et al. illustrate how such trust can be earned through different accountability practices and how it can be strengthened, nurtured, and sustained. Accountability is, therefore, never complete but dynamic, an ongoing practice that involves continuous inward reflectivity to consider possible adjustments. As they state, "accountability is predicated on a system of repeated engagement; it is not a quality for any one actor or implementing organisation to possess or not" (page 257).

Exit Strategies and Sustainability

A longstanding norm within the international development sector, driven mostly by aid from the Global North or Minority World, has been that "aid is by nature temporary" (Heldgaar 2008, 4). The implication of such a temporary status is that, at some point, funders will pull their funding and exit from particular projects and programme areas. And as some scholars and practitioners have noted, such exits are not necessarily always well planned or executed. Perhaps a worse-case scenario includes the work of Jerve and Slob (2008). Reviewing the transformation process of, in this case, 14 bilateral exit cases they found that decisions around programme completion were mostly politically motivated; 13 of these cases were initiated by the funders, and in no case did actors conduct a thorough assessment on whether these programmes would be sustainable post-exit. The most common exit model followed was a "natural phasing out" process where "ongoing commitments are respected and activities simply faded out at the end of a contract period" (Rönngren 2011, 14). While exit has always happened in some shape or form, a global demand for aid effectiveness and sustainability, especially following the 2005 *Paris Declaration on Aid Effectiveness* and the 2008 *Accra Agenda for Action*, brought specific attention to not only whether exit happens but more specifically when and how it takes shape (Rönngren 2011, 13).

These global sentiments placed renewed, and in some cases, new emphasis on processes to ensure programme sustainability post-exit. These processes would include exit strategies. In this case *exit* refers to the "withdrawal of all externally provided programme resources from the entire program areas" (Rogers and Macias 2004, 1). Exit strategies, when they are in place and used by an organisation or implementer, would then be a "tool used by INGOs and other partners to plan and structure the implementation of an exit" (Lewis 2016, 5). A sustainable exit, as James (2016, 16) states, "is the holy grail of development." The intention is that programming continues after interventions and the accompanying technical and financial inputs have ended.

Even if organisations and funders are serious about implementing exit strategies, support is needed. One response to such a need for support came in the form of INTRAC and their Action Learning Set (ALS) formed in 2014. The group's work recognised not only INGOs, limited capacity around designing and implementing exit strategies but also how little sharing has happened around good practices for when and how to exit (Hayman et al. 2016; Popplewell et al. 2016). Their work, by no means exclusive, points to factors essential for successful exit management, including collaborative and all stakeholder involvement in exit strategy planning, strengthening local capacity to ensure programme sustainability post-exit, adaptability, and adjustability to initial exit planning, and transparency throughout the lifecycle of the programme on progress towards exit. Continuous communication between all stakeholders is essential for such transparency (Hayman et al. 2016). Essential to these management successes are community-led principles, for example, including participation, inclusion and voice, recognising, respecting, and using local knowledge, and then paying close attention to context. One exit strategy will not be the same as the next. But what is perhaps most significant is how the durability of community-led development emerged from INTRAC's study on when and why programmes "survive" post-exit. In their follow-up work to determine an INGO's programme sustainability post-exit, Popplewell et al. (2016) found that programmes sustain their activities if they are locally driven, enabling easy take over by communities following exit. Programmes are also more likely to survive if they have access to diversified funding, reducing funding dependency, and continued strong advocacy and awareness components.

From Exit to Transition

Momentum around exit strategies remains helpful, because, as a programme director shared in an INTRAC report, "the manner of leaving can destroy years of good work" (Popplewell et al. 2016, 2). But more recently, strategic thinkers and community-led programmes have started to gravitate towards principles of *transition* as a more appropriate way to rethink exit strategies. Even if exit strategies have been co-developed, implemented, adjusted, and carefully executed in a participatory way to develop local ownership, thereby ensuring programme sustainability, there still remains a question around the relationship between the original implementer and those "left behind." An adjusted way of thinking about such a relationship, Bissonnette and Robillard's chapter demonstrates, is not as an end, but rather a shift that equalises even more explicitly and intentionally power differences in the relationship.

A significant example of transitional thinking is the Stopping as Success (SAS) programme, and its successor, SAS: Locally Led Transitions in Development (SAS+). Central to both the SAS and SAS+ programmes is showcasing and then also supporting shifts in power from traditional development powerholders to local entities, ranging from local nonprofits to community groups and civil society. The emphasis throughout such programming falls on *transition* and *partnership* rather than exit, promoting and strengthening local ownership, leadership, and capacity. All these processes are in response to an overarching objective of equalising, as much as possible, the power hierarchies that might have structured relationships prior to transitioning taking place.

Exemplary in this case, has also been the transition processes of the Nuru Collective – from their expat teams to local country teams and offices. Key factors enabling such transition included clear communication and collective planning, seeing transition as a gradual process rather than immediate action or exit, programming that prioritises and cultivates local ownership, and the presence of servant leadership, networks, and community of practice (Dillan et al. 2018).

Note

1 Kaba's (2021) systematic review of 217 articles across five different disciplines helpfully summarises what scholars focused on NGO accountability agree on.

References

Bovens, Mark. 2007. "Analysing and assessing accountability: A conceptual framework 1." *European Law Journal* 13, no. 4: 447–468.

Denney, Lisa, Gregoire Nimbtik, and Serena Ford. 2023. *UNDP Accountability Ecosystems Analysis*. La Trobe University, Institute for Human Security and Social Change.

Dillan, Haley, Joel Ouma and David Yamron. 2018. *Stopping at Success: Transitioning to Locally Led Development*. Case Study: Nuru Kenya. USAID, CDA, Peace Direct, Search for Common Ground.

Ebrahim, Alnoor. 2003a. "Accountability in practice: Mechanisms for NGOs." *World Development* 31, no. 5: 813–829.

Ebrahim, Alnoor. 2003b. "Making sense of accountability: Conceptual perspectives for northern and southern nonprofits." *Nonprofit Management and Leadership* 14, no. 2: 191–212.

Flinders, Matthew. 2014. "The future and relevance of accountability studies." In Bovens, Mark, Robert Goodin, and Thomas Schillemans (eds), *The Oxford Handbook of Public Accountability* (p. 661). Oxford: Oxford Academic.

Fox, Jonathan. 2007. "The uncertain relationship between transparency and accountability." *Development in Practice* 17, no. 4–5: 663–671.

Fox, Jonathan. 2022. "Accountability Keywords." Accountability Research Center, Working Paper 11.

Gaventa, John, Anuradha Joshi, and Colin Anderson. 2023. "Citizen action for accountability in challenging contexts: What have we learned?." *Development Policy Review* 41: e12697.

Hayman, Rachel, Rick James, Rowan Popplewell, and Sarah Lewis. 2016. *Exit Strategies and Sustainability: Lessons for Practitioners*. INTRAC: Special Series Paper no. 1.

Heldgaar, Jesper. 2008. *Managing Aid Exit and Transformation: Summary of a Joint Donor Evaluation*. Sida.

James, Rick. 2016. "Which way to sustainable exit?" In *Exit Strategies and Sustainability: Lessons for Practitioners*. Hayman, Rachel, Rick James, Rowan Popplewell, and Sarah Lewis. INTRAC: Special Series Paper no. 1.

Kaba, Marcel. 2021. "NGO accountability: A conceptual review across the engaged disciplines." *International Studies Review* 23, no. 3: 958–996.

Lewis, Sarah. 2016. "Development a timeline for exit strategies: Experiences from an action learning set with the British Red Cross, EveryChild, Oxfam GB, Sightsavers and WWf-UK." *INTRAC Praxis Paper* 31 .

Newcomer, Kathryn, Laila El Baradei, and Sandra Garcia. 2013. "Expectations and capacity of performance measurement in NGOs in the development context." *Public Administration and Development* 33, no. 1: 62–79.

Newell, Peter, Joanna Wheeler, and Alison Dunn. 2006. *Making Accountability Count*. Institute of Development Studies.

O'Dwyer, Brendan, and Jeffrey Unerman. 2010. "Enhancing the role of accountability in promoting the rights of beneficiaries of development NGOs." *Accounting and Business Research* 40, no. 5: 451–471.

O'Dwyer, Brendan, and Roel Boomsma. 2015. "The co-construction of NGO accountability: Aligning imposed and felt accountability in NGO-funder accountability relationships." *Accounting, Auditing & Accountability Journal* 28, no. 1:36–68.

Popplewell, Rowan, Rick James, and Sarah Lewis. 2016. "*What remains: Programming for sustainability.*" Praxis Series Paper 1. INTRAC.

Rogers, Beatrice Lorge, and Kathy E. Macías. 2004. *Program Graduation and Exit Strategies: A Focus on Title II Food Aid Development Programs*. Washing-ton, DC: Food and Nutrition Technical Assistance Project, Academy for Educational Development.

Rönngren, Jenny. 2011. *Making Achievements Last: Learning from Exit Experiences.* Kvinna till kvinna Foundation.

Schnable, Allison, Anthony DeMattee, Rachel Sullivan Robinson, and Jennifer N. Brass. 2021. "International development buzzwords: Understanding their use among donors, NGOs, and academics." *The Journal of Development Studies* 57, no. 1: 26–44.

Slob, Anneke, and Alf Morten Jerve. 2008. *Managing Aid Exit and Transformation. Lessons from Botswana, Eritrea, India, Malawi and South Africa. Synthesis Report.* Sida/Norad/Danida/Netherland's Ministry of Foreign Affairs.

Van Zyl, Hyman, and Frederik Claeyé. 2019. "Up and down, and inside out: Where do we stand on NGO accountability?." *The European Journal of Development Research* 31, no. 3: 604–619.

12

FROM ROOTS TO RASIN

The Story of Transition and Transformation in Haiti[1]

Chad Bissonnette and Louino Robillard

The Twa Wòch Dife Approach to Sustainable Development in Haiti

Haiti is located in the Caribbean and has a unique and inspiring history. It is the only country in the world to achieve its independence through a slave revolt (James 1989). Slaves successfully fought their colonisers, the French, and gained their independence in 1804. Today, Haiti is the most economically disadvantaged country in the Western Hemisphere and is currently facing a period of great conflict and social, political, and economic instability.

Robi (R): Haiti is often called the Republic of NGOs because it is a country where the state is weak, institutions are failing the public, and almost all decisions and services are being made and provided by non-governmental organisations (NGOs). In 2010, after a devastating earthquake hit the island country, the number of NGOs operating in Haiti exploded from approximately 3,000 to 10,000. Around that same time, former American President and UN Special Envoy to Haiti Bill Clinton shared that Haiti had the second highest number of NGOs per capita in the world (Trenton 2009). Many of these NGOs are international organisations with good intentions, but it is those same good intentions that are killing the state and weakening local organisations.

R: That Haiti is facing a situation in which the state is becoming weaker every day is no secret. The question now being asked within the humanitarian world is what can be done to better empower local organisations to take the lead and help countries like Haiti develop sustainably. This has led to a movement advocating for the localisation of humanitarian aid. There are institutions and organisations trying to do this but in many cases the methods they use are failing to create stronger, more independent organisations at the local level. To improve this, we need to identify

DOI: 10.4324/9781003377917-17

models and methodologies that are working. We need to document and share them, because Haiti needs more organisations practising approaches to development that do not undermine local groups, but instead empower them. For all these reasons, it is important to tell the story of Rasin Devlopman and Roots of Development and share the details of how their unique partnership is improving quality of life on the island of La Gonave and providing a model for other organisations in Haiti and beyond.

The Backstory: Founding Roots of Development

Roots of Development is a nonprofit organisation based in Washington D.C., U.S.A. It was founded in 2007 by two college friends, Chad Bissonnette and Lindsey Walker, to help the leaders of a community on the Haitian island of La Gonave address some of their development needs.

During its first years in existence, Roots of Development supported several significant infrastructure projects, including the rehabilitation of one of the island's largest water sources and the rebuilding of homes after several natural disasters. The projects helped improve quality of life for the residents of that community and were community-led in most aspects, but it wasn't until the entire programme was handed over to a local, Haitian-run organisation to lead that the efforts began to have a more sustainable and significant impact.

Chad (C): I first visited Haiti in 2005 on an exchange trip with an organisation called Beyond Borders. It was a weeklong trip that brought me to La Gonave (Haiti's largest island) and introduced me to a set of rural communities in the mountains of the island that were both isolated from the world and from the rest of Haiti. I lived with a host family, witnessed the daily life of residents, and learned about the development challenges facing the community from several of its leaders. After my visit to the island, I returned home – and while grateful for such an experience – I had no intention or plans of returning to Haiti anytime soon.

C: I did, however, return to Haiti in 2006. I had remained in touch with my host family and helped them navigate an unexpected and dramatic family emergency a few months after my visit. Communicating regularly and working with them through the situation gave me greater insight into their lives and brought us closer. Still young and without too many formal obligations, I had a lot of flexibility. So, I decided to travel to Haiti again to visit the family and continue learning from their community.

C: On my second visit to La Gonave, the struggles the community faced on a daily basis left a lasting impact on me: no running water or electricity in their homes, food insecurity, lack of access to basic health services, to name a few. It also reminded me of the drive many of the community's leaders had to do something about their situation. One day, on a walk down to the area where residents collect water from a spring, I found a group of men working to protect the spring from surrounding contaminants by building a concrete wall around the point where the water exited the ground and came to the surface.

C: I eventually asked some of the community leaders if I should raise some funds for them to help tackle another need or two in the community. They supported the idea and so upon my return to the United States, I began raising funds from friends and family. Eventually, in 2007, I moved down to Haiti to participate in the first project and manage the funds I had collected. It was at that time that Lindsey Walker, a friend of mine from college who was inspired by the experiences I was having and relationships I was building in Haiti, and I decided to create a formal organisation – a nonprofit – to help raise more funds for our efforts on La Gonave.

C: Over the next eight years, Roots of Development supported numerous community-led development initiatives on the island of La Gonave. Community-led because they were chosen by the community and relied heavily on local knowledge, skills, and resources. I, accompanied by staff and/or volunteers, would raise funds and travel to and from the island a few times a year to help implement these diverse projects that brought clean water, new homes, solar lighting, and more to the community that had received me all those years ago.

Progress and Yet, Problems

Chad (C): While we made progress, we also experienced several project setbacks. Most of these setbacks were related to my lack of understanding of the culture and my level of involvement in the work. They resulted in frustration, exhaustion, and wasted resources. There were times when I didn't have a good sense of how much money was appropriate to inject into the community through a particular project. Miscalculating that drove up the stakes of the project and, in the most extreme cases, fuelled existing mistrust within the community.

C: No matter how well I got to understand the culture or speak the language, I could not ever fully comprehend the dynamics of a community that was not mine; the dynamics that are deeply connected and influence how development happens or doesn't in any given community. And I certainly wasn't the type of foreign aid worker who lives in a fancy apartment in the capital city –Port-au-Prince, in this case – who travels everywhere in a white SUV. I was deeply immersed in the culture and life on La Gonave right from the beginning. I lived with a host family, didn't have a cell phone, and walked everywhere or took public transportation, which was initially on the back of a pick-up truck and then on the back of a motorcycle when they began to arrive on the island. I spent every Friday at the local market to help my host mother sell goods. There I saw how people made a living, how they negotiated, and heard the latest drama between families. I learned the language quickly and spoke it fluently. I was there when the community was grieving a death, celebrating a marriage, talking about an upcoming election. I heard all the small-town gossip and knew who was dating who, who was angry with who, and why.

C: Yet, I missed seeing the "elite capture" that started to take place within APDAG, the community-based organisation we first worked with in Gran Sous. I interpreted doubt and concerns expressed by the community about certain members of the group as being ill-informed and part of the mistrust and jealousy that I had been told existed in the community for years. But this lack of a nuanced understanding of the community, its history, and the behaviour of some of its leaders allowed problems to develop and eventually worsen.

C: Similarly, there was a time when I prepared a presentation for a new and exciting organisational management concept with the members of APDAG but was fundamentally unable to bridge the cultural gap and explain the concept to them. This not only wasted everyone's time but also exposed insecurities that existed within members of the group, negatively impacting the group dynamic instead of bringing everyone closer together. A few years later, when I participated in a presentation given to the same group by a Haitian professional, I learned how powerful and effective anecdotes and stories are for learning and teaching in that environment.

C: Another example that remains clear in my memory is the day I used the Creole word *fok*, meaning "must", instead of *bezwen* which means "needs to". Emotions were already running high due to ongoing frustrations between the leaders of APDAG, its members, and us, Roots of Development. Due to this single misuse of a word by me, a foreigner unable to understand the nuances between words, the situation and the relationship deteriorated further.

C: Over the years as I began to see and understand these patterns, I realised that our work would never be as strong, that we could never be as effective as an organisation led by people from that community and from that very culture; as an organisation led by Haitians.

C: My very presence in a room or in a meeting as a foreigner had an influence and an impact. It changed the way people talked about a subject, how they acted with each other or how much they participated. In many cases, it felt like one eye was always on me, no matter what was going on in the room. Foreigners are often seen as resources; people who have greater access to money, goods, and opportunities. And in these environments, where resources can be limited, "access" to that foreigner can make the difference between going to school or not, buying a motorcycle, visiting another country, or in some cases eating or not. Being a foreigner was something I could never change and it had an impact on our ability to succeed. It led to a waste of resources, stymied growth and continued to uphold colonial relationships and power dynamics.

Robi (R): Roots of Development, which has been working on the island of La Gonave since 2007, has witnessed a lot in Haiti. Not only has Roots seen many projects implemented on the island by NGOs that do not know or come from the island – projects that have failed, despite any good intentions that may have been behind them – but it also witnessed the biggest influx of international NGOs, money, and aid into Haiti in the modern era. On January 12, 2010, an earthquake hit

Haiti that caused a loss of more than 200,000 lives, more than 1.5 million displaced people, and a promise of international aid that exceeded US $13 billion.

R: Despite all the attention, efforts, money, and good intentions that were mobilised for Haiti after the earthquake, very little can be shown for it today and the state has become less functional than it was before. In so many instances during that period of relief, which lasted years, the state was bypassed and local organisations were ignored. So institutions became weaker and local organisations stopped operating and lost staff to larger international NGOs (INGOs) – many of which would not remain in Haiti once the attention shifted to another crisis elsewhere and the aid money dried up. International organisations thought they knew best or were best equipped to deliver aid but it was clear pretty immediately and for years after that efforts in Haiti won't be as effective or sustainable without Haitians in the lead.

R: All of these events, all of these lived experiences, added to Chad's recognition that for all his good intentions, the time he might spend in Haiti, the resources he could mobilise and love he had for the country, he would not be able to change Haiti. With more experience and time, witnessing the same thing happening in Haiti repeatedly, Chad understood that for Roots of Development to be effective and help improve people's lives on the island, the work would have to be led by a local organisation and local leaders.

R: So in 2015, Chad set out to create a Haitian organisation, led entirely by Haitians; an organisation that would then lead the work on La Gonave. This led to the birth of Rasin Devlopman.

The Birth of Rasin Devlopman

Chad (C): The creation of Rasin Devlopman came from a recognition that my understanding and capacity was limited, that the influence I had on things – knowingly and unknowingly – was flawed and problematic, and from my concerns about our impact not being sustainable. It was becoming clearer and clearer that the best way to serve the community, to accomplish the goals and mission of the organisation, would be by handing over operations to people from the community. In this case, to Haitians.

C: Once I decided to establish Rasin, we undertook a step-by-step process to shift the power. The first and most important step was to set up a legal organisation in line with the laws of the country. We identified and spoke with a reputable law firm to understand the different options for legalising Rasin Devlopman and worked with them to successfully incorporate the organisation. Then, I worked with friends and contacts in Haiti to identify an initial set of board members – all Haitians living in Haiti – to serve as stewards of the new organisation. I picked these individuals based on their understanding of our approach to development, their past support, their reputation, and their wide network of personal and professional contacts. Together with the first set of board members, we began hiring employees, based on a commitment to and shared set of values. We knew it was morally important and strategically effective to recognise and find human and social capital locally.

C: Rasin's first employee was Lineda Paul. We found Lineda by sharing a scope of work within our network in Haiti. She came recommended by a friend who had been working with her at *Techo Para Mi Pais*. We purposefully did not hire anyone from the communities Roots had been working with before then, in order to avoid any sort of conflict of interest and to not exacerbate issues between the community (leaders) there. We did eventually hire Marclidens ("Bousthing") St. Vil, who was from Gran Sous and the son of APDAG's Vice-President, but he was never a formal member of APDAG and at that point no longer lived in Gran Sous. He knew the island well and how and where to access the resources that Rasin needed. For organisations to be effective and sustainable, they need actors who are connected and know where and how to access resources. This is strongest when it is locally sourced and an important ingredient of community-led development.

C: Faradhia Moise, who became Rasin's first COO, was hired through a traditional job search using a classified ad and online Haitian employment platforms. Louino ("Robi") Robillard, who was initially brought on as a consultant, became Rasin's Programme Director. Robi's influence on Rasin's success was and is tremendous because of his understanding, background in, and commitment to community-led development. I had first been introduced to Robi by a friend in Haiti and had heard about him through like-minded organisations.

Robi (R): I was born in Haiti and grew up in one of its largest underprivileged areas called Cite Soleil. It is a place that is considered a failure by most NGOs and the Haitian state. I grew up in a place where the community does not control its own destiny. Everything is done by the "blan" (foreigner). All children grow up in an environment where they do not think they have any role in their destiny.

R: I used to hear about the work that Roots of Development was doing in the third communal section of Gran Sous, on the island of La Gonave. I was used to hearing about so many "blan" (foreign) organisations in the country though, all of whom thought of themselves as saviours – the only ones who will change Haiti. So I imagined Roots was just another such organisation until a friend of mine told me about Chad, a "blan" who was helping in Gran Sous but who saw things differently. That friend, who knew my work well and also knew of Chad's work on the island, organised for us to meet. When we first spoke, I was surprised to hear Chad say "I really care about La Gonave, but I'm starting to understand that it is not my role to change La Gonave. I can be there as a supporter through Roots, but it is really the people of La Gonave – Haitians – who must be in control and lead their own development." He went on to share that it was for those very reasons Roots was backing off to play a different kind of role; it would still be there but only when, and in the ways Lagonavians wanted them to be there. It was those rare words that made me believe that together we could create a beautiful, participatory development model driven by local people on the island.

R: I got involved in Rasin Devlopman to help create a model of development that is based on the values and principles of community solidarity, what we call *konbit* in Haitian Creole, where the community is in the driver's seat.

Chad (C): To ensure a lasting commitment to this "new" approach to development, we made sure to establish a system of checks and balances, and transparency within and between Roots and Rasin. This included me sitting on Rasin's board and the two organisations maintaining regular communications.

C: To accomplish these steps, we reached out to and relied on the network I had developed from my ten or so years working in Haiti, and connections and contacts I had been introduced to by my wife and her family over the latter half of that period. (Yes, my wife is from Haiti!) It is undeniable that developing a large network and engaging a lot of people over the years in Roots' work helped us navigate challenges and accomplish these goals.

Perils of a Road Less Travelled: What Often Prevents a "Transition of Power"?

Chad (C): "Exiting" and ensuring equality is not easy. For organisations interested in supporting a truly sustainable and community-led approach to development, here are a few of the challenges or obstacles that may prevent them from achieving their goals:

- As it is in most of life's greatest challenges, ego is often at play. To accept that you are not the best person to lead efforts on the ground, that there is still a lot you don't know about a culture (even after spending years ingrained in it), or that your very presence may be preventing the work from being more successful requires a real ego check. It requires you to be humble and to accept that you may not be able to keep doing aspects of the work that you find most interesting or that make you most happy. Handing over power always means sacrifice.
- There is also a real fear of handing over power, even when you know it is for the best. A lot of people refer to Roots as my baby. Giving up the direction or management of your baby can be very difficult. So how do you manage that fear? How do you trust? Trust is something that you build, it is not necessarily found. You identify opportunities and strategies and then test them, try them out. And, in our case, we set up checks and balances along the way, like me holding a seat on Rasin's board, to help manage that trust and the transfer of power.
- I have found that foreigners are regularly given more credit than they deserve. Our ideas are given more value, simply because they are foreign – even when trust has not yet been developed – and that can be a real challenge to navigate, a challenge to developing a strong and honest partnership from the start. Some foreigners may not even recognise it. Either because of decades and centuries of false narratives or out of strategy, a foreigner's idea will be accepted as "best". When I say strategy, I mean, because a foreigner often comes with

access to additional resources and opportunities, local partners may consciously or subconsciously interpret the foreigner's idea as what he or she wants to do and therefore choose that as the "best" idea. It can be a way of motivating the foreigner to staying involved and sharing access to those additional resources. This means even the direction of the conversation can be influenced by the presence or engagement of a foreign actor.

- An organisation may not know what is available in a country or how to access it. Or in more unfortunate cases, they don't believe what they will find is of good enough quality or skill or trustworthy.
- Money comes with influence and power and funders will sometimes consciously or unconsciously influence decisions or the direction of a project with that power.
- Many international organisations are attempting to respond to the current trend of localising development by implementing workarounds; by *nationalising* their offices. They will take their local offices and register them locally with a local name and maybe even a local board. It is simply a cosmetic change; power does not shift. The direction and leadership are still connected to the headquarters and decisions are influenced by funder schemes and structures.

  Here, it is worth noting that *local* doesn't always mean better development. Just because something is local doesn't mean it is community-led. A great deal of local development is led by professionals who have spent a good deal of their career working in organisations that practise traditional development. When you are in the traditional system long enough, it can be hard to see things differently or believe in and trust a different approach. It can distort what people think of as success and cause you to focus on and serve more traditional priorities like spending the budget and impressing the donor.
- Further, many organisations don't understand community-led development (CLD) or how to support it. They think that going into a community and engaging with people or asking a handful of leaders what they want is CLD.
- Many organisations start reflecting on – or get serious about – this approach way too late. The relationships and expectations between actors are already established and too much dependency has been created.

From Exit to Transition: What Shifting the Power Entails

Chad (C): For some time now, exit strategy has become an important part of organisational strategy in our sector. Yet, many organisations think about the exit strategy too late or they misunderstand what it means. Often it is introduced towards the end of a project to ensure sustainability or community ownership because project funding is about to run out. Yet organisations should do their due diligence to learn about and commit to the practice of community-led development before they begin to operate or get involved in a project. They should understand their role as a partner and commit to remaining within the boundaries of that role.

C: When development is community-led in its purest form, there is no exit strategy needed, because it is the community doing for itself. The community doesn't need to go anywhere. It lives there and is addressing its own issues and maintaining its own development with its own resources. "Exit strategy" is more applicable to an *external* partner of a community or a project.

C: To plan a strong exit strategy from the beginning, define your roles and responsibilities together, early, and carefully, and ensure that role is supportive and your responsibilities are complimentary. Support local leaders and emphasise (and rely on) local resources first. Abandoning a local partner is not the objective. Instead, it is about limiting your role and responsibilities and avoiding dependency. In fact, depending on your relationship and the goals of your organisation, exiting may not be the right approach or even necessary. If the programme is built on a long-term partnership, it may be more about shifting (transitioning) power to the local partner, like in the case of Roots and Rasin.

C: It is important for an external partner to avoid taking on a leadership role from the beginning. The more years you have been operating in a traditional manner, the more things are reliant on you, the harder it will be to reverse course and shift that power. What too often happens is that an organisation begins working in a community to help address its immediate needs. But it does so by leading that effort, either in decision-making or with the resources it brings to the table. The efforts, the systems, and structures put in place to address those needs, become dependent on that organisation. And organisations only start seriously discussing how to hand over leadership, management, and maintenance of those efforts to the community when they begin struggling to provide those resources and maintain those systems. That's when they think about sustainability and talk about true local leadership. Instead of a planned exit developed within the framework of a sustainable partnership, what the organisation is really doing at that point is transferring its risk, which is unfair and often precarious.

C: It is much more difficult to "exit" (to shift the power) later in a traditional relationship because people have gotten used to your role and the resources you bring. They now rely on it, in some cases for survival, and will not risk losing it. Few residents, for the benefit and pursuit of "long-term sustainability", will be interested in or willing to risk losing those resources or services after they have been established. At times, they may even fight for the "unsustainable" or status quo, in order to preserve access to it.

C: What made Roots different from most organisations was that it was founded on a commitment to never support a project that would require its ongoing (financial) support to continue operating. This was something I had learned while studying international development and living and travelling overseas, and I took it very seriously from the start of my work in Haiti. This early commitment allowed us to avoid starting any unsustainable initiatives with APDAG. Later on, when we realised we needed to further shift the power, we were able to focus on redefining our roles and responsibilities and establishing a local entity that would take over the programme.

Understanding and Defining Roles and Responsibilities

Robi (R): If you are an international organisation teaming up with a community or a community-based organisation once or twice on a specific project, it is important to define the roles and responsibilities of each partner, while ensuring that the local partner is truly in charge of deciding the direction of the programme. Your role is to compliment the strengths and weaknesses of the local organisation and support its efforts. The truth is we all need partners and benefit from the support of others throughout our lives. In Haiti, and on La Gonave especially, certain materials, financial resources, and technical expertise are limited. A partner who can help you acquire some of those to enable you to achieve your goals is tremendously useful.

R: Rasin Devlopman, in partnership with Roots of Development, was created intentionally to be more sustainable and to serve as an example for others. There were many organisations working on the island that Roots had interacted with since it was first formed. Organisations that were implementing projects that increased the dependency of communities on them, instead of decreasing it. Organisations that were run by a handful of people making major decisions about projects in offices far away from the island. Roots of Development knew that it could not help the people of La Gonave or create sustainable change operating in the same manner.

R: Rasin Devlopman was formed out of a synergy of people who represent diverse segments of Haitian society, who are very aware of the fact that the way we do things in Haiti must change, and that it begins with strengthening the capacity of local leaders. Rasin Devlopman was formed by Lagonavian leaders, leaders in the private sector, and representatives of Roots of Development. We refer to this collaboration between three key partners as three fire rocks (in Haitian Creole, "twa wòch dife"). We use the same name for our programme on La Gonave. Many Haitians cook by placing their pot on three rocks and lighting a fire underneath. The point is that the pot will not stay upright, and the family will not be able to achieve their objective (in this case, cooking) if they try propping the pot up on just one or two rocks. It takes three rocks to keep it balanced and upright.

R: Rasin's work operates the same way. One of our three rocks, or partners, is a collection of local community groups and community leaders. We refer to them as the "bottom up" group. The "top down" group and second rock is the state, a collection of locally elected officials and entities associated with the government. And the third rock are other groups and organisations from outside the community, like Roots of Development. Together, the three groups form a productive partnership founded on a common goal and a commitment to developing a system of independence rather than dependence.

R: Every group and the individuals that make up that group commits itself to this shared vision and to understanding his or her roles and responsibilities. Roots of Development, for example, knows that its role is to help Rasin implement its mission. Rasin Devlopman knows its responsibility is to support and strengthen the capacity of local authorities and community leaders. And those local authorities and community leaders understand that they are responsible for using that capacity, and the opportunities that arise, to improve the lives of the residents they serve. The relationships are based on mutual respect and an understanding and appreciation of each partner's role. It is like the bond that exists between the three fire rocks; a bond that allows the pot to sit well so that the food can be cooked.

R: One of the ways we ensured our partnership would be equal was by reaffirming our shared commitments and by very clearly defining our roles. Rasin is a community-based, Haitian organisation that develops and implements programmes with its local community groups. Roots of Development is an international organisation that helps mobilise resources and awareness for the work in Haiti. None of the organisations is more important than the other. Both have their roles and each of those roles is uniquely important. Communication between the two organisations is strong and regular, which helps both organisations do their jobs.

R: Roots, as an organisation with access to resources, partners, and opportunities uses those connections to help Rasin strengthen its organisational and administrative capacity so it can do what it does well even better. One of the most recent examples of that was Roots helping Rasin find and finance a Haitian firm to help it develop a system of monitoring and evaluation, so it can better assess and communicate its impact. Roots also helps Rasin identify opportunities that can help it stand on its own financially, by, for example, renting out a portion of its office space and building the La Gonave Community Leadership & Development Center.

Chad (C): Before Roots handed things over to Rasin, I participated and weighed in on project decisions, I engaged with member groups, I volunteered my time digging ditches and carrying stones, I received and critiqued project proposals, and raised funds. I would be part of APDAG meetings and in attendance for voting. I was available for people to come and speak with me about a project.

C: Now Roots responsibilities include fundraising and supporting communications about Rasin's work and our shared community-led approach to development. We visit from time to time in order to better understand (and share) what is going on in the community and we do strategic planning with Rasin.

What Made Roots of Development's "Exit" Successful?

Robi (R): Since I was young, I have been involved in creating social movements that help empower communities to take their destiny into their own hands; movements and organisations with a commitment to development without dependency. However, this work is not easy. It is not easy to get NGOs and the state to accept the need and value of handing power over to the communities to control their own destiny. It is the top-down approach that has made the lives of Haitians miserable and dependent for decades.

R: In our case, both Rasin and Roots know that they are in a long-term relationship. Neither one is in a hurry to stop supporting the other. Both organisations have committed to working together to provide a model for Haiti and the rest of the world. We demonstrate how an international organisation can support a local organisation without trying to replace it or undermine its leadership. Roots of Development serves Rasin by helping to strengthen its capacity so that it is even more effective and capable of creating lasting change. And Rasin Devlopman knows that it is here to collaborate with Roots as an equal partner to help local leaders acquire the skills and resources they need to improve the lives of their communities.

Chad (C): The relationship between Rasin Devlopman and Roots of Development is based on trust and transparency. And things only move at the speed of trust. A commitment towards a long-term relationship made our partnership strong and a transition possible. Our plan was never to establish Rasin and then leave, or to implement a single project with Rasin and then move on.

C: Both our organisations share a commitment to the same alternative way of doing development for long-term change. We share an understanding, experiences, and values. Roots and Rasin are both committed to a shared journey. We see La Gonave as a puzzle we are trying to figure out together. And it is exactly that…a journey. A process. And should be looked at as such.

We believe in accountability, *not* control. Accountability can be mutual, control cannot.

C: We also avoid entering into any relationship that causes a local leader or community to feel like we need them to carry out our mission. Our mission is to support them, at their pace and based on their level of engagement. We have been careful to avoid creating an unhealthy dependence on one another.

The Results of Roots' "Exit" and Rasin's Leadership

Chad (C): Our efforts on La Gonave are now less vulnerable and more sustainable because they rely on local resources, both human and material. The current crisis in Haiti would have posed huge challenges to continue operations if Roots had stuck to its original model. It is almost impossible to travel to the island now or transport goods back and forth. So, my colleagues and I would have been trying to make decisions and support activities from afar, with little understanding of things in the community. On the other hand, now with Rasin our shared mission continues. In fact, it has grown and our programme has become stronger.

C: Under Rasin's leadership, it has been easier for us to scale our efforts and grow our impact. With local knowledge of the island, its leaders, and the activities taking place there, Rasin can more easily identify strong leaders and exciting community-led efforts to bring into its network and offer support. Within two years of Rasin being founded, our work went from taking place in one of La Gonave's 11 communal sections to 7 out of the 11.

C: With its knowledge of popular Haitian Facebook groups and other social media channels, some of which are specific to La Gonave, Rasin has been able to tap into and engage with the Haitian diaspora. This has allowed us to share more about the work we are doing together on the island and encourage others to get involved. With its ability to more easily and effectively communicate in Creole, Rasin is engaging with a larger audience and helping to advocate for an alternative, more sustainable approach to development in Haiti and beyond.

C: With Roots of Development's decision to shift the power, Rasin Devlopman's strong leadership, and a shared commitment to the principles of community-led development, our impact in Haiti continues to grow and evolve. Every year, Rasin Devlopman brings more leaders, partners, projects, and communities into its network and is currently exploring ways to share its impact with others on mainland Haiti. Meanwhile, Roots of Development is speaking with leaders of community-based organisations outside of Haiti to see how it may replicate this type of partnership to help fight poverty and sustainably improve quality of life for communities elsewhere in the world.

Robi (R): The Rasin Devlopman team is 100 per cent Haitian, with 50 per cent of its staff from (and based on) La Gonave. The dream is for Rasin to one day reach 100 per cent of the people on La Gonave and have the ability to send staff, as consultants, to other communities in Haiti and internationally, to share lessons learned and help guide other communities and their leaders through the community-led process. No community alone has everything it needs to develop itself. We understand that independence and interdependence must co-exist. The Roots and Rasin model serves as an example of a true partnership for sustainable development that can help Haiti.

Ann kontinye fè konbit (let's continue the practice of *konbit*).

Note

1 In memory of Sabina Carlson Robillard

References

James, C.L.R. 1989. *The Black Jacobins: Toussaint L'Ouverture and the San Domingo Revolution*. New York: Vintage Books.

Trenton, Daniel. 2009. "Bill Clinton tells diaspora: 'Haiti Needs You Now'." *Miami Herald*, August 10.

13

ACCOUNTABILITY IN COMMUNITY AND LOCAL LEADERSHIP

The Nuru Collective Approach to Uniting People through Place and Purpose

Simon Eli, Amy Gaman, Casey Harrison, Matt Lineal, Abiy Meshesha, and Pauline Wambeti

Introduction

Accountability is intrinsic to power. For leaders in local government and community-based organisations, with the privilege of position and power comes the weight of responsibility to serve the population according to the goal and purpose of their charge. Accountability systems reckon the power wielded by local leaders against the results they achieve. The achievements of local leaders are judged on the extent to which they remove or limit the risks and unfreedoms that dominate the oppressed (Freire 1970) and "that leave people with little choice and little opportunity of exercising their reasoned agency" (Sen 1999, xii).

People are the change agents that exercise power and implement the accountability practices and systems implied. Local and community-based leadership recognises the power of people as the point of departure. For the purposes of this chapter, the functional definition of local is geographic with implications of physical proximity and boundaries, while community-based or community-led terminology implies the collectivised will and shared purpose. Taken together, local and community-led are the union of place, people, and purpose.

Accountability is a form of trust that must be earned and proven every single day. While accountability is intrinsic and inalienable to power, high standards according to principled application cannot be assumed. It should never be taken for granted and must be nurtured through continuous non-judgmental interactions between people. Expanding on this central argument, this chapter proposes fundamental principles of accountability predicated on and applied to the work of the Nuru Collective, a group of not-for-profit, non-governmental organisations (NGOs) with a shared vision, working with rural communities in international contexts. The Nuru Collective hosts formal and technical accountability mechanisms, such as

DOI: 10.4324/9781003377917-18

governance councils, reporting procedures, and communication norms. In a deeper sense, these interactions forge a relationship of mutual and reinforcing engagement in which an evolving and interwoven shared identity creates a sense of belonging, duty, service, fealty and, ultimately, allegiance.

The first section of this chapter introduces the Nuru Collective and the Nuru model. It delves into concepts like servant leadership and agency that are the backbone of this model. The next section describes the four principles of accountability and further applies them to the work of the Collective with practical examples. The concluding section brings together how organisations practising community-led development can practise accountability.

The Nuru Collective

The Nuru Collective is a group of not-for-profit NGOs with member representation from the United States of America, Kenya, Ethiopia, Nigeria, and Burkina Faso. The Nuru Collective's vision is cultivating lasting, meaningful choices in the world's most vulnerable and marginalised communities. In pursuit of this vision across varied geographies and approaches, Nuru Collective members embrace accountability as an intrinsic part of every action they take when implementing the Nuru model.

The Nuru Model and Cooperative Principles

The Nuru model provides business development services, livelihood and healthcare, and leadership mentorship services to cooperative agribusinesses. The cooperatives are rural private-sector entities, community-owned and managed by elected local leaders. One of the primary objectives of the Nuru model is to support cooperatives to become viable, accountable, and trusted socio-economic partners. These cooperatives, in turn, foster the development of diversified rural livelihoods for rural farming households and, in the process, address drivers of extreme poverty. Cooperatives also support socio-economic interventions like healthcare groups and digital skills training. Cooperatives across the world operate on the basis of seven cooperative principles. These principles guide Nuru's approach and the cooperatives in delivering on the values of self-help, self-responsibility, democracy, equality, equity, and solidarity that are core to all cooperative businesses (International Cooperative Alliance [ICA] 2023). Specifically, the seven cooperative principles codified by the International Cooperative Alliance (2017) are as follows:

1. Voluntary and Open Membership
2. Democratic Member Control
3. Member Economic Participation
4. Autonomy and Independence
5. Education, Training, and Information

6. Cooperation among Cooperatives
7. Concern for Community

Throughout their support of cooperatives, Nuru practitioners use human-centred design tools grounded in co-creation principles with a shared goal of seeing cooperatives become financially sustainable and managed transparently by their leadership. These two frameworks provide the foundation for the Nuru local design process, which meets the collective needs of supported communities while contextualising best practices from international development. By taking this intentional approach to co-creation throughout Nuru's engagement with rural communities, discrepancies in visible, hidden, and invisible power are laid bare over time (Hong 2016). To this end, the Nuru local design process delivers meaningful choices to individuals, develops socio-economic interventions that cooperatives can sustain, and works with diverse local actors to build a shared belief in their collective power to produce desired results.

Servant Leadership

An integral focus of the Nuru model is strengthening the capacity of local leaders who oversee their respective cooperatives' ongoing management and operations. Underpinning such training is servant leadership, a framework proposed by Robert K. Greenleaf in 1977. This framework is predicated on service-oriented leaders achieving more by bringing out the best in those they lead. Model leadership behaviours include admitting mistakes, leading by example, and seeking to understand different points of view. Accountability is fundamental to servant leadership and manifests in the positive behaviours of cooperative leaders.

Local Accountability, Impact, and Change

The unique local interventions Nuru NGOs support share a common approach to cooperative development, improving rural livelihoods, and addressing drivers of extreme poverty. Across the Nuru Collective, leadership training and grassroots business development have positively impacted rural households and generated local economic growth led by cooperatives. In 2021, Nuru-supported farmers in Ethiopia increased their rural livelihood income by 73%; in 2022, supported dairy farmers in Kenya increased their incomes by 180%. The farmers who experienced these gains were all members of cooperative agribusinesses that had progressively improved their capacity to lead their member-oriented businesses, further enhancing the farmer members' individual socio-economic benefits and motivating local economic activity (Prince et al. 2022).

Positive change also exists beyond economic indicators. Partners within the Nuru Collective consider cooperatives viable when they can conduct business activities, build trust, sustain agency, and create access to socio-economic services for their remote, rural communities (Cook 2018). Over five to seven years, Nuru NGOs maintain a close relationship with supported cooperatives, acting as coaches, trainers, and mediators. A project cycle does not determine this period, but rather the time commitment is set by the Nuru Collective, partner communities, and cooperatives in the joint pursuit of shared goals. This collaborative approach also requires the communities to deliver on their commitments and meet key milestones.

To evaluate progress towards meeting these goals, all stakeholders participate in transparent evaluations using internal and external monitoring, evaluation, and learning (MEL) tools. Such tools include leadership indices, business capacities, econometrics, and financial analysis. However, to help objectively determine if a cooperative has viable, transparent, and trusted leadership that can sustain it through shocks, Nuru NGOs work with third-party local accounting firms to measure profitability, and a business intelligence company, SCOPEinsight, to measure business capacity improvements. This combination of MEL tools, local and global partnerships, and direct day-to-day interaction allows Nuru NGOs to determine how to tailor their support to cooperatives at different business development stages and scale up their activities in new communities while scaling-down activities in other communities.

From day one, Nuru NGOs work closely with multiple stakeholders across government, private, and local institutions to ensure services meet communities' needs and interests. In addition, Nuru NGOs are accountable to these stakeholders, with ultimate accountability resting within the expressed socio-economic goals of the supported cooperatives that democratically represent their communities. These impacts manifest at the county, *woreda* (districts in Ethiopia are called *woreda*), ward, municipal, and sub-municipal levels along road networks, natural boundaries, and between communities (Grashuis and Ye 2019).

Agency

Accountability manifests in the collective agency of members and local leaders. Agency is the actualised will of local leaders representing the collective ambition of the people in a place. Individual agency is the ability of people to act on their beliefs, dreams, and aspirations. Local leaders succeed when they reduce hardships and limitations that prevent people from being free. These limitations, as described by Freire (1970), stop people from making their own choices and, according to Sen (1999), leave them with few opportunities to act based on their own reasoning. Leaders, individuals, and the greater collective exist in a dynamic transactional environment of aggregating self-interests (Bandura 2001). For example, as Bandura (2001, 75) discussed, "people's shared belief in their collective power to produce desired results is a key ingredient of collective agency." However, it should not be assumed that the aggregation of self-interests will align with positive collective action, which will still require leadership, trust, and accountability in decision-making.

Nuru locally led NGOs support cooperative agribusinesses that are community-owned and managed by elected local leaders. The cooperatives are private-sector entities that are guided by the seven cooperative principles discussed above. This approach is inherently driven by private-sector engagement with the cooperative businesses acting as the leaders of economic growth and self-reliance outcomes in supported communes. All the countries where Nuru locally led NGOs operate have a legal framework for cooperatives that requires, at a minimum, the establishment of by-laws, mission and goals, and the adherence to democratic principles on which their internal governance is structured. It is through these governance mechanisms that cooperative leaders and members hold each other accountable. When collective will becomes manifest through shared action, and positive impact is achieved repeatedly over time, it establishes a reinforcing pathway for exercising responsibility and accountability.

Nuru engages with the populace at large through these cooperative agribusinesses, which engender a sense of ownership over their own development outcomes. For example, Nuru Kenya facilitates the creation of revolving fund accounts to support the cooperative members, the community of farmers, to access inputs timely and affordably. The cooperatives ensure they do not deplete the fund by fulfilling their individual input loan repayment obligation every farming season. Open forum dialogue sessions are held to deliberate how non-compliance shall be handled. The non-compliance is often as a result of drought, inflation, and policy changes affecting the farming productivity and market access. In addition, Nuru Kenya has supported cooperatives to institute financial and governance systems that promote transparency in operations. The systems instituted have increased the confidence of the members to utilise the various platforms.

Principles of Accountability

When proper accountability is present and codified through actions, NGOs can act as a source of inspiration and lifeblood to a thriving civil society (Lewis et al. 2020). They can elevate the dispersed voices of remote, marginalised populations, as Arnstein (1969) would say, "into a chorus." The chorus is only possible if trust and good governance are the norms in community-led development. Moreover, good governance is fragile, and trust will erode without accountability. To prevent such discord, the Nuru Collective draws from the principles of accountability. These principles support practitioners in their day-to-day decision-making and inform the Collective's long-term strategic thinking. The Nuru Collective observes and endorses overlapping principles of accountability:

- Accountability is *multi-directional*
- Accountability is *dynamic*
- Accountability is *endemic*
- Accountability is *complex*

Applying the Principles of Accountability

The remainder of this chapter expands on the Nuru Collective's efforts to ensure transparency in local leaders' policies, decisions, and actions, to reduce and mitigate corrupting influences, and to demand that development initiatives best serve the interests of local communities. The chapter ties together the shared vision, purpose, and approach Nuru locally led organisations share as part of the Nuru Collective. The contributions of the directors of Nuru Kenya, Nuru Nigeria, and Nuru Ethiopia provide concrete examples that reinforce accountability, an immutable pillar of community-led development.

Accountability manifests in various ways through Nuru Collective members, the cooperatives they support, and their interactive network of stakeholders. Over time, each locally led NGO has developed unique tools and tactics to advance the shared vision and values while remaining primarily accountable to the communities they serve. These tools and tactics evolve into a sequential set of daily, monthly, and annual activities that ensure programming is accountable to communities and adapts to a dynamic local context. In the examples below, we share some of the local and global accountability systems active across (1) collective members' operations, (2) at a cooperative level, and (3) a broader government and wider stakeholder level. The systems consist of tools, procedures, and culture that orient staff, strategy, and partners towards realising rural communities' development aspirations.

Multi-Directional Accountability

Accountability requires equal and opposite lines of responsibility (Bergsteiner and Avery 2003). Collective strength and shared purpose have the potential to bridge physical distances between local, regional, and international actors and generate shared understanding and compassion. As noted by Waldo Tobler in the first law of Geography (1970, 234), "everything is usually related to all else, but those which are near to each other are more related when compared to those that are further away." Bringing together dispersed actors helps shorten the distance and increase our ability to relate. To this end, the Nuru Collective offers an applied example demonstrating that an aggregation of local leaders can be brought into cooperation in a way that each additional part creates a greater whole (Nuru International 2023).

Nuru Kenya's approach is based on mutual accountability, that is, "accountability between the providers and recipients of development cooperation, for the effectiveness of that cooperation in producing development results" (United Nations 2023, para 1). In the case of Nuru Nigeria, state government actors play an enhanced role in an integrated system of interaction between the NGO, government, and communities. Nuru Ethiopia has taken a more structural approach. They institutionalise accountability through contiguous policies that protect the environment and community from harm and have cascaded these policies to the cooperatives they serve.

At Nuru Kenya, community accountability develops through weekly and monthly training and coaching services that Nuru Kenya staff provide to cooperative business leaders and farmer members. These services are co-created to meet community needs. They are followed by quarterly stakeholder meetings where farmers, Nuru Kenya staff, and respective county government officials discuss progress, challenges, and their potential solutions. Nuru Kenya then conducts an annual customer satisfaction survey and stakeholder feedback reports to identify areas for improvement. Through iteration, the Nuru Kenya team applies this aggregated learning to its community development activities and services. It is this iteration and adaptive management approach that allows Nuru Kenya to respond to the emerging issues the farmers and communities are facing. Through these accountability actions, Nuru Kenya understands community perceptions and responds to evolving needs while maintaining trust with communities.

Multi-directional accountability also manifests within cooperatives, specifically between leadership and members. In this example from Kenya, former informal groups became credible vehicles for development, promoting the transition of the livelihoods of their members to agribusinesses. The cooperative members are shareholders and hold each other accountable for their own development by participating meaningfully in poverty reduction efforts. Applied accountability practices produce tangible benefits. Cooperative members demonstrate bankability, business prudence, and community stewardship. This builds a profile of professionalism to acquire necessary resources and attract investors. They have demonstrated commitment to their goals in the face of challenges. They jointly devise ways of mitigating these challenges, leading to remarkable growth in their leadership.

These approaches to community-based accountability structures have evolved over time. Nuru Kenya began implementing poverty reduction strategies by working with community members through informal groups with no legal identity. Despite shared values and trust in the informal groups, it became increasingly difficult to demonstrate commitment to long-term developmental goals and implement mechanisms of holding one another accountable for agreed outcomes, especially when faced with challenges. The lack of legal status also made investing and ownership of assets impossible. In 2015, Nuru Kenya revised its poverty reduction strategy and started mobilising smallholder farmers to register as cooperatives. These cooperatives are still farmer-led but have legal status and standardised documentation systems. The members have shared values and goals that are transparently articulated in their offices. There is an outlined governance structure that provides guidelines on how to undertake activities, and minutes are taken for all activities. The members can engage with other legally recognised entities, build business partnerships, and provide financial support to members from external institutions.

The relationship between Nuru Kenya and the cooperatives has evolved further over the years. Formal agreements are in place between the farmers and the organisation, leading to effective planning, monitoring, and evaluation of activities. The allocation and utilisation of resources have become more efficient and impactful. The accountability measures incorporated and enforced through Memoranda of Understandings (MOUs) between Nuru Kenya and the cooperatives in the development projects have enhanced ownership and productivity. The MOUs are a formal measure that keeps the two-way accountability between Nuru Kenya and cooperatives open, transparent and provides space for grievances and feedback.

In sum, the members of the initial informal groups become financial and strategic shareholders in their cooperatives. They have indicated how the transition has impacted their lives. They are now able to invest in their farmer-led cooperatives. They seek out and attend capacity-strengthening activities provided by the cooperative. They have adopted the various practices, policies, and technologies promoted by Nuru. They are more empowered to not only resolve the challenges they face but also own the outcomes of their efforts.

With Nuru's support, the cooperatives have developed transparent, functional governance structures that have built their credibility. They continue to demonstrate high levels of integrity and are now receiving funds directly from government and allied institutions for their development projects. One such cooperative has been able to access funding that has led to the acquisition of land and equipment for use in the value addition activities of the farm produce. The households that benefit from Nuru's work have demonstrated remarkable growth and resilience over the years as evidenced in MEL impact reports and third-party assessments.

The lessons learned by Nuru since inception have continued to shape how the organisation evolves in delivering its mandate to the community. Cooperatives are a force multiplier in targeted and cost-effective scaling of Nuru's overall vision. A virtuous feedback loop of trust-building has emerged. Participant engagement with their cooperatives has built trust with Nuru, and Nuru has leveraged this engagement to build trust with cooperatives and community members.

Local and national governmental bodies are critical pillars in multi-directional accountability. With an active ecosystem of communities, cooperatives and NGOs such as Nuru, there are ample opportunities to link to government services. Cooperatives have afforded legal status and opened civic space to formally engage with different sectors of government. On the governmental side, engaging with collective community groups makes their work more efficient by decreasing the transaction costs of serving remote rural communities. Nuru Kenya's work is an example of this dynamic, where scaling up into additional counties has necessitated a new way of doing business. The organisation is proactively engaging with the county governments through joint work plans. This has facilitated the joint identification of priorities and collaboration in the implementation of planned activities. The new approach has substantially increased collaboration with county and national government bodies. This close working relationship has also resulted in instances where the local government donated equipment and financial support to the organisation to facilitate its work in the community.

Nuru Nigeria provides an additional example of multi-directional accountability in terms of regular formal reporting mechanisms. Nuru Nigeria provides quarterly updates to traditional leaders and local government administrators to keep them informed about the progress of its activities, get constructive feedback, and resolve any issues. These quarterly coordination meeting reports include information on the number of households participating and the impact on the local economy. Nuru Nigeria shares this information with the broader community through town hall meetings and other communication channels.

Rather than being strictly top-down or bottom-up, at any point in time accountability is multi-directional. Recognising this dynamic of mutual accountability between multiple parties lays the groundwork for cultivating it. In the best case scenario, accountability mechanisms provide an opportunity for virtuous feedback loops where accountability is strengthened not just between one party to another, but rather in a broadly encompassing way.

Dynamic Accountability

Accountability is not built overnight. It requires trust established over time with repeated interactions grounded in transparency and servant leadership. In Nuru's context, this involves a complex array of actors, including community members, civil society organisations, local government, cooperatives, and others. A localisation approach rooted in community leadership implies closer relationships between people and interests in this ecosystem. However, accountability is not assumed and must be nurtured through continuous non-judgmental interactions between staff (internal) and partners (external). Overlapping systems, norms, and cultures of accountability create a reinforcing ecosystem. This is an active, long-standing, and dynamic endeavour.

Accountability is dynamic because it changes over time and as a result of the interactions between actors in the ecosystem. In the best case scenario, actors build trust on the basis of continuous interactions. This creates confidence in a reliable system and predictable response. On the other hand, accountability dynamics can degrade if trust is broken by one party or another. Moreover, accountability systems change and morph as a result of sweeping changes to laws and governing institutions, as well as the introduction of new actors. In this regard, accountability is constantly evolving; there is no finish line.

Accountability is in a constant state of change. To accomplish long-term goals amidst change, Nuru orients its work with the co-creation, use of and regular updation of strategic plans. These plans are rooted in farmer-first values, which underpin all decision-making in a co-creative way. The input from multiple stakeholders regularly is used to update, adapt, and inform activities.

Nuru Kenya focuses on facilitating the transformation of farmer-led cooperatives. It guides these cooperatives to institute functional accountability mechanisms as key ingredients of leadership and financial sustainability. Nuru Kenya assists the cooperatives in developing disclosure tools and reports that ensure compliance with the regulatory framework set by oversight agencies. For instance, these include financial statements for tax authorities, obtaining business registration with cooperative authorities, and securing operating permits for conducting business in regulated sectors such as commerce and food safety. These reports are also disseminated to the shareholders during annual general meetings and other relevant forums. Disclosure tools, such as publicly sharing annual financial reports, form part of the social auditing process for farmer organisations.

In operationalising strategic plans, standard operating procedures are socialised, updated, and benchmarked with industry standards to ensure fair and transparent enforcement. This ideal is held up in Nuru's work within its organisation and is promulgated and instilled at Nuru-supported entities such as cooperatives as well. Decision-making is conducted based on a documented system. The way decisions are made, implemented, and communicated follows a standard template called by its acronym RAPID (Huggett and Moran 2007). This system framework has discrete steps of Recommend, Agree, Perform, Input, and Decide. A documented decision-making framework acknowledges the actions and parties involved in a decision to promote efficiency, transparency, and quality. This considers the local knowledge and context, and a clear policy is implemented on when and how the senior leadership will consult and involve staff and their representatives in decision-making.

There is not a discrete moment where accountability is accomplished. It is in a constant state of movement. Nuru's outlook towards the dynamism of accountability is constant improvement. Using formal mechanisms such as reports and decision-making processes, Nuru's work and that of Nuru-supported cooperatives leverage each opportunity to build incremental positive steps towards increased accountability between actors.

Accountability Is Endemic

Endemism is a biogeographic principle describing the natural connection between an organism and a geographic location, a concept we are extending to social science to reinforce the inherent and unique connection between the agency of people and their geographic place in the world. According to Cooley, "the most important spheres [of influence] of this intimate association and cooperation – though by no means the only ones – are the family, the play-group of children, and the neighbourhood or community group of elders" (Cooley 1922, 24). At the core of accountability is the primary group (e.g., the household and the community), a relationship that can only be found naturally in a specific place. Therefore, accountability must be endemic for effective community-led development to be achieved, especially when it comes to locally based leadership initiatives. According to Ostrom (1990), people with a grounding in place and endowed with driving purpose – strong local leaders – are the foundation of successful community-led development. However, being a local leader and working towards a collective goal does not automatically guarantee success. Instead, "the core of organisation [and collective action] involves changes that order activities so that sequential, contingent, and frequency-dependent decisions are introduced where simultaneous, noncontingent, and frequency-independent actions had prevailed" (Ostrom 1990, 39). Leadership must therefore demonstrate, in a contingent and consistent way, accountability to their purpose and the community they represent and strive for quality results with integrity. Only by uniting development aspirations into collective experience and action can change agents bring about their desired lives and livelihoods (Poteete et al 2009).

Local leadership is not inherently destined to be good or bad but must be continuously held accountable by the people that this leadership intends to serve. A community is composed of people in a place. At a practical level, what makes community-led development work is the convergence of people power. This is predicated on leveraging the advocacy, organising, and legal strategies necessary to create meaningful choices by motivating individual self-interest to operate interdependently with society and the broader enabling environment. Therefore, ensuring that opportunities for individual and collective redress and growth are aligned with community interests and needs is vital to successful impact and change.

From a compliance perspective, local leadership accountability means being legally recognised and registered. In turn, local organisations also gain legitimacy when going through legal registration processes, which can sometimes be costly and time-consuming. They achieve this by subjecting themselves to norms, rules, and regulations, which imply certain time and resource expenses. Moreover, by making themselves accountable to government authorities, local organisations, both civil society and private sector, also gain access to resources and can begin to exercise their reasoned agency.

People are at the heart of organisational accountability within the Nuru Collective. Staff roles, responsibilities, and performance criteria are clearly defined and documented. Core job responsibilities are determined based on the organisation's vision, values, mission, and individual job requirements. Individual performance is assessed based on shared Nuru values: servant leadership, transparency, bold action, equity, and fail fast, learn fast. Nuru leadership provides staff with regular and ongoing feedback through weekly one-on-ones, departmental meetings, and bi-annual staff performance evaluations. These systems keep staff accountable to management, the organisation's overall aims, and to the communities they serve.

Organisations in the Nuru Collective have their own bespoke and context-specific accountability mechanisms. Nuru Kenya, for instance, has a formally constituted board that oversees all organisation operations and ensures that compliance reports are submitted to the regulators and donors as required. These reports comprise annual NGO returns, statutory audits, and implementation reports that provide information on funds received, expenditure, accomplishments, and pending activities. For Nuru Kenya, this evolved over time. While the organisation continued to grow in scope and evolve its strategy to align with community needs, it needed to strengthen its administrative capacity for operational efficiency. Initially, the organisation did its finance and human resources manually. Unfortunately, the increased operations led to a commensurate increase in paperwork, tedious work routines, frequent errors, and cases of misappropriation of funds. Transitioning to a digital financial platform led to faster transaction turnaround time and enhanced transparency and accuracy. For instance, since payments are made directly through cashless platforms, the organisation was able to eliminate cash handling from its operations. Reviewing organisational policies to align with new organisation trends led to better reports that instil more confidence and trust in stakeholders.

Nuru Kenya operates in concert with authorities and policies governing NGOs in the country. Nuru Kenya develops joint work plans with local county governments where it works. Each county develops and maintains County Integrated Development Plans detailing the priorities of the county governments and how these are addressed by the various partners (Ministry of Devolution and Planning 2017). Through periodic stakeholder meetings, the county can monitor the implementation of the prioritised activities by each organisation. The complex interaction between the county governments and Nuru Kenya generates a dynamic agenda-setting, action, and iteration environment.

Nuru Nigeria has a distinct experience implementing 360-degree accountability in the context of formal local government area (LGA) administrators and traditional leaders. In this context, Nuru Nigeria implements the same strategies to reach the different stakeholders:

- Transparent monitoring and evaluation: Nuru Nigeria ensures transparency in its monitoring and evaluation process by setting clear goals and objectives for its agricultural programme. The organisation also collects and analyses data to track progress and identify areas for improvement. Nuru Nigeria shares this information with traditional leaders and local government administrators, who are encouraged to provide feedback and suggestions for improvement.
- Community engagement: Nuru Nigeria fosters community engagement by involving traditional leaders and local government administrators in every stage of activity design and implementation. This includes identifying the needs and priorities of the community, developing agricultural plans, and running and monitoring the activities. Community members are also encouraged to participate in activities and provide feedback on their effectiveness.
- Feedback mechanisms: Nuru Nigeria has established mechanisms to ensure that traditional leaders and local government administrators can provide input and suggestions. Such mechanisms include regular meetings, consultations,

and online and offline surveys and questionnaires. Nuru Nigeria also provides suggestion boxes placed in strategic areas of the community to enable it to receive anonymous feedback that can improve its endeavours.

Nuru Nigeria is registered with the National Planning Commission, Adamawa State Planning Commission, the Corporate Affairs Commission, and other legal bodies to formalise their legal status and framework at multiple levels of government. Following registration, the organisation gets accreditation and certification by a third party, fulfilling the nationally established standards and policies. The legal status, accreditation, and certification have helped in partnerships with governments and donor agencies at national and international scales. It also provides a platform for Nuru Nigeria to elevate the dispersed voices of the remote, marginalised populations they serve.

Accountability Is Complex

The concept of localisation is now a mainstream international development best practice (United States Agency for International Development [USAID] 2022). However, embracing localisation requires international, local, or community-based interventions to achieve measurable change, transcend siloed approaches, and leverage cooperation in an environment of increasing complexity.

Accountability is complex because it involves multiple actors in repeated interactions, it is constantly open to newcomers to the accountability system, it changes over time, and it changes on the basis of interactions between actors within this ecosystem. There is no finish line or mission accomplished when it comes to accountability. Moreover, there is no single direction of positive or negative change. The quality of accountability depends on a changing set of actors over time.

In 2021, the Nuru NGOs established the Nuru Global Advisory Council comprising representatives from each NGO. The Council aims to increase diversity and inclusion in decision-making for key elements of Nuru's global operating model. This purpose ensures that all Nuru partner NGOs are accountable to a shared vision, values, and to each other (Nuru International 2021).

Nuru International works to continuously improve internal and external accountability by aligning its mission to international frameworks (e.g. Gender Minimum Standards, 1% for the Planet, AIM for Climate, Principles for Digital Development), improving its MEL practices, and leveraging internal systems like Objectives and Key Results (OKRs) and collaborative annual planning.

Nuru NGOs provide financial records to the relevant stakeholders, such as donors, and internally for transparency and accountability. These include accounting or significant financial records, critical information, and evidence used in preparing, verifying, and auditing the financial statements. They indicate asset ownership for the purpose and creation of liabilities and provide proof for monetary and non-monetary transactions.

The broader range of civil society organisations, businesses, and global community has complex and, at times, punctuated impact on accountability. Nuru's posture is openness to partnerships and collaborations with various other organisations to meet its development goals. The organisation participates in networks where partners share their plans and develop shared values and priorities. These networks build social capital necessary for partners to mobilise needed resources, allocate responsibilities, and disseminate progress reports. For instance, Nuru Kenya is a member of the Migori Innovation Platform, National Conservation Agriculture Hub, and Agribusiness Market Ecosystem Alliance (AMEA).

The Nuru Collective also implemented a robust MEL system across all members with managerial staff within each local NGO. The system includes regular monitoring reports that enable corrective action organisations can take when environmental, social, or economic challenges arise. Annual evaluations are conducted, with and the analysis take out done externally and results published. The organisational culture of transparency and accountability is reflected in the publication and sharing of programme reports that detail successes, lessons learned, and challenges. These reports not only inform the stakeholders about the organisation's activities but provide learning for external stakeholders to ensure activities benefit farmers and rural communities.

Conclusion

Accountability takes root and emanates from within an organisation through its values, principles, and ethical standards that guide staff conduct and operations. A diverse array of tools and procedures ensure that accountability is transparent to both external stakeholders and internal staff.

Organisations that implement community-led development, such as Nuru, deliberately cultivate a culture of accountability in their approach to eradicating poverty. Nuru facilitators initiate this culture during the design phase, mobilising communities to participate in a co-creation process to identify feasible solutions to their poverty-related challenges. This co-creation process facilitates ownership of the interventions. Accountability is predicated on a system of repeated engagement; it is not a quality for any one actor or implementing organisation to possess or not. Accountability is a virtue that should be inculcated by community members and development facilitators so that they not only commit to what they undertake but also own the outcomes. This is key, especially since interventions change and adapt as they are rolled out based on information collected in the communities. The unpredictability of shocks and stressors may lead to unexpected and adverse outcomes where a collaborative problem-solving approach becomes appropriate but can also lead to misunderstandings amongst community members. This is why organisations should have dynamic accountability practices so they can shoulder change and meet every changing context. Such accountability requires regular and consistent communication with stakeholders and communities.

Locally led development aims to help people determine the lives they value and expand their freedoms to include ownership over their own choices (UNDP 2022). It is the responsibility of civil society to take great care with the power afforded them by the communities they aim to serve. Thus, the Movement for Community-led Development (MCLD) defines accountability as "the expectation that power comes with responsibility." The Nuru Collective takes great care and utilises limited resources to ensure transparency in their leaders' policies, decisions, and actions, to reduce and mitigate corrupting influences, and to demand that development initiatives best serve the interests of the communities. Moreover, this investment in accountability and transparency requires long-term and patient investment to unite community development aspirations into collective experience and action that meaningfully changes lives and livelihoods. Through repeated application, success, and iterating past challenges and failures along the way, communities will adopt the behaviours and begin to invigorate their livelihoods, improve their lives, and lead their people and place into the future.

References

Arnstein, Sherry A. 1969. A Ladder of Citizen Participation. *Journal of the American Institute of Planners*, 35(4), 216–224.

Bandura, Albert. 2001. Social Cognitive Theory: An Agentic Perspective. *Annual Review of Psychology*, 52(1): 1–26.

Bergsteiner, Harald, & Gayle Avery. 2003. Responsibility and Accountability: Towards an Integrative Process Model. *International Business & Economics Research Journal (IBER)*, 2(2). https://doi.org/10.19030/iber.v2i2.3763

Cook, Michael L. 2018. A Life Cycle Explanation of Cooperative Longevity. *Sustainability*, 10(5): 1–20.

Cooley, Charles Horton. 1922. *Human Nature and the Social Order*. New York: Charles Scribner's Sons.

Freire, Paulo. 1970. *Pedagogy of the Oppressed*. New York: Continuum.

Grashuis, Jasper, & Ye Su. 2019. A Review of the Empirical Literature on Farmer Cooperatives: Performance, Ownership and Governance, Finance, and Member Attitude. *Annals of Public and Cooperative Economics*, 90(1): 77–102.

Greenleaf, Robert. (1977). *Servant Leadership* (pp. 7–17). New York: Paulist Press.

Hong, Thomas. 2016. "Nuru Leadership Program Manual 2.0". Nuru International, pp. 1–36. Accessed June 1, 2023. www.nuruinternational.org/wp-content/uploads/2016/09/Nuru-Leadership-Program-Manual_v2.pdf

Huggett, Jon, & Caitrin Moran. 2007. RAPID Decision Making: What It Is, Why We Like It, and How to Get the Most Out of It. Accessed June 8, 2023. www.bridgespan.org/getmedia/34fd3f75-3067-4162-ba86-5707a365aee0/RAPIDDecisionMaking.pdf

International Cooperative Alliance (ICA). 2017. "Cooperative Identity, Values & Principles." COOP. Accessed January 5, 2023. www.ica.coop/en/cooperatives/cooperative-identity

Lewis, David, Nanzeen Kanji, & Nuno Themudo. 2020. *Non-Governmental Organizations and Development*. New York: Routledge.

Ministry of Devolution and Planning – Government of Kenya. 2017. *Guidelines for Preparation of County Integrated Development Plans*, pp. 1–26. Accessed June 8, 2023.

https://countytoolkit.devolution.go.ke/sites/default/files/resources/CIDP_GUIDELINES_REVISED_2017_15.09.2017.pdf

Nuru International. 2021. "2021 Annual Report." Accessed May 5, 2023. https://annualreport.nuruinternational.org/

Nuru International. 2023. "Our Model." Accessed January 5, 2023. https://nuruinternational.org/what-we-do/our-model/

Ostrom, Elinor. 1990. *Governing the Commons: The Evolution of Institutions for Collective Action.* Cambridge: Cambridge University Press.

Poteete, Amy, Marco Janssen, & Elinor Ostrom. (2009). *Working Together: Collective Action, the Commons, and Multiple Methods in Practice.* Princeton, NJ: Princeton University Press.

Prince, Heath, Ashweeta Patnaik, Tatek Amataw, Casey Harrison, Matt Lineal, & Ian Schwenke. (2022). Nuru Ethiopia 2021 Impact Report. Ray Marshall Center for the Study of Human Resources at the University of Austin at Texas. Accessed June 1, 2023 from https://sites.utexas.edu/raymarshallcenter/2022/06/20/nuru-ethiopia-2021-impact-report/

Sen, Amartya. 1999. *Development as Freedom.* Oxford: Oxford University Press.

Tobler, Waldo. 1970. A Computer Movie Simulating Urban Growth in the Detroit Region. *Economic Geography*, 46(Supplement): 234–240.

UNDP (United Nations Development Programme). 2022. *Human Development Report 2021–22: Uncertain Times, Unsettled Lives: Shaping our Future in a Transforming World.* New York.

United Nations. 2023. "ECOSOC." United Nations Economic and Social Council. Accessed January 5, 2023. www.un.org/en/ecosoc/newfunct/dcf_account2.shtml

USAID (United States Agency for International Development). 2022. *Local Capacity Strengthening Policy.* Accessed October 27, 2022. www.usaid.gov/sites/default/files/documents/LCS-Policy-2022-10-17.pdf

PART V

Monitoring and Evaluation/ Facilitation

Elene Cloete and Gunjan Veda

Most chapters in this volume focus on the characteristics of community-led development, with authors describing how these characteristics manifest through locally-led activities. The chapters in this section, however, are written to bring attention to community development processes, specifically those associated with monitoring and evaluation, and facilitation. In Rafique et al.'s chapter, we learn about The Constellation's approach to monitoring and evaluation – how the organisation's methodology normalises these processes as simply part of what they do when facilitating locally-led action. It stands perhaps in stark contrast to the prescriptive, sometimes punitive perceptions associated with mainstream and top-down monitoring, evaluation, and learning practice. Fernando and Ariyaratne's introduction to the Sarvodaya Shramadana Movement in Sri Lanka exemplifies facilitation's instrumental role in community-led work. What emerges from their chapter is that without thoughtful, well-planned, and quality facilitation, meaningful community-led work cannot happen. To lay the ground for these chapters, this section introduction briefly pauses to identify how and where the monitoring and evaluation as well as facilitation processes described in both Rafique et al. and Fernando and Ariyaratne's chapters align with broader sentiments within the development sector.

Framing Community-Led Monitoring and Evaluation

The rising tide of localisation and emphasis on local ownership, as mentioned in the introduction, has not excluded monitoring and evaluation practice. On the contrary, increasingly advocates for more localised and decolonised development practices are looking to evaluators, asking them how, where, and when they can prioritise local voices, contexts, and input when conducting evaluations. The local

DOI: 10.4324/9781003377917-19

ownership agenda, as Levine and Grino (2015) urge, must extend to all parts of the programme cycle, including monitoring and evaluation.

The present momentum towards community-led monitoring and evaluation activities has at least three decades worth of "alternative" approaches to draw from (Cousins and Whitmore 1998; Shulha et al. 2016; Chouinard and Cousins 2021). Within evaluation circles, questions about power inequalities, as well as the usability and applicability of evaluation results, have given rise to several, yet closely aligned, participatory and collaborative approaches. These include transformative participatory evaluation (Cousins and Whitmore 1998), transformative evaluation (Mertens 1999, 2009), empowerment evaluation (Fetterman and Wandersman 2005), developmental and utilisation-focused evaluation (UFE) (Patton 2008), and participatory rural appraisal (Chambers 1994). Collectively, they represent Collaborative Approaches to Evaluation (CAE) (Shulha et al. 2016), and within all of these approaches, community members are direct collaborators working with and alongside evaluators.

What is perhaps most important, especially when considering broader localisation and decolonisation conversations, is how CAE reflects pragmatic, political, and philosophical interests (Chouinard and Cousins 2021). A *pragmatic* interest considers the extent to which evaluation results leverage change. The interest includes both an instrumental aspect, such as making programming decisions, and a learning aspect, with community members not only learning about programme functionality but also about the evaluation process itself. The instrumental aspect of monitoring and evaluation is often what receives the most attention. But as Chouinard and Cousins (2013) state elsewhere, its learning focus is how participatory evaluation "stands apart from other forms of evaluation." Learning, including the educative and training components of participatory evaluation, translates into active and meaningful participation of all stakeholders. Herein also lies the possibility of evaluation to strengthen programme participants' capacity to evaluate, learn, and gather knowledge useful to them in the future.

A *political* interest pertains to both the transformative and democratisation potential of evaluation. Evaluation holds the potential for local people who directly benefit from interventions to also learn more about their circumstances and, in the process, recognise which forces contribute to their oppression (Chouinard and Cousins 2021, 5). Evaluation processes should also be inclusive and representative of diverse populations and sociocultural contexts. As discussed in section three and emerging from the chapters of Behal and Metz, participation cannot be separated from inclusion and voice. When conducting evaluations, it is similarly crucial to ensure activities are inclusive, data is reflective of all groups, and the dissemination of data reaches all relevant stakeholders in the same way.

A *philosophical* reason to implement collaborative monitoring and evaluation is that the eventual product will be more representative and, thus more relevant to all stakeholders. Collaboration produces knowledge that is both grounded in local realities and reflective of historical, sociopolitical, economic, and cultural factors (Chouinard and Cousins 2021). Along similar lines, Culturally Responsive Evaluation (CRE) also emphasises a culturally grounded understanding of the community and programmes under study (Hood et al. 2015). It not only pays close attention to but also uses culturally defined ethics, norms, values, beliefs, and traditions to inform evaluation design, methods, and processes (Kawakami et al. 2007; Martinez et al. 2018; Chouinard and Cram 2019). A deep awareness of local context and culture not only holds the potential for evaluations to "create a deeper understanding of complex psychosocial phenomena" (Chouinard and Cousins 2021, 5) but also to contribute to co-created and thus shared knowledge (Chouinard and Cousins 2013, 2).

The pragmatic, political, and philosophical interests embedded in CAE represent by no means a conclusive list of ideals for addressing the power asymmetries active within mainstream evaluation practices. However, they do represent community-led advocates' call that monitoring and evaluation practices should prioritise the meaningful inclusion and collaboration of all stakeholders – from the design of the evaluation to the dissemination of its results and follow-up action planning (Chouinard and Milley 2018). These actors are also committed to strengthening the capacity of local community members and local nonprofits to participate in evaluation activities (Nandi et al. 2015).

The chapter on The Constellation demonstrates what collaborative and locally owned monitoring and evaluation, as envisioned by Jill Chouinard and colleagues, can look like. From an instrumental side, and in this case, the pragmatic interest that drives collaborative evaluation, Rafique et al. provide numerous examples of how community-led evaluation activities, built into The Constellation's CLCP methodology, can produce evidence of change. The results that emerge from the self-assessments in particular can very much provide the evidence community groups need to assess whether their activities were fruitful or not. But evidence on whether change happened, or whether an intervention was successful, is not the only pragmatic interest linked to collaborative evaluation. A second interest relates to the capacity participants gain from being actively involved in the evaluation activities. As Rafique et al. describe, such learning within the context of The Constellation is cyclical. Communities assess themselves multiple times, each time learning from what they have done, using such learning to improve their activities during the next iteration of their work, and then, again, assessing their progress towards reaching their target, or in the language of The Constellation, The Dream. Such circles of learning, scholars like Kolb (2014) would argue contribute to meaningful social learning – learning needed to encourage actors to reflect and then change their initial assumptions about their realities, contexts, and beliefs.

Learning also links to changes in people's perceptions with regard to their environment and contexts. Collaborative and locally-led evaluation can increase people's awareness about what they have access to as opposed to what they legitimately should have access to. Producing and then owning the data they themselves have collected gives local communities the content needed to advocate for themselves to get what is legitimately theirs. We see such advocacy work in Rafique et al.'s chapter, with Assamese communities in India increasing their awareness of water access and quality in their region, and using such knowledge to engage local authorities towards improved access. These practices are transformative, producing, at minimum, results that local participants and practitioners use in their planning and future actions towards addressing social injustices (Hopson 2014).

What is also present in Rafique et al.'s chapter is how The Constellation's evaluation tools, such as the self-assessment tool, are built into the organisation's community-led methodology. Evaluation is, therefore, not treated as something done at the end of a programme, during an one-off activity, or even deployed by external actors, but is integrated into the organisation's community-led practice. By normalising evaluation practice in such a way, and anchoring it within a community-led methodology, The Constellation actively demonstrates the locally relevant possibilities and potential of evaluation. No longer is it something done by only external experts using their knowledge towards extracting information to make decisions at a funder and implementer level. Instead, monitoring and evaluation become something applicable, usable, and valued at a local level. And in the process, as Clarke et al. (2022) mention, practising participatory evaluation demystifies the evaluation activities, increasing local people's confidence in their capacity and ability to track their own progress. In this case, the Self-Assessment Tool, as embedded in The Constellation's community-led methodology, is deepening people's appreciation of their own knowledge and their abilities, skills, and agency to be the central stakeholder in their own evaluations. This is how and where community-led forms of monitoring and evaluation are at the core, both political and philosophical. To make the pragmatic, political, and philosophical objectives of community-led monitoring and evaluation a reality, implementing organisations need skilful facilitation and skilled facilitators – the backbone of community-led development.

Facilitation

Facilitation, within the context of community-led development, captures the processes of engaging people towards co-creation, planning, and implementing collectively envisioned development. In this case, facilitation *is* participatory development – it is how change happens – not in a top-down prescriptive way, but instead through co-creation, collaboration, and inclusive engagements. And as the chapter by Fernando and Ariyaratne explains, such co-creation never stops. Over the course of the Sarvodaya Shramadana movement's history, its approach to development has constantly evolved, perpetually responding and adjusting to local communities' needs. But facilitation is also about *how* such co-creation and collaboration takes place, including the techniques needed to create safe and inclusive spaces of engagement for those often excluded from development activities. Additionally, facilitation is about the *who* – the main actors doing the activities, their skill sets, the support they receive, and the levels of ongoing learning they engage in to increase their receptiveness to local dynamics and contexts. The quality and success of community-led interventions depend on these actors' receptive attitudes and open commitment to learning by doing (Chambers 2012).

Enabling environments that cultivate local ownership requires not only practical skill and experience but also an awareness among practitioners of how their engagement with community members can disempower as easily as it can empower them. In considering both processes of facilitation as well as the role of the practitioner, Toomey's (2011) typology of practitioner roles is especially helpful in describing facilitation within community-led contexts. These roles are structured within clear hierarchies of power. Whereas traditional roles such as the rescuer, provider, moderniser, and liberator reflect vertical relationships with the practitioner on the top, alternative roles such as the catalyst, ally, advocate, and facilitator are more horizontal in nature, structured around collaboration and partnerships. These alternative roles are focused on cultivating local ownership over activities rather than creating dependency on external actors and initiatives.

Facilitators of community-led development are therefore tasked with co-creating conditions and environments for people to work together with the clear intention of "get[ing] out of the way" (Watkins and Mohr 2001). They must, as Weisbord and Janoff (2007) would say, "just not do something, but stand there!" Rather than being teachers or leaders, community-led facilitators who actively work towards meaningful participation are tasked with the challenging role of being present and initiating change while facilitating local ownership. For such ownership to take root, it is crucial that facilitators are attentive to local voices, particularly those marginalised. Toomey (2011) in referencing Wilson (1996) recognised such facilitation in the work of the Sarvodaya Movement: "They bring no blueprints for change, but rather good listening skills with which to empower the villagers" (Wilson 1996, 623).

To take on these facilitating roles, practitioners need skills. And while classroom training can initiate such skills development, scholars and practitioners alike agree that facilitators' actual skill develops through hands-on training in the communities and in real-time. As Fernando and Ariyaratne's chapter describes, such skills development is also directly responsive to changes in local contexts, which can range from emergency situations to the context-specific needs communities might have. Unfortunately, an approach based on experiential learning that is not necessarily time-bounded flies in the face of funder requirements for project completion dates. Even more damaging is how, by ignoring the time needed to train quality facilitators, the quality and subsequent sustainability of programming hangs in the balance.

Closely related is training that creates awareness of power relations and norms that negatively impact the quality of participation. Since inclusion is essential to meaningful participation, facilitators should be prepared to recognise power differences, including the people and systemic practices that support them, and have the skills to navigate and address such differences in a culturally appropriate and sensitive manner. One approach is building rapport with "influential members who can act as gatekeepers and champions for social inclusion" (Dey de Pryck and Elias 2023, 125).

As Toomey (2011, 183) reminds us, "Practitioners are people, not models" and therefore bring to their work their own histories, worldviews, and personalities. Even if facilitators have all the tricks and strategies at hand on how to facilitate inclusive activities, their attitude towards the work and the people is key (Dey de Pryck and Elias 2023). Their attitude also extends to the ongoing experiential learning that accompanies community development practice. On-the-job training and learning as-you-go are approaches to expanding skill sets that cannot be obtained either in a classroom or preparatory training (Evans et al. 2020). What adds to such learning is adopting thoughtful reflexivity, i.e., self-awareness and critical reflection on the activities that should be done as well as activities that have already happened (Dey de Pryck and Elias 2023, 123). Such critical reflection, as a core component of experiential learning, enables a deeper level of awareness of the issue and contexts at hand while strengthening ideals of perpetual learning and growth.

Fernando and Ariyaratne's chapter outlines the necessity of transitioning between Sarvodaya facilitators and new facilitators emerging from local communities and contexts. As these facilitators emerge, communities decrease their dependence on external facilitators, which in turn not only enables a smooth transition for development practitioners and organisations but also increases the likelihood of sustainable development. In the case of Sarvodaya, local volunteers are crucial in filling facilitator roles. They also undergo on-the-job training alongside Sarvodaya social workers so that they are equipped with the experiences to face whatever challenges might emerge in the future.

References

Carden, Fred. 2013. "Evaluation, not development evaluation." *American Journal of Evaluation* 34, no. 4: 576–579.

Chambers, Robert. 1994. Participatory rural appraisal (PRA): Challenges, potentials, and paradigm. *World Development* 22: 1437–1454.

Chambers, Robert. 2012. "Sharing and co-generating knowledges: Reflections on experiences with PRA 1 and CLTS 2." *IDS Bulletin* 43, no. 3: 71–87.

Chouinard, Jill A., and J. Bradley Cousins. 2013. "Participatory evaluation for development: Examining research-based knowledge from within the African context." *African Evaluation Journal* 1, no. 1: 9.

Chouinard, Jill Anne, and J. Bradley Cousins. 2021. "Developing an ethical rationale for collaborative approaches to evaluation." *Evaluation* 27, no. 3: 364–381.

Chouinard, Jill Anne, and Fiona Cram. 2019. *Culturally responsive approaches to evaluation: Empirical implications for theory and practice.* Sage Publications.

Chouinard, Jill Anne, and Peter Milley. 2018. "Uncovering the mysteries of inclusion: Empirical and methodological possibilities in participatory evaluation in an international context." *Evaluation and Program Planning* 67: 70–78.

Clarke, Gretchen S., Elizabeth B. Douglas, Marnie J. House, Kristen EG Hudgins, Sofia Campos, and Elizabeth E. Vaughn. 2022. "Empowering Indigenous communities through a participatory, culturally responsive evaluation of a Federal Program for Older Americans." *American Journal of Evaluation* 43, no. 4: 484–503.

Cousins, J. Bradley, and Elizabeth Whitmore. 1998. "Framing participatory evaluation." *New Directions for Evaluation* 80: 5–23.

Dey de Pryck, Jennie, and Marlène Elias. 2023. "Promoting inclusive facilitation of participatory agricultural research for development." *Development in Practice* 33, no. 1: 122–127..

Evans, Kristen, Anne M. Larson, and Selmira Flores. 2020. "Learning to learn in tropical forests: Training field teams in adaptive collaborative management, monitoring and gender." *International Forestry Review* 22, no. 2: 189–198.

Fetterman, David M., & Wandersman, Abraham (Eds.). 2005. *Empowerment evaluation principles in practice*. Guilford Press.

Hopson, Rodney K. 2014. "Justice signposts in evaluation theory, practice, and policy." *New Directions for Evaluation* 2014, no. 142: 83–94.

Hood, Stafford, Rodney K. Hopson, and Karen E. Kirkhart. 2015. Culturally responsive evaluation: Theory, practice, and future implications. Newcomer, Kathryn E., Harry P. Hatry, and Joseph S. Wholey, eds. *Handbook of practical program evaluation*. pp. 281–317. Jossey-Bass & Pfeiffer Imprints, Wiley.

Kawakami, Alice J., Kanani Aton, Fiona Cram, Moris K. Lai, and Laurie Porima. 2008. "Improving the practice of evaluation through indigenous values and methods: Decolonizing evaluation practice—Returning the gaze from Hawai'i and Aotearoa." *Fundamental Issues in Evaluation* 4, no. 1219–242.

Kolb, David A. 2014. *Experiential learning: Experience as the source of learning and development*. FT press.

Levine, Carlisle, and Laia Grino. 2015. "Local ownership in evaluation: Moving from participant inclusion to ownership in evaluation and decision making." *Briefing Paper, Interaction*. https://protection.interaction.org/resources/local-ownership-in-evaluation-moving-from-participant-inclusion-to-ownership-in-evaluation-decision-making

Martinez, Art, Paulette Running Wolf, Dolores Subia BigFoot, Carlette Randall, and Malia Villegas. 2018. "The process of becoming: A roadmap to evaluation in Indian country." *New Directions for Evaluation* 2018, no. 159: 33–45.

Mertens, Donna M. 1999. "Inclusive evaluation: Implications of transformative theory for evaluation." *American Journal of Evaluation* 20, no. 1: 1–14.

Mertens, Donna M. 2009. *Transformative research and evaluation*. Guilford Press.

Nandi, Rajib, Rituu B. Nanda, and Tanisha Jugran. 2015. "Evaluation from inside out: The experience of using local knowledge and practices to evaluate a program for adolescent girls in India through the lens of gender and equity." *Evaluation Journal of Australasia* 15, no. 1: 38–47.

Patton, Michael Quinn. 2008. *Utilization-focused evaluation*. Sage publications.

Shulha, Lyn M., Elizabeth Whitmore, J. Bradley Cousins, Nathalie Gilbert, and Hind al Hudib. 2016. "Introducing evidence-based principles to guide collaborative approaches to evaluation: Results of an empirical process." *American Journal of Evaluation* 37, no. 2: 193–215.

Toomey, Anne H. 2011. "Empowerment and disempowerment in community development practice: Eight roles practitioners play." *Community Development Journal* 46, no. 2: 181–195.

Watkins, Jane Magruder, and Bernard Mohr. 2001. "Appreciative inquiry: Change at the speed of imagination." *Organization Development Journal* 19, no. 3: 92.

Weisbord, Marvin R., and Sandra Janoff. 2007. *Don't just do something, stand there!: Ten principles for leading meetings that matter*. Berrett-Koehler Publishers.

Wilson, Patricia A. 1996. "Empowerment: Community economic development from the inside out." *Urban Studies* 33, no. 4–5: 617–630.

14

WHO OWNS THE RESPONSE?

How Self-Assessment Catalyses Ownership in the Work of The Constellation

Essa Mohamed Rafique, Rituu B. Nanda, Marlou de Rouw, and Philip Forth

What Is The Constellation?

"The Constellation," a nonprofit registered in Belgium, emerged following the success stories of communities that had started to turn the tide on HIV/AIDS by taking the issue into their own hands. The Constellation's founders dreamt of "a world where communities would take charge of their own lives and connect for sharing and support" (Lamboray 2016 in Google Books, n.d.). They would not teach or preach but appreciate community strengths. Thus, they would facilitate communities to achieve their dream, like a midwife helping to deliver a baby (Lamboray 2016). This idea of ownership is at the heart of The Constellation's approach. In the context of The Constellation, ownership means that the community decides on the action that it wishes to take and that it takes this action based on its resources and strengths available or within reach.

When it began its work in 2004, The Constellation's purpose was to support communities to deal with the HIV pandemic. Soon, it became clear that The Constellation could help communities to address a much broader range of issues. Since then, it has worked with communities in more than 70 countries. As of 2024, The Constellation is connecting a growing network of resilient, self-responsive communities. The organisation has found this approach to be helpful across a wide range of issues, including child health, maternal health, immunisation, nutrition, cholera, diabetes, Ebola, AIDS, malaria, poliomyelitis, water, sanitation and hygiene, palliative care, sexual and reproductive health, drugs, suicide prevention, living together, peace-building, and ageing with dignity. Though these communities work in different geographic and thematic areas, they are bonded into a single network by the SALT and The Community Life Competence Process (CLCP) approach, just like a Constellation in the starry skies.

DOI: 10.4324/9781003377917-20

In this chapter, we introduce The Constellation's approach to community-led development. Co-authored by the founders of the organisations and seasoned practitioners in our process to community development, we first summarise what our process is and how it works and then elaborate more on how monitoring and evaluation are integral to the process. We then delve into the self-assessment tool, embedded in the CLCP process, including how it has been used across different communities and organisations. Here we also emphasise the importance of facilitation. Community-owned monitoring and evaluation do not happen automatically. It requires intentional facilitation. We conclude by listing challenges we have encountered in using the CLCP approach, including its monitoring and evaluation component.

About Definitions

Words like "community," "facilitation," and "community competence" are often used within the development context loosely, assuming that all readers are on the same page about what these concepts mean. Therefore, we briefly share how we interpret and apply these concepts throughout the rest of our chapter.

What is a community? McQueen et al.'s (2001) curiosity about what community means to a diverse group of people across the United States led to the following definition: "A group of people with diverse characteristics who are linked by social ties, share common perspectives, and engage in joint action in geographical location or setting" (p. 1936). Similarly, for The Constellation, a community is a group of people with a shared interest or geographic area. For, in a geographical area, through facilitation, a group of people emerge who take on a challenge and involve others. The Constellation has also worked with groups of similar issues and interests, like youth groups, LGBTQI communities, indigenous groups, sex workers, those who use drugs, people with HIV, immigrants, and refugees, the corporate sector, trade unions, and United Nations agencies. For example, the International Labour Organisation (ILO) South Asia used The Constellation's approach to cultivate participatory leadership (Nanda 2017), as did a group of families in France for a housing project. As far as location or setting goes, this can also be digital. Keeping up with digitalisation and tapping into the potential of online communities, members of The Constellation used this process with a WhatsApp community of around 650 doctors from a medical college to establish a medical journal (Rafique 2022).

What is a Competent Community? For The Constellation, a community is competent not only when it can respond to existing challenges and their root causes, but also when it is prepared to address any new challenges that may arise. When engaged in community-led practices, including collaboratively analysing, planning, and addressing their challenges, communities are more resilient against shock, as demonstrated by the COVID-19 pandemic. For example, Kaza et al. (2022) found that communities exposed to the SALT approach responded to the pandemic far better than other communities in the area.

What Is Facilitation? The foundation of the CLCP approach is facilitation, where careful steps are taken towards community ownership of problems and solutions. Facilitators of CLCP use SALT to guide their facilitation, or *Way of Working* (WoW). Guiding their facilitating process are activities grounded in appreciating, listening, and learning from the lived experience of the communities. This helps facilitators to let go of top-down approaches that teach or provide solutions. In turn, when community members experience this facilitation, it gives them a sense of confidence. For years, outsiders, who are perceived as more educated professionals, have told them what is good for them, which has eroded their belief in their own capacity. Alternatively, this new-found confidence in themselves and others in their community motivates them to do something together for the community. Thus, as we illustrate in this chapter, focused on the work of The Constellation, facilitation in SALT and CLCP is a transfer of power and ownership from the facilitator to the community.

A Report Card on the Health of a Village

"It is when we did our self-assessment the second time that I realised it was like the report card our children get from school." Pointing to the self-assessment sheet, an Anganwadi[1] worker laughed and added, "This seems to be the report card of our village dream. Initially, we did not take this assessment seriously, but slowly, we are learning. It is an important step for the village."

Like her, others in this Assamese village in India were aware of their problems but not the extent of the problem. However, through their collective self-assessment, they gained clear insight into the village's status on immunisation, why some of them were not completing the immunisation schedule, and which population group was left entirely out. Soon, a joint reflection on their self-assessment motivated the village to take collective action to achieve their shared goals around immunisation (Nanda 2017). After these sessions, men who were not previously involved in immunising children also joined the collective action to ensure complete immunisation for their village. When community members, like those in the Assamese village mentioned above, assess their own situation in relation to their collective dream, the assessment is more authentic than when done by a third party. After all, who knows the dream better than the dreamer? Who knows better the areas they are currently excelling at and where they can do better than those who are concerned?

The Learning Mix: SALT and CLCP

It is about a dream that is identified collectively and serves as a beacon for communities in their development journey. It marks the point of success they are aiming for. How close they get to achieving their dream marks their success. For a community to establish its collective dream, members must first recognise their strengths. Therefore, facilitators working with The Constellation begin by stimulating the community to appreciate their strengths so that at the end of the introductory session, attendees are wonder-struck to see the long list of strengths they never knew they had.

By appreciating its strengths, practitioners can support the community to move from thinking to action (VHAI 2022). Facilitators do this by using an open-source technique called "Way of Working," which draws from Appreciative Inquiry and its focus on engaging people in learning and co-constructing the change that they want (Watkins et al. 2011; Cooperrider et al. 2003). The acronym SALT abbreviates the Constellation's Way of Working (Duongsa 2021). Initially, SALT included *support*, *appreciate*, *listen*, and *transfer*, but over the two decades of its use, it has accrued three more sets of words (see Figure 14.1) (The Constellation 2015).

Thus, coaches of The Constellation, who have facilitated SALT in countless learning communities, have witnessed SALT evolve and adjust through added experiential learning.

The Constellation combines its Way of Working (SALT) with its CLCP learning cycle. SALT and CLCP make a productive evaluation, learning, and knowledge management combination (Zaveri et al. 2016; Nandi et al. 2018). CLCP is designed to further encourage communities to take ownership of their development challenges. The idea is that when people take ownership of their challenges, they can take action to overcome them. Ownership, by this definition:

- goes beyond consultation, engagement, and empowerment;
- drives action that will not be dependent on external stimulus;

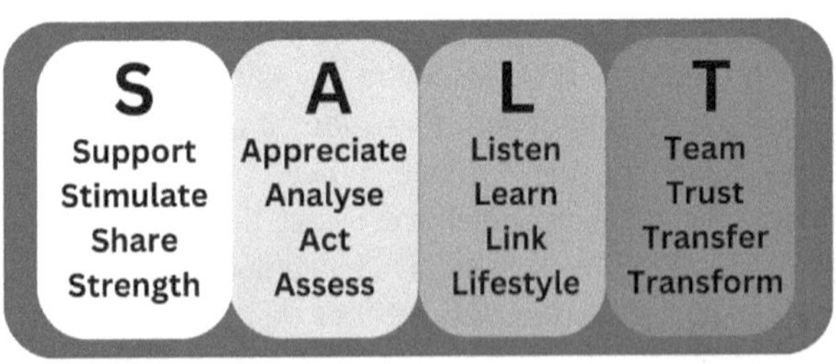

FIGURE 14.1 The constellation has accumulated four distinct sets of words that represent the acronym of SALT.

Source: Rafique (2017).

- entails people asking for the resources and expertise they need to execute their own plans;
- involves a community appreciating the strengths it already has as the basis of further actions and;
- is based on the notion that a community can take sustainable action only when its members recognise their shared interest in a better future. This recognition comes through dialogue (De Rouw et al. 2020).

However, how can such ownership emerge? How is such ownership cultivated? Figure 14.2 shows the steps of the CLCP learning cycle in facilitating and deepening ownership. Throughout this process, SALT is always present, guiding facilitators in engendering engaging questions, conversations, and shared learning.

The first step in CLCP is when the community comes together to establish a common identity grounded in recognising mutual humanity. The community begins by exploring "who are we?" which helps them recognise their strengths and capacity, consider who needs to be part of the conversations, and identify their key issues or concerns.

During the second step, the community defines their "shared dream," which is the common objective the community will work towards. During this step, members also discuss the important practices needed for them to achieve their dreams.

In step three, the community defines its current performance through a self-assessment designed to stimulate productive dialogue as members discuss their current level of achievement, and in step four, the community creates an action plan to move from its current situation to its desired one.

Step five involves the community carrying out its action plan while regularly reflecting on its actions. Questions guiding these reflection sessions include "What went well?" and "What can we do better next time?"

FIGURE 14.2 The six steps of the community life competence process (CLCP) cycle.

During the CLCP's final step, the community reflects on its progress to prepare for the next cycle. The community explores the lessons it has learned thus far and also the information and materials it can share with peers interested in engaging in the same progress. Such learning is then shared through "Learning Festivals" or "Knowledge Fairs," which typically cultivate additional joint learning.

During each step of the CLCP, a participating community builds ownership by designing, implementing, taking action, and evaluating its dream. As the community moves through the process, each step documents progress, but the real measure of ownership lies in the depth of discussion, the consistency of engagement, and the joy of achievement accompanying these steps (The Constellation 2015). As the group completes one cycle, the subsequent one begins as new dreams and issues emerge. Communities repeat these cycles as much as they need and choose to.

Who Develops, Owns, and Does the Self-Assessment?

Suppose the dream is the end-point of the CLCP journey. In that case, the initial self-assessment, inspired by the work of Chris Collison and Geoff Parcell (the latter is also one of the founders of The Constellation) and done during step 3 of the CLCP process, marks the starting line (Collison 2004). Within the CLCP process, a community first reviews its action plan to establish a standard set of practices (Schomaker 2019). These action areas are important to measure consistently for achieving the community's dream (Parcell and Collison 2010). Thus, the initial self-assessment sets a community-formulated and collectively agreed-upon baseline.

After the community has built its common dream community members identify the practices they need to do to reach their dream. In the self-assessment framework, these practices are measured. Each community will, therefore, have its own dream and an accompanying locally developed self-assessment based on the community's dream. Hence, the self-assessment emerges from the local context and uses the terminology of the group rather than externally imposed languages, concepts, or indicators. This ensures ownership of the group's self-assessment. In The Constellation, facilitators do not provide a ready-made self-assessment. Instead of prioritising standardisation and uniformity, a common approach in traditional monitoring and evaluation, The Constellation's self-assessment framework prioritises context.

Next, community members draw their self-assessment framework, marking the level reached for each practice (Nanda 2015). Herein, level one is the minimum level of awareness about the importance of the practice, while level five indicates that the practice is embedded in people's lifestyles, whereby they may have achieved the dream (Collison 2010). Table 14.1 is an example of a particular practice, in this case, handwashing, and the corresponding levels that community members identified and their corresponding descriptors.

TABLE 14.1 Levels of self-assessment for a single practice – "washing my hands"

Self-Assessment Levels: Washing My Hands				
1. Aware	*2. React*	*3. Act Occasionally*	*4. Act Continuously*	*5. Lifestyle or Dream*
I know everything but I have never washed my hands	I wash my hands only when my spouse or partner insists	I wash my hands only when I have to attend a party, wedding, or a function	I frequently wash my hands, but forget whenever I drink or have friends visiting	Washing my hands is my life. There is no one in the world better than me at it

Source: Lamboray (2021).

Table 14.2 includes a set of dozen individual practices as identified by Health Care Workers (HCW) in Bangkok during COVID-19. It reflects the self-assessment that the HCW community already went through with corresponding levels for each of its practices.

What Is the Impact of Using Self-Assessments?

The self-assessment is a linchpin holding the rationale for community-led activities while establishing the baseline competency level of a group (Nanda 2019a). From the baseline, a community can measure its growth during the next cycle of CLCP. So, progress continues constantly, and measuring such progress becomes a reflex, conventional, and established practice for community members (Marsharing 2022). We have seen the self-assessment enabling ownership at both a community and organisational level.

At a community level, the self-assessment tool and, therefore, local groups' active evaluation of their own activities contributed to 50–70% of people in an Assamese village starting to boil or filter water (Islam 2019a, 2019b, 2019c). Moreover, their increased knowledge of water conditions in their community increased their motivation to act and draw on local knowledge. They wrote to the authorities for water supply and used their native wisdom to restart their old practice of indigenous water filters. What better sign is there that a community has benefitted from their self-assessment than them taking action and implementing clean water practices (Nanda 2022b)?

In a different village in Assam, a self-assessment generated conversations around gender, leading to changes in roles and responsibilities (Nanda 2017). Fathers and grandparents realised that they too must take the responsibility of immunisation of children and it cannot be the sole responsibility of mothers. After their evaluation sessions, wives reported that men took more responsibility for household chores (Nanda 2020). In Kenya, a community recognised that

TABLE 14.2 Example of an individual self-assessment carried out on COVID-19 response

No	*Individual Practices*	*SA Level**
1	I act out of care, not out of fear	3 Act Occasionally
2	I wash my hands before each meal, after I go out, & after toilet	4 Act Continuously
3	I only touch my face to wash it	3 Act Occasionally
4	I avoid physical contact, keep a distance with others of 1 metre	3 Act Occasionally
5	I cough and sneeze in the fold of my arm	2 React
6	I regularly clean my workspace, mobile phone, ID, purse, etc.	2 React
7	I work from home and reduce all face-to-face meetings	2 React
8	I avoid intergenerational encounters	4 Act Continuously
9	I follow the guidelines for individuals given by authorities, especially on stigma and discrimination	4 Act Continuously
10	If I test positive, I follow strictly the quarantine and other procedures	#NA
11	I volunteer if possible	3 Act Occasionally
12	I seize the opportunity to check on the quality of my life	3 Act Occasionally

Source: Lamboray and Rafique (2021).

Notes:

* SA Levels were marked during pilot testing.

\# NA as there was no confirmed case in the district.

discrimination is decreasing (Forth 2012), and in the Philippines, self-assessments are elevating relationships between government and local communities (Tablante 2019, 2022).

The CLCP self-assessment has also been used with sex worker collectives in Cambodia and India (Slater and Ganesh 2012). In their respective countries, the Women's Network for Unity (WNU) and Durbar Mahila Samanwaya Committee (DMSC) teams, working on the rights of sex workers, felt the tool and self-assessment exercises were of great value. Specifically, WNU determined the need to shift approaches as a primary concern during their first self-assessment exercise, particularly in their discussions on WNU's vision. During that session, WNU advisors and secretariat members determined a need to acquire relationship-building skills to engage in cooperative advocacy approaches. One sex worker, marking WNU on Level 2 for the practice of monitoring and evaluation during their self-assessment, stated: "Through the self-assessment tool, we came to know where we stand. I liked it because we are assessing ourselves, not outsiders who are evaluating us."

Similarly, a lead figure in the WNU secretariat shared the following about The Constellation's self-assessment:

> I will take this tool with me everywhere. It's very dear to us. We find it easier than before. And useful to learn where we are now and where we can go. It is helpful because it teaches us to analyse ourselves, and we don't need money to hire external evaluators.
>
> *(Slater and Ganesh 2012, 12)*

The self-assessment process is not only applicable to local contexts. In addition to The Constellation groups, the CLCP Self-Assessment has been used by different nonprofits, agencies, and organisations. At the Global Fund for Children's (GFC)[2] India project on anti-trafficking, four NGO partners developed their own self-assessments based on their dreams. Similarly, their communities also developed their own self-assessments. These self-assessments have become vital as they shift the power of monitoring and evaluation in a cascading fashion from the funding agency to the GFC, to the NGOs, and finally to the communities (Nanda 2022a). One of GFC's local Indian partners, Faith Foundation, has done the self-assessment five times. A staff member noted, "Self-assessments help us to think about why and when we do these activities and how to conduct the program activities in more effective ways." Avani, another partner NGO, stated that the capacity of children to solve their own problems has moved from level 2 to level 3.5 in its third self-assessment in 2023. Other NGOs have conducted self-assessments with youth in ethnic communities (Nanda 2022a). When local NGOs themselves take ownership of their monitoring and evaluation, rather than merely adopting the processes prescribed by funders, it becomes easier for them to facilitate a similar process in the communities.

The CLCP has also been used by or integrated into large-scale government and multilateral-funded research initiatives. In Cambodia, the Consultative Group on International Agricultural Research (CGIAR) Research Program on Aquatic Agricultural Systems conducted participatory action research using CLCP (Nurick and Apgar 2014). Similarly, evaluators used CLCP to assess a Government of India programme for the development and empowerment of adolescent girls. They found that their data was richer, resulting in findings and recommendations that are more useful than other top-down and externally imposed evaluations. Evaluators also recognised that the CLCP's participatory approach resulted in learning and transformative experiences for the participants, in this case, adolescent girls (Nandi et al. 2015).

Facilitation Is Critical

When a community begins to use the CLCP, it needs the support of an experienced facilitator. Equally so, an impactful self-assessment is dependent on good facilitation. SALT, as described above, captures the mental model facilitators use when they accompany communities. They would stimulate, share, appreciate, listen, learn, link, transfer, engage in teamwork, and cultivate trust.

Uniquely, CLCP and SALT are mutually reinforcing because when communities appreciate their strengths, they can base their actions on them. Alternatively, when they take action and reflect on it, they recognise their strengths. Table 14.3 lists the different questions, corresponding facilitation methods, and learning types guiding facilitation during the CLCP process.

The facilitator also makes the community aware that it is not alone in working in this way on similar challenges. The facilitator will often connect neighbouring communities, or with the help of technology, worldwide to share experiences, hopes, and concerns. As time passes, the skills exercised through CLCP develop within the community, and the need for an external facilitator dissipates (Kivlehan 2014). Such independence from external facilitators and the transfer of facilitation skills to community members is essential for the community to sustain itself and act collectively.

Facilitators use different guiding questions throughout the various steps of the CLCP cycle to initiate a conversation, choosing from the facilitation methods best suited for each cycle step. As seen in the table below, these facilitation methods could range from only asking questions to eventually supporting communities in organising a learning fair. While the CLCP cycle consists of six formal steps, here we have added two interim steps that take place between the action and the learning festival (Figure 14.2) – self-assessment of change and reflection after this assessment that enables community members to not just measure success but also learn from their process.

Who Owns the Process?

Across The Constellation's activities, we have seen different manifestations of ownership emerge after groups have participated in the CLCP process. One example is when community members demand government services to support their actions. This happened in 30 villages in Bongaigaon, Assam, when community members requested that banners showing immunisation schedules be put up in their villages so that the dropouts would be zero. Subsequently, the government began to respond (Islam 2019a, 2019b, 2019c).

Another example of ownership is seen at Satgaon village in Kamrup District of Assam. Here, Tubur Ali, a motivated community member, took the lead in including children of migrant labourers in the routine immunisation programme, as these children had till then been denied immunisation because of their migrant status (Roy 2019).

What does the facilitator do if every part of the process is of, by, and for the community? In her blog on the result of a six-day CLCP learning event in Ambon, Indonesia, chapter co-author Marlou articulates the earlier simile that the facilitator

TABLE 14.3 Matrix for facilitating the CLCP cycle with questions, learning outcomes, knowledge management cycle, and facilitatory methods

CLCP Cycle Steps	*Step 1: We Are Human*	*Step 2: Dream*	*Step 3: Self-Assessment*	*Step 4: Action Planning*	*Step 5: Action*	*Step 6: Self-Assessment of Change*	*Step 7: After Event Reflection*	*Step 8: Knowledge Fair*
Guiding Questions	Who are we?	Where do we want to go?	Where are we now?	How do we get there?	Just do it!	Where have we reached?	What did we learn?	How do we transfer?
Knowledge Cycle Step	Knowing ourselves	Imagine our future	Interpreting our present	Theorising our way	Experience our way	Interpreting our way	Validating the better way	Gather wisdom for knowledge asset
Learning Type	Social, cognitive, affective learning	Externalise tacit, implicit, social learning	Collaborative learning. shared understanding	Learning before	Learning during	Learning after	Internalise and mentoring learning	Retain, reuse, and sharing learning
Facilitation Method	Socratic question and role play	Go wild	Round robin	Reverse brain-storm or peer assist	Meta planning or affinity diagram	Consensus	Group or peer review	Knowledge fair

Source: Rafique (2017).

is the midwife ensuring the safe and healthy delivery of the community's dream (De Rouw 2015). The facilitator supported and stimulated the community to deliver their beautiful "baby." The community members are the ones who did the hard work and own the success. Facilitators applaud and take a place in the background. Rituu and Ruchira emphasise the midwife role of the facilitator in "accompanying" the community right from the genesis of its dream (Nanda 2018). Thus, the community takes collective action as an index of ownership (Neog 2018).

Challenges Faced in the CLCP Approach

The SALT-CLCP approach involves community members identifying their strengths and challenges and developing their own responses. It is not uncommon for communities to face new challenges when the context changes. Therefore, as communities internalise the approach and use it to develop their action plan, it takes some time as this process challenges the power outsiders hold over communities (Nanda 2019a).

Alternatively, it is easier for outsiders to provide schemes and services to communities. Similarly, communities that have become accustomed to receiving materials and funds from outsiders take much time to take responsibility for responding to their own issues. Furthermore, as the entire community must change their mindset from the receiving mode to one of initiating and sustaining the response, this unlearning and relearning takes time.

Another challenge in CLCP is attributing group activities to the group's achievements because measuring the impact of the group's activities on the community is difficult. Moreover, the impact of the group's activities may not be immediately visible or measurable (Lamboray 2017). For example, in the case of the Health Rise India Transition project implemented across Shimla and Udaipur, even though most of the lifestyle behaviours of participants significantly improved from baseline to end-line evaluations, we cannot attribute the positive behaviour change solely to SALT-CLCP (RICHPHI 2021). This challenge in CLCP to attribute the success of the group's activities solely to the SALT Way of Working or the process per se is because the success of the group's activities may be influenced by external factors such as government policies, funding, and other community groups (Haldane et al. 2019; Pramanik et al. 2020).

Who Owns the Response?

Rather than just engaging or consulting the community, the facilitators seek to accompany the community's journey along the path to ownership of their own challenges. Ownership transfer happens better when the facilitators accompany the community as it applies CLCP with the SALT approach. At the same time, communities' ownership over their own contexts, information, and progress emerges when they themselves are directly involved in measuring and evaluating such change. In this case, the data they use is actionable, informing their next steps and activities. It is their communities, it is their dream, it is their success.

The Constellation's experience is that communities can and do respond to the challenges they face when they take ownership of them. As co-author, Philip, once described such ownership: "When I decide what to do, and I do it, then I have taken ownership" (Nanda 2019a). And one important way of enabling such ownership is through community-led evaluation practices. By doing so, communities set their own baseline, identify indicators of success according to their own capacities, objectives, and goals, and then return to evaluate themselves against such goals. Most important then is to turn such results into action-planning. It is an ongoing cyclical process, with communities deciding the speed and scope of work.

That The Constellation has thousands of facilitators is evidence that CLCP, with SALT and tools such as a self-assessment, has been influential. As Amber Phalen, Interim Key Correspondent Coordinator of Health and Development Networks (HDN) and a facilitator, shared: "Every day I get a bit saltier. This has made all the difference in the world, much like the Constellation with their SALT approach does every day."

Notes

1 An *Anganwadi* is a rural child care centre in India established under the government's Integrated Child Development Scheme.

2 Global Fund for Children invests in community-based organisations globally to help children and youth reach their full potential and advance their rights.

References

Collison, Chris. 2010. *Knowledge Management and Benchmarking – River Diagram.* YouTube. www.youtube.com/watch?v=Ai7LcCzOJo8, Accessed, 16 Sep 2023.

Collison, Chris, and Geoff Parcell. 2004. *Learning to fly.* Chichester: Wiley.

Cooperrider, David. L., Diana Whitney, and Jacqueline M Stavros. 2003. *Appreciative Inquiry Handbook.* Lakeshore.

De Rouw, Marlou. 2015. *Salty Seeds in Fertile Ground in Ambon – Results and Coaching Team Lessons from First Learning Event.* 5 March. Accessed Oct 25, 2022. https://aidscompetence.ning.com/profiles/blogs/salty-seeds-in-fertile-ground-in-ambon-results-and-coaching-team

De Rouw, Marlou, Alice Kuan, Philip Forth, Rituu B. Nanda, and Luc Barriere Constantin. 2020. "Four principles of community-based primary health care." In *Achieving Health for All: Primary Health Care in Action*, by Meike Schleiff and David Bishai. Johns Hopkins University Press.

Duongsa, Usa. 2021. *In SALT We Trust.* 29 June. Accessed Oct 19, 2022. https://aidscompetence.ning.com/profiles/blogs/in-salt-we-trust

Forth, Philip. 2012. *Measuring Change & Adapting Our Response.* 2 Feb. Accessed Oct 15, 2022. https://aidscompetence.ning.com/page/measuring-change-adapting-our

Google Books. n.d. *What Makes Us Human: The Story of a Shared Dream*. www.google.com/books/edition/What_Makes_Us_Human/JbBqDQAAQBAJ?hl=en&gbpv=0 . Accessed, Feb 23, 2024.

Haldane, Victoria, Fiona L. H. Chuah, Aastha Srivastava, Shweta R. Singh, Gerald C. H. Koh, Chia Kee Seng, and Helena Legido-Quigley. 2019. "Community participation in health services development, implementation, and evaluation: A systematic review of empowerment, health, community, and process outcomes." *PLoS ONE* 14, no. 5: e0216112. https://doi.org/10.1371/journal.pone.0216112

Islam, Baharul. 2019a. *Are We Drinking Properly Filtered Water?* 30 Aug. Accessed Oct 20, 2022. https://aidscompetence.ning.com/profiles/blogs/are-we-drinking-properly-filtered-water

Islam, Baharul. 2019b. *L for Link in SALT: CLCP Generates Demand, Government Fulfils*. 9 Feb. Accessed Oct 20, 2022. https://aidscompetence.ning.com/profiles/blogs/l-for-link-in-salt-clcp-generates-demand-government-fulfills

Islam, Baharul. 2019c. *Self-Assessment Helps the Village in Improving Its Immunization Status*. 9 Feb. Accessed Oct 20, 2022. https://aidscompetence.ning.com/profiles/blogs/self-assessment-helps-the-village-in-improving-its-immunization

Kaza, Santhosh Kumar, Pallavi Gupta, Ruchi Vaidya, Nooyi, Shalini Chandrashekar, and Nayanjeet Chaudhury. 2022. "Effect of COVID-19 lockdown on lifestyle habits and self-care practices of diabetic and hypertensive patients in rural Shimla and Udaipur – Findings from the HealthRise India program." *Indian Journal of Public Health*, 66, no. 4: 466–472.

Kivlehan, Shea. 2014. *The Community Life Competence Process – On SlideServe*. 21 July. Accessed Mar 13, 2023. www.slideserve.com/shea/the-community-life-competence-process

Lamboray, Jean-Louis. 2016. *What Makes Us Human?* Balboa Press.

Lamboray, Jean Louis, and Essa Mohammed Rafique,. 2021. *COVID-19 Self Assessments: For Individuals, Communities, and Health Care Workers*. Bangkok: Creative Commons as Google Docs PowerPoint Presentation, 21 Oct. https://docs.google.com/presentation/d/1a423gNXxbdiTIUYYiIcRewaxnDkzN_NYKpEmgBIKvJU/edit#slide=id.p1

Lamboray, Marie. 2017. *Impact Assessment of the SALT Approach*. 1 June. Accessed Mar 21, 2023. https://aidscompetence.ning.com/profiles/blogs/impact-assessment-of-the-salt-approach

MacQueen, Kathleen M. Eleanor McLellan, David S. Metzger, Susan Kegeles, Ronald P. Strauss, Roseanne Scott, Lynn Blanchard, and Robert T. Trotter. 2001. "What is community? An evidence-based definition for participatory public health." *American Journal of Public Health* 91, no. 12: 1929–1938.

Marsharing, Peacefully. 2022. *The Journey to Achieving Our Dreams Begins by Appreciating Our Strengths*. 25 Feb. Accessed Dec 29, 2022. https://globalfundforchildren.org/story/the-journey-to-achieving-our-dreams-begins-by-appreciating-our-strengths/

Nanda, Rituu B. 2015. *Self-Assessment & SALT Visit to Homes of Domestic Workers*. 18 Jul. Accessed Dec 22, 2022. https://aidscompetence.ning.com/profiles/blogs/salty-home-visits

Nanda, Rituu B. 2017. *Self-Assessment Triggers Conversation on Gender Roles*. 25 July. Accessed Oct 20, 2022. https://aidscompetence.ning.com/profiles/blogs/self-assessment-triggers-conversation-on-gender-roles

Nanda, Rituu B. 2018. *Accompanying a Community When It Faces a Hurdle in Taking Action*. 7 July. Accessed Oct 25, 2022. https://aidscompetence.ning.com/profiles/blogs/accompanying-a-community-when-it-faces-a-hurdle-in-taking-action

Nanda, Rituu B. 2019a. *We Knew We Had Problems But Not the Extent.* 5 Dec. Accessed Oct 20, 2022. https://aidscompetence.ning.com/profiles/blogs/we-knew-we-had-problems-but-not-the-extent

Nanda, Rituu B. 2019b. *Ownership of Evaluation and Evaluative Mindset in Communities – Key to Achieving the Goal of "No One Left Behind."* https://aidscompetence.ning.com/profiles/blogs/ownership-of-evaluation-evaluative-mindset-in-communities-key-to-

Nanda, Rituu B. 2020. *Shift in Gender Roles and Responsibilities.* 9 Feb. Accessed Oct 20, 2022. https://aidscompetence.ning.com/profiles/blogs/shift-in-gender-roles-and-responsibilities

Nanda, Rituu B. 2022a. *Shared Organisation Dream – A Driving Force for the Staff.* Mar 18. Accessed Feb 20, 2023. https://aidscompetence.ning.com/profiles/blogs/a-shared-organisation-dream-a-driving-force-for-the-staff

Nanda, Rituu B. 2022b. *Village Celebrates Improvement in Immunisation and Use of Water Filters.* 25 Oct. Accessed Dec 28, 2022. https://aidscompetence.ning.com/profiles/blogs/village-celebrates-improvement-in-immunisation-and-use-of-water-f

Nandi, Rajib, Rituu B. Nanda, and Shiny Saha. 2018. "Sense of ownership as capacity building: experience of using SALT among domestic workers for systematic self-assessment." In *New Directions for Evaluations: Visibility, Voice and Value*, by Anuruddha Brahamchari and Samik Ghosh. Daya Publishing House.

Nandi, Rajib, Rituu B. Nanda, and Tanisha Jugran. 2015. "Evaluation from inside out: The experience of using local knowledge and practices to evaluate a program for adolescent girls in India through the lens of gender and equity." *Evaluation Journal of Australasia 15*, no. 1: 38–47. https://doi.org/10.1177/1035719X1501500106

Neog, Ruchira. 2018. *Recognising Inner Strengths, Taking Collective Action and Fostering Ownership.* 29 Oct. Accessed Oct 25, 2022. https://aidscompetence.ning.com/profiles/blogs/recognising-inner-strengths-taking-collective-action-and

Nurick Robert, and Apgar Marina. 2014. *Participatory Action Research: Guide for Facilitators.* Penang, Malaysia: CGIAR Research Program on Aquatic Agricultural Systems. Manual: AAS-2014-46.

Parcell, Geoff, and Chris Collison. 2010. *No More Consultants: We Know More Than We Think.* John Wiley & Sons.

Pramanik, Santanu, Arpita Ghosh, Anirban Goswami, Tiken Das, Sandra Albert, Philip Forth, and Rituu Nanda. 2020. "Impacts of the Stimulate, Appreciate, Learn, and Transfer community engagement approach to increase immunisation coverage in Assam, India, 3ie Grantee final report." *New Delhi International Initiative for Impact Evaluation (3ie)* (2020).

Rafique, Essa. 2017. "Community life competence process (CLCP) in behaviour change (BC)." In *Field Health Supervisors' Refresher Training in CLCP, Wayanad District, Kerala. 9 Jan 2020*. Kalpetta: Office of the District Medical Officer, Wayanad District. 39.

Rafique, Essa. 2022. "Proposal for Thanjavur Medical Journal." *Submitted to the Chair of the Thanjavur Medical College Alumni Association (TMCAA)*. Thanjavur: Thanjavur Medical College Alumni (ALM) Publications: https://tmcjournal.blogspot.com/2022/07/journal-proposal-to-tmcaa.html 23 July.

Roy, Raju. 2019. *Community Member Tracks Immunisation Drop Outs in Nearby Brick Kiln.* 24 Jan. Accessed Oct 20, 2022. https://aidscompetence.ning.com/profiles/blogs/community-member-tracks-immunisation-drop-outs-in-nearby-bricklin

RICHPHI. 2021. *The HealthRise India Transition project Flyer, by Ramaiah International Center for Public Health Innovations.* 23 June. Accessed Apr 20, 2023. https://ricphi.org/files/userfiles/2021/06/23/files/HealthRise_flyer.pdf

Schomaker, Birgitta. 2019. *Community-Based Self-Reflection by Climate Activists – How Are We Doing with Our Values and Principles?* 4 Nov. Accessed Dec 30, 2022. https://aidscompetence.ning.com/profiles/blogs/community-based-self-reflection-by-climate-activists-how-are-we

Slater, Dirk, and Indira Maya Ganesh. 2012. *Using Technology to Document Violations: Enabling Sex Worker Communities to Document Violence against Them in India and Cambodia.* 5 July. Accessed Oct 25, 2022. https://docs.google.com/document/d/1dT86rAGGkFJLjqNVJWV0s6IMGy0BY06Y7uwcMyv2e-8/edit

Tablante, Evelyn Bacarra. 2019. *CLCP Makes Sure Government Funds Are Not Wasted.* 1 Dec. Accessed Dec 28, 2022. https://aidscompetence.ning.com/profiles/blogs/clcp-makes-sure-government-funds-are-not-wasted

Tablante, Evelyn Bacarra. 2022. *Department of Science and Technology Regional Office No. VIII Values Community Role in Rural Development.* 26 Sep. Accessed Oct 25, 2022. https://aidscompetence.ning.com/profiles/blogs/department-of-science-and-technology-regional-office-no-viii

The Constellation. 2015. *Our Way of Working: The Community Life Competence Process.* 20 Aug. Accessed Oct 25, 2022. http://multiplelanguageconstellation.weebly.com/our-way-of-working-the-community-life-competence-process.html

VHAI, Voluntary Health Association of India. 2022. *SALT: Stimulate, Appreciate, Learn & Transfer – Community Participation & Ownership.* 20 Jan. Accessed Oct 25, 2022. https://vhai.org/our-work/salt-stimulate-appreciate-learn-transfer/

Watkins, Jane Magruder, Bernard Mohr, and Ralph Kelly. 2011. *Appreciative Inquiry: Change at the Speed of Imagination.* Jossey Bass/Pfeiffer.

Zaveri, Sonal, Renu Khanna, and Rituu B. Nanda. 2016. "Approaches to Evaluation Using a Feminist Lens." In *A Resources Pack on Gender Transformative Evaluations*, by Shraddha Chigateri and Shiny Saha. Series in Feminist Evaluation, no. 3. Available at SSRN: https://ssrn.com/abstract=4050501

15

WE BUILD THE ROAD AND THE ROAD BUILDS US

The Sarvodaya Shramadana Movement's Participatory Community Development Model

Udesh Fernando and Vinya Ariyaratne

The Genesis of Sarvodaya – Awakening of All

'We build the road, and the road builds us' is a call-to-action echoed from Sarvodaya's urban headquarters in Moratuwa[1] to multitudes of rural villages in all districts of Sri Lanka. This call-to-action carries sentiments of inspiration, empowerment, and community ownership from the very beginning of any development activity. It embodies Sarvodaya's role as a facilitator utilising a community-centric, bottom-up graduation process.

Since its inception, the Sarvodaya Shramadana Movement has echoed and operationalised this sentiment, fitting into the country's historical milestones and development trajectory. Significant demographic, social, cultural, and economic changes shaped Sri Lanka's development discourse after independence. Sarvodaya weathered those changes as an indigenous grassroots development movement (Ariyaratne 2019).

The Sarvodaya Shramadana Movement was founded by A.T. Ariyaratne – known as 'Ari'. In 1958, Ari became a high school science teacher at Nalanda College in Colombo. Inspired by the Gandhian approach to village development, he took his students to work side-by-side with residents of one of the poorest villages in the country. Two years later, he married his first full-time volunteer, Neetha Dhammachari Ariyaratne, who was already a social activist. Their self-help process expanded, village by village, for the next decade with no outside financial support. In 1969, in honour of Mahatma Gandhi's 100th birth anniversary, Sarvodaya intensified and systematised its activities in a '100 village development programme', which also included building schools in all the villages – an initiative led by Ari's wife and outfitting them with books funded by UNESCO. That

DOI: 10.4324/9781003377917-21

year Ari's work was honoured with the Ramon Magsaysay Award,[2] raising the movement's profile internationally.

Sarvodaya is inspired by Gandhian philosophy and nurtured by Buddhism and other rich faiths and philosophical values. The Sarvodaya development model is often perceived as a holistic development archetype because it encompasses spiritual, moral, cultural, social, economic, and political aspects when planning and facilitating community development. 'Sarvodaya has always believed in the inherent capacity of even the most impoverished communities to surmount their plight if the barriers that prevent them from unleashing their potential are removed' (Ariyaratne 2019).

The word 'Sarvodaya' was initially coined by Mahatma Gandhi in his exploration of communal welfare. It comes from the Sanskrit words '*Sarvam*' and '*Udayam*' meaning welfare of all. Influenced by Gandhian philosophy, the Movement adopted this term in a deep Buddhist context to mean the 'awakening of all' i.e., to enable awakening of individuals, communities, the planet, and all its beings (Ariyaratne 2014; Ariyaratne 2019). The term '*Shramadana*' means gifting of voluntary labour. This was popular during the Movement's beginning years when Shramadana was used to build roads across the island. Hence the Movement became known in Sri Lanka as the 'Sarvodaya Shramadana Movement', with people recognising the voluntary nature of its operations and its focus on self-realisation through community development.

The dawn of the Movement in 1958 was exactly ten years post-independence from British rule. The socio-political context on the island at that time was driven mainly by nationalistic sentiments, embracing the momentum of independence. Electoral narratives, as well as local political developments, focused on transformation. People aspired to exercise their rights to language, culture, religion, education, and politics. A sense of national renaissance was entwined in almost all aspects of public life. In this context, the Movement had four priority endeavours (Ariyaratne 2014). The first was to use the momentum to gather the country's youth to drive the national transformation. Second, to generate awareness among villagers and rural communities of the transformation happening in the country. Third, to address concerns of caste, creed, and social disparities and to facilitate human development via justice and ten identified basic human needs. Fourth, to connect with the world; to embrace positive global values as well as to harness international cooperation for development activities. In all endeavours, *Shramadana* played 'a key function in transmitting ideology, generating a sense of community, and providing a forum for discussion of village needs' (Macey 1996, 58).

Since its start, the Movement has regularly reviewed its strategic direction, responding to development narratives of the nation and catering to the aspirations of the communities it serves. Participatory community action has always been welcomed and appreciated. For example, Sarvodaya receives a call for assistance from a rural village. Its District Centre will activate its Social Mobilisation Officer to visit the village leaders, faith leaders, and other already-established social groups to form a more nuanced understanding of the challenges at hand. This psycho-social approach is followed by a process to engage with the villagers through village-level meetings. These initial engagements focus on 'awakening' rather than immediately intervening. There are two approaches for awakening – personal awakening and communal awakening – and they are interrelated.

The saying 'I cannot awaken myself unless I help awaken others, and others cannot unless I awaken myself' (Bond 1994, 15) depicts the extent to which spirituality contributes to community development through 'action to awaken masses of rural people, to exploit their own development potential through self-help and self-reliance' (Sarvodaya Movement 1980, 67). From its inception, recognising human potential and, therefore, social capital has been interwoven in Sarvodaya's mode of operations. This orientation has enabled communities to embody and recognise development not only as a technical or physical need but to appreciate it as a spiritual requirement that enhances purposeful engagement and humanity on a larger scale.

Apart from the multiple physical engagements and work, Sarvodaya capitalises on the spiritual values of society and promotes spirituality when programmes and initiatives are rolled out, be it grassroots development or national-level engagements (Rajkobal 2020; Bond 1994). In that regard, Sarvodaya is often seen as a spiritual movement and an organisation which values and puts faith and philosophy into practise.

For over six decades, this spiritual nature of Sarvodaya's work has attracted both individuals and communities as they do not feel as if their communal values are encroached upon. Today, diverse communities from all over the island gather in the same spirit, recognising the purposeful nature of working with Sarvodaya. By its fifth decade, Sarvodaya had reached over 15,000 villages in Sri Lanka by facilitating community development activities. Out of those, Sarvodaya has facilitated the development of over 5,400 village societies (Sarvodaya Shramadana Societies) revolving around the Sarvodaya Village Development model. This spirituality drives individual inspiration and collective drive to self-realise community development. Communities have implemented small- to large-scale donor-funded projects. From infrastructure development, community health, and educational awareness, the types of projects implemented have been diverse but largely falling in the areas of the ten basic human needs explained later.

Self-help and external funding of development work is intricately balanced. Sarvodaya, as an organisation, often plays the role of neutral arbiter between donors who are keen to assist activities and with communities who are recipients of such assistance.

The Sarvodaya Movement looks into the future to realise the Movement's greater transformational purpose to 'build a just, sustainable, compassionate social order that fulfils the basic human needs of communities through individual and collective awakening'. In doing so, Sarvodaya facilitates and extends development programmes in consultation with local communities to satisfy their basic human needs through purposeful community-led action, movement, and organisational building. This chapter will illustrate how community-led development facilitation is accomplished by the Sarvodaya Shramadana Movement. It will discuss how practitioners use the five-step village development graduation model to enable grassroots development. It will also show how Sarvodaya negotiates a balance between donors and communities to facilitate development assistance. Finally, it will illustrate how a new initiative, Suwodaya, is implemented both at the national and grassroots levels.

On Practising Development Facilitation

'Facilitation is a co-creative and adaptive process in which a facilitator enables local actors to set common goals, take ownership of these goals, build on existing strengths, and work towards achieving their goals [...]' (Veda et al. 2021). Throughout its six decades of existence, Sarvodaya has been supporting communities to establish their own locally based organisations, known as the Sarvodaya Shramadana Societies. To date, such societies are active in an estimated 5,400 communities and are helping their members improve their own capacities to implement and direct their own development initiatives (Ariyaratne 2019). These Sarvodaya Shramadana Societies are fully operated by the communities themselves. The Movement operationalises its support via the Shramadana Societies unit, based in the Movement's Colombo office. The Unit, in turn, coordinates its efforts through 25 regional district centres directly linked to community-level activities.

This growth from the hundred villages programme in 1969 has been gradual. The programme is a balancing act between community demands and donor support frameworks. Donors demand evidence-based action; communities seek much-focused development cooperation. The result is targeted involvement within a framework that balances resources, expectations, and delivery while involving communities in realising solutions to their development challenges.

'As from its inception, the Sarvodaya Shramadana Movement has been closer to traditional concepts of social development than to modern ones' (Ratnapala 1999); such traditional concepts encompassed understanding the demographics, social and cultural norms as well as other community dynamics with great emphasis to understanding the social psyche of the communities.

The recent 'Suwodaya National Initiative' (Covid response) is a prime example of how Sarvodaya identified real-time challenges such as vaccine hesitancy and how it utilised locally relevant mechanisms to make communities aware as well as partnered with the government to roll out inoculation efforts effectively. The same project utilised targeted risk communication campaigns to address stigma and discrimination surrounding the pandemic, utilising spiritual messages from all key religious traditions practised in Sri Lanka, to counter communal level discrimination, misinformation as well as the need to help others during challenging times.

The Movement fosters and helps communities realise the integrated nature of needs and achieve development through self-help and awakening in all its core programmes as well as in interventional development partnerships.

On *Shramadana*, a Tool to Facilitate Development

Since the initial decades of the Movement, *Shramadana* (voluntary labour) has been the tool to mobilise communities towards village development. Scholars around the world view *Shramadana* to be a 'revolutionary technique, to awaken people to their own potential based on their own culture and innovative abilities' (Ratnapala 1999). It lays the foundation for the physical requirements of villages, and its social aspects build the capacities and inspiration to foster the momentum for integrated development (Bond 1994). Additionally, its 'contribution to grassroots development lies in the way it combines physical work with town meetings' (Macey 1996). By transcending the traditional approach, in the mid-1980s, Sarvodaya took to the drawing board to develop the five-step approach to village development as part of its 10,000 village development programme, a larger ambition and a response to the mass-scale requests it received from communities across the island.

The five-step graduation model to village development

Based on the Gandhian concept of *Gram Swaraj* (Village self-government), communal realities such as culture and faith have been strong elements in laying out development partnerships among communities. Communities embraced this approach as they feel Sarvodaya does not encroach on their existing communal value systems.

The Movement's five-step model is the basis to co-develop communities with community members, Sarvodaya and donors coming in alignment to address development challenges. Cultural and faith rituals play a significant role when initiating activities, whether it is a small-scale committee meeting, a large-scale conference, or a very practically involved activity such as building a road or a community construction project. Often, multicultural and faith rituals are performed as befitting the realities of the communities. Apart from this basis to formalise development activities, implement a monitoring framework as well as measure progress, the model had been formalised and presented to Sarvodaya's network of village communities as well as its pool of donors. It not only functions as a framework for the communities to graduate in the ambition of realising '*Gram Swaraj*', i.e., a commonwealth of independent, self-sustaining villages, but also stands as a framework to engage with donors and mobilise necessary and required support while engaging in impact assessments and monitoring related praxis. The model is a pathway for prospective villages to invite Sarvodaya to facilitate physical and social infrastructure development. The existing network of villages took it as an opportunity to realise development on their own, evaluate and expand their work, and become 'model-villages'. 'It was a useful way of helping the village communities visualise the gradual development process' (Bond 1994). The process does not prescribe an exact time frame and each village community has their own trajectory of development.

The Stages of Village Graduation

At the first stage of village development (Figure 15.1), goodwill creation and networking play a crucial role. Addressing barriers of dependency and patronage helps address challenges in a more holistic way. 'All these [barriers] must be broken down since psychological infrastructure has to be created not only among the members of the community but also among the people who serve the community' (Ratnapala 1999). Psychological infrastructure (individual and collective awakening) precedes social infrastructure to identify and address community-level challenges. 'The most important outcome in the first stage is the opportunity the people get to think together, plan together and to work together and to feel that they have a greater potential for self-development' (Ratnapala 1999). During this first stage, Sarvodaya introduces the ten basic human needs (Table 15.1), which is a point of reference to understand community-level development challenges in depth. It also serves as a set of minimum standards and a tool to evaluate community requirements. Trained development facilitators, also known as Sarvodaya District Mobilisation Officers and the district staff use the ten basic human needs as a reference to stimulate dialogue and mediation and to make the communities aware of their needs. Sarvodaya workers, in general, and the district staff go through

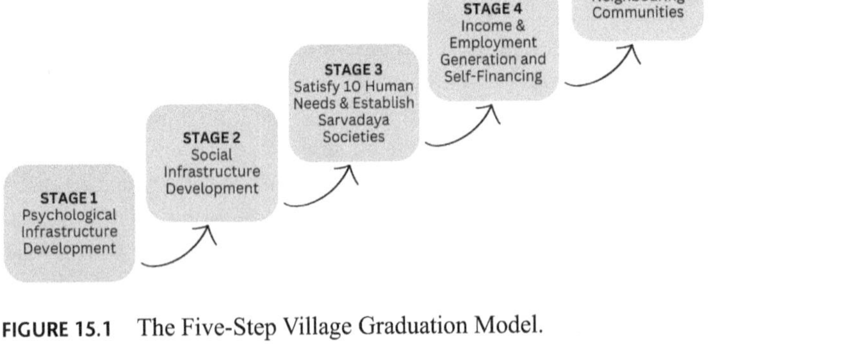

FIGURE 15.1 The Five-Step Village Graduation Model.

TABLE 15.1 The ten basic human needs

A clean environment	Primary health care
Clean and adequate water supply	Communication and technology
Minimum clothing requirements	Minimum energy requirements
A balanced and nutritious diet	Holistic education
Housing	Cultural and spiritual needs

constant training on facilitating dialogue and partnerships at different intervals as well as based on the needs of special and rapid response programmes.

Hesha Perera, Manager of the End Child Poverty Knowledge Initiative funded by Arigatou International,[3] utilises some of the steps in the village graduation model in her own work to mobilise children, parents, and teachers when she facilitates programmes.

> When I receive a request to intervene or facilitate an identified initiative, I make a few visits to the community going through a particular challenge related to child poverty. I mobilise community leaders, consult their faith leaders and most importantly, in my line of work, the children who would be mostly impacted. I even consult my programme participants (children) on what they want to achieve at the end or simply ask them whether they would like to be exposed to a programme that would better their lives and work with them on the building blocks that would compose a tailor-made programme. We even contextualise international material to serve our local contexts and needs. I actively listen to their stories and then try to stimulate them to discover working solutions. By utilising this bottom-up approach, the work I have been engaged in has been impactful and fulfilling at an individual and a communal level.

The model utilises 'key components of effective facilitation [that] are guiding discussion, asking questions, consensus-building, mediation and ensuring diverse voices are heard, all within a relationship of mutual learning and partnership' (Veda et al. 2021). The field-level social workers of Sarvodaya employ such skills in their deliberations as well as 'a team of experienced camp organisers specially oriented for the purposes reside[s] in the village and work[s] along with the community' (Ratnapala 1999). This approach largely helped to gain the trust of the village communities, to immerse themselves in the day-to-day relations of the village, and to understand the challenges and their social dynamics in depth.

In the initial stages of the Movement, Shramadana Camps played a significant role where community mobilisers, development facilitators, or simple technical experts would work in a community. From the inception of the Movement, the mode of operations has not changed. Camp organisers and social workers' organisational training requires them to sharpen these facilitation skills. There is also frequent dialogue and alternative training to sharpen their skills.

Especially during the first step of the process, *Shramadana* activities are organised to fulfil the basic human needs. Social workers and trained volunteers of Sarvodaya play a decisive role in mobilising people and guiding activities. From the first step to the second, 'the psycho-social infrastructure that is laid in a village, therefore, satisfies the prerequisites for an economic development founded on self-reliance' (Ratnapala 1999) and the many activities that may unfold for the betterment of communities.

At stage two, children's groups, mother's groups, and other formal groups are created. Typically, at the onset, deeper inclusion of all community members is not a strict requirement but, over time, becomes more encouraged. The participants, who will also take on eventual leadership positions, are typically self-nominated or nominated by the larger group. Forming these groups and stimulating local leadership manages the village population into micro-sectors. The respective groups' needs also become more apparent. Children's groups play a key role in bringing the communities together as most homes will have children attending pre-schools or schools in which Sarvodaya operates. The End-Child Poverty Knowledge Initiative, mentioned above, is an example of how Sarvodaya successfully rolled out programmes on the Sustainable Development Goals (SDGs) for children. Several batches of children have already been trained to be trainers for their own schools and children's clubs, where they will be ambassadors to promote SDGs.

At stage three, the formation of Sarvodaya Societies provides the base to extend the Movement's activities at the village level and to initiate village-to-village development partnerships. Model villages further reinforce their strengths and extend support to the ones at the periphery. The Sarvodaya Shramadana Societies become the focal points to serve village development in the Movement's structure. Whereas social organising during stages one and two is more informal, communities can choose to become more formalised during stage three. In this case, the Sri Lankan government expects societies and community groups to register themselves under the Societies Ordinance, especially if groups plan on raising and maintaining funds as a village-level society. Sarvodaya provides communities with the support they need to undergo such formalisation, including financial auditing, bookkeeping, meeting facilitation, and management training.

Office bearers and members are all volunteers and unpaid. They also play a vigorous role in step 4, which is the establishment of income generation activities for their respective communities and of social enterprise models to fund their own social-development activities. The societies also seek to realise further the ten basic human needs at this stage. With the recognition of resources, both human and physical in nature, communities address the challenges at hand in a much more intense and profound way.

The many psycho-social relational activities practised at stages one and two, lead the way to institutionalise Sarvodaya Shramadana Societies. This paves the way to formalise and establish village-level influence, and leaders will make key decisions about the welfare of the village. The Shramadana Societies

Constitution, initially developed via large-scale community consultations, provides instructions on the legal basis of the societies' composition. As part of their social mobilisation, the district teams address issues and challenges related to inclusivity, be it gender, cultural, or faith representations. In predominantly multicultural communities, nominating members representing all communities is always encouraged. The Sarvodaya social workers play an intermediary role in ensuring communal values are respected and that the Sarvodaya ethos is practised throughout the process.

At stage five, village societies govern their own village affairs in a sustained manner. They also have the capacity to share expertise and resources with others. The most important aspects here are the capacity to implement and manage donor-funded projects and generate income for the many activities they plan. Most villages at stage five will have successfully operated village businesses and social enterprises. Profits generated through these activities as well as their own monthly charitable donations will keep the village services running. In most Shramadana Societies, the most successfully run social endeavour happens to be the pre-schools and then other activities such as running their own economic-financing kiosk to offer microloans, advice, and economic partnerships. The Sarvodaya Development Finance, the financial arm of Sarvodaya, plays a larger role in this phase to facilitate financial and economic activities as well as to impart vital information and knowledge.

On the grand scale, the five stages not only become a model for Sarvodaya internally but also a model for the entire country to reciprocate and develop their own village-level communities. Sarvodaya has set benchmarks for community development where voluntary organisations and even successive governments have utilised or reciprocated the five-step model in their own community development programmes at regional and national levels. Similar models have been replicated or adopted in countries such as Bangladesh, Nepal, and many others. SOJAG Bangladesh is a prime example of how the Sarvodaya model has been reciprocated and adapted to the local context of Bangladesh.

From Staff-Led to Volunteer-Led

The graduation model has evolved according to the needs expressed by its communities. Although the implementation of the initial model required staff, successful training, and loyalty of volunteers replaced formal staff representation while establishing a strong network of villages yearning to fulfil the purpose of the Movement. It is especially youth groups from the communities themselves who become key volunteers in mobilising villagers. When there are specific targeted interventions, youth leaders are also the ones contacted. Apart from the donor demands for a clear and coherent programme, Sarvodaya workers have found the model to be a practical approach to viewing village-level development and a tool that was easily understood by the village communities.

The village graduation model enables communities to become active participants in development rather than being passive recipients. In that regard, Sarvodaya provides training to village leaders, youth, faith leaders, and others so that they become owners and shapers of their development requirements through the entire life cycle of the five-stage village development model. These trainings are centrally coordinated by the Sarvodaya Shramadana Societies Unit at the headquarters level in Moratuwa. That includes routine training for Sarvodaya field staff as well as society leaders. From leadership development to technical things knowledge such as bookkeeping for banking needs and entrepreneurial know-how is imparted in these training sessions. Donor-sponsored training programmes are carefully adapted and rolled out in selected communities. Sarvodaya runs the bulk of current programmes at the grassroots level, providing them with vital skills, expertise, and knowledge to address community-level and national-level challenges. This attracts volunteers and contributes to the sustainability of programmes. In return, volunteers play a larger part in implementing community solutions to the diverse challenges they come across. 'Maybe the only one that can bring about development in developing countries, it should be self-aid; it should be self-reliance' (Ratnapala 1999). Therefore, the Sarvodaya village-level development model stands as a model approach to development facilitation. The graduation of the village communities through the step-by-step model aspires to transform the social-governance fabric to a Sri Lankan *Gram Swaraj* i.e., a commonwealth of independent self-ruling villages. Moreover, it helps contribute to the greater transformation of the social order Sarvodaya aspires to establish in the country to realise the awakening of all.

Enabling Development Assistance: Donors and Community Expectations

Working with donors often means that development is delivered, monitored, and evaluated according to the needs and requirements set by donors. The first two decades of Sarvodaya's evolution were completely based on voluntary sharing of labour, material, and local donations (Ariyaratne 2019).

However, when the Sarvodaya message travelled across the country and when development requests flowed for assistance, 'local resource mobilisation alone was not sufficient to respond to those needs' (Ariyaratne 2019). At present, the Movement largely invests time to re-orient projects and often negotiates with donors to re-calibrate their ethos to promote an ambience of community-led development and to hold strong to the bottom-up approach in permitting development at the very grassroots and at the national level.

At the negotiating table, Sarvodaya makes a case with the donors rather than being a passive recipient of aid and assistance. The latest social protection national initiative of the Movement known as 'We Are One' is a prime illustration of how Sarvodaya innovated a new model to assist people in need due to the 2022 economic crisis on the island. When Sarvodaya introduced a working model,

INGOs, UN Bodies, and corporate partnerships rallied around extending their support, and more often than not, Sarvodaya had a larger say in how it wanted to assist and connect with communities in need. In terms of donor assistance, 'Sarvodaya did not shy away from receiving development assistance from a variety of external funding sources' (Ariyaratne 2019) and utilising it for the betterment of communities and for its organisational sustainability to serve Sri Lankan communities in the years to come. This way Sarvodaya has demonstrated how 'not to create a dependency but to enhance community self-reliance and leveraging of local resources' (Ariyaratne 2019) even by welcoming donors and their funds to aid and to extend development.

To overcome the challenges laid out by donor parties, Sarvodaya constantly carries out balancing acts. The five-step graduation model, as illustrated previously, was welcomed by the community as well as donors who came forward to assist. Bond (1994) presents the diverse arguments brought forward by donors and how Sarvodaya balanced certain aspects of donor demands. Although the donors were satisfied with the model, there were events in which the donors wanted to take charge and become more of 'producers of development rather than supportive initiators of development' (Sarvodaya Report 1994; Bond 1994). Balancing donor demand and excessive institutionalisation with the need to keep up the momentum of volunteership, Sarvodaya introduced progressive changes to the graduation model and introduced village categories to the existing village structure.

In a more participatory-community development approach, Sarvodaya's institutionalised system from the headquarters to the very village level has created multiple layers for development issues to be taken into consideration. Such layers also mean that there are frequent consultations with the Sarvodaya Shramadana Societies and their representatives, making the Movement fully aware of the grassroots development needs and requirements. This serves as a key strength when challenges, solutions as well as assistance are to be paired among communities and donors. The donors most often rely on Sarvodaya to tap into this wisdom and respect Sarvodaya for creating this space, effectively lessening the pressure they usually exercise with other development organisations. In a more communal sense, Sarvodaya gains more credibility and trust because it pairs resources and assistance to address community-level challenges while respecting their actual needs.

Balancing acts and the role played as an intermediary therefore becomes crucial in facilitating development at the community level. It is also vital to be aware of the reality that 'liberation-co-operation is what we need most in the world today – an operation to liberate both the rich as well as the poor, "the developed" as well as the "developing"' (Ratnapala 1999). In that regard, Sarvodaya has been advocating a society with 'no-poverty and no-affluence', a social order that works for all. Even in the present times, this spirit is consciously practised, and Sarvodaya often reminds its pool of donors that they must embrace and be aware that they are development partners and not producers. In a more realistic sense, Sarvodaya in the past had its own grim experience with donors not assuming their proper role and abruptly deciding on matters and abandoning partnerships (Bond 1994; Ariyaratne 2019). However, Sarvodaya has successfully addressed and strongly positioned itself on the participatory approach to community development while effectively maintaining its large pool of donor assistance both at local and international level.

Independence of Sarvodaya Shramadana Societies

All Sarvodaya Shramadana Societies have their own legal personality in which respected village leaders play an active role in managing their affairs. This model helps address issues with their identity, ownership, and delegates more authority for village leaders themselves to take charge of their activities. At the Sarvodaya Moratuwa Headquarters level, the Shramadana Societies Unit plays an active role in connecting with their district officers as well as the Societies themselves. Coordinating the societies' portfolio means looking into their legal requirements, troubleshooting, facilitating technical expertise, and conflict resolution as well as raising red flags when malpractices are investigated. Apart from these they coordinate between Shramadana Societies if they need to share expertise among the network. The Shramadana Societies Unit and the District Coordination Unit at the headquarters also plug Sarvodaya technical programme areas with the grassroots. Therefore the role of the Shramadana Societies Unit is to facilitate affairs rather than to centrally manage with authority. The unit reiterates the tenet to enable self-help and inspire communities to express themselves and find solutions to the challenges they identify on their own. 'No two villages are alike in all respects even though certain general factors can be identified' (Sarvodaya Movement 1980). Therefore those who cannot provide for themselves and require extra support and assistance will be catered to accordingly to address their basic functionalities that includes full or partial assistance with resources, technical skills as well as necessary knowledge to address development challenges at hand in those respective communities. It is also vital to find a common ground where the 'developed' and the 'developing' meet. 'We cannot meet at conference tables; we cannot meet as the boss and the obedient servants. We must meet on equal terms. And that place is the rural village of Sri Lanka' (Ratnapala 1999). Sarvodaya plays a greater emphasis in this aspect when development facilitation is to take place and most importantly to understand that it co-learns and co-designs development encounters and experiences to the greater good and the awakening of all.

Suwodaya: Primary Health Care and Community Participation

As illustrated in the previous sections, Sarvodaya inculcates holistic programmes at the community level and lays out a functioning system to support participatory community-led development. This section will demonstrate how Sarvodaya transforms undertakings from the grassroots level to the national level with a special focus on Sarvodaya's public health programme known as Suwodaya i.e., 'awakening health and wellbeing'. The Suwodaya programme was launched in the wake of the Covid -19 pandemic with the ethos that 'the village communities have to get committed to bring about better health as an integral part of total development' (Ratnapala 1999). From the very community level to national ones Sarvodaya partakes in the same philosophy to build initiatives and programmes that affect a mass of people. Even amidst challenging and unprecedented times such as the pandemic, community involvement had been recognised, respected, and utilised to realise better outcomes for all. Health and well-being are one among the ten basic human needs Sarvodaya has identified.

In the 1980s, 'at the community level, everyone had access to a primary health care facility, first aid and preventive medicine awareness' (Bond 1994). At present most Shramadana Societies do not have a requirement to maintain a regular clinic any longer as medical services offered both by the private and public sectors have significantly improved. Sarvodaya initiated community clinics mostly when health care services were inaccessible in the past. However, there exist Shramadana Societies still offering clinics to their own communities in partnership with their local medical service providers. As a pandemic response Sarvodaya re-established community-led health teams at the village level especially in areas where there was a need for greater Covid awareness (mostly rurally). These were named as Suwodaya Committees. The programmes have benefited thousands of people and have prevented escalation of epidemics including Covid-19. Post-Covid-19, 256 of these committees continue to offer services for non-communicable disease prevention. The successes of the campaigns have always depended on the level of community participation and the techniques Sarvodaya utilises to mobilise communities, also respecting that 'every community is in the process of development and has reached a particular technological level peculiar to that community' (Ratnapala 1999). The communities that were part of the programme were not merely recipients but also 'participants' that take the message across to their own members and beyond. Further

> participation and involvement must be a two-way process with mutual respect and equality in association. It must not be a process where some of us with great scientific and technical knowledge want to sit down and plan and expect the community to passively participate.
>
> *(Ratnapala 1999)*

During the pandemic, Sarvodaya operationalised this by reaching out to affected communities virtually and establishing health-committees with technical know-how so they could understand the community health challenges at hand and operationalise relevant mechanisms. The Suwodaya Covid-19 response programme is no different and has ensured that indigenous knowledge is respected, and then new knowledge is respectfully imparted. In the larger national context, community participation, and involvement has played a key role and most of these programmes

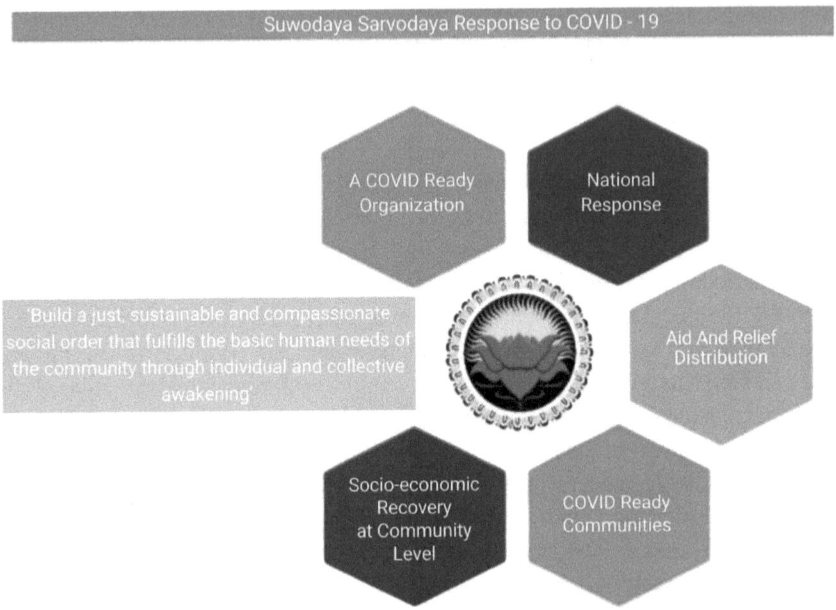

FIGURE 15.2 Suwodaya, the five-pronged approach to Covid-19.

were facilitated by trained volunteers from the very communities Sarvodaya works hand in hand with.

In terms of establishing the five-pronged Suwodaya programme for Covid-19 (Figure 15.2), Sarvodaya consulted the bulk of its headquarters and field-level staff and decided that the organisation required its own introduction of health protocols to operate during the pandemic. As it conducts participatory facilitation at the very grassroots level, the organisation exercised similar approaches within the different levels and layers, cherishing the inclusive and participatory approach when the programme design was concerned. Effective communication played a vital role in transparently and concurrently communicating the new programme amidst many difficulties such as lockdowns, technological connectivity, and the challenges set forth by the pandemic. The lockdowns posed a greater limitation for the social workers who appreciate physical engagements. Meeting virtually meant they had to learn new skills and platforms as well as change their mode of operations. Sarvodaya had to roll out virtual training to onboard people on the platforms.

Yet again, the field staff played a pivotal role in liaising with the headquarters, the health sector officials in their regions as well as in localities.

> Apart from that, Sarvodaya District Representatives constantly communicated with their respective Sarvodaya Shramadana Societies (villages), and adjacent communities to address public health concerns by providing the necessary

awareness material and, most importantly, to offer them solace in this time of crisis, tending to immediate needs of relief.

(Fernando 2021)

The benefit of community interactions, even amidst crisis, paved the way for the Movement to learn and experience how communities react to the pandemic, to learn from them the different ways in which they kept transmission at bay. For example: indigenous medical praxis that kept communicable diseases at bay such as herbal fogging, signs that marked a house has been infected, as well as to know their actual needs and concerns while addressing taboos and myths. Apart from that Sarvodaya played a greater role in relief distribution when local- and national-level lockdowns were imposed, and a greater role was yet again played by the community-level volunteers to facilitate relief distribution and services.

Suwodaya Committees

The Suwodaya Committees formed during the pandemic are auxiliary to the village committees already operating at the Shramadana Society level. The formation of the Suwodaya committees was financially assisted by a diverse pool of donors who were convinced that Sarvodaya will play a bigger part in preventive measures as well as the vaccination campaigns. The mandate of the committees was to facilitate 'Covid Ready Villages'. That is to make entire communities aware of virus transmission, preventive measures as well as the protocol on how to seek assistance when families were affected by Covid-19 (Sarvodaya Public Health Unit 2021). Not only members from communities but also officials working with communities from the localities came to address the issues at hand. Most of the grassroots-level public health volunteers were selected from the high-risk-prone communities. They gained intensive training via virtual means due to the lockdowns. Sarvodaya field workers also obtained permission for the field volunteers to operate and to communicate the messages by adhering to necessary health regulations and protocols. When households were affected, the volunteers collected data, shared them with relevant field-level officials and paved the way to provide relief packs when home quarantine measures were enforced.

> Sarvodaya's response to the pandemic surely provides at least a drop of hope to those ordinary-unsung community-oriented youth, women, volunteers, leaders, and activists, also surely, inspiring the most seasoned humanitarians and those who are celebrated not only in the island but also abroad.
>
> *(Fernando 2021)*

Post-Pandemic Phase

In the post-pandemic phase, the Suwodaya Committees have now been transformed into broader committees for people's well-being. They will roll out grassroots-level public health campaigns that specifically address psychological well-being and non-communicable diseases and assist the public health work run by government health care parties to increase their efficiency and effectiveness. The current and ongoing economic crisis has affected the health sector negatively and Suwodaya hopes to address aspects of preventive care as well to address other immediate needs at the community level, to ease the burden on the public health care system. Suwodaya illustrates how grassroots campaigns are designed both according to national-level priorities and the extent to which communities play a key role when the needs are logically communicated to them. The very successes of public health programmes depend on the effective involvement of communities, and Sarvodaya has demonstrated how effective interventions bring together people, officials, donors, and civil society to address the challenges brought forward by an unprecedented crisis. The public health programme is one among many other participatory community-led programmes Sarvodaya runs at the national level.

Conclusion

Sarvodaya serves as a benchmark within Sri Lanka, the region, and the world to demonstrate how development facilitation is implemented at a grand scale while capitalising on the power of communities. Over six decades, Sarvodaya has addressed community and national-level challenges by utilising a holistic approach to development. The Sarvodaya development approach is also perceived as an integral approach (Schieffer and Lessem 2014) as it values and takes into consideration six key spheres that are spiritual, moral, cultural, social, economic, and political when development interventions are planned.

The international development community could glean valuable insights from the experience of the Sarvodaya Shramadana Movement especially about its five-step village development model. The Movement's success over six decades is strongly rooted in its philosophical approach and, therefore, its recognition of community's cultural and faith orientations that activates a more psycho-social approach to development facilitation.

Another key area is its recognition of self-help, and the broader basis of self-help is emphasised and entwined, recognising the importance of individual and collective awakening. The self-help ethos largely enables an atmosphere that facilitates bottom-up development facilitation and the recognition that communities themselves should be the pioneers of their own development. Fostering this sense of ownership and recognising collective action Sarvodaya facilitates and plugs in other auxiliary stakeholders such as governments, authorities as well as development partners (donors), enabling a partnership-cooperation approach.

Arising from self-help is also the need to sustain action. Sustainability and transition of projects to initiatives and signature programming is intricately balanced by Sarvodaya as an organisation that works at multiple leadership levels from its headquarters to the grassroots village development structure known as the Sarvodaya Shramadana Societies. Based on its holistic development model and reinforced by an approach to volunteerism and cherishing volunteer action in the spirit of *Shramadana*, the Movement underscores the importance of long-term sustained action over short-term project-based engagements that win hearts and minds of the communities it serves.

Learning from its own decades-long experience, Sarvodaya itself is in continuous transformation. The Movement underwent a multi-tiered strategic planning process very recently where it re-calibrated its development plan. These exercises were also participatory and inclusive in terms of diversity of thought and wisdom that strengthens planning. At the time of writing, Sri Lanka is undergoing its worst economic crisis in history, and Sarvodaya's interventions and community empowerment programmes must grow at the community and national level. That includes enabling the next generation of community leaders to take greater responsibility to re-imagine economic systems that work for everyone leading to a shared economy and, most importantly, to establish a social order that works for every Sri Lankan (Ariyaratne 2019). Inclusive participatory community action will still be the way and Sarvodaya will dedicate time, effort, and resources to harness the potential of individuals to facilitate development and to awaken entire communities. Aligned by its purpose to 'build a just, sustainable, compassionate social order that fulfils the basic human needs of communities through individual and collective awakening' (Fernando 2021), Sarvodaya will play a greater role in Sri Lanka's development discourse, especially in these trying and unprecedented times, leaving no one behind and with the most noble aspiration to realise 'Sarvodaya ~ the Awakening of All'!

Notes

1 A large municipality in Sri Lanka, 18 km south of its capital, Colombo.
2 The Ramon Magsaysay Award is an annual recognition of transformative leadership in Asia.
3 The End-Child Poverty Knowledge Initiative is a long-standing partner of the Sarvodaya Movement.

Bibliography

Ariyaratne, Ahanagamage Tudor. 2014. The Power Pyramid and the Dharmic Cycle. Sarvodaya Vishwa Lekha.

Ariyaratne, Vinya. 2019. Practising Development, Upending Assumptions for Positive Change. Edited by Susan H Holcombe and Marion Howard, 65–81. Kumarian Press.

Bond, George D. 1994. Buddhism at Work, Community Development, Social Empowerment and the Sarvodaya Movement. Kumarian Press.

Fernando, Udesh. 2021. Suwodaya the Wellbeing of All: Sarvodaya's Response to COVID-19. Sarvodaya.

Macey, Joanna. 1996. Dharma and Development. Kumarian Press.

Rajkobal, Praveena. 2020. The Sarvodaya Movement, Holistic Development and Risk Governance in Sri Lanka. Routledge.

Ratnapala, Nandasena, ed. 1999. A.T. Ariyaratne Collected Works Volume I. Vol. I. Vishva Lekha.

Sarvodaya Movement. 1980. Ethos and Workplan of the Lanka Jathika Sarvodaya Shramadana Sangamaya. Vishva Lekha.

Sarvodaya Public Health Unit. 2021. Sarvodaya Suwodaya Service, Participatory Approach to Pandemic Preparedness. Sarvodaya Suwodaya Service.

Sarvodaya Report. 1994. The Future Directions of Sarvodaya. Strategic Direction, Sarvodaya Vishva Lekha.

Schieffer, Alexander, and Ronnie Lessem. 2014. Integral Development, Realising the Transformative Potential of Individuals, orGanisations and Societies. Gower Publishing, Routledge.

Veda, Gunjan, Cara Donohue, Ruth Nicholls, Elene Cloete, Holta Trandafili, Molly Wright, Amy Williams, Diana Delgadillo, Matthew Cruse, and Gill Westhorp. 2021. Impact of Community Led Development on Food Security (InCLuDE): A Rapid Realist Review. Rapid Review, The Movement for Community-Led Development & Charles Darwin University.

16
CONCLUSION

Elene Cloete and Gunjan Veda

As we bring this volume to a close, we wanted to reflect on what lies ahead for community-led development as a practice and methodology. It is a journey of potential, considering the human-centredness of community-led approaches, the interests of international and large-scale funders in locally-led development, and the possibilities community-led development holds to decolonise the international development sector. Such potential is woven throughout the volume's different chapters and their examples of community-led activities, interventions, and processes. But the journey is also one of perpetual learning and ongoing reflection, recognising what works and what perhaps needs adjustment.

Practising community-led development is not easy. Its principles come with their own set of challenges and obstacles. The future of community-led development depends on its advocates, implementors, and participants recognising, acknowledging, and then learning from such challenges. In what follows, we briefly problematise some of the dimensions, describing some of the common critique and challenges linked to concepts such as context, participation, local knowledge, and collaboration. We also consider how potential ways of responding to such critique are embedded in the symbiotic relationships that exist between the different dimensions of community-led development.

Context matters, but so does inclusion, equity, and equality

There is no one-size-fits-all community-led intervention. Community-led development prides itself on how it recognises and respects local context. Working with a local context, understanding it and therefore adjusting programming to align with such a context is crucial to getting a programme off the ground while ensuring local buy-in. But at the same time, merely accepting local contexts as is can directly

DOI: 10.4324/9781003377917-22

contradict other principles of community-led development. For example, people in positions of power within a particular community might inappropriately use cultural norms and values to justify their position. In the process, their actions actively discriminate and perpetuate inequalities. Such misuse of cultural and social norms must be addressed. As we have learned from the Amani Initiative, it can be done. But it takes time, skilful facilitation, and, most importantly, a deep understanding that contextual and cultural norms, values, and practices are not static but constantly evolving and allow for alternative possibilities and inclusive futures. Community-led activities therefore include delicate and ongoing negotiations between context and principles of meaningful participation, inclusion, and voice.

Local resources, development responsibilities, and neoliberal critique

Throughout the volume, authors emphasised the value of local resources, and knowledge, and also celebrated local agency and efficacy that can emerge from meaningful participation and engagement. A major takeaway from such an emphasis is that to move the needle on poverty-related challenges, the development sector, its organisations, and practitioners should ignite "the local." They should facilitate collective action among those directly impacted by poverty, encouraging them to use their local resources towards enacting change rather than looking towards external funders and actors, even the government, to provide support. Read differently, the responsibility of addressing poverty therefore falls directly on those affected by it. They are the ones affected. They are, therefore, the ones who should step into action and act on their challenges. They should do so, not only by participating in development activities but also by using their own resources and knowledge. In the process, community-led development can be seen as overlooking the resource poverty imposed by systematic discrimination and absolving those with financial and technical resources of the responsibility to support people in Majority World contexts in addressing poverty-related challenges. At the same time, this approach to development could also seem to absolve governments from providing safety nets and developing development programmes and social infrastructure. Community-led development can, therefore, easily be interpreted as perpetuating a neoliberal agenda, placing the responsibility of community development on already overburdened individuals while exonerating those in positions of economic and political power of any responsibility towards addressing the underlying systemic structures that perpetuate global inequalities.

Promoting individualism over collective and shared responsibilities is not the intention of community-led development. While it does emphasise the importance of strengthening the agency and efficacy of local communities so that they can become more resilient and self-sufficient, such an emphasis is not to relieve those in positions of political and financial power of their responsibility of addressing structural inequalities. On the contrary, igniting local agency is about increasing local awareness of social injustices. It is about re-establishing dignity and pride that might have crumbled under the weight of poverty-related challenges so that people can regain the confidence to insist on improved access to basic needs and services. Therefore, the recognition and use of local resources and knowledge and the corresponding emphasis on participation, inclusion and voice work in conjunction with larger state-driven measures that address social and economic justice. At the same time, the community-led dimension of collaboration also enables shared responsibility, where community-led activities that establish and then strengthen connections between communities and local government agencies are about the equal sharing of resources. What keeps these processes in check are multidirectional accountability, and ongoing monitoring and evaluation, with the latter, in true community-led fashion owned by local communities themselves.

Who has time to participate?

Community-led activities rely heavily on participation and corresponding processes of decision-making, consensus building, reflection, and, if need be, readjustment and replanning. All of these processes take time, a resource that many people living within Majority World contexts do not have. It is especially true for women, who are often the targeted participants of development interventions, and yet have the least time, having to engage in unpaid household labour while also actively contributing to livelihood activities. This over-reliance on women's participation can therefore exacerbate their time poverty, i.e. when "some individuals do not have enough time for rest and leisure after taking into account the time spent working, whether in the labour market, for domestic work, or for other activities such as fetching water and wood" (Blackden and Wodon 2006, p. 6). In this case, the time demands of quality participation, which is needed for inclusive and meaningful community-led development, can become burdensome and thus do more harm than good. Again, skilful and experienced facilitation can address this challenge. Practitioners who have developed trusting relationships with community members should also have the heightened sensitivity to know whether activities are too time-demanding. Additionally, trusting relationships between practitioners and community members also mean that participants will be comfortable sharing their experiences and time constraints with practitioners. Some organisations are now exploring ways of addressing time poverty of the historically marginalised population by providing support services that address factors that contribute to this time poverty. For example, creches or wells in the vicinity reduce the amount of time women spend on fetching water.

Long live participation!

Any discussion about the challenges of community-led development will be incomplete without critical reflections on how grand hopes about participation have resulted in disillusionment. Critics have described the pitfalls of participation, including how it is "the new tyranny" (Cooke and Kothari 2001) and continues to be a development buzzword (Cornwall and Brock 2005). The warnings against tokenistic participation are well noted. However, this critique of participation stems from situations where organisations might view participation through the number of people attending a community meeting rather than who they are and how they participate in the discussion and in any decisions made. And that is exactly what community-led development intentionally guards against, advocating for participation that is representative, that enables true engagement, that is patient, ensuring that all voices are heard in the way they feel most comfortable being heard. Community-led development continues to value meaningful participation because, as we have seen across the different chapters in this volume, it not only comes with significant potential, but it is the impetus behind this approach. Participation, when meaningful, enriches discussions by adding additional opinions; it disrupts the status quo by exposing often unheard experiences and realities; and it is the crucial point of departure for other essential community-led principles, including doing community-led monitoring and evaluation, surfacing local knowledge and resources, and enabling multidirectional accountability. Additionally, collaboration cannot happen without participation, neither can ongoing and sustained collective action. Within the context of community-led development, the responsibility of incubating meaningful, inclusive participation resides with facilitators who, in turn, have to recognise why some people participate and others do not and then negotiate with the underlying power structures that stand in the way of true participation.

Community-led development takes time

Quality interventions that result in long-term impact and sustainable outcomes cannot be rushed. Establishing trusting relationships, the cornerstone of principles, such as accountability, collaboration, and also facilitation processes, does not happen overnight. They require time spent within communities, learning about their contexts, lived realities, and experiences. Additionally, if practitioners want to be responsive to local contexts, as demanded by community-led development, they need to spend time understanding such contexts and doing the necessary research to grasp existing power structures that might not be explicit to outsiders.

But such time also costs money, and typical funding norms demand time-bounded intervention estimates linked to specific outputs and outcomes. With increased changes in funding priorities and with localisation being recognised as a more viable and sustainable way forward, hopefully, funding requirements will become more flexible, and funders will develop a greater awareness of what is required for interventions to be sustainable.

Hopeful futures

Perhaps the cyclical evaluation practices described by the Constellation's authors in their chapter on community-led monitoring and evaluation would be a good way to end this volume. As they described, evaluation is a continuous process that involves not only evaluating what works and what does not but also proactively using such information to either repeat the same process and activity or perhaps make readjustments, recognising that change is needed. But more importantly, because the process is cyclical, it does not stop. It must continue. It must sustain its perpetual circularity.

As a global development community, our work is far from done. We must continue to address systemic inequalities. We must persist at decolonising visible structures of inequality as well as make visible the less obvious yet powerful mindsets, including colonised minds, that often unknowingly sustain global power hierarchies. Within the context of community-led development, authentic collaboration and equitable, inclusive participation are our departure points in doing this work.

Additionally, we are charged with hope because this is the time when we cannot lose hope. At the time of writing, the looming predicaments of climate change and the disheartening violation of human rights across different geographic regions challenge imagining fruitful futures. But we cannot lose sight of the potential of communities, their collective action, and their efforts to ensure sustainable futures for themselves and their children. Investing in such development – development envisioned, planned, implemented, and owned by local communities themselves—is possible. And because of colleagues and diverse stakeholders across different geographic and social regions supporting such work, the future is hopeful. As Arundhati Roy reminds us: "Another world is not only possible, she is on her way. On a quiet day, I can hear her breathing."

References

Blackden, Mark, and Quentin Wodon. 2006. Gender, time use and poverty: Introduction. In Blackden, M. C., & Wodon, Q. (Eds.), *Gender, Time Use, and Poverty in Sub-Saharan Africa* (pp. 1–10). The World Bank.

Cooke, Bill, and Uma Kothari. 2001. *Participation: The new tyranny?* Zed Books.

Cornwall, Andrea, and Karen Brock. 2005. "What do buzzwords do for development policy? A critical look at 'participation', 'empowerment and 'poverty reduction'." *Third World Quarterly* 26, no. 7: 1043–1060.

Tavernaro-Haidarian, Leyla. 2018. "Why efforts to decolonise can deepen coloniality and what Ubuntu can do to help." *Critical Arts* 32, no. 5–6: 104–118. doi:10.1080/02560046.2018.1560341

ANNEX

Participatory CLD Assessment Tool

MOVEMENT FOR
COMMUNITY-LED
DEVELOPMENT

This tool was developed by MCLD's collaborative research team, under the leadership of Gunjan Veda, and reflects the collective work of over a hundred CLD practitioners. A living tool, it was first released on Jan 21, 2021 and has seen multiple updates and adaptations since, including the community version seen here. For any questions on the tool, please reach out to gunjan.veda@mcld.org.

The tool is available in nine languages – Shared here is a condensed copy of English version showing only the questions (not the possible responses) as of August 2024. Fictional responses for a virtual programme have been plugged in to show the spider diagram.

Suggested Citation:

Glossary

- M&E – Monitoring and Evaluation
- Accountability Mechanisms – Accountability mechanisms include parties sharing monitoring reports, accounting for their decisions and spending through public notice boards and through interactive sessions such as public forums, e.g. social audits or quarterly or bi-annual decentralised workshops where all communities can be represented.
- Facilitator – the front-line staff who explain the programme and work with communities on a day-to-day basis to facilitate planning and action. Facilitators may work for NGOs, be community volunteers, etc.

Who Should Complete This Tool and When?

- This tool should be completed through a participatory exercise with community leaders and programme staff.
- Organisations can use this tool at different programme junctures to self-assess how programming aligns with CLD characteristics – during design, mid-programme reviews, or at the end of a programme cycle to inform future programmes.
- Organisations can also use the tool during organisational reviews to understand programming across areas.

Explanation of Sections

1 **Basic Info:** collects basic information on who completed the form, when this took place and any other descriptors an organisation might want for future reference.
2 **Rubric:** collects information on CLD characteristics and processes
3 **Results:** diagrams summarising overall results for characteristics and processes
4 **Data:** options to export, import or delete the data from your local device.

How to Complete the Rubric?

- The response options (and their corresponding points) include insufficient information (0), doesn't try (1), tries (2), progressed (3) and succeeds (4).
- Click the button on responses that best describe your organisation's current work and progress on the different CLD characteristics, and processes based on the discussion with stakeholders.
- The rubric will auto calculate the score for each dimension and display it under results

How Can You Interpret the Results?

- A goal for organisations using CLD approaches should be to eventually reach the outer rim for the components relevant to their contexts, programming and operations.
- Not all dimensions may be relevant to all programmes, but where they are, the position on the graph can help organisations see where they can push their programming further.
- Overall Results: Reflects the outcomes of all of the rubric's segments.
- Breakdowns: The rubric includes further break-downs of dimensions A–G (of the CLD characteristics) and processes (M&E and Facilitation) offering information on how these dimensions might function within a particular organisation. These break-downs are included in graph form in tabs 4 and 5 so that this detail is not lost.
- Please ensure that you discuss the results with community members and participating staff after using the tool with them. Discuss the priorities and what you could do to make your programme more community-led based on the results of using the tool.

Dimensions

A: Participation, Inclusion and Voice
B: Local Resources and Knowledge
C: Sustainability and Transition Strategy
D: Accountability Mechanisms
E: Responsiveness to Context
F: Collaboration
G: Working with Local Government/Civil Society Organisations
H: Monitoring and Evaluation Practices
I: Facilitation

Basic Programme Information

- Organisation Name
- Type of Organisation
- Programme Name
- Programming Country(s)
- Provinces/Regions
- Stage
- Name(s) Completing This Assessment
- Date Completed
- Comment (include information on how the tool was used, number and nature of participants, location etc)

Rubric Questions

A: Participation, Inclusion and Voice

A1. The programme ensures the inclusion of all groups of people in the community (like old and young, men and women, better-off and poor, from different clans, castes, religions)

A2. Community members decide the priorities of the CLD programme BEFORE the actual design of the programme.

A3. Community members play an active role in CLD programme planning in their community.

A4. Community bodies representing all groups and neighbourhoods implement the programme.

A5. The programme builds the voice and confidence of community representatives to influence/shape decision-making.

A6. The programme raises awareness of rights (social, economic and political) and builds skills among local representatives to ask for those rights.

B: Local Resources and Knowledge

B1. The CLD programme builds on Local Resources and Knowledge.

B2. Community contributes their resources (e.g. time, cash, labour, land, materials).

C: Sustainability and Transition Strategy

C1. Communities are central to planning how and when the programme should be completed and handed over to them.

C2. Communities work with the implementing organisations to constantly review and adapt the planning for handover of programmes and transition.

C3. The programme ensures that community structures (like community based organisations, groups implementing programmes) have the capacities to continue working after handover.

C4. After completion, the programme's impact is measured with local participation.

C5. After the programme has been handed over to community/local government structures, community members belonging to all groups (e.g. women, youth, elderly, poor, people with disabilities, minorities) are still benefiting from community-led activities.

D: Accountability Mechanisms

D1. The programme and community structures share important information, for example, what they are doing, why, how and how funds were used.

D2. The programme addresses community grievances/complaints.
D3. The results of monitoring and evaluation are regularly shared with community members.

E: Responsiveness to Context

E1. The programme is responsive to changing community needs and contexts.
E2. The pace of the CLD Program (i.e. timing, frequency and length of engagement with the community) is determined with community members.

F: Collaboration

F1. The programme builds positive relationships between rich and poor; poor and poor.
F2. The programme builds positive relations within the same groups and across different ethnic, caste, religious groups, etc.
F3. The programme builds positive relations between women and women and between men and women.
F4. The programme links local communities or their leaders to other villages and their leaders across districts, provinces or states.

G: Working with Local Government/Civil Society Organisations[1]

G1. The programme's community groups work together with local government structures and actors.

H: Monitoring and Evaluation Practices

H1. Community members monitor the key activities and progress of the programme.
H2. Participatory evaluation is carried out.
H3. Monitoring and evaluation activities look at how the programme works with and benefits different groups of people including women, people with disabilities, the elderly, people from minorities.

I: Facilitation

I1. Facilitators decide the time, place and setting of the meetings such that everyone is able to participate in them.
I2. Project Facilitators are respectful and encourage dialogue.
I3. After attending meetings with the facilitators, we feel:
I4. (For facilitators only) We feel supported (receive regular trainings, understand what we are doing and why, have flexibility and budgets) by the implementing organisation/government agency to do our work.

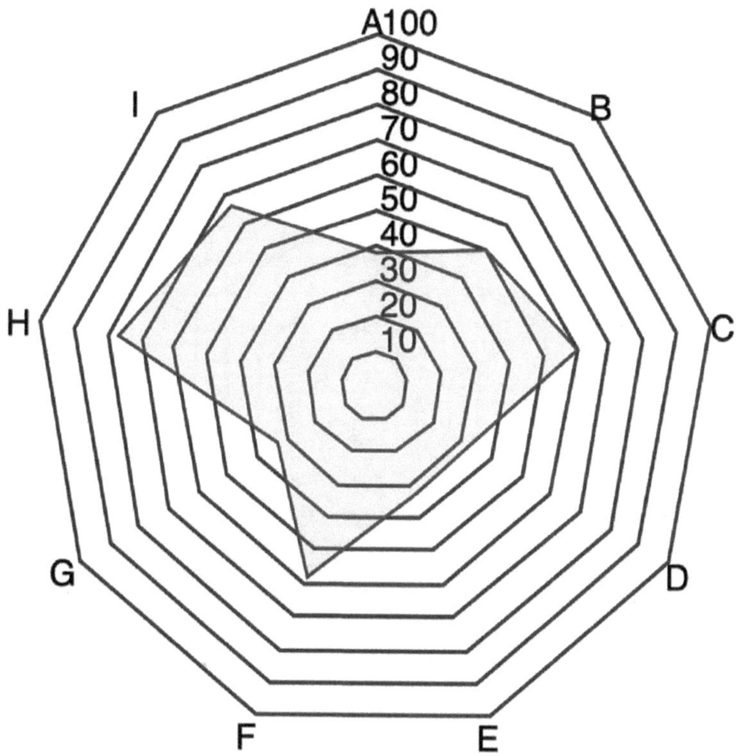

38	A: Participation, Inclusion and Voice
50	B: Local Resources and Knowledge
60	C: Sustainability and Transition Strategy
33	D: Accountability Mechanisms
33	E: Responsiveness to Context
58	F: Collaboration
33	G: Working with Local Government/Civil Society Organizations
77	H: Monitoring and Evaluation Practices
66	I: Facilitation

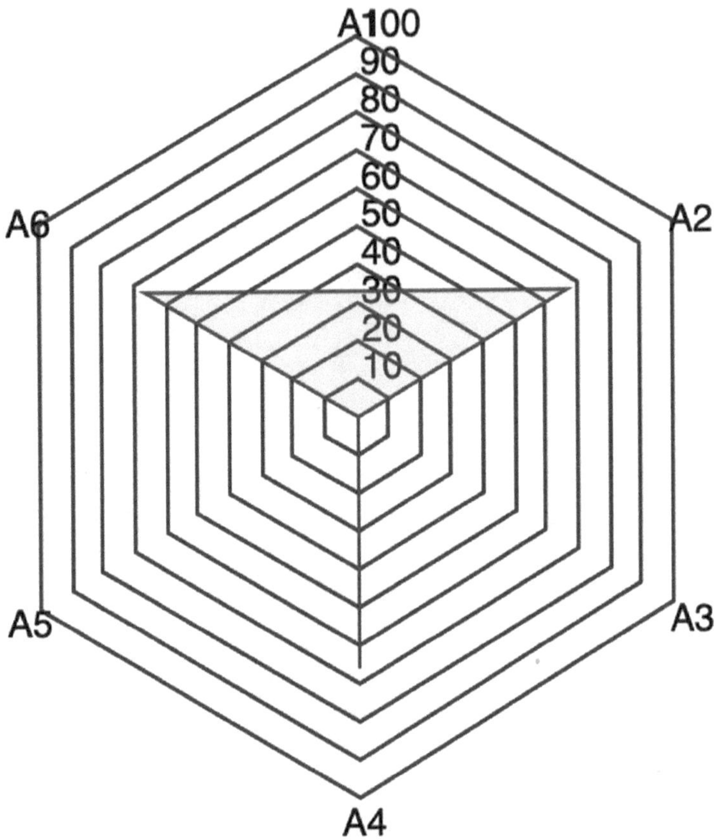

33	A1. The programme ensures the inclusion of all groups of people in the community (like old and young, men and women, better-off and poor, from different clans, castes, religions)
66	A2. Community members decide the priorities of the CLD programme BEFORE the actual design of the programme.
0	A3. Community members play an active role in CLD programme planning in their community.
66	A4. Community bodies representing all groups and neighbourhoods implement the programme.
0	A5. The programme builds the voice and confidence of community representatives to influence/shape decision-making.
66	A6. The programme raises awareness of rights (social, economic and political) and builds skills among local representatives to ask for those rights.

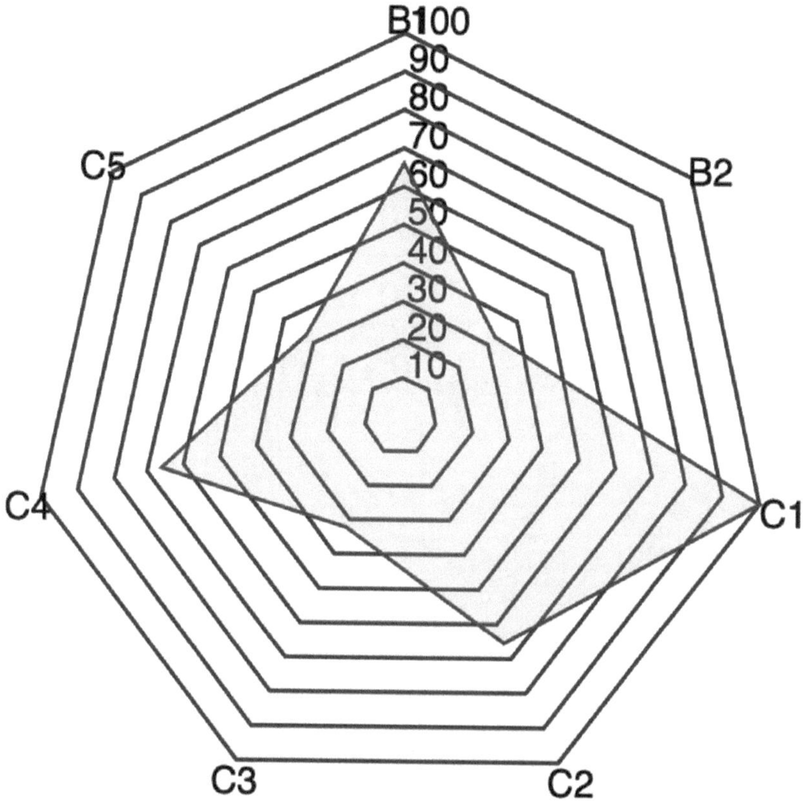

66	B1. The CLD programme builds on Local Resources and Knowledge.
33	B2. Community contributes their resources (e.g. time, cash, labour, land, materials)
100	C1. Communities are central to planning how and when the programme should be completed and handed over to them.
66	C2. Communities work with the implementing organisations to constantly review and adapt the planning for handover of programmes and transition.
33	C3. The programme ensures that community structures (like community based organisations, groups implementing programmes) have the capacities to continue working after handover.
66	C4. After completion, the programme's impact is measured with local participation.
33	C5. After the programme has been handed over to community/local government structures, community members belonging to all groups (e.g. women, youth, elderly, poor, people with disabilities, minorities) are still benefiting from community-led activities.

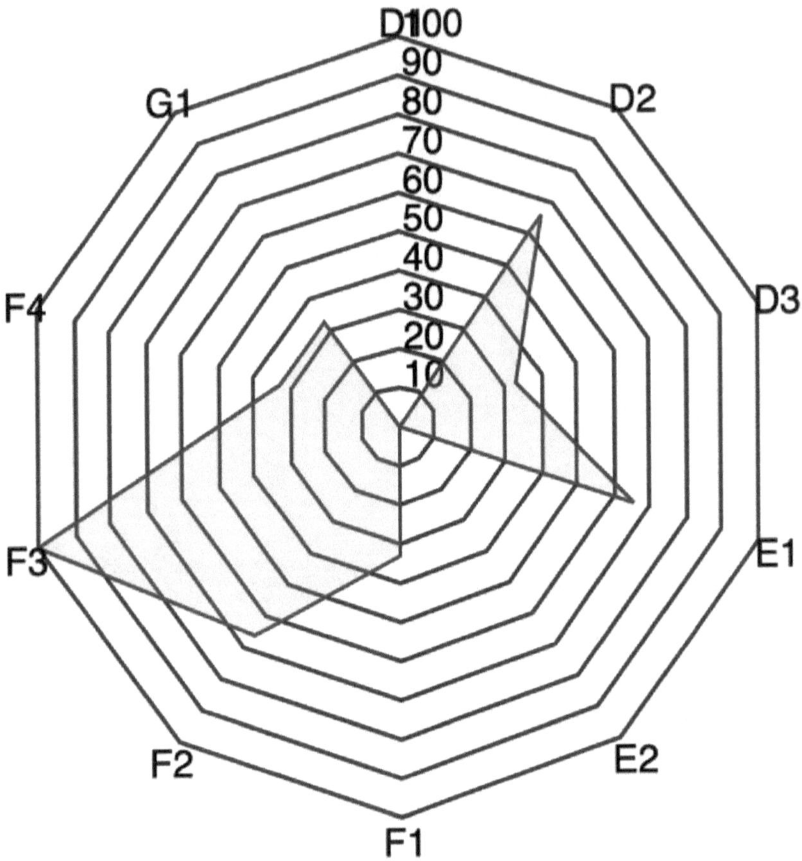

0	D1. The programme and community structures share important information for example what they are doing, why, how and how funds were used.
66	D2. The programme addresses community grievances/ complaints.
33	D3. The results of monitoring and evaluation are regularly shared with community members.
66	E1. The programme is responsive to changing community needs and contexts.
0	E2. The pace of the CLD Programme (i.e., timing, frequency, and length of engagement with the community) is determined with community members.
33	F1. The programme builds positive relationships between rich and poor; poor and poor.
66	F2. The programme builds positive relations within the same groups and across different ethnic, caste, religious groups, etc.
100	F3. The programme builds positive relations between women and women and between men and women.
33	F4. The programme links local communities or their leaders to other villages and their leaders across districts, provinces or states.
33	G1. The programme's community groups work together with local government structures and actors.

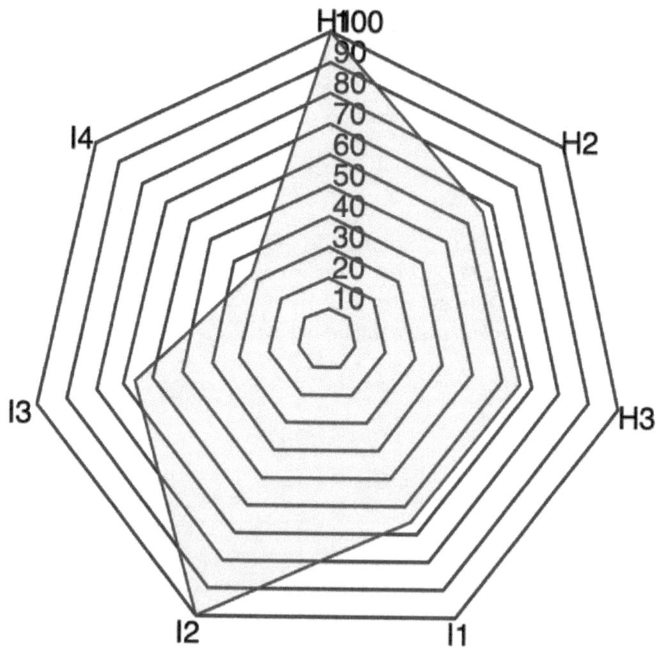

100	H1. Community members monitor the key activities and progress of the programme.
66	H2. Participatory evaluation is carried out.
66	H3. Monitoring and evaluation activities look at how the programme works with and benefits different groups of people including women, people with disabilities, the elderly, people from minorities.
66	I1. Facilitators decide the time, place and setting of the meetings such that everyone is able to participate in them.
100	I2. Project Facilitators are respectful and encourage dialogue.
66	I3. After attending meetings with the facilitators, we feel:
33	I4. (For facilitators only) We feel supported (receive regular trainings, understand what we are doing and why, have flexibility and budgets) by the implementing organisation/government agency to do our work.

Note

1 The questions for this dimension are automatically populated based on type of organisation. This question is for civil society organisations. For local government, a different version of the question comes up

Reference

*Veda, Gunjan, Holta Trandafili, Brigitta Bode, Nelly Mecklenburg, Elene Cloete, Janet Edmond, Diana Delgadillo, Martha Cruz Zuniga, Julie Carandang, Randy Lyness. 2021. Participatory CLD Assessment Tool, New York: The Movement for Communityled Development. https:// mcldto ols.git hub.io/ en.htm*l

INDEX

Kolibri 360 GmbH
Ferdinand-Jühlke-Straße 7
99095 Erfurt, Deutschland
produktsicherheit@kolibri360.de